The Giant Book
of Jokes

The Giant Book of Jokes

Edited by Dave Phillips

Magpie Books, London

Constable & Robinson Ltd
3 The Lanchesters
162 Fulham Palace Road
London W6 9ER
www.constablerobinson.com

First published by Magpie Books,
an imprint of Constable & Robinson Ltd 2005

A copy of the British Library Cataloguing in
Publication Data is available from the British Library

ISBN 1-84529-208-1

Printed and bound in the EU

1 3 5 7 9 10 8 6 4 2

All Creatures Great and Small

In the National Forests of Alaska, a tourist guide was addressing a group of holidaymakers about the dangers of hiking in grizzly bear territory. He warned: 'Most bear encounters occur when hikers, being extra quiet along the trails in the hope of viewing wildlife, unexpectedly stumble into bears. The resulting surprise can be disastrous. To avoid this, we suggest that hikers should wear tiny bells on their clothing to warn the bears of their presence. Finally, exercise added caution when you spot signs of bears in the area, particularly when you see bear droppings.'

One tourist asked: 'How do you identify bear droppings?'

'Easy,' explained the guide. 'They're the ones with all the tiny bells in them!'

Did you hear about the hyena that swallowed an Oxo cube? – He made a laughing stock of himself.

A hunter was crossing a road one day when a frog called out to him and said: 'If you kiss me, I'll turn into a beautiful princess.'

He bent over, picked up the frog and put it in his pocket.

The frog spoke again and said: 'If you kiss me and turn me back into a beautiful princess, I will stay with you for one week.'

The hunter took the frog out of his pocket, smiled at it and put it back in his pocket. The frog then cried out: 'If you kiss me and turn me back into a princess, I'll stay with you and do whatever you want.'

Again the hunter took the frog out, smiled at it and returned it to his pocket.

Finally the frog demanded: 'What is your problem? I've told you that I'm a beautiful princess, I'll stay with you for a week and do anything you want. Why won't you kiss me?'

The hunter said: 'Look, I'm an avid hunter, and when I'm not hunting, I'm fishing. I don't have time for girlfriends, but a talking frog is really cool!'

Why did the bee cross his legs? – Because he couldn't find the BP station.

A New York family bought a ranch out west where they intended to raise cattle. A friend came to visit one weekend and asked if the ranch had a name.

'Well,' said the would-be cattleman, 'to be honest we've had a few arguments over names. I wanted to call the ranch the Bar-J; my wife favoured the Suzy-Q; one son liked the Flying-W; and my other son wanted the Lazy-Y. So we're calling it the Bar-J-Suzy-Q-Flying-W-Lazy-Y Ranch.'

'But where are all your cattle?' asked the friend.

'So far, none have survived the branding.'

A farmer needed to buy a bull to service his cows but, in order to afford it, he had to borrow money from the bank. The banker who lent him the money stopped by a week later to see how his investment was shaping up. The farmer complained that the bull just ate grass and wouldn't even look at the cows, so the banker suggested calling in a vet to take a look at the animal.

The following week the banker returned to see if the vet had been of any use. The farmer looked very pleased. 'The bull serviced all my cows twice,' he said, 'then broke through the fence and serviced all my neighbour's cows three times.'

'Wow!' exclaimed the banker. 'What did the vet do to that bull?'

'Just gave me some pills to give him,' replied the farmer.

'What kind of pills?'

'I don't know,' said the farmer, 'but they sort of taste like chocolate.'

What kind of monkey can fly? – A hot air baboon.

At the height of the Cold War, the Russians and the Americans had got together and decided that the only way to resolve matters was by way of a dogfight. Whichever country lost the fight would lay down its arms. To prepare for the contest, each country had five years in which to breed the world's meanest fighting dog.

Russian experts set to work with a vengeance, rounding up the biggest, nastiest Dobermans and Rottweillers and breeding them with Siberian wolves. They took only the strongest puppy from each litter and made sure that it received all the milk, even at the expense of the rest of the puppies. After five years they came up with a truly fearsome beast – a dog that no human dared approach and which had to be kept in a cage behind five-inch thick steel bars. The Russian dog was a killing machine.

Come the day of the fight, the Russians paraded their awesome animal and waited to see what kind of dog the Americans would offer as a challenger. To the Russians' amazement and amusement, the American handler was walking a nine foot long dachshund. The Russians couldn't believe that after five years, the most brutal hound the Americans could come up with was an elongated sausage dog.

The two animals were left alone in the ring. The Russian dog snarled and growled at its opponent but the American dog simply waddled forward and swallowed it whole.

The Russians were distraught. They said to the Americans: 'Our best scientists have spent five years developing this brutal dog, cross-breeding with wolves. We thought it was unbeatable.'

'Well,' said the Americans, 'we had our best plastic surgeons working for five years to make an alligator look like a dachshund.'

Two cows were talking in a field one day.

The first cow said: 'Have you heard about the Mad Cow Disease that's going around?'

The second cow said: 'Yeah, makes you glad you're a penguin, doesn't it?'

One afternoon in the Arctic, a father polar bear and his polar bear son were sitting in the snow. The cub turned to his father and said: 'Dad, am I a hundred per cent polar bear?'

The father replied: 'Of course, son, you're a hundred per cent polar bear.'

A few minutes later, the cub turned to his father again and said: 'Dad, tell me the truth. I can take it. Am I a hundred per cent polar bear? No brown bear or black bear or grizzly bear?'

The father answered: 'Son, I'm a hundred per cent polar bear, your mother is 100 per cent polar bear, so you are definitely a hundred per cent polar bear.'

The cub seemed satisfied, but a few minutes later he turned to his father once more and said: 'Dad, don't think you're sparing my feelings. I've got to know. Am I a hundred per cent polar bear?'

The father was becoming distressed by the continual questioning and said: 'Why do you keep asking if you're a hundred per cent polar bear?'

The cub said: 'Because I'm freezing!'

A zookeeper needed some extra animals for his zoo, so he decided to write a letter. But unfortunately he didn't know the plural of 'mongoose'.

He started the letter: 'To whom it may concern, I need two mongeese.' But that didn't sound right, so he tried again. 'To whom it may concern, I need two mongooses.' But that didn't sound right either. Then he had an idea. 'To whom it may concern, I need a mongoose, and while you're at it, send me another one.'

A tiny turtle looked up from the ground and slowly began to climb a tree. Inch by inch, it crept up the bark until three hours later it finally reached the top. Then it climbed on to an outside branch, jumped into the air waving its legs and crashed to the ground with a thud.

Saved from injury by its shell, the little turtle started to climb the tree again. Fours hours later it reached the top, climbed on to a branch, jumped into the air waving its front legs and crashed to the ground.

Undaunted, the tiny turtle tried again. This time it took five hours of Herculean effort to reach the top of the tree. Once there, it stumbled on to an outside branch, jumped into the air waving its front legs and crashed to the ground.

As the tiny turtle dusted itself down for yet another laborious ascent of the tree, two birds were watching from above. The female bird turned to the male and said: 'Darling, don't you think it's time we told him he's adopted?'

Once upon a time there was a cattle rancher who, after two years of trying, finally found a buyer for his oldest bull, Caesar. The new owner was the rancher's closest neighbour and lived on the other side of the river across the valley.

'Well,' said the rancher to his cowhands, 'it's time to take this bull across the river to his new home.' So the men roped Caesar and walked him down to the river.

They were about to put him on the boat when the rancher's son, who had helped to raise Caesar, pleaded: 'Can we take him for one last munch in his favourite meadow?'

The other hands thought it was a good idea and led the bull for a snack in the field. With the sun beating down on them, they lost the appetite for work and dozed off until, three hours later, the rancher noticed that the bull was still on his property. Angrily, he rushed down to the valley and ordered the men to wake up immediately. He yelled at them that the beast should have been on the boat and across the river long ago. 'I can't believe this,' he raged. 'We've come to ferry Caesar, not to graze him!'

Two silkworms were having a race, but it ended in a tie.

A tourist guide was talking with a group of schoolchildren at America's Yellowstone Park when one boy asked him whether he had ever come face-to-face with a wolf.

'Yes,' said the guide, 'I did come face to face with a wolf once. What made it worse was that I was alone and unarmed.'

'What did you do?'

'What could I do? First, I tried looking him straight in the eyes but he slowly advanced towards me. I crept back, but he kept on coming, nearer and nearer. I had to think fast.'

'Wow! How did you get away?'

'As a last resort, I just turned around and walked quickly to the next cage.'

Two fish were in a tank. One turned to the other and said: 'Do you know how to drive one of these things?'

Three tortoises went on a picnic. It took them ages to crawl to a suitable spot and when they eventually found one, they realized that they had forgotten the chocolate biscuits. The two older tortoises turned to the youngest and said: 'Will you pop home and fetch the biscuits?'

'Why me?' he asked.

'Because you've got younger legs.'

After much persuasion, he relented, but only on condition that they didn't start drinking the lemonade until he returned.

'We promise not to touch a drop,' they said.

So the young tortoise set off on the long crawl home. After two hours, the others were gasping for a drink and so they took out the bottle of lemonade. As they did so, a little head peered round a nearby rock and said: 'If you do, I won't go . . .'

Two caterpillars were watching a pupae burst open to reveal a beautiful butterfly. As it stretched its wings and flew away, one caterpillar turned to the other and said: 'You'll never get me up in one of those things.'

Once upon a time there were two skunks named In and Out. When Out was in, In was out and when Out was out, In was in. One day, Out was in and In was out and the mother skunk said: 'Out, I want you to go out and bring In in.'

Out went out and returned almost immediately with In.

The mother was amazed and said: 'How did you find him so quickly?'

'Easy,' said Out. 'In stinked.'

A man was driving down a country lane when he spotted the most beautiful horse he'd ever seen, standing in the middle of a field. He slammed on his brakes and stopped to have a quick look. 'I must buy that horse,' he said to himself and immediately went in search of the owner. Arriving at a nearby farmhouse, he knocked on the door.

'Are you the owner of that magnificent animal in the field back there?' he asked.

'Yes,' replied the farmer.

'Then I simply must buy him from you.'

'I can't sell him,' said the farmer. 'He doesn't look so good.'

'What do you mean? He's the most beautiful horse I've seen in my life.'

'Well, okay,' conceded the farmer, 'if you insist. Does a thousand dollars sound reasonable to you?'

'Absolutely,' said the man, and he took the horse home on a trailer.

A few days later, the farmer heard another knock on his door. It was the man with the horse. 'You ripped me off!' yelled the man. 'That horse is as blind as a bat!'

'I tried to warn you,' answered the farmer. 'I told you he doesn't look so good.'

By way of a change from flower arranging demonstrations and talks about pottery, the local women's institute decided to go on a trip to a working farm. Since most of them had lived in the city all of their lives and had never been near a farm, it would be a new and challenging experience.

Dressed for the part, they arrived in their minibus to be greeted by the farmer. As they looked around the various barns and outhouses, one woman was intrigued by an animal she spotted.

'Excuse me,' she called to the farmer, 'can you explain to us why this cow doesn't have any horns?'

The farmer cocked his head for a moment, and then explained patiently: 'Well, ma'am, cattle can do a lot of damage with horns. Sometimes we keep 'em trimmed down with a hacksaw. Other times we can fix up the young 'uns by puttin' a couple of drops of acid where their horns would grow, and that stops 'em cold. Still, there are some breeds of cattle that never grow horns. But the reason this cow don't have no horns, ma'am, is because it's a horse.'

One woodworm turned to the other and said: 'How's life?'

'Boring,' said the other.

A zookeeper spotted a visitor throwing ten-dollar bills into the elephant enclosure.

'Why are you doing that?' asked the keeper.

'The sign says it's okay,' replied the visitor.

'No, it doesn't.'

'Yes it does. It says: "Do not feed. $10 fine."'

There was once a snail who dreamed of becoming a racing car driver. When he learned that his uncle had died and left him a small fortune, the snail realized that this was his chance to fulfil his ambition. So he bought himself a racing car, fine tuned it, and painted large red letter S's all over it.

'Why have you painted it like that?' asked a fellow competitor.

'Because,' said the snail proudly, 'when I go hurtling down the straight past the pits at a hundred and eighty miles per hour, I want everyone in the stand to say: "Look at that S-car go!"'

An explorer in the African jungle heard of a plan to capture the legendary King Kong. And sure enough, when he came to a clearing, there before him, imprisoned in a cage, sat the imposing figure of King Kong. It dawned on the explorer that he could be the first person ever to touch the great ape and so tentatively he inched towards the cage. Since King Kong appeared quite passive, the explorer thought he would take a chance and reach through the bars to touch him. But as soon as he made contact with the gorilla's fur, King Kong went berserk. He immediately rose to his feet, began beating his chest and within seconds had burst out of his cage. As the explorer ran for his life, King Kong set off in hot pursuit. Instinctively the explorer headed for the heart of the jungle, hoping that he might be able to hide from his manic pursuer, but wherever he tried to conceal himself, Kong Kong always sought him out. As night began to fall, the breathless explorer prayed that he would be able to lose the gorilla in the darkness but no matter how fast he ran, the sound of King Kong's pounding footsteps was only ever about a hundred yards behind. For three long days and nights the explorer ran through Africa with King Kong always close behind, occasionally letting out a menacing roar from his vast throat. Eventually the explorer reached the coast. There were no ships in sight for an easy escape, so he realized the only option was to dive into the sea and hope that King Kong couldn't swim. But to his horror, the gorilla jumped straight in after him and demonstrated an excellent front crawl. On and on they swam across the Atlantic – rarely separated by more than fifty yards – until six months later the weary explorer arrived in New York. He scrambled ashore with as much energy as he could muster, only to see the menacing King Kong, still beating his chest ferociously and with steam coming from his nostrils, right behind him. Through the streets they stumbled, explorer and ape equally exhausted, until the explorer took a wrong turn and ended up down a dead end, his escape barred by a twenty-foot high wall. With nowhere left to run, he sank to his knees in despair and pleaded to King Kong: 'Do whatever you want with me. Kill me, eat me, whatever. Just put me out of my misery!' King Kong stalked slowly over to the cowering explorer, prodded him with a giant paw and growled: 'You're it!'

Two slugs were slithering along the pavement. As they went round a corner, they found themselves stuck behind two snails.
    'Oh no!' said one. 'Caravans!'

A man was driving along the highway when up ahead, he saw a rabbit hopping across the road. He swerved to avoid hitting it, but unfortunately the rabbit jumped the wrong way and went under the wheels. Being a sensitive soul as well as an animal lover, the driver pulled over to the side of the road and went back to see whether the rabbit had somehow survived. To his dismay, the rabbit was dead. The man was so upset by the incident that he broke down in tears.
    Seeing his distress, a woman driver stopped her car to ask what was wrong.

'I feel terrible,' he said. 'I've just run over a rabbit and killed it.'

'Don't worry,' she said. 'I may be able to help.'

She reached into the glove compartment of her car and pulled out a spray can. She then walked over to the limp, dead rabbit and sprayed the contents of the can onto the animal's body. Miraculously, the rabbit came back to life, jumped up, waved its paw at the two humans and hopped off down the road. Twenty yards on, the rabbit stopped, turned around, and waved at the two again. Another twenty yards on, it stopped again, turned around and waved, and so on, stopping and waving at similar intervals until it disappeared from view.

The man was amazed. He had never seen anything like it. He went over to the woman and said: 'What on earth was in your spray can? What did you spray onto that rabbit?'

She turned the can around so that the man could read the label. It said: 'Hare Spray: Restores Life to Dead Hare. Adds Permanent Wave.'

A farmer kept a donkey in a stable, but the donkey's ears were so long that they repeatedly hit the top of the door, causing the animal to kick out dangerously. So the farmer decided to raise the height of the doorframe.

He spent all day toiling away with his hacksaw. Seeing that he was struggling to complete the task, his neighbour suggested: 'Instead of lifting the door frame, wouldn't it be easier if you simply dug out the ground in the doorway and made it deeper?'

'Don't be an idiot,' said the farmer. 'It's the donkey's ears that are too long, not his legs!'

What happened to the two bedbugs who fell in love? – They got married in the spring.

A baby camel turned to its father and said: 'Dad, why do we have humps on our back?'

'Well, son,' replied the father, 'our humps contain the fat necessary to sustain us through all the days when we're out in the desert.'

'Oh,' said the baby camel. 'Dad, why do we have long eyelashes?'

'They're to protect our eyes from the sandstorms that rage in the desert.'

'Right. Dad, why do we have big padded feet?'

'Because the sand in the desert is very soft and we need big feet so that we can walk on the sand without sinking.'

'I understand now, Dad. So what are we doing in the city zoo?'

Did you hear about the shepherd who drove his flock through town, and got a traffic ticket for making a ewe turn?

A man was driving down a country lane when his car ground to a halt. As he lifted the bonnet to study the engine, a brown and white cow from an adjoining field lumbered over to the car and stuck her head under the bonnet next to the man's. After a moment or two, the cow turned to the man and said: 'Looks like a dodgy carburettor to me.' Then she walked back into the field and resumed her grazing.

Amazed, the man walked up to the farmhouse and asked the farmer: 'Is that your cow in the field?'

'The brown and white one? Yes, that's old Buttercup.'

'Well,' continued the man, 'my car's broken down, and she just said: "Looks like a dodgy carburettor to me."'

The farmer shook his head and said: 'Don't mind old Buttercup. She don't know a thing about cars.'

Why do birds fly south in the winter? – Because it's too far to walk.

While cleaning out the aviary at a run-down zoo, a keeper spotted that two finches had died of old age. So he put them in a sack and continued with his rounds. At the primate cage he saw that two chimpanzees had also died of natural causes, so he put them in the sack with the finches. With money tight, he decided to use the dead creatures as food for the lion and that afternoon he emptied the sack into the lion's cage. The lion took one look at his meal and grimaced: 'Oh no! Not finch and chimps again!'

A couple's house was plagued by an invasion of flies in hot weather. After the husband went round with the fly swatter, his wife asked him whether he had managed to kill any.

'Yes,' he said. 'Four males and two females.'

'How can you tell?' she asked.

'Four were on a beer can and two were on the phone.'

A mother kangaroo jumped in the air with a squeal before glaring down into her pouch. 'How many times do I have to tell you? No smoking in bed!'

One frozen winter, Jim and John built a skating rink in the middle of a field. A shepherd leading his flock decided to take a shortcut across the rink, but the sheep were afraid of the ice and refused to cross it. So in desperation the shepherd began tugging them to the other side.

'Look at that,' said Jim to John. 'That guy is trying to pull the wool over our ice.'

What's light, white, and sweet and hangs from trees? – A meringue-utan.

A man drove his car into a ditch on a quiet country lane. Fortunately a farmer passed by with a horse.

'Could your horse pull my car out of the ditch?' asked the driver.

'Buddy's a big strong horse,' said the farmer. 'We'll see what we can do.'

The farmer hitched Buddy up to the car and said: 'Pull, Blackie, pull!' Buddy didn't move an inch.

Then the farmer said: 'Pull, Samson, pull!' Buddy didn't move an inch.

Then the farmer said: 'Pull, Troy, pull!' Buddy didn't move an inch.

Then the farmer said: 'Pull, Buddy, pull!' And Buddy effortlessly pulled the car out of the ditch.

The driver was grateful but mystified. 'Tell me,' he said, 'why did you keep calling your horse by the wrong name?'

'Well,' said the farmer, 'you see, Buddy is blind. And if he thought he was the only one pulling, he wouldn't even try!'

An elephant was drinking from a river when he spotted a turtle asleep on a log. Without a word, the elephant went over and kicked it right across the river.

'What did you do that for?' asked a giraffe.

'Because,' said the elephant, 'I recognized it as the same turtle that took a nip out of my trunk fifty-three years ago.'

'Wow, what a memory!' said the giraffe.

'Yes,' said the elephant. 'Turtle recall.'

What do you call a woodpecker that's lost its beak? – A headbanger.

A duck walked into a general store, waddled up to the counter and asked: 'Got any grapes?'

'No,' said the clerk.

The following day the duck was back again. 'Got any grapes?' he asked.

'No,' said the clerk, becoming irritated.

The next day the duck came in again. 'Got any grapes?'

'No,' yelled the clerk. 'I've told you before, we don't have any grapes. I'm getting so fed up with all this that if you come in here again and ask for grapes, I'm going to take a hammer and nail your webbed feet to the floor.'

The next day the duck came in again. 'Got any nails?'

'No,' replied the clerk.

'Good,' said the duck. 'Got any grapes?'

A naturalist found evidence of a hitherto unknown breed of giant elephant living in the rainforests of South America. Eventually he raised sufficient funds to launch an expedition to bring back this direct descendant of the mammoth.

After weeks battling their way through the jungle, the party stumbled upon a three-foot tall pygmy standing next to the dead elephant. The naturalist approached the pygmy and exclaimed: 'My God! Did you kill this elephant?'

'Yes,' replied the pygmy.

'But it's so big and you're so small!'

'Yes,' said the pygmy.

'How on earth did you kill it?' asked the naturalist.

'With my club,' said the pygmy.

'How big is your club?' inquired the naturalist.

'Well, there are about a hundred of us.'

The rarest bird in the world was called, appropriately enough, the Raree Bird. After being hunted to extinction in the nineteenth century, there was only one Raree Bird left on the planet by 1900 and a huge reward was offered for its capture – dead or alive.

The last surviving Raree Bird lived in Africa where it was relentlessly pursued by a hunter eager to claim the reward. After six months of following the Raree Bird across plains and through jungles, the hunter finally tracked it down to a lone tree in the desert. The hunter aimed his rifle at the bird and fired. The bullet narrowly missed but the shock was sufficient to send the Raree Bird toppling from its perch. With an injured wing, it lay on the ground at the hunter's feet and pleaded to be spared.

'Please, Mr Hunter,' begged the Raree Bird, 'don't kill me like this.

Shooting me is so brutal – it's not sporting. Besides, it's your last bullet. What will happen if you're attacked by a lion?'

The hunter thought about what the Raree Bird had said and while he was distracted, the bird hobbled behind a rock. But the hunter spotted a feather protruding from behind the rock and fetched a heavy wooden club from his bag.

'Please, Mr Hunter,' begged the Raree Bird, 'don't kill me like this. If you club me to death, nobody will be able to recognize it as me, and you won't be able to claim the reward.'

The hunter realized that the Raree Bird had a point and so he searched for an alternative instrument of death. While the hunter's back was turned, the bird limped off, only to find itself cornered at the top of a cliff, above a two hundred foot drop. The hunter quickly caught up with the Raree Bird.

'I'm going to push you over the cliff and claim the reward,' snarled the hunter. 'Is that a fitting way for the last Raree Bird to die?'

'No, Mr Hunter, please don't,' begged the Raree Bird.

'Why, what's wrong this time?' demanded the hunter.

The bird wiped a tear from its eye. 'Because it's a long way to tip a Raree . . .'

Three men hired a small plane to hunt moose in Canada, but the pilot warned them: 'This is a very small plane, so you can only bring back one moose.'

Inevitably the men got carried away and ended up killing three moose. When they brought their trophies back to the plane, the pilot was appalled.

'I said one moose only!'

'That's what you said last year,' replied one of the hunters, 'but for an additional hundred dollars you then allowed us to take the three moose on the plane. So, here, take the money now.'

The pilot relented and allowed the three moose on board, but shortly after take-off the plane crashed. Pulling himself from the wreckage, one hunter looked around semi-conscious and asked: 'Where are we?'

One of his colleagues muttered: 'About a hundred yards from where we crashed last year.'

If a spider is in a corn field, does it make cob webs?

A cash-strapped zoo was desperate for a major attraction to boost falling attendances. Unable to afford any new animals, the zoo manager persuaded a visitor to dress up in a gorilla costume and masquerade as a great ape.

The ruse worked well as the man threw himself into the role with great enthusiasm, devouring buckets of bananas, swinging on branches, prowling his cage with menace and beating his chest dramatically. But then one day, he went too far and accidentally fell into the lion cage next door.

'Help! Help!' cried the fake gorilla.

The lion let out an almighty roar, then rushed at him, put his paw on the gorilla's chest and growled: 'Shut up, or we'll both lose our jobs!'

Three mischievous boys went to the zoo one day on a school outing. They decided to visit the elephant enclosure but within an hour, they were picked up by a police officer for causing a commotion. The officer hauled them off to security for questioning and the teacher in charge told them to give the police their names and say what they were doing at the elephant house.

The first boy said: 'My name is Gary, and I was just throwing peanuts into the elephant enclosure.'

The second said: 'My name is Kevin, and all I was doing was throwing peanuts into the elephant enclosure.'

The third boy was a bit shaken up by the ordeal and said: 'My name is Peter, but my friends call me Peanuts . . .'

A happily married man had only one complaint: his wife was always nursing sick birds. One evening he came home to find a woodpecker with a splint on its beak sitting in his favourite chair. In another chair was a condor wrapped in a blanket while in the kitchen his wife was comforting a shivering little wren that she had found in the snow.

The furious husband strode over to where his wife was towelling down the cold little bird. 'I can't stand this any more!' he yelled. 'We've got to get rid of all these darn . . . !'

'Please, dear,' she said, cutting him off in mid-curse. 'Not in front of the chilled wren.'

Two sheep were standing in a field.

One went: 'Baaaa.'

'Huh,' said the second, 'I was going to say that.'

One day a gorilla escaped from the zoo, prompting a huge search of the district and appeals on radio, television and in the newspapers. He was finally discovered a few days later in the city library where zoo officials found him sitting at a desk in the reading room with two books spread out in front of him. The gorilla was deep in concentration. One book was the Bible; the other was written by Charles Darwin.

The zoo keepers asked the gorilla what he was doing. The gorilla replied: 'I'm trying to figure out whether I am my brother's keeper or my keeper's brother.'

If a pig loses its voice, is it disgruntled?

A farmer was helping one of his cows to give birth when he noticed his young son watching wide-eyed from behind the fence. 'Oh dear,' thought the farmer, 'I'm going to have to explain the birds and bees to him.'

So when he had finished, he asked the boy: 'Well, have you got any questions about what you've just seen?'

'Just one,' gasped the boy. 'How fast was that calf going when it hit the cow?'

A hungry lion was scouring the jungle looking for food. In a clearing he spotted two men. One was sitting on a rock, reading a book; the other was scribbling a letter. Without a moment's hesitation, the lion pounced on the man reading the book and ate him . . . because even lions know that readers digest and writers cramp.

Two fleas were planning a trip from the living room to the kitchen. One turned to the other and said: 'Shall we hop or take the dog?'

A police officer saw a man driving a pickup truck full of penguins. He pulled the guy over and said: 'You can't drive around with penguins in this town. Take them to the zoo at once.'

The next day he saw the man still driving around with the penguins, and this time they were wearing sunglasses.

The cop said: 'I thought I told you to take these penguins to the zoo yesterday.'

The man replied: 'I did. Today I'm taking them to the beach.'

A man bought a horse from a farmer. 'This is a very unusual horse,' admitted the farmer. 'He has religious tendencies. You have to say "Hallelujah" to make him go and "Amen" to make him stop.'

The man thanked the farmer for the advice, jumped on the horse, said 'Hallelujah' and rode off. After he had been riding for a while, the man decided that he wanted to go faster, so he said 'Hallelujah' and the horse broke into a trot. Then the man said 'Hallelujah' again and the horse accelerated into a gallop. One more 'Hallelujah' and the horse was running like the wind.

Suddenly the man realized that they were approaching a cliff, and he could not remember how to stop the horse. So he prayed: 'Dear God, please help me remember how to stop this horse, and I will always be grateful. Amen.'

Hearing the magic word, the horse stopped right on the edge of the cliff. A clod of earth was pushed over the side and crashed to the ground two hundred feet below. Realizing how close he had come to death, the man sat back in the saddle and sighed with relief: 'Hallelujah!'

While out walking one day, two men came across an abandoned well. Curious as to how deep it was, they threw a pebble down the well and waited for the sound of it hitting the bottom. But they heard nothing.

So they found a larger rock and threw that down the well. Still they heard nothing.

This experiment clearly called for something bigger and after a quick search, they found a railroad tie. With a superhuman effort, they carried the tie across to the well and dropped it down the hole. As they stood back waiting for the sound of it hitting the bottom, a goat suddenly darted between them and leaped into the open well.

The men were still recovering from the shock when a farmer approached.

'Anyone seen a goat?' he asked.

'Yeah,' they said, 'one just jumped down that well.'

'No, that couldn't have been my goat,' said the farmer. 'Mine was tethered to a railroad tie.'

A mother firefly led her large family of fireflies through the jungle one night. To avoid being eaten by marauding bats or other nocturnal foragers, she ordered everyone to keep their lights out. But after nearly an hour's walking, she turned round to see that one of the youngsters at the back had got his light on.

'What are you doing?' she said. 'You'll get us all killed. I told you: no lights.'

'I know,' said the young firefly. 'But if you've gotta glow, you've gotta glow.'

Bizarre Real-life Animal Laws:
Dogs are forbidden from riding in ambulances in Westport, Massachusetts.
It is illegal to get a fish drunk in Oklahoma.
In Atlanta, Georgia, it is against the law to tie a giraffe to a street lamp.
In Kingsville, Texas, there is a law against two pigs having sex on the city's airport property.
When a man meets a cow in Minnesota, he is required by law to remove his hat.
It is illegal for hens to lay eggs before 8am and after 4pm in Norfolk, Virginia.
Cats in International Falls, Minnesota, are not permitted to chase dogs up telegraph poles.
In Minnesota, it is illegal to tease skunks.
In Alaska, it is illegal to look at a moose from the window of an aircraft.
In Marshalltown, Iowa, a horse will be breaking the law if it eats a fire hydrant.
Ducks quacking after 10pm in Essex Falls, New Jersey, are breaking the law.
In Quitman, Georgia, it is against the law for a chicken to cross any road within the city limits.
It is illegal to start a fire under a mule in Ohio.
It is forbidden to march a goose down a street in McDonald, Ohio.
No one is allowed to shoot bullfrogs on a Sunday in Pennsylvania.
In Minnesota, it is illegal to cross state lines with a duck on your head.
In Statesville, North Carolina, it is against the law to race rabbits in the street.
It is illegal to take a deer swimming in water above its knees in North Carolina.
In Wallace, Idaho, it is illegal to sleep in a dog kennel.
It is forbidden to blow your nose in public places in Leahy, Washington, because the noise might scare a horse and cause it to panic.
In Oklahoma, dogs must have a permit signed by the mayor in order to congregate on private property in groups of three or more.
In Tuscumbia, Alabama, no more than eight rabbits may live on the same block.

In New York City, it is illegal to shoot rabbits from the rear end of a Third Avenue streetcar when it's moving.

Horses are allowed in the taverns of Burns, Oregon, if an admission fee is paid in advance.

People in Oklahoma can be fined for pulling faces at a dog.

A Detroit, Michigan, law prohibits crocodiles from being tied to fire hydrants.

Donkeys are not allowed to sleep in bathtubs in Brooklyn, New York.

In Seattle, goldfish can ride the city buses in bowls only if they keep still.

In Texas, it is illegal to put graffiti on someone else's cow.

In Chicago, it is illegal to take a French poodle to the opera.

It is against the law to ride a mule down the Main Street of Lang, Kansas, in August unless the animal is wearing a straw hat.

A pub landlord was just locking up when there was a ring on the doorbell. He opened the door to find a snail sitting there.

'What do you want?' asked the landlord.

'I want a drink,' said the snail.

'Clear off,' said the landlord, 'we're closed. And anyway we don't serve snails.'

'Please, I'm desperate for a drink.'

'I'm sorry,' repeated the landlord. 'We're closed.'

'Just one drink,' begged the snail.

'No.' And with that the landlord kicked the snail and slammed the door.

Ten months later, the landlord was again locking up when he heard the doorbell ring. He opened the door to see the snail sitting there.

The snail said: 'Why did you do that?'

What's worse than finding a maggot in your apple? – Finding half a maggot.

Night after night, a keen ornithologist stood in his backyard hooting like an owl. After weeks of getting no reply, he suddenly heard an owl hoot back at him. He was overjoyed at the response and for the next nine months man and bird kept up a regular dialogue of hooting. He was fascinated by his ability to relate to a wild creature and kept a thorough record of all their conversations.

Just when he was on the brink of taking his findings to the Natural

History Society, his wife happened to be talking to a neighbour who lived four doors away.

'My husband spends his nights calling to owls,' she confided.

The neighbour said: 'That's funny. So does mine!'

How do you catch a gorilla? – Hide in a tree and make a noise like a banana.

A police drugs raid recovered well over eight hundred pounds of marijuana. Unsure as to how to dispose of it, the authorities decided to burn it and lit a huge fire miles from the nearest town. The illegal drug burned fiercely, sending a vast cloud of thick smoke billowing into the sky. They consoled themselves with the belief that the fire was not having any adverse effect on the environment or wildlife until suddenly a flock of terns, migrating south for the winter, flew straight into the cloud of smoke. Upon exiting the other side, the entire flock mysteriously performed a 180-degree turn and flew back into the cloud of smoke. The effect of this was, alas, to leave no tern unstoned.

Armed Forces

A Navy psychiatrist was interviewing a sailor for a job. To ascertain how the young man might react to danger, the psychiatrist asked: 'What would you do if you looked out of that window right now and saw a battleship coming down the street?'

The young man replied confidently: 'I'd grab a torpedo and sink it.'

'And where would you get the torpedo?'

'The same place you got your battleship!'

When a famous admiral died, the navy wanted to lay on a grand ceremony in his honour. After two hours of speeches and hymns, it was suggested that the event should end with a cannon salute.

That was when the organization of the ceremony threatened to run into trouble for nobody on the four-man planning committee could seem to agree on the number of shots that should be fired in the salute.

'I think one shot would be perfect,' said the first captain. 'It would be moving and deeply symbolic.'

'I think there should be two,' suggested the second captain, 'in honour of the two great battles he won.'

'Well, I think we should have three shots,' said the third captain, 'as a mark of respect to the number of ships he commanded.'

The fourth captain puffed quietly on his pipe until asked for his opinion.

'There's no argument,' he said. 'We must fire four shots at the end of the ceremony to commemorate the late admiral's four decorations for gallantry. In fact, I have already discussed the matter with the Queen, and it has all been approved.'

With that, the other three captains stormed out of the room. One turned at the door and said: 'We wouldn't have bothered coming if we had known it was a four-gun conclusion!'

With his fort about to be attacked by the Sioux, an army captain sent for his trusty Indian scout.

'Now,' said the captain, 'I want you to use all your renowned tracking skills to give me some idea of the strength of the enemy.'

The Indian scout lay down, put his ear to the ground and reported: 'Big war party. Two hundred braves in warpaint. Two chiefs, one on a black horse, one on a white horse. Also a medicine man with a limp.'

'That's amazing!' said the captain. 'You can deduce all that just by listening to the ground?'

'Not really,' replied the Indian. 'I'm looking under the gate.'

What soldiers smell of salt and pepper? – Seasoned troopers.

A knight walked into a blacksmith's shop. The blacksmith said: 'You've got mail.'

A soldier cradled the dying General Custer in his arms at the Little Big Horn. Custer gasped: 'I'll never understand Indians. A few minutes ago they were singing and dancing . . .'

An army sergeant was passing barracks after lights out when he heard some voices from inside. He threw the door open and barked: 'A few minutes ago you all heard me say "goodnight". What you don't seem to have grasped is that when I say "goodnight", what I really mean is "shut the hell up"!'

The room instantly fell silent. But after a few seconds, a small voice could be heard from somewhere at the back of the darkened room: 'Goodnight, sergeant.'

An old British Navy sailor and a retired US marine were chatting about who had experienced the tougher career.

The marine declared proudly: 'I did thirty years in the corps and fought in three of my country's wars. Fresh out of boot camp, I hit the beach at Okinawa, clawed my way up the blood-soaked sand, and eventually took out an entire enemy machine gun nest with a single grenade.

'As a sergeant, I fought in Korea. We pushed back the enemy inch by bloody inch all the way up to the Chinese border, always under a barrage of artillery and small arms fire.

'Finally, I did three consecutive combat tours in Vietnam. We ploughed through the mud and razorgrass for fourteen hours a day, plagued by rain and mosquitoes, ducking under sniper fire all day and mortar fire all night. In a firefight, we'd fire until our arms ached and our guns were empty, then we'd charge the enemy with bayonets!'

'Oh,' said the sailor with a dismissive wave of his hand, 'all shore duty, huh?'

Riding through the forest one day, a medieval duke noticed a number of archery targets on the trees with an arrow smack in the middle of each one. Impressed by such magnificent marksmanship, the duke instructed his followers to find the archer responsible so that he could sign the man up for his private army. An hour so later, they returned with a small boy, carrying a bow and arrow.

The duke could hardly believe his eyes. 'Do you mean to tell me that this mere boy is the master archer?'

'Yes, sire, it is me,' said the boy.

The duke looked at him suspiciously. 'Are you sure you didn't just walk up to the targets and hammer arrows in the middle?'

'No,' replied the boy. 'I swear on my mother's life that I shot them from a hundred paces.'

'Very well,' said the duke. 'I believe you, and hereby admit you into my service. But you must tell me how you came to be such an outstanding shot.'

'Well,' said the boy, 'first I fire the arrow at the tree, and then I paint the target around it.'

A retired army general bumped into his former orderly in a bar and tried to persuade him to come and work for him as a valet.

'Your duties will be exactly the same as they were in the army,' explained the general. 'There's nothing to it – you'll soon catch on again.'

After thinking about it for a short while, the man accepted the job offer. On his first morning at work, at eight o'clock sharp, the ex-orderly entered the ex-general's bedroom, pulled open the curtains and gently woke the general. He then strode around to the other side of the bed, slapped his employer's wife on the bottom and said: 'Okay, sweetheart, it's back to the village for you!'

During the Second World War, the SS picked up a number of Irishmen in Berlin and threw them in jail on suspicion of being spies. Determined to escape, the prisoners started using their combs to file through the metal bars on their cell window, disguising the noise with a cheerful Irish refrain. Alas, the German guards were not fooled. As one guard remarked to another with a little song of his own: 'I can always tell . . . when Irish spies are filing . . .'

Trying out a new army computer, an officer typed in a question: 'How far is it from the mess room to the sentry box?'
  The computer replied: 'Six hundred.'
  The officer typed: 'Six hundred what?'
  The computer replied: 'Six hundred, sir!'

Airman Jones was assigned to the induction centre where he was to advise new recruits about their government benefits, especially their GI insurance.
  After a couple of months his captain noticed that Jones had almost a hundred per cent record for insurance sales – something that had never been achieved before.
  Rather than ask him the secret of his success, the captain decided to stand at the back of the room and listen to Jones's sales pitch. First, Jones explained the basics of the GI insurance to the new recruits, and then said: 'If you have GI insurance and go into battle and are killed, the government has to pay two hunded thousand dollars to your bene-ficiaries. If you don't have GI insurance, and you go into battle and get killed, the government has to pay only a maximum of six thousand.
  'Now,' he concluded, 'which bunch do you think they are going to send into battle first?'

A platoon of rebel soldiers were travelling along a track when they heard a voice call from behind a sand-dune: 'One of the king's men is better than ten rebels!'
  The rebel commander quickly sent ten of his best soldiers over the dune whereupon there was a short, fierce gun battle followed by silence. The voice then called out: 'One of the king's men is better than a hundred rebels!'
  The furious rebel commander reacted by sending his next best hundred troops over the dune. There was a ten-minute battle, then silence until the voice called out again: 'One of the king's men is better than a thousand rebels!'
  The enraged rebel commander mustered a thousand fighters and sent them across the dune. There was a huge battle lasting half an hour, then silence. Eventually one wounded rebel soldier crawled back over

the dune and with his dying words told his commander: 'Don't send any more men. It's a trap. There's actually two of them.'

The admiral was resting in his quarters when suddenly the lookout burst in. 'Two enemy ships spotted on the horizon, sir.'

'Right,' said the admiral. 'Fetch me my red shirt.'

The danger passed but later in the day the lookout burst in once more. 'Three enemy ships spotted on the horizon, sir.'

'Right,' said the admiral leaping to his feet. 'Fetch me my red shirt.'

Again the danger passed but the lookout felt compelled to ask the admiral why he always ordered his red shirt when battle was imminent.

'Well,' explained the admiral, 'it's a question of morale. If I'm wounded while wearing a red shirt, the men won't see the blood and will continue to fight.'

When this answer was relayed to the men, all were agreed that their admiral was a remarkably courageous man.

The next morning, the admiral was resting in his quarters as usual when suddenly the lookout burst in. 'Twelve enemy ships spotted on the horizon, sir.'

'Right,' said the admiral. 'Fetch me my brown underpants.'

A drill sergeant at training camp told his recruits: 'Today, I have good news and bad news. First the good news: Private Mounce will be setting the pace on the morning run.'

The men were overjoyed because Mounce was fat and slow. Then the drill sergeant added: 'Now the bad news: Private Mounce will be riding a motorcycle.'

A young ensign had nearly completed his first overseas tour of duty when he was given an opportunity to display his ability at getting the ship under way. With a stream of crisp commands, he had the decks buzzing with men. The ship steamed out of the channel and soon the port was far behind. The ensign's efficiency was remarkable. In fact, word was going around that he had set a new record for getting a destroyer under way. The ensign basked in the glory and was not at all surprised when another seaman approached him with a message from the captain.

He was, however, rather surprised to find that it was a radio message, and he was even more alarmed to read: 'My personal congratulations upon completing your underway preparation exercise according to the book and with amazing speed. In your haste, however, you have overlooked one of the unwritten rules – Make Sure The Captain Is Aboard Before Getting Under Way.'

The top brass from the Army, Navy and Marine Corps were arguing about who had the bravest troops. They decided to settle the dispute using an enlisted man from each branch.

The army general called a private over and ordered him to climb to the top of the base flagpole, then let go with both hands and salute. The private quickly complied.

Next, the admiral ordered a sailor to climb the pole, polish the brass knob at the top, salute smartly and jump off. The sailor did as he was told and landed on the concrete below.

Finally, the marine was told to do exactly the same as the army and navy men but in full battle gear, pack filled with bricks and loaded weapon carried high. He took one look at the major general and said: 'You're out of your mind, sir.'

The marine commander turned to the others and said: 'Now *that's* guts!'

Sir Geraint and his men returned to the king's castle bearing bags of gold and half a dozen slave women, the fruits of plundering the land for a week.

'Where have you been all this time, Sir Geraint?' asked the king.

'I have been robbing and pillaging on your behalf all week, sire, burning the villages of your enemies in the north.'

'But I don't have any enemies in the north,' protested the king.

'You have now, sire.'

You Might Be In The Army If:

You won't let your wife go to the cinema because the laundry room failed inspection.

You have a fence set up around your house that even Rambo wouldn't want to mess with.

Lights out is at 2200hrs every night.

Your kids must perform ten push-ups before entering the dining room.

Your wife's favourite lipstick colour is khaki.

Your kids wear a beret when they go out to play.

You cut the lawn in a pair of jungle boots.

Your dog's name is Ranger.

Your nicest set of clothes is your uniform.

You think waking up at 7am is sleeping in.

You've ever worn camouflage gear to a wedding.

You refer to sex with your wife as being 'on manoeuvres'.

You spend your spare time polishing your boots.

Your family thinks there's nothing wrong when you disappear for a month.

All your friends are in the army, too.

An army general received word that the mother of Private Philpott had died. At parade, the sergeant major volunteered to break the sad news to Philpott.

'I'll go and tell him, shall I, sir?'

'Steady on, sergeant major,' said the general. 'You can't just barge in and tell the poor man that his mother has died, in front of the rest of the regiment. This calls for tact and diplomacy. Subtlety.'

'Very well, sir,' said the sergeant major. 'I shall be at my most diplomatic and subtle.'

With that, he marched over to the line of soldiers and bellowed the command: 'All those with mothers still alive, one pace forward . . . Not so fast, Philpott!'

As everyone sat around the table for a big family dinner, the youngest son announced that he had just signed up at an army recruitment office. There were audible gasps from the gathering, followed by laughter as his older brothers expressed their disbelief that he could handle army life.

'Oh, come on, quit joking,' snickered one. 'You haven't really signed up, have you?'

'You'd never get through basic training,' scoffed another.

Finally his father spoke up. 'It's going to take a lot of discipline. Are you ready for that?'

Coming under fire on all sides, the new recruit looked to his mother for help. But she said simply: 'Are you really going to make your own bed every morning?'

A new ensign assigned to submarines was eager to impress his commanding officer with all the knowledge he had picked up at submarine school. After listening patiently for five minutes, the senior officer said: 'Listen, it's simple. Add the number of times we dive to the number of times we surface. Divide that number by two. If the result doesn't come out even, don't open the hatch.'

The sergeant was appalled to find that ten of his men were late back to army camp following leave. As he waited impatiently at the barracks gates, one man finally ran up to him, panting heavily.

'Sorry, sir! I can explain. You see, I had a date and it ran a little late. I ran to catch the bus but I missed it. So I hailed a cab but it broke down. I managed to find a farm and bought a horse but it dropped dead. In the end I had to run ten miles, and now I'm here!'

The sergeant was highly sceptical about this explanation, but at least the soldier had made it back eventually so he let him off this time. A couple of minutes later, eight more of his men ran up to the sergeant, panting. He asked them why they were late. Each told the same story.

'Sorry, sir! I had a date and it ran a little late. I ran to catch the bus but I missed it. So I hailed a cab but it broke down. I managed to find a farm and bought a horse but it dropped dead. In the end I had to run ten miles, and now I'm here!'

The sergeant eyed them suspiciously but since he had let the first man go, he decided that it was only fair to excuse them too. A few minutes later, the tenth and last soldier ran up to him, panting heavily.

'Sorry, sir! I had a date and it ran a little late. I ran to catch the bus but I missed it. So I hailed a cab but . . .'

'Let me guess,' interrupted the sergeant. 'It broke down.'

'No, sir. There were so many dead horses in the road, it took forever to get round them.'

A cargo plane was preparing for departure from Thule Air Base in Greenland, and they were waiting for the truck to arrive to pump out the aircraft's sewage tank. The aircraft commander was becoming impatient. Not only was the truck late, but also the airman performing the job was extremely slow in getting the tank pumped out. Finally the commander snapped and promised to punish the airman for his slowness.

The airman replied: 'Sir, I have no stripes, it is twenty below zero, I'm stationed in Greenland, and I am pumping sewage out of airplanes. Just what are you going to do to punish me?'

At drill on a cruiser, the deck officer asked the starboard lookout: 'What would you do if a sailor was washed overboard?'

'I'd yell: "Man Overboard!"'

'Good. Now what would you do if an officer fell overboard?'

The lookout hesitated for a second before answering: 'Which one, sir?'

Thrown from his horse while fleeing the enemy troops, a cavalryman lay helpless on the ground, his leg broken. With the enemy approaching, the terrified soldier called out: 'All you saints in heaven, help me get up on my horse!'

Then with a superhuman effort, he leaped onto the horse's back, only to go straight over the other side. Once again lying on the ground, he called to the heavens: 'Okay, just half of you this time!'

In the year 2000, a Belgian man went to his local priest and confessed: 'Forgive me, Father, for I have sinned. During the Second World War, I hid a Jewish man in my attic.'

'That's not a sin,' said the priest. 'It was an act of great kindness.'

'But I made him agree to pay thirty-five francs for every week he stayed.'

'I admit that wasn't particularly charitable,' said the priest, 'but you did it for a good cause.'

'Thank you, Father,' said the man. 'That is a great relief to me. I have just one more question.'

'What's that?'

'Do I have to tell him the war is over?'

At the recording of a television game show, an army major was in the hot seat for the last big question. The host read the question slowly and carefully but, to his dismay, the major didn't know the answer. However the major was not prepared to miss out on the chance of winning a fortune, so he put his contingency plan into operation. He let out a sudden cough, and from the back of the stage four mounted knights-in-armour appeared, waving their lances threateningly at the host.

The host looked momentarily terrified, but then a steely determination set in as he refused to allow the major to cheat his way to the big cash prize. Suddenly the host leapt into the air and karate kicked the first knight onto the floor. He picked up the lance from the stricken knight and fought off the second, who also fell sprawling to the floor. The second knight's horse shied and bolted, colliding with the third knight in the process.

The game show host was just beginning to enjoy himself now. He waved the spear he was still carrying at the fourth knight, looked back at the contestant and said: 'Is that your final lancer?'

Two military policemen were chasing a fleeing draftee from the army base. He fled into a nearby convent where he spotted a nun sitting in the courtyard.

'Quick, sister,' he begged. 'Hide me. I don't want to be drafted and the military police are after me.'

The nun lifted her skirt and told the young man to hide under it.

'You've got nice legs for a nun,' he remarked from beneath the skirt.

'If you look up a little farther,' said the nun, 'you'll find a set of balls. I don't want to be drafted either!'

A group of soldiers on a first-aid course were tested by the instructor. He asked the recruits: 'If the sergeant major sustained a head injury during an exercise, what would you do about it?'

One soldier piped up: 'I'd wrap a tourniquet around his neck and tighten it until the bleeding stopped.'

A naval officer met a pirate at an inn and couldn't help noticing that the pirate had a wooden leg, a hook and an eye patch.

'How did you get the wooden leg?' asked the officer.

'Well,' said the pirate, 'we were in a storm at sea and I was swept overboard into shark-infested waters. And one of the sharks bit off my leg.'

'That's terrible,' said the officer. 'What about the hook? How did you come by that?'

'Well,' said the pirate, 'we were boarding an enemy ship and in the heat of battle, my right hand was sliced off by an enemy swordsman.'

'How terrible,' said the officer. 'And the eye patch?'

'A seagull dropping fell into my eye.'

'You lost your eye to a seagull dropping?'

'Well, it was my first day with the hook.'

A group of young army parachutists went up in the plane for a jump, but the flight was rough and in the end it became so windy that the officer in charge called it off. The plane headed back to base but as it made a remarkably smooth landing, five of the young parachutists were violently sick.

The officer didn't understand it. 'How come you could put up with that rough flight, but you couldn't handle a smooth landing?'

One of the parachutists replied: 'Well, sir, we've always jumped out of planes, but we've never actually landed in one before!'

On a camouflage training session, an army private was ordered to disguise himself as a tree and stay absolutely silent and still. But suddenly in the depths of the forest he jumped in the air and screamed, a piercing noise which alerted the sergeant.

'What the heck do you think you're doing?' boomed the sergeant. 'Don't you know that if this had been a real military exercise, by yelling and jumping the way you did, you could have endangered the lives of the entire company?'

'I'm sorry, sir,' replied the private. 'But I can explain. I did my best out there. I stood still when a flock of pigeons used me for target practice. And I didn't move a muscle when a large dog peed on my lower branches. But when two squirrels ran up the leg of my pants and I heard the bigger one say: "Let's eat one now and save the other till winter" . . . that did it!'

During World War Two, German soldiers were looting French villages of food, wine and women. In one village, everyone fled in advance except for a young man and his ninety-year-old grandmother who refused to be driven out by the Germans. When the German tanks rumbled into the near-deserted village, the soldiers cornered the young man.

'Bring us food,' they demanded.

'All I have left is a loaf of bread,' said the young man.

'War is war,' said the soldiers, and they forced him to hand over the last crumbs.

Then they shouted: 'Bring us wine.'

'All I have left is a third of a bottle,' said the young man.

'War is war,' insisted the soldiers, and they forced him to hand over the remainder of the bottle of wine.

Then the soldiers shouted: 'Bring us a woman.'

'But there is only one woman left in the village,' protested the young man.

'War is war,' barked the soldiers.

So he fetched his ninety-year-old grandmother. The German soldiers took one look at her and said: 'Er, maybe, we'll let you off this time.'

'No way,' said Granny. 'War is war.'

Many years ago, a tribe of Basques living in a valley in northern Spain came under threat from marauding barbarians. Since the valley only had one way in or out, the Basques thought they could a lay a trap by luring the enemy to their deaths. So the entire Basque army waited in the hills at the valley entrance and when the barbarians passed below, they descended on them. Unfortunately the barbarians were more experienced soldiers, boasting better equipment, and, with no means of escape, the hapless Basques were slaughtered on the spot. The moral of the story is simple: Don't put all your Basques in one exit.

Art

An artist asked the gallery owner if there had been any interest in his paintings currently on display.

'I've got good news and bad news,' replied the owner. 'The good news is that a gentleman inquired about your work and wondered whether it would appreciate in value after your death. When I told him it would, he bought all twelve of your paintings.'

'That's great!' exclaimed the artist. 'So what's the bad news?'

The gallery owner said sombrely: 'The man was your doctor.'

A visitor to an art gallery liked to study every painting for hidden meanings, but even he was puzzled by one picture, which appeared to be nothing more than a blank canvas.

'I don't know who's responsible for this,' he raged to a man standing next to him, 'but it looks to me like a complete waste of space.'

'As a matter of fact, I'm the artist responsible.'

'Then perhaps you can enlighten me as to what it's supposed to be?'

'Certainly,' said the artist. 'That, sir, is a cow grazing.'

'Where's the grass?'

'The cow has eaten it, sir.'

'But where's the cow?'

'You don't think she'd be stupid enough to stay after she'd eaten all the grass, do you?'

A man was standing in a gallery, studying two near-identical pictures by the same artist. Both showed a glass of wine, a basket of bread rolls, a bowl of salad and a plate of smoked salmon. Yet one was priced at a hundred dollars, the other at a hundred and twenty. So he asked the gallery owner to explain why one was more expensive than the other.

'It's easy,' said the owner, pointing at the more expensive painting. 'You get three extra slices of smoked salmon in that one.'

A woman at an art gallery was looking at some abstract paintings. One featured an assortment of black and yellow blobs while the one next to it consisted of a mass of grey streaked with red.

Finally she went over to the artist and said: 'I really don't understand your paintings.'

The artist replied dramatically: 'I paint what I feel inside me.'

The woman said: 'Have you tried Alka Seltzer?'

A millionaire specialized in collecting impressionist paintings. Although he showed interest in the works of French, Italian and Spanish artists, he concentrated on the Eastern Bloc countries and in particular Czechoslovakia, believing that one day works from that region would be greatly sought-after. Over the years he built up an impressive collection of more than three hundred paintings. Individually they were not that valuable but as a collection they were of considerable interest to art historians. Consequently he amended his will and bequeathed his entire collection to his hometown museum.

The millionaire died in 1990, shortly before the break-up of the old Soviet Union, an act that sent the prices of art from Communist countries such as Czechoslovakia rocketing through the roof. His surviving relatives, who had previously shown little interest in his paintings, began to circle like vultures, especially when cataloguing revealed that his collection included a long-lost work by a famous French impressionist – a painting that was now worth a great deal of money. The relatives demanded that the will be contested in court. Some wanted all the paintings for themselves; others were willing to allow the museum to have everything except the French example, but even that was negotiable if the museum was prepared to pay a reasonable price for it.

The judge deliberated for just over a month before concluding that there was no ambiguity whatsoever in the will. He therefore awarded all the paintings to the museum. His ruling in favour of the museum was clear and to the point: 'You get your Monet for nothing and your Czechs for free.'

Babies and Birth

Three men were waiting expectantly outside the labour ward of the city hospital. After a few minutes, a nurse came out to tell the first man: 'Congratulations. You are the father of twins.'

'Twins!' he exclaimed. 'How about that? I work for the Doublemint Chewing Gum Company!'

Five minutes later, a nurse came out to tell the second man: 'Congratulations. You are the father of triplets.'

'Triplets!' he said. 'What an amazing coincidence! I work for the 3M Organization!'

The third man stood up ashen-faced and muttered: 'I need some air. I work for 7-Up!'

Two women sitting in the doctor's waiting room began discussing babies.

'I want a baby more than anything else in the world,' said one. 'But I guess it's impossible.'

'I used to think that,' said the other. 'But then everything changed. That's why I am here. I'm going to have a baby in three months.'

'You must tell me what you did.'

'I went to a faith healer.'

'But I've tried that. My husband and I went to one for nearly a year and it didn't help a bit.'

The other woman smiled and whispered: 'Try going alone, next time.'

A man phoned the hospital in a highly agitated state. 'My wife is pregnant,' he gasped. 'Her contractions are only two minutes apart.'

The doctor asked: 'Is this her first child?'

'No, you fool. This is her husband!'

When a woman discovered that she was pregnant, her four-year-old son overheard his parents' conversation. But he didn't say anything until a week later when a family friend asked him if he was excited about the prospect of a new brother or sister.

'Yes,' said the boy, 'and I know what we're going to name it. If it's a girl, we're going to call her Emily, and if it's another boy we're going to call it Quits.'

A man staggered home from the pub pushing a baby carriage.

His wife went mad. 'You drunken idiot!' she screamed. 'That's not our baby!'

'I know,' he said, 'but it's a nicer pram.'

A couple were at their first pre-natal class. So that the husband could get an idea of what it felt like to be pregnant, the instructor strapped a bag of sand to his stomach.

As he walked around with his new bulge, the husband said: 'This doesn't feel too bad.'

Then the instructor deliberately dropped a pen and said to the husband: 'Now I want you to pick up that pen as if you were pregnant.'

'You want me to do it the way my wife would?' confirmed the husband.

'Exactly the same,' said the instructor.

The husband turned to his wife and said: 'Honey, pick up that pen for me.'

Anyone who says it's as easy as taking candy from a baby has never tried it.

An English soccer fan was about to become a father for the first time, with the baby due to arrive at some point during the World Cup.

His friend said: 'What will you do if your wife is having the baby on the same day that England play?'

'Don't worry, I just bought a VCR. I can watch the birth after the game.'

For weeks, a six-year-old boy had been telling his teacher about the baby brother or sister that was expected at his house. One day his mother allowed him to feel the movements of the unborn child. Although obviously impressed, he didn't say anything and from then on, he stopped telling his teacher about the impending event.

The teacher finally sat the boy on her lap and said: 'Timmy, whatever became of that baby brother or sister you were expecting at home?'

Timmy burst into tears and confessed: 'I think Mommy ate it!'

A young couple were desperate to start a family but after eight years of trying, it seemed that they were destined never to become parents. Having exhausted all medical advice, the wife read in a magazine about the growing trend for proxy fathers. She approached a few male friends to ask them if they would be willing to donate their sperm but all declined on moral grounds. So with her husband's backing, she contacted a stranger who was advertising his services. On the morning that the sperm donor was due to call, her husband set off for work as usual and wished her good luck. She wasn't exactly looking forward to the experience.

As chance would have it, that same morning a travelling baby photographer was also in the neighbourhood and called at her house. She answered the door, expecting the sperm donor.

'Good morning, madam,' said the photographer. 'You don't know me, but I've come to . . .'

'Yes, I know,' she interrupted. 'There's no need to explain. Come in. I've been expecting you.'

'Really?' said the photographer, thinking that his advertising must have paid off. 'I must say I have made a speciality of babies.'

'That's what my husband and I were hoping,' she said. 'So, tell me, where do we start?'

'Well, I usually try two in the bathtub, one on the couch and perhaps a couple on the bed. That seems to work for me.'

'No wonder Eric and I haven't had much luck,' she mused.

'If we try several different positions and I shoot from six or seven different angles, I'm sure you'll be pleased with the results.'

'I do hope so,' she replied, becoming more nervous by the minute. 'Can we get this over with quickly?'

'In my line of work, I have to take my time,' he said. 'It's no good rushing these things. I'd love to be in and out in five minutes, but I think you'd be disappointed with that.'

'That's true,' she sighed knowingly.

The photographer opened his briefcase and pulled out a folder of baby pictures. 'This one was done on top of a bus,' he revealed proudly.

'Really?' she said, a mixture of surprise and horror.

'And these twins turned out really well in view of the fact that their mother was difficult to work with.'

'In what way was she difficult?'

'She insisted that we go outdoors, so I had to take her over to the park to get the job done properly. People were crowding four deep to watch. It took over three hours before we were finished. It was really exhausting.'

By now the wife was sick with worry.

'Right,' he said. 'I'll just get my tripod.'

'Tripod?'

'Yes, I need a tripod on which to rest my Canon.'

At that point the wife fainted.

One night a woman found her husband standing over their newborn baby's crib. Silently she watched him. As he stood looking down at the sleeping infant, she saw on his face a mixture of emotions: disbelief, doubt, delight, amazement, enchantment, scepticism.

Touched by his unusual display of deep emotions, she felt her eyes grow moist. She slipped her arms around her husband. 'A penny for your thoughts,' she whispered in his ear lovingly.

'It's amazing,' he replied. 'I just can't see how anybody can make a crib like that for only thirty-nine ninety-five!'

Two babies were sitting in their cribs when one called over to the other: 'Are you a little girl or a little boy?'

'I don't know,' replied the other baby giggling.

'What do you mean, you don't know?' asked the first.

'I mean I don't know how to tell the difference.'

'Well, I do,' said the first baby chuckling. 'I'll climb into your crib and find out.'

So he carefully manoeuvred himself into the other baby's crib, then quickly disappeared beneath the blanket. After a couple of minutes, he resurfaced with a big grin on his face. 'You're a little girl and I'm a little boy,' he said proudly.

'You're ever so clever,' cooed the baby girl, 'but how can you tell?'

'It's easy,' replied the baby boy. 'You've got pink booties and I've got blue ones.'

A woman in labour with her first child began to shout over and over again: 'Shouldn't, wouldn't, couldn't, can't.'

The worried husband said: 'Doctor, what's wrong with my wife?'

'It's nothing to worry about,' said the doctor. 'She's just having her contractions.'

Cars

A teenage boy had just passed his driving test and to celebrate, the whole family climbed into the car for his inaugural drive. Dad sat in the back, directly behind the driver.

The boy said: 'I'll bet you're back there to get a change of scenery after all those months of sitting in the front passenger seat teaching me how to drive?'

'No,' replied Dad. 'I'm going to sit back here and kick the back of your seat while you drive, just like you've been doing to me for seventeen years.'

'The car won't start,' said a wife to her husband. 'I think there must be water in the carburettor.'

'How do you know?' said the husband scornfully. 'You don't even know what the carburettor is!'

'I'm telling you,' insisted the wife. 'I'm sure there's water in the carburettor.'

'We'll see,' said the husband patronisingly. 'Let me check it out. Where's the car?'

'In the swimming pool.'

A father was driving his son to school when he inadvertently made a wrong turn at some traffic lights. Realizing his mistake, he said: 'Oops, I just made an illegal turn.'

'It's okay, Dad,' said his son. 'The police car behind us did the same thing.'

A woman was out driving when she stalled at a red light. Hard though she tried, she was unable to restart the engine and soon a long queue began to form. The male driver immediately behind her was particularly impatient, honking his horn continuously.

Finally she got out, went up to the driver behind and said: 'I can't seem to get my car started. Would you be a sweetheart and see if you can get it started for me? I'll stay here in your car and lean on your horn for you!'

Used Car Buyers' Guide – The Reality:

MUST SELL . . . before it falls apart.

RUNS FINE . . . I was going to say 'runs excellent' but I had a last-minute conscience attack.

NEEDS SOME BODY WORK . . . was blind sided by a Winnebago.

WELL-MAINTAINED . . . I changed the oil occasionally.

ALL ORIGINAL . . . I never had anything fixed, adjusted or replaced.

LOADED WITH OPTIONS . . . each one more troublesome than the last.

NEVER SMOKED IN . . . unfortunately, that's the best thing I can say about it.

A REAL CHERRY . . . it's the pits.

ONLY ONE OWNER . . . difficult to sell.

GREAT ACCELERATION . . . downhill.

LOOKS LIKE NEW . . . just don't try to drive it anywhere.

GREAT SECOND CAR . . . you wouldn't want to depend on it for primary transportation.

LOTS OF POTENTIAL . . . doesn't run.

NEEDS MINOR REPAIR . . . doesn't run.

An old man was driving on the motorway when his mobile phone rang. It was his wife, saying that she had just heard a news report about a car that was driving the wrong way up the motorway.

'I know,' said the old man. 'But it's not just one car, it's hundreds of them!'

A car mechanic received a repair order that read: 'Check for clunking sound when going around corners.' So he took it out on a test drive and, sure enough, whenever he went round a corner, he heard a clunk.

However he quickly located the problem and returned the repair order to the service manager with the notation: 'Removed bowling ball from trunk.'

A Californian man has invented a robotic parking attendant. He's calling it the Silicon Valet.

A motorist was driving along when he saw a police car behind flashing him to stop. As he stepped out of the car, he threw up his hands in despair.

The officer said: 'Sir, I'm afraid your rear lights aren't working properly.'

'I don't believe this!' screamed the man. 'I can't believe this has happened!'

'There's no need to get so worked up,' said the officer. 'You can easily get the lights fixed at a garage.'

'Damn the lights!' yelled the driver. 'Where's my caravan?'

While working on a car, a mechanic accidentally swallowed some brake fluid. To his surprise, he quite liked the taste. The next day he decided to have another swig and enjoyed it so much that he told his friend.

His friend said: 'You shouldn't be drinking brake fluid. It's bad for you.'

But the mechanic was becoming hooked, each day increasing his intake of brake fluid. His friend became seriously concerned.

'You've got to give it up,' he insisted. 'Brake fluid is poisonous.'

'Don't worry,' said the mechanic. 'I can stop any time.'

If you smuggle cars into the country, are you trafficking?

When her car broke down, a woman called out a local mechanic to repair it. He lifted up the hood, looked in the engine, whacked something with a hammer and said: 'Try it now.'

To her amazement, the car started straight away.

'That's incredible,' she said. 'You've been here less than a minute and you've managed to fix it. I'm so grateful.'

'All part of the job, madam. That'll be two hundred and fifty dollars.'

The smile vanished from the woman's face. 'How much? How can you charge to hundred and fifty dollars when all you did was hit it with a hammer?'

'I can write you out an itemized bill if you like.'

'Yes, please,' she said firmly.

So he wrote out the bill and handed it to her. It read: 'Hitting engine with hammer — $10. Knowing where to hit it — $240.'

An angry motorist went back to the garage where he had purchased an expensive battery for his car six months earlier. He told the garage owner: 'When I bought that battery, you said it would be the last battery my car would ever need. Now six months later, it's dead!'

'Sorry,' said the garage owner, 'I didn't think your car would last longer than that.'

Facts About the Company Car:
It accelerates at a phenomenal rate.
It has a much shorter braking distance than the private car.
It can take speed humps at twice the speed of private cars.
The battery, radiator water, oil and tyres never have to be checked.
The floor is cunningly designed to double as an ashtray.
It never needs to be kept in a garage at night.
It can be driven up to sixty miles with the oil warning light flashing.
It needs washing less often than private cars.
Unusual and alarming engine noises are easily eliminated by turning up the radio.
The suspension is reinforced to allow for the weekend loads of bricks, concrete slabs and other building material.
It needs no security system and may be left anywhere, unlocked and with the keys in the ignition.

A man stood by the side of the road hitch hiking on a very dark night in the middle of a storm. The thunder was rolling and no cars passed. The rain was so torrential that he could barely see a few feet ahead. Then suddenly he saw a car come towards him and stop.

Instinctively, the man climbed into the car and shut the door, only to realise that there was nobody behind the wheel! The car started slowly. He peered through the windscreen at the road ahead and, to his horror, saw a tight corner. Scared to death, he said a silent prayer. He was still in shock when, a few yards before the corner, a hand appeared through the window and turned the wheel. The man, paralysed with terror, watched how the hand appeared every time he approached a corner. Finally he summoned the strength to escape from the moving car and run to the nearest town. Wet and shaking, he found a bar where he started telling everyone about the terrible experience he had been through.

About half an hour later, two men walked into the bar, and one said to the other: 'Look, Denzil, that's the guy who climbed into the car while we were pushing it.'

A scoutmaster was driving along a country lane one morning when a truck suddenly pulled out in front of him. He tried to sound his horn to warn the truck driver, but no noise came out and so he was forced to slam on his brakes. Fortunately his brakes were in good working order and a collision was avoided, but the scoutmaster thought he had better get the broken horn fixed. So he took the car to the nearest garage and explained the problem.

'The horn simply isn't working,' the scoutmaster told the mechanic. 'I can't get a sound out of it – not a honk, a toot or even a gentle beep. I'm on my way to weekend scout camp and I'm already running late, so is there any chance you could get some sort of sound out of it by lunchtime, even if it's just a patched up job?'

'Okay,' said the mechanic, 'I'll have a look at it. Come back in a couple of hours.'

The mechanic fiddled with the wiring and eventually managed to get the horn to make a sound. It was by no means a loud blast, more a beep, but he thought that would satisfy the scoutmaster for the time being.

When the scoutmaster returned to collect his car, the mechanic was out at lunch. But he had left a note on the windscreen. It read: 'Beep repaired.'

For the following jokes you can substitute Skoda or Lada

What do you call a Yugo with a long radio aerial? – A dodgem.

How do you double the value of a Yugo? – Put a gallon of petrol in it.

What do you call a Yugo with a sun roof? – A skip.

Why does a Yugo have a double rear window heater? – To keep everyone's hands warm while they're pushing it.

What do you call a Yugo with twin exhausts? – A wheelbarrow.

What do you call a Yugo driver who says he's had a speeding ticket? – A dreamer.

What happens if you apply rust remover to a Yugo? – It disappears.

Cars

Why do Yugos need two spare wheels? – So you can cycle home.

What's the difference between a Yugo and the flu? – You can get rid of the flu.

A boy was walking along the road when a car pulled up alongside him. The driver leaned out and said: 'If you get in my car, I'll give you a bag of sweets.'

The boy ignored him.

'All right,' said the driver, 'if you get in my car, I'll give you two bags of sweets.'

The boy still ignored him.

'Listen,' persisted the driver, 'if you get in my car, I'll give you all the sweets you want and ten dollars.'

The boy turned to the driver and said: 'Dad, for the last time, I'm not getting into that Yugo!'

An insurance agent was teaching his wife to drive when her brakes suddenly failed on a steep downhill gradient.

'I can't stop,' she shrilled. 'What should I do?'

He said: 'Brace yourself and try to hit something cheap.'

Driving along a busy street, a man became aware of an impatient woman who was tailgating him. She was so close that when he had to brake to allow some children to use a pedestrian crossing, she almost crashed into him. Furious at being delayed, she sounded her horn and began waving her fists in a disgraceful exhibition of road rage.

Before she could move off, she felt a tap on her window. It was a police officer who ordered her to step out of the car. He then asked her to come down to the station where she was searched, fingerprinted, photographed, and put in a cell. A couple of hours later, after vehicle checks had been carried out, she was told that she could collect her valuables and that she was being released without charge.

The woman was extremely indignant at her arrest and demanded an apology. The officer responsible explained the reason for the mistake. 'You see, madam, I pulled up behind your car while you were sounding your horn and loudly cursing the driver in front of you. Then I noticed the "Follow Jesus, Not Me" sticker on the rear window, the "God Is Love" sticker, and the chrome-plated Christian fish emblem on the boot. Naturally, I assumed that you had stolen the car . . .'

One cab driver said to another: 'Why have you got one side of your cab painted red and the other side painted blue?'

'Well, when I get in an accident, the police always believe my version of what happened, because all the witnesses contradict each other.'

A motorist accidentally hit and killed a calf that was crossing the road. Feeling guilty about the incident, he asked the farmer how much the animal was worth.

'About three hundred dollars today,' replied the farmer, 'but in six years it would have been worth nine hundred. So realistically I'm nine hundred dollars out of pocket. That's what I want as compensation.'

The motorist wrote out a cheque and handed it to the farmer. 'Here is the cheque for nine hundred dollars,' he said. 'It is post-dated six years from today.'

Bogged down in a huge, mud-filled hole in the road, a motorist paid a passing farmer five dollars to pull him out with his tractor.

Once back on dry ground, the grateful motorist said: 'If that's all you charge, I bet you're pulling people out of the mud day and night.'

'Can't,' said the farmer. 'At night I haul water for the hole.'

Although he had hardly ever driven in his life, a man always dreamed of owning a sports car, so when he inherited a large sum of money from a dead relative, he headed straight for the car showroom and bought himself a Porsche. Within half an hour he was on a quiet country road putting his new car through its paces. Faster and faster he went until suddenly, at top speed, there was an almighty bang and smoke began pouring from the engine.

Towed back home, he immediately called the car salesman and told him what had happened. The salesman was at a loss for an explanation but, because the customer was so wealthy, he agreed to swap the Porsche for a Lotus. The next day, the man took the Lotus out on its first run, but as he hit a hundred miles per hour, the same thing happened. The car juddered to a sudden halt and the engine exploded.

Highly dissatisfied, the man phoned the car salesman once again and told him what had happened. Eventually the salesman agreed to exchange the Lotus for a Ferrari, but only on condition that he joined the customer on a test drive to see what the problem was.

Together they set off into the country. Soon the customer was picking up speed and going through the gears from fourth to fifth and up to sixth. As he accelerated still more, the car suddenly shook violently and the engine went bang.

'What did you do?' asked the salesman, shaken.

'Well,' said the driver, 'I was going faster and faster, and I ran out of numbered gears. So I put it into R for "Race".'

Why It's Time To Buy a New Car:

Instead of an airbag, there's a whoopee cushion taped to your steering wheel.

You lose the traffic light getaway race to a milk float.

Joyriders have stolen every car in the street except yours . . . even though you leave it unlocked.

For the past five years you've had to settle for making 'vroom vroom' noises while sitting on the driveway.

Only the Garfield on the side window is holding the car together.

You keep losing dates on left turns.

The stench from the bodies in the trunk is becoming unbearable.

A car was speeding along the road when it suddenly crashed through the guard rail, rolled down a cliff, bounced off a tree and landed upside down in a gully, wheels spinning wildly.

As the driver clambered dazed from the wreckage, a passer-by asked: 'Are you drunk?'

'Of course,' said the motorist. 'What do you think I am – a stunt driver?'

An actuary quoted an extremely low premium for an automobile 'fire and theft' policy. When asked why it was so cheap, he said: 'Who'd steal a burnt car?'

A man was annoyed when his wife told him that a car had backed into hers, damaging the front bumper, and that she hadn't got the registration number.

'What kind of car was he driving?' asked the husband.

'I honestly don't know,' she said. 'I can never tell one make of car from another.'

Hearing this, the husband decided it was time for her to learn and for the next few days, whenever they were driving, he made her name each car they passed until he was satisfied that she could recognize every make.

It worked. About a week later she bounded in with a big grin on her face. 'Darling,' she said. 'I hit a Peugeot!'

A guy asked a passer-by: 'What's the quickest way to York?'
  'Are you walking or driving?'
  'Driving.'
  'That's the quickest way.'

Man: My wife drives like lightning.
  Friend: You mean fast?
  Man: No, she hits trees.

A wild drinking party in the woods was prematurely curtailed by a sudden storm – thunder, lightning and torrential rain. Two young men, much the worse for drink, were forced to run for ten minutes in the driving rain before eventually reaching the sanctuary of their car. Just then the rain began to ease off and, although neither was in a fit state to drive, they decided to head for home. So the driver started the engine and put his foot down – the sooner they got home, they thought, the less chance there was of being stopped by the police.

They had been driving for about a minute when an old man's face suddenly appeared at the passenger window. The young men were startled, not least because the speedometer showed they were doing about forty miles per hour.

'What do you want?' they shouted, swigging beer as the old man tapped on the window. The driver put his foot down but when the old man kept tapping, the scared passenger wound the window down part-way.

'Do you have any tobacco?' asked the old man quietly.

The passenger looked aghast at the driver. 'He wants tobacco!'

'Well, give him a cigarette, quick!' shouted the driver, accelerating up to sixty miles per hour.

The passenger fumbled around with the packet, handed the old man a cigarette and yelled to the driver 'Step on it!' before quickly winding the window up.

'God, that was spooky!' said the passenger, taking another swig of beer.

'You're not kidding!' agreed the driver. 'Let's get home — fast!'

But moments later, with the speedometer touching eighty miles per hour, there was another tap at the passenger window.

'I don't believe it!' screamed the passenger. 'It's him again!'

'See what he wants now,' yelled the driver.

The terrified passenger wound the window down a little and the old man asked politely: 'Have you got a light?'

The passenger tossed a lighter out of the window, wound up the window and again ordered the driver to put his foot down.

They were now doing a hundred miles per hour and still guzzling beer, trying to forget what they had just seen, when all of a sudden there was more knocking.

'Oh my God! He's back!'

The passenger, shaking with fear, wound down the window and, in a trembling voice, asked the old man what he wanted this time.

The old man replied softly: 'Do you want some help getting out of the mud?'

Out driving with his wife, a man sped along a country lane in an increasingly reckless fashion.

'Can't you slow down when you're turning corners?' she complained. 'You're scaring the life out of me.'

'Do what I do,' he replied. 'Shut your eyes.'

Over lunch in a fast-food restaurant, a woman was telling her friend about a recent accident in which a teenage boy had driven into the back of her car. 'The boy blamed me and called me every rude, dirty name in the book!'

Two small boys had been listening at the next table and one turned to the other and said wide-eyed: 'There's a book?'

On a bitterly cold winter's day, a man was driving down a lonely country road when heavy sleet began to fall. As the car windows iced up, his worn wiper blades were unable to cope with the conditions and soon fell apart. With no visibility, he faced the prospect of having to stay in his car until the weather improved, but just then he had an idea. Stepping into the surrounding heathland, he overturned a series of large rocks until he found two extremely lethargic hibernating adders. Straightening the snakes out flat, he installed them on the blades and they gave him perfect visibility.

When he relayed the story to his wife, she was puzzled as to what had given him the idea about using the snakes.

'Surely,' he said, 'you've heard of wind chilled vipers?'

A police officer pulled over a car on a quiet country road and walked up to the elderly driver.

'Excuse me, madam,' he said. 'Can you explain why you have been driving so erratically for the past few miles. You've been weaving all over the road.'

'Thank goodness you're here, officer,' she gasped. 'I almost had an accident. I looked up and there was a tree right in front of me. I swerved to the left and there was another tree. So I swerved to the right and there was another tree. It was the most terrifying experience.'

Calmly the officer reached through the side window to the rear view mirror and explained: 'Madam, there are no trees along this road. It was your air freshener.'

A driver was speeding along a twisty country lane when he turned a corner and, to his horror, saw two farmhands standing chatting in the middle of the road. He swerved violently to avoid them but the car ran up an embankment, did a triple somersault and landed in an adjacent field.

One farmhand turned to the other and said: 'That was a stroke of luck. I reckon we got out of that field just in time.'

A man and a woman were driving along the same road from opposite directions. As they passed, the woman leaned out of the car window and yelled: 'Pig!'

The man responded by leaning out of his window and shouting: 'Bitch!'

Each continued on their way until the man rounded the next corner and crashed into a huge pig in the middle of the road.

When a man arrived home from work, his wife was waiting for him. She sat him down and told him she had good news and bad news about the car.

'Right,' he said. 'What's the good news?'

She said: 'The air bag works.'

Two old ladies were out driving in a big car. Both could barely see over the dashboard. They were cruising along at a steady twenty-six miles an hour when they came to a junction and although the light was red, they went straight through. The woman in the passenger seat thought to herself: 'I must be losing it, I could have sworn we just went through a red light.'

Three hundred yards further down the road, they approached another junction. Again the light was red, but again they went through it. The woman in the passenger seat thought to herself: 'I must be seeing things because I'm sure we just went through another red light.'

A couple of minutes later they went through a third red light. This time she turned to the other woman and said: 'Mildred! Don't you know we just went through three red lights! You could have killed us!'

'Oh,' said Mildred. 'Am I driving?'

The owner of an old Datsun Cherry in Canada was upset because his car wouldn't start. He took it to a garage where the mechanic informed him that the engine needed a new cog. Unfortunately, owing to the vehicle's age, that particular line of cogs had been discontinued and the only way to obtain the essential cog was to have one made specially. So the car owner wrote to Datsun head office in Tokyo and ordered a cog for a 1988 Datsun Cherry. But the company wrote back to say that it was simply not economical to manufacture one cog and that they could therefore respond only to a minimum order of hundred. Left with little alternative, the man duly placed an order for a hundred cogs.

The shipment was transported from Japan by air but over Seattle the plane suddenly developed engine trouble. The pilot immediately ordered that all extra weight be jettisoned and the hundred cogs were hurled out of the aircraft. As they fell to earth, a man on the ground turned to his wife and said: 'Hey, Mary, it's raining Datsun cogs.'

The following are genuine statements made on insurance claim forms:
The accident happened because I had one eye on the lorry in front, one eye on the pedestrian and the other on the car behind.
I started to slow down but the traffic was more stationary than I thought.
I pulled into a lay-by with smoke coming from under the hood. I realized the car was on fire, so took my dog and smothered it with a blanket.
The car in front hit the pedestrian but he got up so I hit him again.
The accident occurred when I was attempting to bring my car out of a skid by steering it into the other vehicle.
The gentleman behind me struck me on the backside. He then went to rest in a bush with just his rear end showing.
I knew the dog was possessive about the car but I would not have asked her to drive it if I had thought there was any risk.

I was thrown from the car as it left the road. I was later found in a ditch by some stray cows.

I thought my window was down, but I found it was up when I put my head through it.

Q: Could either driver have done anything to avoid the accident?

A: Travelled by bus.

Chicken Jokes

Why did the chicken cross the basketball court? – He heard the referee calling fowls.

Why did the turkey cross the road? – To prove he wasn't chicken.

Why did the chicken cross the road, roll in the mud and cross the road again? – Because he was a dirty double-crosser.

Why did the skeleton cross the road? – To get to the Body Shop.

Why didn't the skeleton cross the road? – Because he didn't have the guts.

Why did the chicken stop in the middle of the road? – She wanted to lay it on the line.

Why did the chicken cross the playground? – To get to the other slide.

Why did the sheep cross the road? – Because it was tied to the chicken.

Why did the turtle cross the road? – To get to the shell station.

Why did the dinosaur cross the road? – Because chickens hadn't evolved yet.

Why did the hedgehog cross the road? – To see his flat mate.

Why did the horse cross the road? – It was the chicken's day off.

Famous people give their answers to the question: why did the chicken cross the road?

Albert Einstein: Whether the chicken crossed the road or the road moved beneath the chicken depends on your point of reference.

Bill Gates: I have just released the new Chicken Office 2004, which will not only cross roads, but will lay eggs, file your important documents, and balance your cheque book.

Rene Descartes: Since the chicken does not really exist, it was only an illusion that the chicken crossed the road. This illusion was only in my mind. Therefore I created the chicken that crossed the road.

Charles Darwin: Over great periods of time, chickens have been naturally selected in such a way that they are now genetically disposed to cross roads.

Douglas Adams: Forty-two.

Martin Luther King: I envisage a world where all chickens will be free to cross roads without having their motives called into question.

Richard Nixon: The chicken did not cross the road. I repeat, the chicken did not cross the road.

Bill Clinton: I did not cross the road with THAT chicken. What do you mean by chicken? Could you define chicken, please?

George W. Bush: The chicken was misinformated as to what attractivation was on the other side.

Captain James T. Kirk: To boldly go where no chicken has gone before.

Mark Twain: The news of its crossing has been greatly exaggerated.

Fox Mulder: You saw it cross the road with your own eyes. How many more chickens have to cross the road before you believe it?

Colonel Sanders: I missed one?

A keen gardener liked to show off his floral display to his grown-up son, but was disappointed with the results one summer. 'It's those damn free range chickens from next door,' he moaned. 'They're always coming through the hedge and pecking my flowers. I've tried everything, but I don't know how to stop them.'

When the son next came to visit a month later, he was immediately struck by how much healthier the flowerbed looked. It was a riot of colour.

'It looks like you've solved the problem with your neighbour's chickens. How have you managed to keep them off?'

'Well,' replied the father, 'it was easy in the end. One night I hid half a dozen eggs under a bush in the flowerbed, and the next morning I made sure that my neighbour saw me picking them up. Since then I haven't been troubled by his chickens!'

After the egg hunt on Easter Sunday, a farm boy decided to play a prank. He sneaked into the chicken coop and replaced every egg with a brightly coloured one.

A few minutes later the rooster walked in, saw all the coloured eggs, then stormed outside and beat up the peacock!

A man was driving along the road when to his amazement he was overtaken by a three-legged chicken. The man accelerated to try and keep up, but the faster he went, the faster the chicken went too. He couldn't believe that a chicken could run that fast. After ten minutes, the man could no longer keep pace with the bird and saw it disappear from view, but, determined to discover the origins of this curious fowl, he followed its tracks down a country lane. At the end of the lane he found a farmer leaning on a gate.

'Did you see a three-legged chicken go past here?' asked the man.

'Sure,' said the farmer. 'I breed them.'

'You breed three-legged chickens? Why?'

'Well,' said the farmer. 'I like a leg, my wife likes a leg, and my son likes a leg.'

'I see,' said the man. 'What do they taste like?'

'Darned if I know,' replied the farmer. 'They run so fast I can't catch them!'

A farmer specialized in the fertilized egg business. He had several hundred young layers – or pullets – and a dozen roosters whose job it was to fertilize the eggs. In order to make the business as profitable as possible, he attempted to keep a strict record of each rooster's performance, but found the chore to be exceedingly time-consuming. Then one day he spotted a set of bells for sale at market and hit on the idea of tying a bell around each rooster's neck. Whenever a rooster mated with a pullet, the bell around its neck would ring and since each bell played a different tune, he was able to monitor the workrate of the various male birds from the comfort of his porch.

The farmer's favourite rooster was called, appropriately, Randy. But one morning the farmer was surprised because he didn't hear Randy's bell ring once. On closer investigation, he discovered that the crafty old bird had put its bell in its beak to prevent the bell ringing.

Randy would then sneak up on a pullet, do the business and move on to the next bird.

The farmer was so impressed by Randy's ingenuity that he entered the rooster for the county fair. Randy was a sensation and picked up two awards. Not only did he win the No Bell prize but also the Pullet Surprise.

Children

A young boy wanted to earn some pocket money, so he knocked on the rear door of a big mansion. When the house owner – a wealthy banker — answered the door, the boy asked whether there were any odd jobs he could do to earn a dollar.

The banker was not in the habit of being generous, so he decided to make the youngster earn every cent of his dollar. 'Okay, son,' he said, 'I'll give you a dollar if you paint my porch. You'll find a tin of paint and a brush in the garage.'

An hour later the boy knocked on the back door again.

'Finished already?' said the banker.

'Yes, sir,' said the boy. 'But I think I ought to tell you. It's a Mercedes you've got, not a Porsche.'

A small boy turned to his Aunt Edna and said: 'My God, you're ugly!'

His mother overheard the remark and was appalled. She took him to one side and gave him a real telling-off before ordering him to go back and say sorry to Aunt Edna.

Suitably chastened, the boy went over and said quietly: 'Aunt Edna, I'm sorry you're ugly.'

A little girl made a cup of tea for her mother.

'I didn't know you could make tea,' said Mom taking a sip.

'Yes, I boiled some water, added the tea leaves like you do, and then strained it into a cup. But I couldn't find the strainer, so I used the fly swatter.'

'What!' exclaimed Mom, choking on her tea.

'Oh, don't worry. I didn't use the new fly swatter. I used the old one.'

A salesman saw a young boy sitting on a porch and said: 'Hi, son, is your Mom at home?'

'She sure is,' replied the boy.

The salesman rang on the bell, but there was no reply. So he pressed again, and then for a third time. Still no reply. Finally he turned to the boy and said: 'I thought you said your Mom was at home?'

'She is,' answered the boy. 'But I don't live here.'

A mother was putting her young son to bed at the height of a violent thunderstorm.

'Mommy,' he asked nervously, 'can I sleep with you tonight?'

'I'm sorry, darling,' she said. 'But I have to sleep with Daddy tonight.'

'It's not fair,' said the boy. 'Tell the big coward not to be such a baby.'

The boss of a big company needed to speak urgently to one of his management team at the weekend, so he phoned him at home.

The phone was answered by a small boy in hushed tones.

'Hello,' said the boss. 'Is your daddy home?'

'Yes,' whispered the child.

'May I talk with him?'

'No.'

The boss was not used to hearing his requests rejected. 'Well, is your Mommy there?'

'Yes,' whispered the boy.

'May I talk with her?'

'No.'

The increasingly impatient boss tried again: 'Is anyone else there?'

'Yes, a policeman.'

The boss was startled to hear that the police were there. 'Well, may I speak with him?'

'No, he's busy,' whispered the boy.

'Busy doing what?'

'Talking to daddy, Mommy and the firemen.'

Just then, the boss heard a strange whirring sound down the phone. 'What's that noise?' he asked.

'A helicopter,' whispered the boy.

'Exactly what is going on there?'

'The search team just landed the helicopter,' confided the boy.

'What are they doing there?'

'They're looking for me.'

The boy stood on the burning deck. But he was just trying to stop his pack of cards from going up in smoke.

A six-year-old boy was standing with his father in front of the polar bear enclosure at the zoo. The father was telling the boy how dangerous polar bears were and that, of all the animals in the zoo, they were the ones that the keepers feared most.

Eventually the boy said: 'Dad, if the polar bear escapes and eats you up . . . ?'

'Yes, son?'

'Which bus do I catch home?'

A group of Boy Scouts from the city were on a camping trip. The mosquitoes were so persistent that the youngsters had to hide under the blankets at night to avoid being bitten. Then, on seeing some lightning bugs, one boy said to his friend: 'We might as well give up. They're coming after us with flashlights.'

Arriving home, a boy confessed to his mother that he had accidentally broken a lamp at his friend's house while playing football in the living room. 'But, Mom,' he added, 'you don't have to worry about buying another one because Craig's mother said it was irreplaceable.'

A small boy came home from school with a sofa slung across his back and armchairs under his arms. His father said angrily: 'I told you not to accept suites from strangers.'

A little boy was excited when his father finally agreed to take him to the zoo. When they got home, his mother asked whether he had a good time.

'It was great,' said the boy, 'and Dad really enjoyed himself too – especially when one of the animals came in at twenty to one.'

Two young boys were staying the night at their grandparents' house. At bedtime they knelt beside their beds to say their prayers. The younger brother said in a really loud voice: 'I pray for a new bike, a portable TV and a Nintendo!'

The other brother said: 'Why are you shouting your prayers? God isn't deaf.'

'No, but grandma is!'

The Differences Between Boys And Girls:

You throw a little girl a ball, and it will hit her in the nose. You throw a little boy a ball, and he will try to catch it. Then it will hit him in the nose.

You dress your little girl in her Sunday best, and she'll look just as pretty when you make it to church an hour later. You dress a boy in his Sunday best, and he'll somehow find every muddy puddle from your home to the church, even if you're driving there.

If a girl accidentally burps, she will be embarrassed. If a boy accidentally burps, he will follow it with a dozen fake belches.

Boys grow their fingernails long because they're too lazy to cut them. Girls grow their fingernails long so that they can dig them into a boy's arm.

By the age of six, boys will stop giving their dad kisses. By the age of six, girls will stop giving their dad kisses unless he bribes them with sweets.

A little girl will pick up a stick and look in wonderment at what nature has made. A little boy will pick up a stick and turn it into a gun.

When girls play with Barbie and Ken dolls, they like to dress them up and play house with them. When boys play with Barbie and Ken dolls, they like to tear off their clothes.

Girls are attracted to boys from an early age. At the same age, boys are attracted to dirt.

Girls will cry if someone dies in a movie. Boys will cry if you turn off the DVD player after they've watched the *Teenage Mutant Ninja Turtles* movie three times in a row.

Girls turn into women. Boys turn into bigger boys.

A little girl was looking at a picture book when she asked her mother: 'Mommy, where do babies come from?'

'The stork, darling,' replied the mother.

The girl went back to her book, but a few moments later asked: 'Mommy, who keeps bad people from robbing our house?'

'The police, darling,' answered the mother.

The girl returned to her book, but seconds later asked: 'Mommy, if our house was on fire, who would save us?'

'The fire department, darling.'

The girl briefly resumed leafing through her picture book until she asked: 'Mommy, if I'm sick, who will make me better?'

'The doctor, darling.'

The girl glanced at her book, then asked: 'Mommy, where does our food come from?'

'The butcher, darling.'

The girl closed her book and asked: 'Mommy, what do we need Daddy for?'

A man called his children together, held up a chocolate bar and asked them who should get it.

'Me . . . me . . . me,' they chorused.

'I'll tell you who will get it,' continued the father. 'Who never talks back to mother and does everything she says?'

Three small voices answered in unison: 'Okay, Dad, you can have it.'

When she got home from school, a seven-year-old girl told her mother that Tommy had kissed her after class.

'How did that happen?' asked the mother, shocked.

'It wasn't easy. Three other girls had to hold him down for me!'

Much to the concern of his parents, an eight-year-old boy had never spoken a word in his life. Then one day after lunch, he turned to his mother and said: 'Soup's cold.'

His mother hugged him and exclaimed: 'Son, I've waited so long to hear you speak! Your father and I have been worried sick. So why have you never said a single word in all these years?'

The boy said: 'Up until now, everything's been okay.'

A young girl and a young boy were at nursery. She said: 'Hey, Paul, do you want to play house?'

'Sure. What do you want me to do?'

'I want you to communicate.'

'That word is too big. I have no idea what it means.'

'Perfect,' she said. 'You can be the husband.'

A small boy was passing his time at home drawing.

'What are you drawing, son?' asked his father.

'I'm drawing God,' replied the boy.

'That's quite hard because nobody knows what God looks like.'

The boy said: 'They will when I'm finished.'

After losing another tooth, seven-year-old James became even more curious about the elusive tooth fairy. Finally putting two and two together, he came right out and asked his mother: 'Mom, are you the tooth fairy?'

Thinking that he was now old enough to hear the truth, she confessed: 'Yes, I am.'

James thought about this revelation for a moment and then said: 'So how do you get into the other kids' houses?'

While watching a vicar perform a baptism, a little girl turned to her father and said: 'Why is he brainwashing that baby?'

A schoolboy was told by a classmate that most adults are hiding at least one dark secret, and that this makes it very easy to blackmail them by simply saying: 'I know the whole truth.'

The boy decided to go home and try it out. Greeted by his mother, he announced: 'I know the whole truth.' She quickly handed him twenty dollars and said: 'Please don't tell your father.'

Pleased with himself, the boy waited for his father to arrive home from work and greeted him with: 'I know the whole truth.' The father promptly handed him fifty dollars and said: 'Please don't say a word to your mother.'

Delighted with the profit, the boy was on his way to school the next day when he saw the postman at the front door. Deciding to try the plan again just for fun, he said to the postman: 'I know the whole truth.'

The postman immediately dropped his mail, opened his arms and said: 'Then come and give your father a big hug.'

A little boy was performing in the school play when he suddenly fell through a large crack in the floorboards.

The audience gasped, but the boy's mother calmly turned to her friend and said: 'Don't worry, it's just a stage he's going through.'

A mother took her five-year-old son with her to the bank on a busy Friday. They got into line behind an overweight woman wearing a business suit, complete with pager. As the mother waited patiently, the boy looked at the woman in front and observed loudly: 'She's fat.'

The big woman turned around immediately and glared at the child, causing the embarrassed mother to reprimand him quietly.

However, a minute later, the unrepentant boy spread his hands as far as they would go and said loudly: 'I bet her butt is *that* wide!' Again, the woman turned and gave him a withering look, forcing the mother to give him a stricter telling off.

But a couple of minutes later the boy stated loudly: 'Look how the fat hangs over her belt!' The woman turned and told the mother in no uncertain terms that she ought to teach her son some manners. The mother responded by issuing threats if he did not behave himself. The boy promised to keep quiet.

Three minutes later, the large woman got to the front of the queue but just as she did so, her pager began to emit its distinctive tone. The boy could not help himself. 'Run for your life, Mom!' he yelled in panic. 'She's backing up!'

One evening, a mother said to her young son: 'Will you pop outside and fetch the broom?'

'Do I have to, Mom? It's dark outside.'

'There's nothing to be frightened of,' said the mother reassuringly. 'Jesus will look after you.'

'Can't it wait until morning?'

'No, I need it now. Don't be afraid. Jesus will keep an eye on you.'

But the boy remained unconvinced. Nervously he made his way to the back door and peered outside into the gloom. Putting a tentative foot over the step, he called: 'Jesus, if you're there, can you hand me the broom?'

One evening a teenage boy volunteered to babysit so that his mother could enjoy a rare night out. At bedtime he sent the youngsters upstairs and settled down to watch the football on the television. One child repeatedly crept downstairs, but the teenager kept waving him back up so that he could concentrate on the match.

Then at about nine o'clock the doorbell rang. It was the woman from next door asking whether her son was there.

'No,' said the teenager brusquely.

Just then a little head appeared over the banister and a voice said: 'I'm here, Mom, but he won't let me go home!'

A mother asked her young son: 'Why on earth did you swallow the money I gave you?'

'You said it was my lunch money.'

A woman getting her hair cut asked the hairdresser when would be the best time to bring in her two-year-old son for his first haircut. The hairdresser replied: 'When he's four.'

Two children were talking. One said: 'I'm really worried. My dad works twelve hours a day to give my family a nice home and plenty of food. My Mom spends the whole day cleaning and cooking for me. I'm worried sick!'

'What are you worried for?' asked his friend. 'It sounds as if you've got it made.'

'Yeah,' said the first, 'but what if they try to escape?'

Rather than drag his tired three-year-old daughter around the shopping mall, a kindly father gave her a ride on his shoulders. But after a few minutes, she started tugging at his hair.

'Stop that, darling,' he said. 'It hurts.'

'But daddy,' she replied, 'I'm only trying to get my gum back.'

Timmy's father was a rector in a small church, and when the bishop came to visit, Timmy was very excited. The bishop arrived late in the evening, well past Timmy's bedtime, but the next morning the boy asked his father if he would be allowed to meet the important guest.

His father thought about this and decided to let Timmy take the bishop his tea and wake him up. The following instructions were issued: 'First, knock on the door of the bishop's room and then say to him: "It's the boy, my Lord, it's time to get up."'

Timmy rehearsed his lines, repeating them over and over. Finally the tea was ready and he picked up the tray and headed for the bishop's room. A few minutes later, the bishop, still in his pyjamas, was seen running out the door and down the lane.

The father turned to his son and said: 'What happened?'

'I'm sorry,' said Timmy. 'I was so nervous I messed up my lines. I knocked on the door and said: "It's the Lord, my boy, your time is up!"'

A couple had two little boys, aged eight and ten, who were always getting into trouble. Having seemingly exhausted every avenue of discipline, their harassed parents heard of a fire and brimstone preacher who had met with some success in correcting the behaviour of wayward children. So they contacted him and he agreed to help.

He asked to see the boys individually, starting with the eight-year-old. The preacher sat him down and asked sternly: 'Where is God?'

The boy did not answer, so the preacher repeated the question, more forcefully: 'Where is God?'

Again the boy made no attempt to answer, so the clergyman raised his voice even more and shook his finger in the boy's face: 'Where is God?'

At that, the boy bolted from the room, ran straight home and shut himself in his bedroom. His older brother asked: 'What happened?'

The younger boy replied: 'We are in BIG trouble this time. God is missing and they think we did it!'

A young boy became separated from his father at the funfair and asked a police officer to help find him.

'Right,' said the officer, searching for a description. 'What's your father like?'

'Beer and women,' replied the boy.

A salesman rang the doorbell of a smart suburban house and was greeted by an eight-year-old boy smoking a cigar and clutching a bottle of whiskey. Stifling his surprise, the salesman asked: 'Is your mother home?'

The kid nonchalantly flicked the ash from his cigar and said: 'What do you think?'

On a visit to his impoverished sister, a man was obliged to share a room with his young nephew. Entering the bedroom, he saw the little boy crouched down at the far side of the bed with his head bowed. Thinking the child had been brought up to say his prayers, the man decided to follow his example and kneeled at the near side of the bed with his head bowed.

The boy said: 'What are you doing?'

'The same as you.'

'You'll be in trouble with my Mom. The pot's on this side!'

Signs That You Were a Bad Child:

You put at least three teachers into retirement.

Your parents used to ground you in advance in order to save time.

Your parents moved without telling you.

Half the animals buried in your backyard weren't dead when you buried them.

Your principal had your name, address, and other school related information on a rubber stamp to save time when writing up your referral sheet.

You spent more time in detention than in regular class.

Your teacher offered you an automatic 'A' grade if you promised not to go to school.

Your name was frequently raised at P.T.A. meetings, along with the words 'thug', 'fight' and 'expelled'.

The wooden paddle in the teacher's desk is shaped like your butt.

You were a frequent subject in other people's therapy.

Clothes

Harry wanted a new suit so he bought a nice piece of cloth and tried to find a good tailor. The first tailor he visited looked at the cloth, measured Harry, then told him there was not enough cloth to make a suit.

Harry found this hard to accept, so he went to the tailor next door who measured both Harry and the cloth before announcing that there was enough cloth to make a three-piece suit.

A week later, Harry returned to collect his suit and noticed that the tailor's son was wearing trousers made of the same cloth. Puzzled, Harry asked: 'How come you have been able to make a three-piece suit for me and trousers for your son when the chap next door could not even make a suit?'

'Simple,' said the tailor. 'The guy next door has two sons.'

Did you hear about the second-hand Indian clothing store called Whose Sari Now?

A man said to his friend: 'How come you're only wearing one glove? Did you lose one?'

The friend said: 'No, I found one.'

A wife was throwing out some old clothes for a charity jumble sale when she reached into the pocket of one of her husband's old suits and discovered a shoe repairer's ticket. She showed the ticket to her husband.

'This ticket must be more than twenty years old,' he said. 'I must have forgotten to collect those shoes. That shop is still there, so I'll take the ticket in and see whether they've still got my shoes.'

'They won't have them after all this time,' said the wife.

'You never know,' said the husband. 'It's worth a try.'

So he went back to the shoe shop with the ticket. The sales assistant said: 'They'll be ready Thursday.'

A wife said to her husband: 'Darling, I need a new dress.'

'What's wrong with the one you've got?' he said.

'Well, it's too long and, besides, the veil keeps getting in my eyes.'

A man walked into a shoe shop and tried on a pair of shoes.

'How do they feel?' asked the sales assistant.

'A bit tight.'

The assistant bent down to check the shoes and said: 'Try pulling the tongue out.'

'They thtill feelth a bith tighth.'

On a day trip to Amsterdam, a young man fell madly in love with a Dutch girl and after a whirlwind romance they got married. For the first six months they were blissfully happy but then she was stricken down with a mysterious foot disease, which meant that she had to wear special inflatable Dutch shoes. Her husband hoped that the inflatable shoes would cure her illness but sadly her condition continued to deteriorate until one day he was devastated to learn that she had popped her clogs.

A man told his friend: 'My wife only has two complaints: nothing to wear and not enough closet space.'

The manager of a ladies' dress shop realized that it was time to give one of her sales staff a pep talk. 'Paula,' she said, 'your figures are the lowest in the department by a long way. In fact, unless you can improve your sales record soon, I'm afraid I'll have to let you go.'

'I'm sorry, ma'am,' said a humbled Paula. 'Can you offer me any advice on how to do better?'

'Well,' said the manager, 'there is an old trick I can tell you about. It sounds silly, but it's worked for me in the past. Get hold of a dictionary and go through it until you find a word that has particular power for you. Memorize it, work it into your sales pitch whenever it seems appropriate, and you'll be amazed at the results.'

Sure enough, Paula's sales figures shot up, and at the end of the month the manager called her in again, this time to congratulate her.

'Did you try my little trick?' she asked.

Paula nodded. 'It took me a whole weekend to find the right word, but I did in the end.'

'And what is it?'

'Fantastic.'

'Yes, that's an excellent word,' said the manager encouragingly. 'And how have you been using it?'

'Well, my first customer on Monday was a woman who told me her little girl had just been accepted at the most exclusive prep school in the city. I said, "Fantastic." She went on to tell me how her daughter always got straight As and was the most popular girl in class. I said, "Fantastic", and she bought five hundred dollars worth of clothing.

'My next customer said she needed a formal dress for the spring ball at the country club, which she was organising. I said, "Fantastic." She went on to tell me she had the best figure of anyone on the committee and that her husband makes the most money. "Fantastic", I said, and she not only bought a two thousand dollar designer gown, but hundreds of dollars of accessories. It's been like that all week: the customers keep boasting, I keep saying, "Fantastic", and they keep buying!'

'Excellent work, Paula,' said the manager. 'You're a credit to the department. Just as a matter of interest, what did you used to say to customers before you discovered your power word?'

Paula shrugged. 'It was usually, "Who gives a damn?"'

Did you hear about the man who put on a pair of clean socks every day? — By the end of the week he couldn't get his shoes on.

An inventor took his latest idea to a bra manufacturer. He said. 'I've come up with a new bra, specially designed for middle-aged women. I call it the "sheepdog bra".

'Why do you call it that?' asked the manufacturer.

'Because it rounds them up and points them in the right direction!'

A man walked into a shoe shop and asked for a pair of shoes, size eight.

The sales assistant said: 'Are you sure, sir? You look like a size twelve to me.'

'Just bring me a size eight,' insisted the customer.

So the assistant fetched a pair of size eight shoes and the man squeezed his feet into them with obvious discomfort. He then stood up in the shoes, but with considerable pain.

'Listen,' he explained, 'I've lost my house to the taxman, I live with my mother-in-law, my daughter ran off with my best friend, and my son just told me he's gay. The only pleasure I have left is to come home at night and take my shoes off!'

A teenage boy with spiked hair, a nose ring and baggy clothes told his friend: 'I don't really like dressing like this, but it stops my parents from dragging me everywhere with them.'

Woman: Whenever I'm down in the dumps I buy myself a dress.
    Friend: I've always wondered where you got them.

A couple decided to take their teenage daughter out for a birthday dinner at a local restaurant. The girl came downstairs wearing a short skirt and a tight top, thereby prompting a tirade from her father about the state of her clothes. The mother was more sympathetic and reminded him that when they were young, she used to dress the same way.
    'Yeah,' said the husband. 'Well if you remember, I had something to say about that, too.'
    'Yes, dear,' said his wife. 'You did. You asked me for my phone number.'

Country music star Kenny Rogers was about to go on stage for the biggest concert of his life. But as he stepped out of the dressing room, he suddenly felt his left leg give way beneath him. The heel of his cowboy boot, that he had been meaning to get repaired for some time, had finally fallen off. So while the audience waited, Kenny had to hunt around frantically for a spare pair, all the time muttering to himself: 'You picked a fine time to leave me, loose heel.'

A small boy put on his shoes by himself, but his mother spotted that he had got them mixed up.
    'Sweetheart,' she said, 'you've put your shoes on the wrong feet.'
    The boy looked at her and said: 'But these are the only feet I've got!'

After his dog chewed through an expensive new training shoe, a man took the footwear to the shoe repairer in the hope that something could be salvaged.
    'What do you recommend?' the man asked.
    The repairer looked at the shredded trainer and said: 'Give your dog the other shoe!'

A man walked into an army surplus store and asked if they had any camouflage trousers.

'Yes, we have,' replied the assistant, 'but we can't find them!'

A man went into a store to buy a bra for his wife.

'Certainly,' said the clerk. 'What type do you want?'

'Oh,' said the man. 'Is there more than one type?'

'Well, yes. For a start, there's our religious order of bras – there are three types, each performing a different function.'

'I don't understand.'

'Let me explain,' said the clerk. 'The Catholic type supports the masses, the Salvation Army type lifts up the fallen, and the Baptist type makes mountains out of mole hills.'

What does a one-legged ballerina wear? – A one one.

While making a tour of the provinces, a Turkish sultan was so impressed by a salesman's ornate fez that he invited him to the royal palace six months later to display his line of headgear. When the salesman arrived at the palace for his audience, he was ushered with others into the sultan's waiting room. The sultan passed by shortly afterwards and glanced at the salesman. 'I don't recall your name,' said the sultan pleasantly, 'but your fez is familiar.'

Cowboys

A Texas cowboy received a visit from his city-slicker cousin and decided to impress him by showing him the workings of the local Indian tribe. So they headed into the wilds where they discovered an Indian lying on his stomach with his ear to the ground.

The cowboy said to his cousin: 'See that Indian? He's listening to the ground. He can hear things for miles in any direction.'

Just then the Indian looked up. 'Covered wagon,' he said, 'about two miles away. Have two horses, one brown, one white. Man, woman, child, household effects in wagon . . .'

'That's incredible!' exclaimed the cousin. 'Just from listening to the ground, this Indian knows how far away they are, how many horses, what colour they are, who is in the wagon, and what is in the wagon.'

The Indian continued: ' . . . Ran me over about twenty minutes ago.'

After weeks on the trail, a cowboy paid his first visit to a city church, an experience that he later relayed to his fellow ranch hands.

'I parked my old truck in the corral . . .'

'You mean the parking lot,' corrected Charlie, one of the more worldly-wise members of the group.

'I walked up the trail to the door . . .'

'The sidewalk to the door,' explained Charlie.

'Inside I was met by this dude.'

'That would be the usher,' said Charlie.

'The usher led me down the chute . . .'

'You mean the aisle,' corrected Charlie.

'Then he led me to a stall and told me to sit there.'

'Pew.'

'Yeah, that's what the pretty lady said when I sat down beside her.'

A sheriff walked into a bar and said: 'Has anyone seen Brown Paper Jake? He wears a brown paper hat, a brown paper waistcoat, a brown paper shirt, brown paper boots, brown paper pants, and a brown paper jacket?'

The bartender asked: 'What's he wanted for?'

The sheriff said: 'Rustlin'.'

A cowboy strolled out of a saloon, ready to ride out of town. But he saw that someone had painted his horse green from head to hoof. The cowboy stormed back into the saloon.

'Which one of you painted my horse green?' he demanded.

'I did,' said a huge, mean-looking guy rising to his feet.

'Right,' said the cowboy. 'Just letting you know that the first coat's dry.'

Two cowboys staggered out of a zoo with their clothes in shreds and their faces covered in cuts and bruises. One turned to the other and said: 'That lion dancing sure ain't as restful as they made out.'

A slow-witted country boy desperately wanted to be a cowboy. For months he pleaded with a local rancher to take him on until eventually the rancher agreed to give him a chance.

On his first day, the rancher showed him a rope. 'This,' he said, 'is a lariat. We use it to catch cows.'

'I see,' said the new recruit, apparently taking everything in. 'And what do you use as bait?'

A tough old cowboy told his grandson that if he wanted to live a long life, the secret was to sprinkle a little gunpowder on his oatmeal every morning. The grandson did this religiously and lived to the age of ninety-eight. When he died, he left sixteen children, twenty-nine grandchildren, thirty-seven great grandchildren, and a fifteen-foot hole in the wall of the crematorium.

Looking for a new horse, a cowboy called at a ranch run by an old timer who was advertising a horse for sale. The cowboy liked the look of the animal and the old man sang its praises but warned: 'There's just one snag with him. He loves sitting on watermelons. If he sees a watermelon, you can be sure he'll sit on it.'

Even so the cowboy bought the horse and was mindful of avoiding watermelons at all cost. On their first day out together, he was riding along pleasantly when they came to a stream. To the cowboy's surprise, the horse suddenly stopped in midstream and sat down.

'Come on boy, up you get,' urged the cowboy, pulling on the bridle. But the horse refused to shift. Over the next half-hour, the cowboy pushed, shoved, pulled and cajoled without success until finally the horse clambered to its feet. The cowboy couldn't take any more of this and so he rode straight back to the ranch where the old man had sold him the horse.

When the cowboy angrily recounted the incident, the old man simply replied: 'Oh, yeah, I forgot, he also likes to sit on fish.'

A cowboy was trying to buy health insurance.

'Ever had an accident?' asked the man from the insurance company.
'Nope.'
'Not any kind of accident, ever?'
'Nope, never.'
'But it says on the application form that you filled in that you were bitten by a snake once. Wouldn't you consider that an accident?'
'Hell no. That dang varmint bit me on purpose!'

Why did the cowboy buy a dachshund? – He wanted to get along little doggie . . .

Three cowboys were hanging out in the bunkhouse, waiting for the fourth member of their gang to return.

The first said: 'Tex is so full of himself that I bet you anything you like as soon as he gets back, he'll start bragging about that new foreign car he's bought.'

The second said: 'No, he won't even mention the car. Tex will just come in and say "hello".'

The third said: 'I know Tex better than either of you. And he's smart. He'll figure out a way to do both. Here he comes.'

Moments later, Tex threw open the doors and said: 'Audi, partners!'

A cowboy rode into town and stopped at a saloon for a drink. The locals had a tendency to play cruel practical jokes on strangers and when he finished his drink, he found that his horse had been stolen. He strode back into the bar, flipped his gun into the air, caught it, and fired a shot into the ceiling . . . all in one movement.

'Which one of you varmints stole my horse?' he yelled menacingly.
Nobody answered.

'Right,' he said, 'I'm gonna have another beer and if my horse ain't back outside by the time I finish, I'm gonna do what I done in Tombstone! And I don't want to have to do what I done in Tombstone!'

Hearing this, some of the locals shifted uneasily. True to his word, the cowboy had another beer, marched outside and saw that his horse had been returned. As the cowboy saddled up ready to ride out of town, the bartender wandered out and asked: 'Hey, out of curiosity, just what did happen in Tombstone?'

The cowboy said: 'I had to walk home.'

Lost in the desert for weeks, two cowboys were close to starvation. As they stumbled on, hoping for salvation in the form of an oasis, they suddenly spied, through the heat haze, a small tree in the distance. As they got closer, they could see that the tree was draped with rasher upon rasher of bacon. There was smoked bacon, crispy bacon, and streaky bacon.

'Look!' said one of the cowboys excitedly. 'It's a bacon tree. We're saved!'

His partner couldn't contain himself and raced towards the tree, positively salivating at the prospect of food. But when he got to within five feet of the tree, he was shot down in a hail of bullets.

His friend ducked down behind a nearby rock and called over to him: 'What happened?'

With his dying breath, the wounded cowboy called back: 'Get out of here . . . now . . . It wasn't a bacon tree at all . . . It was a ham bush.'

Dating

A girl brought home her fiancé, a theology student, to meet her parents for the first time. Her father was keen to learn what prospects the boy had.

'How do you plan to make a living?' asked the father.

'I don't know,' said the student, 'but God will provide.'

The father raised his eyebrows. 'Do you own a car?'

'No,' said the student, 'but God will provide.'

'I see. And where are you thinking of living once you're married?'

'No idea, but I'm sure God will provide.'

Later the mother asked the father what he thought of their prospective son-in-law.

'Not a lot, really,' sighed the father. 'He's got no money and seems to have given precious little thought to the future. But on the other hand, he thinks I'm God!'

A jealous guy caught his girlfriend talking quietly on the phone and immediately confronted her.

'Who was that you were talking to?' he demanded. 'Is there somebody else?'

'Of course not,' she groaned. 'Do you honestly think I'd be going out with a loser like you if there was somebody else?'

Two actresses were sitting in a bar when one noticed that the other was no longer wearing her huge diamond engagement ring.

'What happened?' she asked. 'Is the wedding off?'

'Yes,' replied her friend. 'I saw him in his swimming trunks last week, and he looked so different without his wallet.'

A young couple parked in a lovers' lane. 'It's lovely out here tonight,' she sighed romantically. 'It's so quiet and peaceful. Just listen to the crickets.'

'They're not crickets,' replied her boyfriend. 'They're zippers.'

A girl rushed home to tell her mother: 'I've found a man just like Dad!'

The mother replied: 'What do you want from me? Sympathy?'

On his first visit to a girl's house, a guy waited in the living room while she prepared a snack in the kitchen. Left alone, he noticed a small, attractive vase on the mantelpiece. He picked it up and was looking at it when the girl walked back in.

'What's this?' he asked.

'Oh, my father's ashes are in there,' she said.

'Oh my God! I'm so sorry . . .'

'Yeah, he's too lazy to go to the kitchen and get an ashtray.'

A boy promised his girlfriend: 'We're going to have a great time Saturday. I got three tickets for the big game.'

'Why do we need three?' she asked.

'One for your father, one for your mother, and one for your kid sister!'

Jill: Whatever happened to that couple who met in the revolving door?

Jane: I think they're still going around together.

An aspiring young actor had been dating a girl for ten months, but when their thoughts turned to marriage, her father voiced his disapproval in the strongest possible terms.

'There is no way that any daughter of mine is going to marry an actor,' he boomed. 'It is a career riddled with insecurity. I will not give my blessing.'

However the young man was not willing to give up without a fight and said: 'Perhaps if you came to see me in my current play, you would revise your opinion about the acting profession. At least give me a chance.'

Reluctantly the father agreed to watch the young man perform at the theatre and he phoned him the very next morning.

'You were right,' said the father. 'I have changed my mind. You have my permission to marry my daughter because one thing is for certain – you're definitely no actor!'

Following the loss of his wife, a widower in his seventies started attending a senior citizens club so that he had a bit of social life. He made a lot of new friends there, including two widows, Kathryn and Edith, both of whom appeared to take a shine to him. He was lonely and enjoyed their company enormously, but the problem was, he couldn't decide which of the two he preferred. Kathryn shared his love of gardening and walking, while Edith was a marvellous cook and raconteur.

As the weeks passed, he became set on asking one of them to be his wife. To help him choose, he took them on separate holidays. He took Kathryn to the Lake District and Edith to Cornwall, but even that couldn't help him make up his mind. Both women were wonderful. The torment of having to make a decision was keeping him awake at night. Finally it was the women themselves who issued him with an ultimatum. Fed up with competing for his affection, they told him he had to make a decision.

The moral of the story is: you can't have your Kate and Edith too.

Two girlfriends met up for the first time in months.

'How's Dave?' asked one.

'He's fine. And how's Kevin?'

'Oh, my feelings towards him changed, so I broke off the engagement.'

'Right. Then why are you still wearing his ring?'

'Because my feelings for the ring haven't changed.'

A protective father took his daughter's first boyfriend to one side for a little chat. 'I hope you're going to treat my daughter properly,' he said. 'I want her to know the difference between right and wrong.'

The boy said: 'I imagine you've brought her up to know what's right, haven't you?'

'Yes, I have.'

'That's good. Well, now I'm taking care of the other side.'

'How was your blind date?' a college student asked her twenty-one-year-old roommate.

'Terrible!' she moaned. 'He showed up in his 1932 Rolls-Royce.'

'Wow! That's a very expensive car. What's so bad about that?'

'He was the original owner.'

For some months a guy had been dating a girl named Lorraine who worked in the same office. They got on really well, but his interest began to wane after a new girl, Joanne Clearly, arrived to work in his department. He became truly besotted with the newcomer and, because he wasn't the sort of person who two-timed someone, he realized he'd have to finish with Lorraine. For weeks he agonised about dumping her but couldn't bring himself to do it. Finally he was put out of his misery when, as luck would have it, she was transferred to a new job in Australia. Joyously he broke the news to a colleague: 'I can see Clearly now Lorraine has gone . . .'

Death

Three nuns were killed in a car crash and went to heaven, only to find a sign at the gates saying, 'Closed for Building Work.' Nevertheless they knocked on the gates and St. Peter eventually emerged.

'What do you want?' he said. 'There are no new arrivals this weekend. We're closed for building work. Didn't you read the sign?'

'I'm sorry,' said one nun, 'but we're dead, so we can't really go back, much as we would like to.'

'Now that's where you're wrong,' said St. Peter. 'For this weekend only we're operating a special scheme whereby we will send you back to Earth for two days as whoever you want to be and then, when the rebuilding is complete, we'll accept you back into heaven.'

'That sounds interesting,' the nuns chorused.

'So who would you like to be?' he asked the first nun.

'Tonight, Peter, I would like to be Joan of Arc, because she gave her life to God and died so tragically young.'

'Fine. We can do that,' said St. Peter.

The second nun suggested: 'I would like to be Mother Theresa because she lived such a fulfilling life, selflessly devoting herself to others.'

'Okay,' said St. Peter. 'That's no problem.'

The third nun said: 'I want to be Alice Kapipelean.'

St. Peter looked perplexed. 'Who?'

'Alice Kapipelean,' repeated the nun.

'Sorry,' said St. Peter, flicking through his notes, 'but we have no record of any Alice Kapipelean being on Earth.'

'Well, your records are incomplete,' stormed the nun. 'Look, I have proof right here.' And she handed a newspaper article to St. Peter.

St. Peter glanced at the cutting. 'No, sister, you have misread the article. It says that the *Alaska Pipeline* was laid by five hundred men in six months!'

A widow from New York decided to prepare her will and make her final requests. She told her solicitor that she wanted to be cremated and that she wanted her ashes to be scattered all over Bloomingdale's.

'Why Bloomingdale's?' asked the solicitor.

'That way I can be sure my daughters will visit me twice a week.'

A vicar died and went to heaven where he was dismayed to notice a London taxi driver with more crowns.

The vicar complained to St. Peter: 'I devoted my whole life to my congregation and yet that cabbie has got more crowns than I have. It's not fair.'

St. Peter said: 'We reward results. Did your congregation always pay attention when you gave a sermon?'

The vicar admitted: 'Occasionally someone would fall asleep.'

'There you are,' said St. Peter. 'When people rode in that guy's taxi, they not only stayed awake, but they usually prayed!'

Did you hear about the man who looked up synonyms for 'death' in a thesaurus? – He found himself at words for a loss.

While sunning himself in the Bahamas, a wealthy English businessman received a telegram from his butler, which read simply: 'Cat dead.' Distraught at the loss of his beloved pet, the businessman cut short his holiday and returned home. After giving the cat a decent burial in the garden, he remonstrated with his butler for the cold-hearted nature of the telegram.

'You should break bad news gently,' he said. 'If I had been telling you that your cat had died, I would have sent a telegram saying: "The cat's on the roof and can't get down." Then a few hours later I would have sent another telegram, saying: "The cat's fallen off the roof and is badly hurt." Finally, a couple of hours after that, I would have sent a third telegram, saying: "The cat has sadly passed away." That way, you would have been gradually prepared for the bad news and would have been able to deal with it better.'

'I understand, sir,' said the butler. 'I will bear that in mind in future.'

With that, the businessman booked another ticket to the Bahamas and resumed his holiday.

Two days later, he received another telegram from his butler. It read: 'Your mother's on the roof and can't get down.'

An eccentric bachelor passed away and left a nephew nothing but a collection of four hundred and thirty-three clocks. The nephew is now busy winding up the estate.

An archaeologist was digging in a desert in Israel when he found a casket containing a mummy. After examining it, he called the curator of a world-famous museum to report excitedly: 'I've just discovered a three thousand-year-old mummy of a man who died of heart failure.'

The curator replied: 'Bring it in, we'll check it out.'

A month later, the curator called the archaeologist. 'That's amazing. You were spot on about the mummy's age and cause of death. How on earth did you know?'

'Easy,' said the archaeologist. 'There was a piece of paper in his hand that said, "10,000 Shekels on Goliath".'

Unable to attend his father's funeral, a son who lived far away called his brother and said: 'Do something nice for Dad and send me the bill.'

A few weeks later, he received a bill for two hundred dollars, which he duly paid. Then the next month he got another bill for two hundred dollars, which he again paid, thinking it was some unforeseen expense. But when the bills for two hundred dollars kept on arriving each month, he phoned his brother to find out what was going on.

'Well,' said the other brother, 'you said to do something nice for Dad. So I rented him a tuxedo.'

A woman went to a psychic in an attempt to make contact with her recently deceased husband. After a few false alarms, he finally came through loud and clear.

'How are you, George?' she asked. 'Are you keeping well?'

'I'm fine,' said George. 'I'm standing in this field looking at beautiful cows.'

'Can you see any angels?' asked the wife.

'No, but who needs angels when you're surrounded by cows? There's a real looker standing right in front of me. Lovely long eyelashes . . .'

'What about God?' interrupted the wife. 'Have you met him yet?'

'No, I haven't seen God either. Wow! That cow's a real knockout!'

The wife was becoming irritated. 'Why do you keep going on about cows all the time?'

'Oh, sorry, I should have told you,' said George. 'I've come back as a bull.'

A man was telling his friend: 'My grandfather predicted in advance the very year in which he was going to die. What's more, he knew the exact month he was going to die, the precise day he was going to die, and even the time of day he was going to die. And he was right on every count.'

'That's amazing,' said the friend. 'How did he know all that?'

'The judge told him.'

While driving home from a restaurant with his wife, a man was involved in a terrible car crash and died instantly. After a short journey through a dark tunnel with a light at the end, he found himself at the gates of heaven. St. Peter was awaiting his arrival and beckoned him towards the Pearly Gates.

'Sir,' began St. Peter, 'you have proved yourself to be a kind and generous soul. You are worthy of passing through these gates. In order for you to enter heaven, I ask only one thing: that you spell one simple word, a word that epitomizes the philosophy of heaven. The word is "love."'

'That's easy,' said the man. 'L-O-V-E.'

And St Peter opened the Pearly Gates, enabling the man to enter.

Just as the man stepped into the kingdom of heaven, St. Peter's pager went off. God needed him for an emergency meeting. 'Excuse me,' said St Peter to the man he had just admitted, 'could you watch the gates for me while I'm in this meeting? I shouldn't be more than ten minutes. All I ask of you is that you let nobody in unless they spell the word correctly.'

The man agreed, and St. Peter vanished, leaving him with a bright silver key to the gates.

A few minutes later, the man's wife appeared in front of the gates.

'Hello, dear,' she said.

'What are you doing here?' he asked.

'Well, they rushed me to hospital and for a while it seemed as though I might pull through, but I didn't make it. I died of internal haemorrhaging.'

Obeying the instructions of St. Peter, the husband said: 'My beloved, in order for you to pass through the gates of heaven, you only need to spell one simple word. And the word is . . . "onomatopoeia."'

Taking flowers to a cemetery, a woman noticed an old Chinese man placing a bowl of rice on a nearby grave.

Thinking it a strange form of memorial, she said: 'When exactly do you expect your friend to come up and eat the rice?'

The Chinese man smiled: 'The same time your friend comes up to smell the flowers.'

A man died penniless and went to heaven where he met St. Peter sitting in a great hall, surrounded by millions of clocks.

'What are all those clocks for?' asked the man.

St. Peter explained: 'There is one clock for every living person Earth, ticking out the days of their lives.'

'Why are the hands on some of the clocks moving faster than others?'

'Every time you tell a lie,' said St. Peter, 'you lose one hour of your life and your clock speeds up.'

'Huh,' said the man. 'Have you got one for Mr Hart, the lying, cheating bank manager who swindled me out of thousands?'

'Sure,' said St. Peter. 'It's in the back room. We use it as a ceiling fan.'

A woman was talking to her friends about her husband who had passed away recently.

'When he was on his death bed, George told me that he had three envelopes in his desk drawer that would take care of all the arrangements. Well, he died shortly afterwards, so I opened the drawer, and there were the three envelopes, just like he had said.

'On the first envelope, George had written "for the coffin". There was five thousand dollars in the envelope, so I bought him a nice coffin.

'On the second envelope, George had written "for the expenses". There was four thousand dollars in that envelope, so I used the money to pay all the funeral bills.

'On the third envelope, George had written "for the stone". There was three thousand dollars in that.'

Holding her hand out to her friends, she said: 'Isn't it beautiful?'

A little boy told his teacher: 'My uncle Ronnie died last week.'

'I'm sorry to hear that,' said the teacher. 'What did he die of?'

'I don't know,' said the boy, 'but apparently it wasn't anything serious.'

After enduring forty years of miserable marriage, a man was not too upset by the death of his wife. He refused to spend anything on her funeral and, to save on burial costs, he arranged for her to be buried privately in their back garden.

A week later, a friend of the deceased came round to pay her respects and was surprised to see the wife's bottom sticking up out of the ground.

'Did you bury her like that as a token of affection?' asked the friend. 'So that there would always be something visible to remind you of her?'

'Certainly not,' said the husband. 'It's somewhere to park my bike!'

While an old man lay dying in his bedroom, his family sat in the living room discussing his funeral arrangements.

Son Jerome said: 'We'll make a real big thing out of it. We'll have five hundred people, and we'll order fifty limos.'

Daughter Grace disagreed. 'Why do you want to waste money like that? We'll have the family and just a few friends. One limo for us will be plenty.'

Grandson Tom proposed: 'We'll have lots of flowers. We'll surround him with dozens of roses and lilies.'

Granddaughter Emma said: 'That's a complete waste! We'll have one little bouquet – that will be enough.'

Eventually the rest of the family agreed that it would be foolish to spend lots of money on the funeral. They would keep costs down to the bare minimum.

'No use throwing money away,' said son Michael.

Suddenly the voice of the old man could be heard, wafting weakly from the bedroom: 'Why don't you get me my shoes? I'll walk to the cemetery!'

A woman went to a local psychic in the hope of contacting her dearly departed grandmother. Soon the psychic's eyelids began fluttering, her voice started to quiver, her hands floated up above the table, and she began moaning. Eventually a coherent voice emanated, saying: 'Granddaughter? Are you there?'

The woman, wide-eyed and on the edge of her seat, responded: 'Grandma, is that you?'

'Yes, granddaughter, it's me.'

'It's really, really you, grandma?'

'Yes, it's really me, granddaughter.'

The woman looked puzzled. 'You're sure it's you, grandma?'

'Yes, granddaughter, I'm sure it's me.'

The woman paused for a moment. 'Grandma, I have just one question for you.'

'Anything, my child.'

'When did you learn to speak English?'

Once upon a time there was a very rich businessman who was near death. Having worked hard all his life, he desperately wanted to be able to take some of his wealth with him to heaven and was eventually given special permission by God to bring one suitcase. Overjoyed, the businessman gathered his largest suitcase, filled it with pure gold bars and placed it beside his bed.

Shortly afterwards the man died and showed up at the Pearly Gates where he was greeted by St. Peter. Seeing the suitcase, St. Peter said: 'Wait, you can't bring that in here.'

The businessman explained that he had been granted permission by God. St. Peter checked out the story and confirmed: 'Yes, you have permission to bring in one case, but I must check its contents before letting it through.'

So St. Peter opened the suitcase to inspect the worldly items that the businessman found too precious to leave behind. As the lid sprang back to reveal the gold, St. Peter exclaimed: 'You brought pavement?'

Two old ladies met in the street. After inquiring about each other's health, the topic of conversation turned to their respective husbands.

'Oh,' said one. 'George died last week. He went out to the garden to dig up a cabbage for dinner, had a heart attack and dropped dead in the middle of the vegetable patch.'

'Oh my!' said the other. 'What did you do?'

'I opened a can of peas instead.'

An old man called on his solicitor to make a will. 'What exactly do I have to do?' he asked.

'It's perfectly straightforward,' said the solicitor. 'Just answer a few questions then leave it all to me.'

The old man looked worried. 'I quite like you,' he said, 'but I was planning to leave some of it to my wife.'

A young preacher new to the area was asked by the local funeral director to conduct a graveside service at a small country cemetery. There was to be no funeral, just the graveside ceremony, because the deceased had outlived all his family and friends.

The new preacher set off early for the cemetery, but soon became lost. After a number of wrong turns, he finally arrived half an hour late. There was no sign of the hearse, and the workmen were relaxing under a nearby tree, eating their lunch. The preacher went over to the open grave and found that the vault lid was already in place. He took out his book and read the service.

As he returned to his car, he overheard one of the workmen say: 'Do you think we should tell him that's a septic tank?'

A middle-aged woman suffered a heart attack and was rushed to hospital. While on the operating table, she underwent a near-death experience. Seeing God in her vision, she asked: 'Is my time up?'

God answered: 'No, you have another thirty-eight years, three months and sixteen days to live.'

Soon the woman made a full recovery and was so relieved to be alive that, while in hospital, she decided to roll back the years with a facelift, liposuction and a tummy tuck. She even had her hair coloured to disguise the grey streaks. On being discharged, she was making her way home when she was knocked down and killed by a car.

Arriving in heaven, she berated God: 'I thought you said I had another thirty-eight years! Why didn't you pull me away from the path of the car?'

God said: 'I didn't recognize you.'

A young woman was in floods of tears at work. Her boss asked her what the problem was.

'I'm sorry,' she sobbed, 'but this morning I got a phone call saying that my mother died.'

'That's terrible,' said the boss sympathetically. 'Why don't you take the rest of the day off?'

'No, it's all right,' she answered. 'Being at work and being surrounded by people helps me take my mind off it.'

'Well, only if you're sure,' he said. 'Remember, if you need time off or someone to talk to, just come and see me.'

'That's very kind of you,' she said, 'but I'm sure I'll be fine now that I've had a little cry.'

Even so he continued to keep an eye on her and was horrified to see her sobbing her heart out all over again a couple of hours later.

'What's happened?' he asked.

'It's too awful,' she said. 'I've just had a phone call from my sister and her Mom died, too!'

Three guys were standing on the roof of the Empire State Building. The first said: 'You know, the wind currents here in New York are so strong that you could step off the edge of this building and literally float in mid-air due to the upward thrust of the thermal air current.'

'You're crazy,' said the second guy.

'You don't believe me?' said the first. 'Watch this.'

And with that, the first guy stepped off the edge of the Empire State Building, floated around in mid-air for thirty seconds and returned safely to the roof.

'That was incredible,' said the second guy. 'I have to try that.'

So the second guy stepped off the roof, but instead of floating he dropped like a stone to the street below.

Seeing this, the third guy, who had remained silent until then, turned to the first guy and said: 'You know something, there are times when you can be a real jerk, Superman.'

A famous Hollywood director died and went to heaven. St. Peter was waiting at the Pearly Gates and informed the director that God wanted him to make one last movie.

The director wasn't keen. 'I've had enough of making movies. I'm sick of all the backbiting and talentless wannabes in Hollywood. I've come up here hoping for a nice rest.'

Then St. Peter announced the list of names that had already signed up for the project. 'Wolfgang Amadeus Mozart has agreed to write the score, Michelangelo says he'll design the set and William Shakespeare is penning the screenplay.'

'I must say that's a real impressive line-up,' conceded the director.

'It should be fantastic,' gushed St. Peter.

'Okay then, you've talked me into it. I'll do it.'

'Great!' said St. Peter. 'There's just one little snag. God's got this girlfriend who thinks she can act . . .'

A lawyer was reading out the will of a rich man to the various people mentioned in the will. 'To you, my loving wife Mary, who stood by me throughout our marriage, I leave the house and two million. To my daughter, Jodie, who kept the business going, I leave the yacht, the business, and one million. And to my brother Dan who hated me, argued with me constantly, and thought that I would never mention him in my will, well you are wrong. Hi, Dan!'

Two guys were driving down the road on a motorcycle. The driver was wearing a leather jacket that didn't have a zip and finally he stopped the bike to tell his pillion passenger: 'I can't drive anymore with the wind hitting me in my chest.' So he decided to put the jacket on backwards to block the air from hitting him.

They set off again but a mile down the road they took a corner too fast and smashed into a tree. A farmer that lived nearby was first on the scene.

Shortly afterwards a police car pulled up. Surveying the wreckage, the officer asked the farmer: 'Are either of them showing any signs of life?'

The farmer said: 'Well, that first one was until I turned his head around the right way.'

A dead British aristocrat and his dead butler bumped into each other in hell.

'I did not expect to see you here, sir,' said the butler.

The aristocrat sighed: 'I'm here because I lied, cheated and stole to pay the debts run up by that wastrel son of mine. But what about you? You were a faithful, loyal servant to my family for forty years. What are you doing here?'

The butler replied: 'For fathering your wastrel son.'

A man died and went up to heaven where he was greeted by St. Peter.

'And who are you?' asked St. Peter.

'My name is Michael Hodgson.'

'And what do you do for a living?'

'I work for the Gas Board.'

'I see. And have you ever done anything good in your life?'

'Well, yes, I have actually. A little old lady who lived down the road was having trouble with her gas supply. She thought she had got a faulty connection and could smell gas in her living room. And I agreed to go round and take a look at the problem, even though it was my day off.'

'That's highly commendable,' said St. Peter, flicking through his files, 'but I can't see any report of the incident. When did it happen?'

'About five minutes ago.'

Two guys walking home after a Halloween party decided to take a short cut through the cemetery for a laugh. As they picked their way through the graves, they were startled by a tapping noise coming from somewhere in the misty gloom. They looked at each other nervously, unsure whether to flee the scene or try and trace the source of the mysterious sound. Choosing the latter option but trembling with fear, they found an old man with a hammer and chisel, chipping away at one of the headstones.

'You scared us half to death,' they said, breathing a huge sigh of relief. 'For a moment we thought you were a ghost! Anyway what are you doing working here so late at night?'

The old man replied: 'They misspelled my name.'

Quasimodo, the demented bell ringer of Notre Dame, put an advert in the papers for an assistant bell ringer. There was one applicant, but he had no arms.

'How are you going to assist me?' asked Quasimodo.

'That's easy,' replied the man, and he ran at the bell and banged it with his head.

'That's amazing!' enthused Quasimodo. 'Can you show me that again?'

'Sure!' said the man, and he ran at the bell again, but this time he missed the swinging bell and fell out of the tower. A crowd huddled around the poor man lying in the street and a police officer asked: 'Does anyone know who he is?'

Quasimodo replied: 'I don't know his name, but his face rings a bell.'

The day after the guy with no arms fell to his death, his brother turned up to audition for the bell ringer's job. Quasimodo took him to the bell tower where the guy picked up the wooden mallet and began ringing the bells. Alas he misjudged one huge swing, missed the bell, and plunged to his death from the balcony.

Quasimodo ran outside and the policeman asked him who the fellow was. Quasimodo said: 'I never got his name but he's a dead ringer for his brother!'

Education

An inflatable boy at an inflatable school was sent to the inflatable headmaster for bringing a drawing pin to school. The headmaster told him: 'You've let me down, you've let the school down, but worst of all you've let yourself down.'

A teenage boy went off to university, but about a third of the way through the semester, he had foolishly squandered the money his parents had given him. Desperate to get more money out of his father, he came up with a cunning plan.

Phoning home one weekend, he said: 'Dad, you won't believe the educational opportunities that are available at this university! Why, they've even got a course here that will teach Fido how to talk!'

'That's incredible!' said the gullible father. 'How do I enrol him on the course?'

'Just send him down here with a thousand dollars, and I'll make sure he gets on the course.'

So the father sent the dog and a thousand dollars, but about two-thirds of the way through the semester, that money had also run out. The boy called his father again.

'How's Fido doing?' asked the father.

'Awesome, Dad, he's talking brilliantly. But you just won't believe this, they've had such great results with the talking dogs course that they're starting up a new one to teach the animals how to read!'

'Read?' echoed his father. 'No kidding! What do I have to do to get him on that course?'

'Just send two thousand five hundreddollars. I'll get him on the course.'

His father duly sent the money, but at the end of the semester, the boy was faced with a problem: how to conceal from his father the fact that the dog could neither talk nor read. So the boy decided to take drastic action and shot the dog. When he arrived home, his father was waiting expectantly.

'Where's Fido?' asked the father. 'I just can't wait to hear him talk or listen to him reading something.'

'Dad,' said the boy solemnly, 'I've got some bad news. This morning, when I got out of the shower, Fido was in the living room reading the morning paper, like he usually does. Then suddenly he turned to me and asked: "So, is your Dad still messing around with that little blonde at number forty-four?"'

The father's face turned red with rage and he shouted: 'I hope you shot that lying dog!'

'I sure did, Dad.'

'That's my boy!'

Two young men who had just graduated from university climbed into a taxi wearing their graduation gowns.

'Are you graduates from the city university?' asked the cab driver.

'Yes, sir,' they announced proudly. 'Class of '99.'

The cabbie extended his hand. 'Class of '67.'

The geography teacher was giving a lesson on map reading, and trying to explain to his class about latitude and longitude, degrees and minutes. Towards the end of the lesson, he asked his students: 'Suppose I ask you to meet me for lunch at latitude 19 degrees, seven minutes north and longitude 39 degrees, thirteen minutes east?'

After a confused silence, one student volunteered: 'I guess you'd be eating alone, sir!'

A college student took a part-time job delivering pizza. On his first day, he had to deliver to a renowned skinflint.

'What's the usual tip?' growled the customer.

'Well,' said the student, 'this is my first delivery, but the other guys said that if I got a quarter out of you, I'd be doing great.'

'That so?' grunted the man. 'In that case, here's five dollars.'

'Thank you, I'll put it in my college fund.'

'Oh, what are you studying?'

'Applied psychology.'

A junior school class was being tested on the Kings and Queens of

England.

'Who followed Edward VI?' asked the teacher.

'Mary,' answered a little girl at the front.

'And who followed Mary?' asked the teacher.

A boy at the back called out: 'Her little lamb!'

One day, God decided to descend to Earth for a good look round. He was walking along when he met a man crying by the roadside.

'Why are you crying?' asked God.

The man wailed: 'I am blind and have never seen a sunset.'

With that, God touched him and gave him vision. The man immediately stopped crying.

Further along the road, God met another man sobbing by the roadside.

'Why are you so sad?' asked God.

'I have been crippled since birth and will never be able to walk.'

So God touched him and restored the use of his limbs. The man stopped crying straight away.

Half a mile further along the road, God met another man in floods of tears.

'Why are you crying?' asked God.

'I'm a teacher at an inner-city elementary school.'

God sat down and cried with him.

A little girl came home from school and said: 'Mommy, today in school I was punished for something I didn't do.'

'That's terrible! I'm going to speak to your teacher about it. Now what was it that you didn't do?'

'My homework.'

A conscientious student stayed up all night to prepare for a zoology test the next day. As he entered the classroom, he saw ten bird cages, each partially covered with a sheet so that only the birds' legs were visible. The new professor announced that the students had to identify the different species of bird purely from their legs.

Having spent the night poring over textbooks, the student thought he knew the subject by heart – the Latin names, the habitats, the nesting sites – but he certainly hadn't expected anything as silly as having to recognize birds by their legs. He said the task was ridiculous and impossible, but the professor was unmoved. Eventually in sheer frustration, the student tore up the test paper and stormed towards the door.

'Hey, you!' shouted the professor. 'Where do you think you're going? What's your name?'

The student rolled up his trouser legs and said: 'You tell me!'

A child told her mother: 'My teacher thinks I'm going to be famous. She said all I have to do is mess up one more time and I'm history!'

A group of students at medical school were struggling with a physics lecture and let the professor know of their disquiet. One student rudely interrupted the lecture to ask: 'Why do we have to learn this stuff?'

'To save lives,' replied the professor.

'How does physics save lives?' the student persisted sarcastically.

The professor shot back: 'It keeps idiots like you from graduating medical school.'

Teacher: Well, at least there's one thing I can say about your son.
    Father: What's that?
    Teacher: With grades like these, he couldn't have been cheating!

The children at school were asked to talk about a recent exciting event in their lives. One small boy put up his hand and said: 'Daddy fell down a well last week.'

'My goodness!' exclaimed the teacher. 'Is he all right now?'

'He must be,' replied the boy. 'He stopped yelling for help yesterday.'

Worst Analogies (taken from genuine high school papers):

She caught your eye like one of those pointy hook latches that used to dangle from screen doors and would fly up whenever you banged the door open again.

Her hair glistened in the rain like a nose hair after a sneeze.

The little boat gently drifted across the pond exactly the way a bowling ball wouldn't.

Her eyes were like two brown circles with big black dots in the centre.

He was as tall as a six foot three inch tree.

The hailstones leapt from the pavement, just like maggots when you fry them in hot grease.

Her date was pleasant enough, but she knew that if her life was a movie this guy would be buried in the credits as something like 'Second Tall Man'.

Long separated by cruel fate, the star-crossed lovers raced across the grassy field toward each other like two freight trains, one having left Cleveland at 6.36pm travelling at fifty-five miles per hour, the other from Topeka at 4.19pm at a speed of thirty-five miles per hour.

The politician was gone but unnoticed, like the period after the Dr. on a Dr Pepper can.

John and Mary had never met. They were like two hummingbirds who had also never met.

The thunder was ominous-sounding, much like the sound of a thin sheet of metal being shaken backstage during the storm scene in a play.

The red brick wall was the colour of a brick-red Crayola crayon.

Her vocabulary was as bad as, like, whatever.

When a student returned home for Christmas, his mother asked: 'How's your history paper coming along?'

'Well, my history professor suggested I use the Internet for research and it's been extremely helpful.'

'Really?'

'Yes. So far I've located fifteen people who sell them.'

A teacher asked her young class: 'Give me a sentence about a public servant.'

One boy wrote: 'The fireman came down the ladder pregnant.'

The teacher called the boy to one side to correct him. 'Jamie,' she said, 'do you know what pregnant means?'

'Yes,' replied Jamie breezily. 'It means carrying a child.'

A professor was delivering a lecture to his philosophy class. He picked up a jar, filled it with golf balls and asked the students if they thought the jar was full. They agreed that it was. Then he picked up two handfuls of pebbles and poured them into the jar. As he shook the jar, the pebbles dropped into the gaps between the golf balls. He then asked the students if they thought the jar was full. They said it was. Next he picked up a tin of sand and poured that into the jar. Once again he asked the students if they thought the jar was full. They agreed that it was.

The professor then picked up two cans of beer and poured them into the jar. 'Right,' he said. 'I want you to appreciate that the contents of this jar represent your life. The golf balls represent the essential things – your family, your health, your friends. If everything else were lost and only they remained, your life would still be full. The pebbles represent the other important things, such as your house and your job. The sand represents everything else – the minutiae of everyday life, things about which we sometimes worry too much. If you put the sand into the jar first, there's no room for the pebbles or the golf balls. But finally, remember: no matter how full your life might seem, there's always room for a couple of beers.'

The schoolchildren had all been photographed and their teacher was trying to persuade them each to buy a copy of the group picture. 'Just think,' she said, 'how nice it will be to look at when you are all grown up and you can say, "There's Jenny, she's a lawyer" or "There's David, he's a doctor."'

A small voice piped up at the back of the room: 'And there's teacher, she's dead.'

The teacher asked her class whether anyone could remember the chemical formula for water.

'Sure,' said one student. 'It's HIJKLMNO.'

'It's what?' said the teacher angrily.

'Well, you told us last week it was H to O.'

Worried that their son would refuse to learn maths at school, his parents sent him to a Catholic school, which had a fine reputation in the subject. But after his first day at the new school, he came home, ran straight to his room and slammed the door. This behaviour went on every school night for the next two months, at the end of which his parents were asked along to meet the teachers. They feared the worst but instead their son's maths teacher revealed that the boy was doing excellent work and was top of the class.

'So what changed your mind about learning maths?' they asked when their son came home.

'Well,' said the boy, 'on the first day I walked into the classroom, I saw a guy nailed to a plus sign at the back of the room, and I knew then that they meant business!'

You Might Be a Teacher If:

You can't have children because there is no name you can think of that doesn't give you high blood pressure.

You have an overwhelming urge to nod and say, 'Now I understand why your child behaves like that,' after meeting the parents.

You believe 'shallow gene pool' should have its own box on report cards.

You hand pieces of paper to your friends and make them spit out their gum in front of you.

You have chalk marks on your forehead from banging your head against the blackboard all day.

You correct a total stranger's grammar errors.

You think people should get government permits before they can reproduce.

You cringe whenever someone says, 'At least you get three months' holiday.'

Having seen their twelve-year-old son finish bottom of the class in every subject, a couple decided to send him to a special tutor. Six weeks later, they asked the tutor how he was doing.

'He's getting straight As,' said the tutor.

'That's great,' said the relieved parents.

'Mind you,' added the tutor. 'His Bs are still a bit wonky.'

A woman began a job as a junior school counsellor and was eager to help with the children's welfare. One day she noticed a small boy standing by himself on one side of the playing field while the rest of the children were at the other end enjoying a game of soccer.

So she decided to approach him and ask him if he was all right. He said that he was, but ten minutes later she saw that he was still in the same spot and still by himself.

'Would you like me to be your friend?' she asked gently.

'If you want,' said the boy.

'So, tell me, why are you all on your own? Why don't you join in with the others?'

'Because,' he sighed, 'I'm the goalie!'

As a kindergarten class settled down to their colouring books, one little boy went up to the teacher and said: 'I ain't got no crayons, miss.'

'No, Ricky,' said the teacher, 'you mean, I don't have any crayons. You don't have any crayons. We don't have any crayons. They don't have any crayons. Do you see what I'm getting at?'

'Not really, miss. What happened to all them crayons?'

'What's your father's occupation?' asked the school secretary filling in the necessary forms on the first day of a new academic year.

'He's a magician,' said a new boy at school.

'How interesting! What's his favourite trick?'

'He saws people in half.'

'Gosh! Now, next question. Any brothers or sisters?'

'Yes. One half-brother and two half-sisters.'

School Answering Machine:

Hello. You have reached the automated answering service of your child's school. In order to assist you in connecting to the right staff member, please listen to all options before making a selection:

To lie about why your child is absent, Press 1.

To make excuses for why your child did not do his/her work, Press 2.

To complain about what we do, Press 3.

To verbally abuse our staff members, Press 4.

To request another teacher for the third time this year, Press 5.

To complain about bus transportation, Press 6.

To complain about school lunches, Press 7.

To complain about why your child was not given the lead role in the school play, Press 8.

To tell us that your child is innocent and that it was all Sarah Mooney's fault, Press 9.

If you want us to raise your child, Press 0.

A linguistics professor was lecturing his class. 'In English a double negative forms a positive. In some languages, however, such as Russian, a double negative is still a negative. But there is no language where a double positive can form a negative.'

A student at the back called out: 'Yeah, right.'

On the first day of college, the dean addressed the students. 'The female dormitory,' he stated, 'will be out of bounds for all male students, and the male dormitory to all female students. Anybody caught breaking this rule will be fined twenty dollars the first time, sixy dollars the second time and the third time. Any questions?'

One male student asked: 'How much for a season ticket?'

A group of third, fourth and fifth graders accompanied by two teachers went on a field trip to the local racecourse to learn about thoroughbred racehorses. During the tour some of the children wanted to go to the toilet, so it was decided that the girls would go with one teacher and the boys would go with the other.

As the teacher assigned to the boys waited outside the men's toilet, one of the boys came out and told her that he couldn't reach the urinal. Having no choice, the teacher went inside and began hoisting the little boys up by their armpits, one by one. As she lifted one up by the armpits, she couldn't help but notice that he was unusually well-endowed for an elementary school child. 'I guess you must be in the fifth,' she said.

'No, ma'am,' he replied, 'I'm in the seventh, riding Silver Bullet. Thanks for the lift anyway.'

When a woman decided to improve her computer skills, she threw herself into the task with enthusiasm, borrowing two or three instructional books from the library each week.

After about a month, the librarian commented: 'Wow! You must be getting really knowledgeable about this stuff.'

'Thanks. What makes you say that?'

'Well,' said the librarian, 'only one of the books you're taking out this week has "For Dummies" in the title.'

A small boy was struggling with his maths homework. After a while, he turned to his father and said: 'Dad, can you help me?'

The father said: 'I could. But it wouldn't be right, would it?'

'Probably not,' said the boy. 'But you could at least give it a try.'

On his first day at a new school, a headmaster was making his rounds when he heard a terrible commotion from one of the classrooms. Marching in, he spotted one boy, taller than the others, who seemed to be making most of the noise. So he seized the lad, dragged him to the hall, and told him to wait there until he was excused.

Returning to the classroom, the headmaster restored order and lectured the class for ten minutes on good behaviour.

'Now,' he concluded. 'Any questions?'

One girl stood up timidly and asked: 'Please, sir. May we have our teacher back?'

'Yes, where exactly is your teacher?'

The girl replied: 'He's in the hall, sir.'

At a school careers' evening, a fifteen-year-old boy was asked what he wanted to do when he left school. 'I want to be a stamp collector,' he replied.

The careers advisor was sceptical. 'What about teaching? There's always a shortage of teachers.'

'No, I want to be a stamp collector.'

'Or how about studying law? There's good money to be made as a lawyer.'

'No, I want to be a stamp collector.'

'Or journalism? That can lead to all manner of different career opportunities – public relations, sports writing, a career in television ...'

'No, I want to be a stamp collector.'

The careers advisor threw up his hands in despair. 'But don't you see, philately will get you nowhere!'

The Holy Scripture may have turned out somewhat different if it had been written by college students:

The Last Supper would have been eaten the next morning – cold, with Coke.

The Ten Commandments would actually be only five – double-spaced, with wide margins, and written in a large font.

Forbidden fruit would have been okay, simply because it wasn't cafeteria food.

Paul's letter to the Romans would have become Paul's e-mail to abuse@romans.gov.

Reason Cain killed Abel: They were roommates.

Reason why Moses and his followers walked in the desert for forty years: They didn't want to ask for directions and look like freshmen.

Instead of God creating the world in six days and resting on the seventh, he would have put it off until the night before it was due and then pulled an all-nighter.

A boy was sitting a school test that consisted solely of either/or questions. As he hadn't done any revision, he decided that tossing a coin was as good a way as any of answering the questions. If the coin came up 'heads', he would tick answer 'A'; if it came up 'tails', he would tick answer 'B'.

Using this technique, he raced through the paper and chose to use the remaining time re-reading the paper, tossing the coin again, and occasionally cursing under his breath.

As the swearing became audible, the teacher came over to ask if there was a problem.

'It's okay,' said the boy. 'I finished the test a while back. Now I'm just checking my answers.'

The kindergarten teacher noticed a little puddle under Mary's chair. 'Oh, Mary!' said the teacher. 'You should have put your hand up.'
    'I did,' said Mary. 'But it still trickled through my fingers.'

A small boy was dawdling all the way to school.
    'Hurry up,' said his mother. 'You'll be late!'
    'What's the rush?' he asked. 'They're open till 3.30.'

In junior school science class the teacher wanted to instruct his young pupils about the evils of alcohol, so he produced an experiment involving a glass of water, a glass of whiskey, and two worms.
    'Now, children,' he said. 'Watch the worms.'
    And with that he put the first worm into the glass of water and saw it writhe about. Then he put the second worm into the glass of whiskey and saw it contort in pain before sinking to the bottom, dead as a doornail.
    'So what lesson can we learn from this experiment?' he asked.
    A boy at the back raised his hand and said: 'Drink whiskey and you won't get worms!'

Actual Excuses Notes To Teachers:
Please excuse Roland from P.E. for a few days. Yesterday he fell out of a tree and misplaced his hip.
    My son is under a doctor's care and should not take P.E. today. Please execute him.
    Please excuse Gloria from Jim today. She is administrating.
    John has been absent because he had two teeth taken out of his face.
    Carlos was absent yesterday because he was playing football. He was hurt in the growing part.
    Megan could not come to school today because she has been bothered by very close veins.
    Please excuse Ray Friday from school. He has very loose vowels.
    Please excuse Tommy for being absent yesterday. He had diarrhoea and his boots leak.
    Maryann was absent December 11-16, because she had a fever, sore throat, headache and upset stomach. Her sister was also sick, fever and sore throat, her brother had a low grade fever and ached all over. I

wasn't the best either, sore throat and fever. There must be something going around, her father even got hot last night.

Please excuse Jimmy for being. It was his father's fault.

I kept Billie home because she had to go Christmas shopping because I don't know what size she wears.

Sally won't be in school a week from Friday. We have to attend her funeral.

My daughter was absent yesterday because she was tired. She spent a weekend with the Marines.

Please excuse John from being absent on Jan 28, 29, 30, 31, 32, and also 33.

Please excuse Jason for being absent yesterday. He had a cold and could not breed well.

Gloria was absent yesterday as she was having a gangover.

Please excuse Burma, she has been sick and under the doctor.

Please excuse Mary for being absent yesterday. She was in bed with gramps.

Please excuse Jennifer for missing school yesterday. We forgot to get the Sunday paper off the porch, and when we found it Monday, we thought it was Sunday.

Families

A couple were admiring their garden from the kitchen window. The wife said: 'Sooner or later, you're going to have to make a proper scarecrow to keep the birds off the flower beds.'

'What's wrong with the one we've got?' asked the husband.

'Nothing. But mother's arms are getting tired.'

A newlywed farmer and his wife were visited by her mother who immediately demanded an inspection of the place. While they were walking through the barn, the farmer's mule suddenly reared up and kicked the mother-in-law in the head, killing her instantly.

At the funeral service a few days later, the farmer stood near the coffin and greeted people as they walked by. The pastor noticed that whenever a woman whispered something to the farmer, he would nod his head 'yes' and say something. But whenever a man whispered something to the farmer, he would shake his head 'no' and mumble a reply.

Curious, the pastor later asked the farmer what that was all about. The farmer replied: 'The women would say, "What a terrible tragedy", and I would nod my head and say, "Yes, it was." The men would ask, "You wanna sell that mule?" and I would shake my head and say, "Can't. It's all booked up for a year."'

A husband was late home from work one evening. 'I'm sure he's having an affair,' said his wife to her mother.

'Why do you always think the worst?' said the mother. 'Maybe he's just been in a car crash.'

A couple were travelling through Eastern Europe with the wife's aged aunt. The old woman had done nothing but moan from the outset, complaining about everything – the food, the hotels, the weather, the people. Finally she went too far and insulted a small nation's queen. As a result, all three members of the family were sentenced to corporal punishment in the form of fifty lashes. However, because the nation did not wish to be viewed as hostile to tourists, the queen agreed that each be granted a wish before receiving the punishment.

The wife said: 'I would like a pillow to be tied to my rear end.' The pillow was tied in place and the wife received her fifty lashes.

Next it was the aunt's turn. Seeing her niece's pain, she said: 'I would like two pillows – one to be tied to my rear end and one to be tied to my back.' The pillows were tied in place and the aunt received her fifty lashes.

Finally, it was the husband's turn. 'I have two wishes, if that is possible,' he said.

The chief of police consulted with the queen before saying it was possible for the husband to be granted two wishes. 'Now, what are your two wishes?'

'Firstly, I would like to be given a hundred lashes instead of fifty.'

'Are you sure?' said the chief of police. 'That is a most unusual request.'

'I am sure. I definitely want a hundred lashes.'

'And what is your second wish?'

'I want my mother's aunt to be tied to my back.'

A man took his dog to the vet and asked the vet to cut off its tail.

'Why do you want to do that?' asked the vet.

'Because my mother-in-law is arriving tomorrow, and I don't want anything to make her think she's welcome.'

After talking on the phone for about half an hour, a teenage girl suddenly hung up.

'Wow!' exclaimed her father sarcastically. 'That was short. You usually talk for two hours. What happened?'

'Wrong number.'

An American man went on vacation to the Middle East with most of his family, including his mother-in-law. While they were visiting Jerusalem, the mother-in-law died. With the death certificate in hand, he went to the American Consulate Office to make arrangements to send the body back to the United States for proper burial. The Consul warned that to send a body back to the US for burial was an extremely expensive business and could cost as much as ten thousand dollars. 'In most cases,' advised the Consul, 'the person responsible for the remains normally decides to bury the body here. That would only cost three hundred.'

The man gave it some careful thought before answering: 'I don't mind how much it's going to cost to send the body back home; that's what I want to do.'

The Consul remarked: 'Considering the difference in price, you must have been extremely fond of your mother-in-law.'

'No, it's not that,' said the man. 'You see, there was a case many years ago of a person that was buried here in Jerusalem. On the third day he rose from the dead. I just can't take that chance!'

Two men were walking down the street when one spotted six men kicking and punching his mother-in-law.

'Are you going to help?' asked his friend.

'No,' he said. 'Six should be enough.'

Three mothers were sitting on a park bench in Miami Beach, talking about how much their sons loved them.

Hettie said: 'You know the Gauguin painting hanging in my living room? My son, Arnold, bought that for me for my seventieth birthday. What a good boy he is. How he loves his mother!'

Zelda said: 'You call that love? You know the Chevrolet I just got for Mother's Day? That's from my son Bernie. What a boy!'

Rose said: 'That's nothing. You know my son Stanley? He's in analysis with a therapist on Park Avenue, no less. Five sessions a week, two hundred and fifty dollars an hour, and what does he talk about all the time? Me.'

On a beautiful summer's day, a father and his eight-year-old son were lying on the grass by the riverbank, looking up at the sky and watching the wisps of cloud float gently overhead. After a few minutes of silence, the boy turned to the father and said: 'Dad, why are we here?'

'That's a good question, son. I think we're here to enjoy days such as this, to experience nature in all its glory, the vastness of the sky, the beauty of the trees, the song of the birds, the rippling flow of the water. We're here to help make the world a better place, to pass on our wisdom to future generations who will hopefully profit from our achievements and learn from our mistakes. We're here to savour the small triumphs of life – passing your school exams, the birth of a new member of the family, promotion at work, a win for the home team. And we're here to comfort those dearest to us in times of distress, to provide kindness and compassion, support and strength, to let them know that, no matter how bad a situation may seem, they are not alone. Does that answer your question, son?'

'Not really, Dad.'

'No?'

'No, what I meant was, why are we here when Mom said to pick her up forty minutes ago?'

A little girl said: 'Daddy, you're the boss of the house, right?'

'Yes, sweetheart,' he said, 'I'm the boss of the house.'

'And I know why you're the boss of the house, Daddy.'

'Why's that?'

'Because Mommy put you in charge.'

A couple were going out for a rare night on the town. They put on their best clothes, called a cab, and put the cat out. The taxi arrived but as the couple walked out of the front door, the cat shot between their legs, back into the house and up the stairs. Knowing that the cat would wreck the house while they were gone, the husband ran upstairs to chase the cat out again while the wife waited in the taxi.

Since she didn't want the cab driver to know that the house would be left unoccupied, the woman explained to him: 'My husband is just going upstairs to say goodbye to my mother.'

A few minutes later, the husband reappeared and climbed into the taxi. 'Sorry I took so long,' he said. 'Stupid old thing was hiding under the bed, and I had to poke her with a coat hanger to get her to come out!'

Fresh out of ideas as to what to get his mother-in-law for her birthday, a man decided that a novel present would be to buy her a large plot in an exclusive cemetery. The following year he didn't buy her anything, prompting her to complain bitterly.

'Listen,' he said. 'You still haven't used the present I got you last year!'

A woman came from a large family of five sisters and four brothers. One day she was looking through the family photo album when she noticed that in picture after picture, all of the children were dressed in matching outfits. Later, she asked her mother why everyone – even the baby – was dressed identically.

Her mother replied: 'When we had just four children, I dressed you alike so that we wouldn't lose any of you. Then when the other six came along, I started dressing you alike so that we wouldn't pick up any that didn't belong to us!'

A little boy greeted his grandma with a hug and said: 'I'm so happy to see you, Grandma. Now maybe Daddy will do the trick he has been promising us.'

'What trick's that?' she asked.

'Well,' said the little boy excitedly, 'I heard Daddy tell Mommy that he would climb the walls if you came to visit us again.'

Having missed the last bus, a teenage girl was forced to stay at a friend's house overnight. Knowing that her mother would be worried sick, she called home first thing in the morning to let her know that she was safe.

The words came out in a breathless torrent. 'Mom, It's Emma. I'm fine. I knew you'd be worried, but I didn't get a chance to call you last night. I missed the last bus and by the time I got back to Sophie's house, I knew you'd have gone to bed, and I didn't want to wake you. Please don't be mad with me.'

By now, the woman on the other end of the phone realized that the caller had got the wrong number. 'I'm sorry,' she said, 'I don't have a daughter named Emma.'

'Gee, Mom, I didn't think you'd be this mad!'

A big game hunter went on safari with his wife and mother-in-law. One evening, the husband and wife were sitting around the camp fire having supper when she realized that her mother was missing. The hunter picked up his rifle and, with his wife close behind, set off into the jungle to look for the missing woman. After searching for over an hour, they finally spotted her backed up against a cliff with a huge lion facing her.

'What are we going to do?' shrieked the wife.

'Nothing,' said the husband. 'The lion got himself into this mess . . .'

A son made a long-distance phone call to his mother.

'How are you doing, Mom?'

'Not too good. I've been very weak.'

'Why have you been weak?'

'Because I haven't eaten in thirty-four days.'

'Why on earth haven't you been eating?'

'Because I didn't want my mouth to be filled with food when you called.'

A modern mother was explaining to her little girl about the pictures in the family photo album. 'This is the geneticist with your surrogate mother and here's your sperm donor and your father's clone. This is me holding you when you were just a frozen embryo.'

'Mommy,' said the little girl. 'Who is the lady with the worried look on her face?'

'That's your aunt Kim. She's the family genealogist.'

A lawyer cabled his client overseas: 'Your mother-in-law passed away in her sleep. Shall we order burial, embalming or cremation?'

Back came the reply: 'Take no chances – order all three.'

Reading a letter at the breakfast table, a wife suddenly looked suspiciously at her husband. 'Henry, I've just received a letter from mother saying she isn't accepting our invitation to come and stay, as we don't appear to want her. What does she mean? I told you to write and say that she was to come at her own convenience. You did write, didn't you?'

'Er, yes,' said the husband. 'But I couldn't spell "convenience", so I made it "risk".'

The scoutmaster was surprised to see a young boy arrive for summer camp with an umbrella.

'Why did you bring an umbrella to camp?' he asked.

The boy sighed: 'Did you ever have a mother?'

Two fathers were discussing their daughters. 'I don't know whether to send my daughter to college or not,' said one. 'Is it worth it? What do you think?'

The other said: 'Well, it cost me a thousand dollars a year to send Debbie to college and it took her four years to find a husband. I spent three hundred to send Kelly to the beach for two weeks and she came home married. I recommend the beach.'

Jim was plagued by his spiteful mother-in-law who, much to his dismay, lived with the family. Each morning, just as he was about to leave for work, the mother-in-law would take him to one side and hiss: 'If you don't treat my daughter right after I'm dead, I'll dig up from the grave and haunt you!'

It was the same when Jim came home for lunch. The mother-in-law would sidle up to him and whisper menacingly: 'If you don't treat my daughter right after I'm dead, I'll dig up from the grave and haunt you!'

And at night, she would collar him on his way to bed and snarl: 'If you don't treat my daughter right after I'm dead, I'll dig up from the grave and haunt you!'

He recounted his awful life with the old woman to a friend who, after not seeing Jim for a couple of months, asked him how his mother-in-law was feeling.

'She isn't feeling anything,' said Jim. 'She died three weeks ago.'

'Aren't you worried about her ominous threat?' asked the friend.

'Not really,' replied Jim, 'but just to be sure, I buried her face down. Let her dig!'

A little girl noticed that her mother had a few grey hairs appearing on her head. 'Why is that?' she asked.

'Because,' explained the mother, 'every time you do something naughty and make me unhappy, one of my hairs turns white.'

The child thought for a moment and said: 'Is that why all of Grandma's hair is white? You must have been really hard work!'

'I'm ashamed of the way we live,' a young wife said to her layabout husband who refused to find a job. 'My father pays our rent, my mother buys all our food, my sister buys our clothes, and my uncle bought us the car. I'm just so ashamed.'

The husband rolled over on the sofa. 'So you should be ashamed,' he agreed. 'Those two worthless brothers of yours never give us a cent!'

Two sisters came home from school in floods of tears. 'Whatever is the matter?' asked their mother.

The first sister sobbed; 'The kids at school make fun of my big feet.'

'There, there,' soothed the mother. 'Your feet aren't that big.' She turned to the second sister. 'Now why are you crying?'

'Because I've been invited to a ski party, and I haven't got any skis.'

'That's okay,' said the mother. 'You can borrow your sister's shoes.'

A woman in Florida was going on and on about her two remarkable grandchildren. Eventually a weary fellow sunbather asked: 'Tell me, how old are your grandsons?'

The woman replied: 'The doctor is four and the lawyer is six.'

A census taker in a rural area went up to a farmhouse and knocked on the door. When a woman answered, he asked her the names and ages of her children.

She said: 'Let's see now, there are the twins, Billy and Bobby, they're seventeen. And the twins, Seth and Beth, they're sixteen. And the twins, Benny and Jenny, they're fifteen.'

'Wait a minute!' said the census taker. 'Did you get twins every time?'

'Heck no,' answered the woman. 'There were hundreds of times we didn't get nothin'.'

A man told his neighbour: 'I took my dog to the vet today because it bit my mother-in-law.'

'Oh,' said the neighbour. 'Did you have it put to sleep?'

'No, I had its teeth sharpened.'

A man came into work one Monday morning with his neck heavily bandaged.

'What happened to you?' asked his boss.

'Well, I was playing golf yesterday with my mother-in-law and on the second hole she sliced her ball into a field. She wasn't going to give the ball up for lost and so she insisted that we search for it. We looked for a quarter of an hour, but there was no sign of the ball, just one old cow standing in the field. Still my mother-in-law insisted that she wouldn't leave until we had found her ball. We searched for another twenty-five minutes, but still couldn't find it. I was on the point of giving up when I thought I'd better check that the ball hadn't somehow got lodged in the cow. So I lifted up the cow's tail and, sure enough, a ball was stuck there. I called my mother-in-law over and said: "Does this look like yours?" And she hit me in the throat with a five-iron.'

Food and Drink

A man walked into a bar and said to the barman: 'Beer for me, beer for you, and beer for everyone who is in the bar now.'

After finishing his beer, the man turned to leave.

'Hey,' said the barman. 'What about paying?'

'Sorry, I've got no money.'

Hearing this, the angry barman hit him and threw him out onto the street.

The following evening the man returned to the same bar and told the bartender: 'Beer for me, beer for you, and beer for everyone who is in the bar now.'

Thinking that the man wouldn't be dumb enough to try the same trick twice, the barman poured the pints, but again, after finishing his drink, the customer turned to leave.

'Hey, you haven't paid!' called the barman.

'Sorry, I've got no money,' said the man.

The barman was so furious that he hit him hard and hurled him out onto the street.

The next evening the man again walked into the bar and said to the barman: 'Beer for me, and beer for everyone who is in the bar now.'

Disgusted, the barman said: 'What, no beer for me this time?'

'No,' answered the man. 'You get violent when you drink.'

Two fonts walked into a bar. The bartender said: 'Sorry, we don't want your type in here.'

Every evening Bill would head for the local pub before staggering home around midnight, considerably the worse for wear. He invariably struggled with getting his key into the keyhole with the result that the noise would wake his wife who would be forced to come downstairs and let him in. She would then yell at him for going out every night and coming home drunk. But still he continued his nightly routine.

One day the long-suffering wife was moaning to a friend about Bill's behaviour and how it was damaging their marriage. The friend suggested: 'Why don't you treat him a little differently when he comes home? Instead of shouting at him, why don't you give him some loving words and welcome him home with a kiss? You never know, he might change his ways.' The wife decided it was a good idea.

That night, Bill took off again and arrived home in his usual drunken state around midnight. His wife heard him at the door and quickly let him in. Instead of screaming at him, she took him by the arm and led him into the living room. There, she sat him down in his favourite chair, put his feet up on the foot stool, took his shoes off and fetched his slippers. After cuddling up to him for a few minutes, she whispered: 'It's pretty late, Bill. I think we should go upstairs to bed now.'

Bill slurred: 'We might as well. I'll be in trouble anyway when I get home!'

An ice cream man was found lying on the floor of his van covered in hundreds and thousands. Police say he topped himself.

A man came into a bar and ordered a martini. Before drinking it, he removed the olive and carefully put it into a jar. Then he ordered another martini and did the same thing. After an hour, by which time he was full of martinis and the jar was full of olives, he staggered out.

'Well,' remarked a customer, 'I never saw anything as strange as that!'

'What was strange about it?' asked the barman. 'His wife had sent him out for a jar of olives.'

A man went into a bar with a banana on his head. As he served him, the bartender said: 'Look, I don't know if you realize this, but you've got a banana on your head.'

'That's okay,' said the man. 'I always wear a banana on my head on Tuesdays.'

'But today's Wednesday,' said the bartender.

'It's not, is it?' said the man. 'Oh no! I must look a right fool!'

What's smelly, round and laughs? – A tickled onion.

A blacksmith living in a remote German village was cut off during a particularly harsh winter. With the roads impassable, he was unable to get to the nearest shops for food supplies. The weather showed no signs of abating and his plight became increasingly desperate. Eventually with no one else to turn to, he contacted his brother who lived over two hundred miles away in Munich and asked him to send a food parcel by helicopter.

'What sort of food would you like me to send?' asked the brother.

'Some bread, some milk, oh, and some sausage. Definitely some sausage. It has been weeks since I have tasted a good German sausage.'

The brother promised to send the parcel immediately but two days later it had still to arrive. 'I don't know how much longer I can go on,' wailed the blacksmith. 'I am tired and frail, I have no gas or electricity, snow is piled against the front door, and the wurst is yet to come!'

A drunk reeled into a funeral parlour and ordered a scotch. The mortician tried to explain where he was, but the befuddled drunk simply repeated the order.

'Look,' said the mortician, 'we do not serve scotch here. Do you understand?'

'OK,' said the drunk. 'Give me a beer.'

A little-known fact about William Tell is that apart from being an expert with the crossbow, he was an accomplished chef. One day he had prepared a new dish for his Swiss friends, but, ever the perfectionist, he felt there was something missing with the sauce.

'More berries in the sauce?' he suggested.

'No, no,' they said. 'I think you have just the right amount of berries.'

'More salt, then?'

'No, the amount of salt is perfect,' they insisted.

'Herbs, that's it,' he said triumphantly. 'I should have put in more herbs. What do you think?'

'Hmm,' they pondered, tasting the sauce. 'Perhaps only thyme, Will Tell.'

A police officer stopped a drunk wandering through the streets at six o'clock in the morning.

The policeman said: 'Can you explain why you're out at this hour?'

The drunk replied: 'If I could, I'd be home by now!'

A man went into a fishmonger's carrying a trout under his arm.
'Do you make fishcakes?' he asked.
'Yes, we do,' replied the fishmonger.
'Great,' said the man. 'It's his birthday.'

A termite walked into a pub and asked: 'Is the bar tender here?'

A smartly dressed man entered a trendy bar and took a seat. The bartender came over and said: 'What can I get you to drink, sir?'
'Nothing, thank you,' replied the man. 'I tried alcohol once, but I didn't like it, and I haven't drunk it since.'
The bartender was puzzled but being a friendly sort of guy, he pulled a packet of cigarettes from his pocket and offered one to the man.
But the man refused. 'I tried smoking once, didn't like it, and I have never smoked since. Look, actually, I wouldn't be in here at all except that I'm waiting for my son.'
To which the bartender replied: 'Your only child, I presume?'

A man ordered a takeaway pizza. The waiter said: 'Shall I cut it into six pieces or twelve?'
'Six please. I could never eat twelve.'

What is the best way to make an apple crumble? – Torture it for ten minutes.

A drunk boarded a bus late one night and lurched along the centre gangway. Suddenly he stopped and shouted that everyone in the seats to his right was an idiot and that everyone in the seats to his left was an asshole.
An angry passenger stood up and said: 'How dare you! I'm not an idiot!'
The drunk yelled back: 'So move to the other side then.'

Two biscuits were walking down the street when one was crushed by a passing car. The other said: 'Crumbs!'

Reasons For Allowing Drinking At Work:
    It's an incentive to show up.

Employees tell management what they think, not what management wants to hear.

It helps save on heating costs in the winter.

It encourages carpooling.

It increases job satisfaction because if you have a lousy job, you don't care.

It eliminates holidays because people would rather come to work.

It makes fellow employees look better.

It makes the cafeteria food taste better.

Bosses are more likely to hand out raises when they are drunk.

Breaking wind during a meeting isn't so embarrassing.

No one will remember your strip act at the Christmas party.

After a heavy day's drinking, a tramp fell asleep on a park bench as night closed in. But no sooner had he dozed off than a passer-by, spotting the watch on his wrist, tapped him on the shoulder and asked him for the time.

Roused from his slumbers, the tramp grumpily replied, '11.30' and went back to sleep.

A few minutes later, another passer-by prodded the tramp and asked him the time. '11.34,' said the tramp irritably and settled back down to sleep.

He had barely shut his eyes before another pedestrian woke him to ask the time. '11.39,' muttered the tramp wearily.

When another three people stopped to ask him the time in the space of ten minutes, the tramp could take no more. So he took a piece of card, wrote on it 'I cannot tell the time', and placed it where everyone passing the bench could read it. Then he dozed off to sleep. Two minutes later, a man tapped him on the arm.

'What do you want?' snapped the tramp.

The man said: 'It's a minute to twelve.'

A woman collared her husband as he stumbled through the door. 'What's the big idea coming home half drunk?'

'Sorry, honey. I ran out of money.'

Did you hear about the bailiff who moonlighted as a bartender? – He served subpoena coladas.

One day a little girl was watching her mother prepare roast beef. The mother cut off the ends, wrapped it in string, seasoned it, and placed it in the roasting tin. The girl asked her mother why she always cut off the ends of the roast. She replied that she didn't really know why – but it was the way her mother had done it.

That night, grandma came to dinner and the little girl and her mother asked her why she had always cut the ends off the roast before putting it in the oven. Grandma replied that she didn't know why – but that was the way *her* mother had done it.

Great grandmother was very old and confined to a nursing home. But the next time the little girl, her mother and her grandma went to visit, they asked her the same question. 'Why did you cut the ends off the roast before cooking?'

Great grandmother looked at them in surprise and explained simply: 'We were poor and had a small oven in those days. I cut off the ends so the roast would fit.'

As a punishment for his naughty behaviour all day, a mother decided to give one of her sons short rations at dinner time. So while the rest of the family tucked into chicken, potatoes, carrots, peas and beans, the naughty boy had to make do with chicken, potatoes, carrots and beans.

'Why haven't I got my favourite vegetable?' he wailed.

'Because you've been a bad boy,' explained his mother. 'And you know what they say: no peas for the wicked.'

Two British executives staggered out of a company party in New York. Keith crossed the street while Maurice stumbled into a subway entrance. When Keith reached the other side, he noticed Maurice emerging from the subway stairs.

'Where have you been?' slurred Keith.

'I don't know,' said Maurice, 'but you should see the train set that guy has in his basement.'

A farmer was pulling a cartload of horse manure down the lane.

'What are you going to do with that?' asked his dim-witted farmhand.

'I'm going to put it on my strawberries,' said the farmer.

'That's strange,' said the farmhand. 'We put cream and sugar on ours.'

A woman suffering from anxiety about her growing weight went to see a therapist. She told him that no matter how hard she tried, she had never been able to stick to diets, whereupon he advised her: 'The key to a happy and successful life is: always finish what you start.'

The woman took these words on board and when she returned for her next appointment, she had a much more optimistic outlook.

'I feel better already,' she told the therapist. 'So far today I've finished a giant bag of crisps, a pack of custard creams and a chocolate cake.'

A drunk phoned Alcoholics Anonymous.

'Is that AA?' asked the drunk.

'Yes,' said the switchboard girl. 'Would you like to join?'

'No,' said the drunk. 'I'd like to resign.'

Wife: The two things I cook best are meatloaf and apple pie.

Husband: And which is this?

A young man was sitting outside his local pub one day, enjoying a quiet beer and generally feeling good about life, when a nun suddenly appeared at his table and began sounding off about the evils of drink.

'You should be ashamed of yourself, young man! Drinking is a sin. Alcohol is the blood of the devil!'

After five minutes of listening to her lecturing, the young man decided it was time to retaliate. 'How do you know all these things, sister?'

'My Mother Superior told me.'

'But have you ever had a drink yourself?'

'Don't be ridiculous – of course I haven't.'

'Then how can you be sure that what you're saying is right?'

'Well, er . . .'

'Look. Let me buy you a drink. If you still believe afterwards that drink is evil, I will give up alcohol for life.'

'But how can I, a nun, sit outside a public house drinking?'

'I'll get the barman to put it in a teacup for you, then nobody will know.'

'Well, I suppose so.'

The young man went into the pub and walked over to the bar. 'Another pint for me, and a triple vodka on the rocks.' Lowering his voice, he said to the barman: 'And could you put the vodka in a teacup?'

'Oh no!' said the barman. 'It's not that bloody nun again!'

Did you hear about the man who bought a plate with four corners so he could enjoy a square meal?

An Englishman was widely considered to be the world's foremost authority on tea. One day he was chatting with a friend who had just returned from Australia. The friend told him that he had heard of an unusual tea brewed in a small Outback town named Mercy. The connoisseur scoffed at the suggestion, stating that no tea came from the Outback because there was nowhere to grow it.

'Oh, no, it doesn't come from leaves,' said the friend. 'They brew it from koala fur.'

The expert was so intrigued that he booked a flight to Australia the very next day. On arrival, he hired a guide to take him deep into the Outback to the remote town of Mercy. Once in town, he found the only bar and ordered a cup of the mysterious beverage. The cup was placed before him, and he spent several minutes studying the colour, the aroma, and the viscosity. Finally he took a small sip and was pleasantly surprised by the taste. He then followed with a big mouthful, but suddenly started gagging and spitting, clutching at his mouth.

'What is this?' he exclaimed, holding up a handful of what appeared to be short, coarse threads.

'Oh, that's koala fur,' said the bartender.

'You mean to tell me that you don't strain out the fur?' asked the expert, incredulous.

'Of course not,' replied the bartender. 'The koala tea of Mercy is not strained.'

A wife served some homemade cinnamon rolls for breakfast and waited eagerly for her husband's reaction. When none was immediately forthcoming, she said: 'If I baked these commercially, how much do you think I could get for one of them?'

Without looking up from his newspaper, he replied: 'About ten years.'

A drunk was floundering down an alleyway carrying a box with holes in the side when he bumped into an old friend.

'What have you got there?' asked the friend, nodding towards the box.

'A mongoose,' replied the drunk.

'What have you got a mongoose for?'

'Well, you know how drunk I can get. When I get drunk, I see snakes and I'm scared to death of snakes. That's why I got this mongoose, for protection.'

'But those snakes are imaginary.'

'That's okay. So is this mongoose.'

A Zen Master walked up to a hot-dog seller and said: 'Make me one with everything.'

A wife was still in a foul mood the morning after a party. She told her husband crossly: 'You certainly made a fool of yourself last night. I just hope nobody realized you were sober.'

'How were your sandwiches today, darling?' asked the wife as her husband returned home from work.

'They were fine,' he replied.

'Are you sure they tasted okay?'

'Yes, they were really good.'

'You don't feel ill at ill?'

'No, never felt better. Why?'

'Oh, it's just that tomorrow you're going to have to clean your shoes with fish paste.'

A guy went into a bar and ordered five pints of beer. The bartender was baffled by the request since the customer was alone, but nevertheless he poured him five pints and lined them up along the bar. The guy proceeded to down all five in quick fashion before wiping his mouth and saying: 'That was good.'

As soon as he had finished, he ordered four more pints. Again they were lined up on the bar and the guy knocked them back quickly. By the last pint, he was definitely beginning to feel a little groggy.

Undaunted, he ordered another three pints. These took a bit longer to sink and by the end he was slurring his words.

Even so, he ordered another two pints. After drinking these, he could hardly manage to sit on his stool.

Nevertheless he ordered one more pint.

'I think you've had enough,' said the bartender.

As the guy struggled to focus on him, he said: 'Yeah, you know, it's funny. The less I drink, the drunker I get.'

Arriving home drunk one night, a husband cut himself when he walked into an overhanging shelf in the garage. With blood trickling from facial wounds, he went straight upstairs to the bathroom to carry out repairs.

The next morning, his wife said: 'You came home drunk last night, didn't you?'

'No,' he replied, mustering all the sincerity at his disposal.

'Then perhaps you can explain to me why there are plasters all over the bathroom mirror . . .'

You Know You've Had Too Much To Drink When:
You lose arguments with inanimate objects.
Your doctor finds traces of blood in your alcohol stream.
You notice your tie sticking out of your fly.
Someone uses your tongue for a coaster.
You start kissing the portraits on the wall.
You see your underwear hanging from the chandelier.
You have to hold on to the floor to keep from sliding off.
Every woman you look at seems to have a twin.
You strike a match and light your nose.
The back of your head keeps getting hit by the toilet seat.
You hear someone say, 'Call a priest.'
You hear a duck quacking, and it's you.
You complain about the small bathroom after emerging from the wardrobe.
You refill your glass from the goldfish bowl.
You tell everyone you have to go home . . . even though the party's at your place.
You tell your best joke to the rubber plant.
You realize you're the only one under the coffee table.

Why did the raisin go out with the prune? – Because she couldn't find a date.

A priest and a rabbi were walking down the street together when they both fancied a drink. There was just one snag: neither had any money.

'No problem,' said the priest. 'I know how we can get free drinks.'

While the rabbi watched from outside, the priest walked into the busy bar and ordered a whisky. The priest downed his drink and then the barman handed him the bill.

'But my son,' said the priest innocently, 'I've already paid for the drink.'

'Oh, I'm really sorry, Father,' said the barman. 'It's been so busy in here I must have forgotten.'

Graciously accepting the apology, the priest left.

A few minutes later, the rabbi walked in and ordered a gin and tonic. After the rabbi had finished his drink, the barman presented him with his bill.

The rabbi protested: 'But I paid you when I ordered the drink.'

The barman said: 'I'm terribly sorry, rabbi, I don't know what's wrong with me. This is the second time that's happened today. Please accept my apologies.'

'That's all right,' said the rabbi. 'No offence taken. Now just give me change for the twenty dollar bill I gave you, and I'll be on my way.'

Grossly overweight, a man was bullied by his work colleagues into going on a diet. For three weeks, he resisted temptation, even changing his route to work to avoid his favourite bakery. But then one day, to the horror of his workmates, he turned up at the office clutching a huge chocolate cake.

When his colleagues berated him, he was quick to offer an explanation. 'I accidentally drove by the bakery this morning and there were loads of tasty treats in the window. I felt this was fate, so I prayed to God, saying: "If you want me to have one of those delicious chocolate cakes, show me a sign – let there be a parking space directly in front of the bakery." And sure enough, the eighth time around the block, there it was!'

A couple were sound asleep in bed at three o'clock in the morning when they were woken by a pounding on their back door.

'You answer it,' said the wife.

So the husband reluctantly trudged downstairs and opened the door to find a drunk leaning against the wall. 'I need a push,' said the drunk, slurring his words.

'Sorry,' said the husband. 'It's three o'clock in the morning, it's pouring with rain, and you don't look as if you should be driving anyway. So there's no way I can give you a push.' And with that he slammed the door.

When he returned to the bedroom, his wife asked him who had been at the door. 'It was just some drunk,' he explained. 'He wanted a push, but I sent him packing.'

The wife reminded him that they had once been in a similar predicament and had been forced to knock on a stranger's door in the middle of the night. 'Remember how grateful we were when that guy came to our assistance?'

Now feeling guilty, the husband got dressed, put on a raincoat, and ventured out into the miserable night. But the drunk was nowhere to be seen.

'Hey,' shouted the husband, trying not to wake the neighbours, 'Do you still need help? Do you still need a push?'

In the distance he heard a slurred response. 'Yeah, I still need a push.'

'Where are you?'

The drunk said: 'I'm over here on the swing!'

A pork pie walked into a bar. The barman said: 'Sorry, we don't serve food in here.'

A man walked into a bar and ordered a double scotch. He downed it in one and immediately ordered another. He knocked that back and ordered another straight away. This quick-fire drinking went on for an hour until the bartender felt compelled to comment: 'You look unhappy. What's the problem?'

The man said: 'My wife and I got into a fight and she vowed not to talk to me for a month . . . And tonight's the last night.'

A husband took his young daughter to the grocery store where, in addition to the carefully prepared list of healthy items, they bought a box of sugar-rich cookies.

When they arrived home and unpacked the items, his wife immediately glared at the cookies.

'It's okay, honey,' he said. 'This box of cookies has one-third fewer calories than usual.'

'How come?' she asked.

'Because we ate a third on the way home.'

Back in the 1920s, there was no such thing as sliced bread. That is, until a customer at a small bakery complained that she had cut her hand while slicing a loaf and announced that in future she wanted the baker to slice it for her. The baker was happy to oblige and the pre-sliced bread proved so popular that soon the whole village was asking for it. The demand became such that the baker started using a longer knife so that he could slice two — and then even three — loaves at a time. Determined to keep pace with his increasing trade, he then searched for a knife long enough to slice four loaves simultaneously, but was unable to find a suitable implement. For weeks on end, he visited every hardware shop in the area but was still unable to find a knife capable of slicing four loaves.

Then one night while he and his wife were visiting a neighbouring village, something in a shop window across the street caught his eye. As he walked over and stared intently into the window, his wife sidled up next to him and asked what had so captured his attention.

Excitedly the baker replied: 'I'm looking over a four loaf cleaver that I overlooked before!'

A vicar, a priest and a rabbi walked into a pub. The bartender said: 'Is this some kind of joke?'

A guy walked into a bar and said: 'Bartender, give me two shots – one for me and one for my buddy here.'

The bartender said: 'Do you want both drinks now or do you want me to wait till your buddy arrives to pour his?'

'No, it's okay,' said the guy, 'I've got my best buddy in my pocket here.' With that, he pulled out a little three-inch man from his pocket.

'That's amazing,' said the bartender. 'Can he walk?'

The guy flicked a coin down to the end of the bar and said to his tiny friend: 'Hey, Cliff, go and get that coin.'

Cliff duly ran along the bar, fetched the coin and brought it back to the guy.

The bartender was impressed. 'What else can he do? Can he talk?'

'Talk?' said the guy. 'Sure he talks. Hey, Cliff, tell him about that time we were on safari in Africa and you insulted that witch doctor.'

Late at night, a drunk was on his knees beneath a street-light, obviously searching for something. A passer-by offered to help.

'What have you lost?' he asked.

'My watch,' replied the drunk. 'It fell off when I tripped over the pavement.'

The passer-by joined in the search but after twenty minutes, there was still no sign of the watch. 'Where exactly did you trip?' he asked.

'About three hundred yards up the street,' answered the drunk.

'Then why are you looking for your watch here if you lost it three hundred yards up the street?'

The drunk said: 'Because the light is much better here.'

Fork: Who was that ladle I saw you with last night?

Spoon: That was no ladle. That was my knife.

After a night on the town, a husband lurched home at three o'clock in the morning. Just as he got through the door, the cuckoo clock started and cuckooed three times. Thinking on his feet because he knew that the clock would almost certainly wake his wife, he cuckooed another nine times.

The next morning his wife asked him what time he had arrived home last night.

'Twelve o'clock,' he answered.

When she didn't dispute it, he was convinced that he had got away with it. He was really pleased with himself.

Then she added: 'We really must get a new cuckoo clock. Last night it cuckooed three times, said "damn", cuckooed another four times, belched, cuckooed another three times, cleared its throat, cuckooed twice more and giggled.'

A man walked into a bar and ordered a glass of white wine. After taking a sip of the wine, he hurled the remainder into the bartender's face. Before the bartender could recover from the shock, the man began weeping.

'I'm sorry,' he sobbed. 'I'm really sorry. I keep doing that to bartenders. I can't tell how who embarrassing it is to have a compulsion like this.'

Far from being angry, the bartender was sympathetic and suggested that the man see an analyst about his problem. 'I happen to have the name of a good psychiatrist,' said the bartender. 'My brother and my wife both go to him, and they say he's the best there is.'

Six months later, the man was back. The bartender remembered him. 'Did you do what I suggested?' he asked, pouring the man a glass of white wine.

'I certainly did,' said the man. 'I've been seeing that psychiatrist twice a week.' Then he took a sip of the wine and threw the rest into the bartender's face.

The flustered bartender wiped his face with a towel. 'The doctor doesn't seem to be doing you any good,' he spluttered.

'On the contrary,' claimed the man. 'He's done me the world of good.'

'But you threw the wine in my face again!'

'Yes, but it doesn't embarrass me anymore.'

In the window of a seafood restaurant, a man spotted a sign saying 'Lobster Tails $2 each.'

Sensing a bargain, he went inside and asked the waitress why they were so cheap. 'They must be very short tails for that price,' he suggested.

'No,' replied the waitress. 'They're normal length.'

'Then they must be pretty old.'

'No, they're fresh today.'

'There must be something wrong with them . . .'

'No, they're just regular lobster tails.'

'Okay,' said the man, 'for two dollars I'll have one.'

So the waitress took the man's money, sat him down and said: 'Once upon a time there was a big red lobster . . .'

What did the grape say when it was trodden on? – Nothing. It just let out a little wine.

A man had spent all day drinking in a bar. By ten o'clock at night, he was blind drunk but still wanted more. However he had run out of money.

'I've got to have another drink,' he told the bartender. 'Can't you give me one on credit?'

'You know the rules,' replied the bartender. 'No credit. But I'll tell you what I'll do. It's a quiet night in here and I fancy a bit of fun. So I'll make a deal with you: you can have another drink if you carry out three tasks.'

'Sure,' said the drunk. 'Anything you want. Just name it. I'm listening.'

'Okay,' began the bartender, 'first I want you to go up to that big doorman and knock him out cold; then I want you to pull a loose tooth belonging to Satan, the pit bull terrier in the back room; and finally I want you to have sex with the town's sleaziest woman, who is sitting over there, alone at the end of the bar.'

'No problem,' said the drunk, levering himself off his stool. He staggered over to the doorman and, taking him by surprise, felled him with a single blow. The bartender was amazed and pointed to the back room where the pit bull was waiting. The drunk lurched through the back door and the bartender waited to hear the commotion. Any second, he expected to see the drunk rush out, hotly pursued by Satan. Instead there was silence. Then after a few minutes the dog started whimpering.

Five minutes later, the drunk emerged with a big grin on his face. 'Right,' he said, 'now where's the woman with the loose tooth?'

People who eat metal paper fastenings have a staple diet.

A police officer saw a drunk staggering home in a posh neighbourhood. Suspicious when the man struggled to get his key in the lock, the officer asked: 'Are you sure this is your house, sir?'

'Certainly,' said the drunk. 'And if you follow me in, I'll prove it to you.'

As they entered the living room, the drunk said: 'See that piano? That's mine. And see that television? That's mine, too.'

Then he led the officer clumsily up the stairs. 'See,' slurred the drunk. 'This is my bedroom. See the bed? That's mine. See the woman lying in the bed? That's my wife. And see the guy lying next to her . . . ?'

'Yeah?' said the officer, more suspicious than ever.

'Well, that's me!'

Did you know it takes forty pigs to make four thousand sausages? Isn't it amazing what you can teach them?

A female American tourist travelling in south-east Asia was horrified to be served bird's nest soup.

'Do you mean to say this is an actual bird's nest?' she grimaced.

The chef assured her that it was, explaining that the bird built the nest using its own saliva as glue.

'Are you saying I'm supposed to eat saliva from a bird?' she demanded. 'That's gross. I cannot imagine anyone eating birds' saliva.'

Realising that there was no hope of converting her, the chef asked her whether there was anything she would like instead.

She said: 'Oh, just fix me an omelette.'

What food will reduce a woman's sex drive by fifty per cent? – Wedding cake.

A wife was throwing a posh dinner party at the family apartment and had invited the cream of city society to attend. To ensure that she was serving only the freshest food at the party, that afternoon she sent her husband down to the beach to fetch some snails. But while he was collecting the snails, he met a beautiful woman. One thing led to another and they ended up going back to her place, drinking several bottles of wine and making passionate love.

He was so smitten with her that he completely forgot about the time and it was ten o'clock in the evening before he woke up.

'My God!' he thought. 'My wife's dinner party! She'll kill me!'

Frantically he got dressed and ran back home. But he was in such a hurry that as he reached the top of the stairs leading to their apartment, he dropped the bucket of snails and they fell to the floor. There were snails all the way down the stairs.

Hearing the crash of the bucket, his wife opened the door. She was furious. 'Where the hell have you been?' she screamed.

He looked at her and then at the trail of snails down the stairs. 'Come on guys,' he said. 'We're nearly there.'

When a clock is hungry, does it go back four seconds?

A husband was standing on the bathroom scales, desperately holding his stomach in.

His wife, thinking he was trying to reduce his weight, remarked: 'I don't think that will help.'

'It does,' he said. 'It's the only way I can read the numbers!'

Count Dracula had thoroughly enjoyed his night on the town, drinking Bloody Marys in clubs and biting the necks of unsuspecting women. Shortly before sunrise he was making his way home when he was suddenly hit on the back of the head. Looking round, he saw nothing, but on the ground was a small sausage roll.

A mystified Dracula carried on his way until a few yards further along the road he felt another blow to the back of the head. Again he turned around quickly but could see nothing except, lying on the pavement, a small triangular sandwich. More puzzled than ever, he resumed his journey, only to feel another bang to the back of his head. He whirled round instantly but there was no sign of the culprit. Furious, he looked down and saw a cocktail sausage lying on the pavement. He stood motionless for a few seconds, peering into the darkness of the night. Nothing.

He had walked only a short distance further along the road when he felt a tap on the shoulder. With a swirl of his cape, he turned as fast as he could. Just then he felt a sharp pain in his heart. He fell to the ground clutching his chest, which was punctured by a small cocktail stick laden with a chunk of cheese and a pickle. As he lay dying on the pavement, Dracula looked up and saw a young woman. 'Who the hell are you?' he gasped.

She replied: 'I'm Buffet the Vampire Slayer.'

A man was staggering home drunk in the early hours of the morning when he was stopped by a police officer.

'What are you doing out at this time of night?' asked the officer.

'I'm going to a lecture,' slurred the drunk.

'And who's going to give a lecture at this hour?'

'My wife.'

Two sausages were sizzling in a pan. One looked at the other and said: 'It's hot in here.' The other one said: 'My God, a talking sausage!'

A man rushed into a bar and ordered a double whisky. He downed it in one gulp, put five dollars on the bar and dashed straight out again. Not thinking anyone was watching, the barman picked up the money and tucked it in his shirt pocket, but he turned round to see the bar manager standing in the doorway staring at him accusingly.

Thinking on his feet, the barman said: 'Boss, did you see that chap just now? Came in here, bought a double whisky, give me a five-dollar tip, and rushed out without paying!'

What do you get if you divide the circumference of a pumpkin by its diameter? – Pumpkin pi.

A drunk rolled into a bar, but the bartender refused to serve him. 'You've had too much to drink,' he said. 'I'm not letting you have any more.'

Five minutes later, the drunk came in again. The bartender stood firm. 'There's no way I'm serving you more alcohol. You've had more than enough already.'

Five minutes later, the doors opened and the drunk lurched in once more. 'Listen,' said the bartender. 'I'm not serving you. You're too drunk.'

The drunk nodded. 'I guess I must be,' he said. 'The last two places said the same thing.'

Good King Wenceslas rang his local pizza parlour. 'The usual, please,' he said. 'Deep pan, crisp and even.'

A husband went out for a few drinks with his pals one Friday evening but ended up getting so drunk at their flat that by the time he came round, it was Sunday lunchtime. Realizing that his wife would give him hell over the missing day and a half, he knew he had to come up with a plausible explanation. He was really struggling to think of a good excuse until he had a sudden brainwave. Calling home, he yelled down the phone: 'Don't pay the ransom, darling! I've managed to escape!'

A customer in a bar ordered a beer but as he drank it, he couldn't help noticing that it didn't taste as good as it should.

'Excuse me, bartender,' he said, 'but this beer's a bit warm.'

The bartender glared at him. 'Just shut up and drink your beer!' he snapped.

Upset by the bartender's attitude, the customer decided to take a small measure of revenge when it was time to pay for his drink. Instead of giving the bartender three dollar bills, he threw thirty dimes behind the counter and watched amused while the rude bartender had to get down on his hands and knees to pick them up.

In the hope that things had improved, the customer returned to the same bar the following day, waving a five dollar bill. Still seething from yesterday, the bartender thought about kicking him out before remembering that he couldn't really afford to turn away custom. Once again, the beer was rather warm, but the man refrained from complaining. When it was time to pay, he duly handed over the five dollar bill. The bartender went to the till to get the change, but, instead of taking out two dollar bills, he took out twenty dimes and threw them all over the pub. 'There!' he said triumphantly. 'There's your bloody change!'

The customer surveyed the scene but remained perfectly calm. Then he took out ten dimes, threw them behind the counter and said: 'Gimme another beer!'

A family of tomatoes were walking down the street but after a while the little boy tomato started to lag behind. The father tomato turned round and called: 'Ketchup!'

A drunk phoned the police to report that thieves had been in his car. 'They've stolen the dashboard, the steering wheel, the brake pedal, even the accelerator,' he moaned.

Five minutes later the phone at the police station rang again. It was the same drunk. 'Sorry,' he slurred. 'I just realized I got in the back seat by mistake.'

When the plums dry on your tree, it's time to prune.

Two students were talking about food.

'I've got a cookery book,' said one. 'But I've never been able to use it.'

'Why not?' asked the other. 'Were the recipes too complicated?'

'Not really, but each one began the same way: take a clean dish . . .'

A man went into a butcher's shop and asked for half a rabbit.

'I'm sorry,' said the butcher. 'I don't want to split hares.'

A businessman walked into a bar and ordered a hot dog and a Budweiser. He downed the beer, put the hot dog on his head, smashed it with his hand and walked out before the bartender could say anything.

The next day the businessman returned and once again ordered a hot dog and a Budweiser. The bartender watched in amazement as the businessman drank the beer, put the hot dog on his head, smashed it with his hand and walked out.

The businessman was back again the following day and placed his regular order of a hot dog and Budweiser. But this time the bartender was waiting to catch him out. 'I'm sorry,' he said. 'We're out of hot dogs.'

'Okay,' said the businessman without missing a beat. 'I'll have a cheeseburger and a Budweiser.'

He downed the beer, put the cheeseburger on his head, smashed it with his hand and headed for the door.

'Wait!' called the bartender, unable to contain his curiosity any longer. 'Why did you smash that cheeseburger on your head?'

The businessman replied: 'Because you didn't have any hot dogs.'

A short-sighted good Samaritan was on his way home one evening when he met a drunk slumped in the doorway of an apartment block.

'Do you live here?' asked the Samaritan, peering through his thick glasses.

'Yeah,' said the drunk. 'On the second floor.'

'Would you like me to take you upstairs?'

'Yeah, thanks.'

The Samaritan slowly led the drunk up to the second floor but decided that he didn't really want to face the wrath of an angry wife. So he opened the first door he came to and pushed the drunk through it.

Having done his good deed for the day, the Samaritan went back downstairs where, to his surprise, he found another drunk. The man said he, too, lived on the second floor, so the Samaritan led him hesitantly up the stairs, pushed him through the same door and went back down the stairs with the intention of resuming his journey home. But when he got to the bottom of the stairs, he found yet another drunk who said he lived on the second floor. So the Samaritan guided him up the stairs, pushed him through the same door and went back downstairs.

Once again a drunk was standing there, leaning against the wall and looking decidedly the worse for wear. But before the Samaritan could do anything, the drunk staggered over to a passing police officer and said: 'Officer, protect me from this madman! He keeps taking me upstairs and throwing me down the elevator shaft!'

What do you get if you cross a door knocker with some courgettes, tomatoes, onions, and garlic? – Rat-a-tat-a-touille.

A man walked into a pub and saw a gorilla serving behind the bar.

'What's the matter?' said the gorilla, realizing he was being stared at. 'Have you never seen a gorilla serving drinks before?'

'It's not that,' said the man. 'I just never thought the giraffe would sell this place.'

Following a beer festival in London, all the brewery presidents decided to go out for a beer.

Corona's president said: 'I would like the world's best beer, a Corona.'

The barman handed him a bottle of Corona.

Next Budweiser's president said: 'I'd like the best beer in the world, a Budweiser, the King of Beers.'

The barman reached up to the shelf and handed him a bottle of Budweiser.

Then the president of Coors said: 'I'd like the best beer in the world, a Coors, the only one made with Rocky Mountain spring water.'

The barman served him a bottle of Coors.

The three men were then joined by the president of Guinness who said: 'Give me a Coke.'

The other brewery presidents looked across and said: 'Why aren't you drinking a Guinness?'

The Guinness president replied: 'Well, if you guys aren't drinking beer, neither will I.'

A woman was in bed with her lover when she suddenly heard a noise downstairs.

'My God! Your husband is home,' said the lover. 'What am I going to do?'

'Don't worry,' said the wife. 'Just stay in bed with me. He's probably so drunk, he won't even notice you here with me.'

The lover took her advice and sure enough, the husband didn't notice anything untoward when he blundered his way into the bedroom. He crawled into bed and it wasn't until he pulled the covers over himself and exposed six feet at the end of the bed that he became suspicious.

'Honey!' he yelled. 'What the hell is going on? I see six feet at the end of the bed.'

The wife replied calmly: 'Dear, you're so drunk, you can't count. If you don't believe me, count them again.'

The husband got out of bed and counted: 'One, two, three, four . . . Dammit, you're right, honey.' And he climbed back into bed and went to sleep.

A man had been drinking at a bar for eight hours when he happened to mention that his girlfriend was in the car. The bartender, concerned because it was such a cold night, thought he had better go out to check on her but when he peered inside the car he saw the drunk's buddy Mick and the girlfriend going at it on the back seat. The bartender shook his head, came back in and told the drunk it might be a good idea to check on his girlfriend.

The drunk staggered outside, saw Mick and the girl entwined, then walked back into the bar laughing.

'What's so funny?' asked the bartender.

'That fool Mick, he's so drunk, he thinks he's me!'

A drunk fell into one of the fountains in Trafalgar Square. As he splashed around aimlessly, he looked up and saw Nelson standing on his column.

'Don't jump!' yelled the drunk. 'This is the shallow end!'

A man sat at the bar looking thoroughly dejected. After a while, the bartender asked: 'What's wrong, mate?'

The man sighed: 'I'll never understand women. The other night my wife threw me a birthday party. She told me that later on, as her gift to me, I could do with her whatever I wanted.'

'Wow!' said the bartender. 'Sounds like a great gift! Then why are you so miserable?'

'Well,' said the man, 'I thought about it and sent her home to her mother. Now she won't even speak to me.'

A guy rushed into a bar, ordered four expensive, thirty-year-old single malts and asked the barman to line them up in front of him. Then without hesitating, he quickly downed each one.

'Wow!' said the barman. 'You seem to be in a hurry.'

The man said: 'You would be too if you had what I have.'

'Why, what do you have?' asked the barman sympathetically.

'Fifty cents.'

A businessman was sitting quietly at the bar, staring blankly into his drink. To the amusement of a gang of bikers, after forty-five minutes he had still not taken a sip, so one of them decided to play a little joke by suddenly grabbing the businessman's drink and knocking it back in one.

The biker laughed his head off. 'So what you gonna do about that?' he snarled.

'Nothing,' said the businessman quietly. 'You see, today has been the worst day of my life. I lost my job, my wife has left me, my car was stolen, my dog was run over, and the one week I forgot to do the lottery, my numbers came up! And now just when I've decided to end it all, you come along and drink my poison!'

As a fire engine sped down the road with bells and sirens wailing, a drunk was desperately running behind it. After chasing it for two hundred yards, he realized he could no longer keep up and slumped to the ground exhausted. Shaking his fist at the engine as it disappeared into the distance, he yelled: 'Fine! You can keep your bloody ice-cream!'

An elderly couple died in a car crash. They had been in excellent health for years through exercizing regularly and also because the wife was obsessed with health foods, keeping a strict watch on both their diets. So when St. Peter welcomed them to heaven, they were keen to take advantage of the first-rate relaxation facilities. The husband was particularly impressed by the eighteen-hole golf course and the Olympic-sized swimming pool.

'This really is a fantastic place you've got,' he told St. Peter.

'And there's more,' said St. Peter. 'Let me show you the restaurant.'

As they observed the sumptuous buffet serving every food imaginable, the husband asked; 'Where's the low fat table?'

'Oh, you don't have to worry about things like that,' said St. Peter. 'You can eat whatever you want, no matter how fatty it is, and it's all free. After all, this is heaven!'

With that, the husband threw his hat to the ground in a fit of temper.

'What's the matter?' asked St. Peter.

Turning to his wife, the husband snapped: 'This is all your fault, Mildred. If it weren't for your blasted bran muffins, I could have been here ten years ago!'

A horse walked into a bar and ordered a drink. The bartender said: 'Why the long face?'

A cannibal king in a remote jungle territory had a particular taste for missionaries. Somehow their meat always tasted sweeter. And the king was an expert on food, for there was nothing he enjoyed more than sitting down to a sumptuous banquet.

On one particular evening he was tucking in heartily to the huge platter of thinly sliced missionary before him. It was easy to see why he weighed in at over twenty-five stone. Whilst his people were happy to see the king enjoying himself – he had a ferocious temper when things did not meet with his approval – they were fervently hoping that there would be a few scraps left over for them. For whereas the king was decidedly rotund, his subjects were thin from near starvation. So with each slice of meat that he devoured, their hearts sank a little further. It was beginning to look as if there would be nothing left.

The natives began to mutter among themselves. 'It doesn't look good,' said the cannibal who had felled the missionary with a poison dart. 'He is going to eat the lot! It's always the same when we bring him back one of these religious types.'

'He certainly has a liking for these men of God,' agreed a fellow subject. 'There's obviously something about their delicate skin.'

'Well, it's simply not good enough,' said the first native, becoming increasingly irate. 'It's about time we followed the example of the Watumbabibi tribe down river and refused to hunt until the king shows us more consideration and allows us a fair helping of his missionary meals.'

'You mean,' queried his fellow cannibal, 'that we should ask him to implement some kind of Prophet-sharing scheme?'

An old drunk stumbled across a baptismal service one Sunday afternoon down by the river. He proceeded to walk down into the water and stand next to the preacher. The minister turned around, spotted the drunk and said: 'Mister, are you ready to find Jesus?'

The drunk replied: 'Yes, preacher, I sure am.'

The minister then dunked him under the water and pulled him right back up. 'Have you found Jesus?' he asked.

'Nooo, I didn't,' spluttered the bedraggled drunk.

So the preacher dunked him under for a bit longer, brought him up and said: 'Now, brother, have you found Jesus?'

'Nooo, I did not, preacher.'

In disgust, the preacher then held him under for at least thirty seconds before bringing him back to the surface and demanding: 'My God, man, have you found Jesus yet?'

His head drenched, the old drunk spat out water and, wiping his eyes, said to the preacher: 'Are you sure this is where he fell in?'

The bartender asked the guy sitting at the bar: 'What'll you have?'

The guy answered: 'A scotch, please.'

The bartender handed him the drink and said: 'That'll be five dollars.'

The guy said: 'What are you talking about? I don't owe you anything for this.'

A lawyer, sitting nearby and overhearing the conversation, said to the bartender: 'You know, he's got you there. In the original offer, which constitutes a binding contract upon acceptance, there was no stipulation of remuneration.'

The bartender was not happy, but said to the guy: 'Okay, you beat me for a drink. But don't ever let me catch you in here again.'

The next day, the same guy walked into the bar. The bartender said: 'What the heck are you doing in here? I thought I told you to steer clear of this joint. I can't believe you've got the nerve to come back!'

The guy said innocently: 'What are you talking about? I've never been in this place in my life.'

Fearing that he had made a mistake, the bartender backed down.

'I'm very sorry, but the likeness is uncanny. You must have a double.'
The guy replied: 'Thanks. Make it a scotch.'

A skeleton walked into a bar and said: 'I'd like a beer and a mop . . .'

Two guys were sitting in a Dublin bar when one turned to the other and said: 'You see that chap over there? Don't you think he looks just like me?'

The man went over to his doppelganger and said: 'Excuse me, but I couldn't help noticing that you're a dead ringer for me.'

'You're right, I do look like you.'

'Where are you from?'

'Dublin.'

'Me too.'

'Which street?'

'Kilkenny Avenue.'

'Kilkenny Avenue? That's incredible. That's my street too. What number?'

'Forty-eight.'

'Forty-eight. I don't believe it. Me too. What are your parents' names?'

'Pat and Mary.'

'Pat and Mary. Unbelievable. So are mine.'

Just then, the bartenders changed shifts. 'Anything happened?' asked the new bartender.

'Nothing much,' said the old one. 'Oh, except the O'Malley twins are drunk again.'

A drunk staggered to the men's toilet in a large restaurant. Meandering back, he suddenly stopped and put his hand on a woman's shoulder. The woman recoiled in horror.

'Excuse me,' he said. 'Did I step on your foot about five minutes ago?'

'Yes,' she snapped. 'You certainly did!'

'That's good,' he said. 'I knew my table was around here somewhere.'

Vincent Van Gogh walked into a bar.
The bartender asked: 'Would you like a drink?'
Van Gogh said: 'No thanks, I've got one 'ere.'

A Texan walked into a pub in Ireland and announced: 'I hear you Irish are a bunch of heavy drinkers. Well, I'll give five hundred dollars to anybody in here who can drink ten pints of Guinness back-to-back.'

The room fell silent with nobody willing to take up the Texan's offer. One man even left. Thirty minutes later the same Irishman who had left returned and tapped the Texan on the shoulder.

'Is your bet still good?' asked the Irishman.

'Sure,' said the Texan, and he asked the barman to line up ten pints of Guinness.

Immediately the Irishman sank all ten pints to the accompaniment of loud cheering. Handing over the five hundred dollars, the stunned Texan said: 'Tell me, my friend, where did you go to for that thirty minutes?'

The Irishman replied: 'I had to go to the pub down the street first to make sure that I could do it!'

Shakespeare walked into a bar and asked for a beer. 'I can't serve you,' said the bartender. 'You're bard.'

A man walked into a bar with an ostrich behind him. He ordered a beer and said to the ostrich: 'What will you have?'

The ostrich said: 'I'll have the same.'

'That's four ninety,' said the bartender.

The man reached into his pocket and without looking or counting, handed the bartender exactly four dollars, ninety cents.

The following day the man and the ostrich called in again. 'I'll have a whiskey,' said the man. 'And what do you want?' he asked the ostrich.

The ostrich said: 'I'll have a rum and coke.'

'That's six thirty-three,' said the bartender.

The man reached into his pocket and immediately produced exactly six dollars and thirty-three cents.

The next day the man and the ostrich were back again. The man ordered a gin and tonic and the ostrich asked for a glass of Chardonnay and a packet of nuts.

'That's six ninety-eight,' said the bartender.

The man reached into his pocket and handed over exactly six dollars, ninety-eight cents.

The bartender said: 'There's something I have to ask you. How do you manage to bring out the precise amount of change from your pocket without ever counting it?'

The man explained: 'Last year I was clearing out the attic when I came across an old lamp. For fun, I thought I'd rub it to see whether a genie appeared and, to my amazement, one did. Not only that, but he granted me two wishes. My first wish was that if I ever had to pay for anything, I could just put my hand in my pocket and the right amount of money would always be there.'

'That's great,' said the bartender. 'So many people wish for untold wealth, expensive holidays or fast cars. One other thing though: what's with the ostrich?'

The man said: 'My second wish was for a chick with long legs.'

If you sent a cauliflower through the Internet, would it arrive as e-coli?

A millionaire was driving along in his stretch limo when he saw a humble man eating grass by the roadside. Ordering his chauffeur to stop, he wound down the window and called to the man: 'Why are you eating grass?'

'Because, sir, we don't have the money for real food.'

'Come with me then,' said the millionaire.

'But, sir, I have a wife and six children.'

'That's fine – bring them all along.'

The man and his family climbed gratefully into the limo. 'Sir, you are too kind. How can I ever thank you for taking all of us with you, offering us a new home?'

'No, you don't understand,' said the millionaire. 'The grass at my home is four feet high. No lawn mower will cut it!'

A man walked into a bar with a strip of tarmac under his arm.

'What'll you have?' asked the bartender.

The man said: 'I'll have a beer, and one for the road.'

A guy in a bar noticed that a woman came in regularly by herself. After the second week, he decided to make his move. He bought her a drink and asked her if she fancied coming back to his place.

'No, thank you,' she said. 'It may sound rather odd in this day and age, but I'm keeping myself pure until I meet the man I love.'

'That must be difficult,' said the guy.

'Oh, I don't mind too much. But my husband gets pretty upset.'

According to popular legend, Mrs Descartes was throwing a lavish New Year's Party to celebrate the arrival of 1630. She had been making preparations for weeks and had invited all the local dignitaries. Shortly before the guests began to turn up, she issued her philosopher husband Rene with strict instructions regarding the pastries on the pantry table. To make sure that the guests did not leave immediately after midnight, she insisted that the pastries should not be eaten until the early hours. In fact she decided that an hour into the New Year was the ideal time to allow the guests to tuck into her cooking and keep the party in full swing. Rene was given the job of guarding the pastries until that time. Although deep in thought, he agreed to mind the table.

As the party started to warm up, Descartes found himself involved in an absorbing philosophical discussion with Van Dyck about art and life in general. To hear each other better, they drifted away from the drawing room and towards the pantry. With Descartes lost in thought, Van Dyck helped himself to one of the precious pastries even though it was barely ten o'clock. When Descartes suddenly realized what the artist had done, he discreetly wrote a message on a napkin and handed it to Van Dyck so as not to attract his wife's attention. Van Dyck was eager to see what gem of inspiration Descartes' brilliant mind had come up with now. However before Van Dyck could read it, they were interrupted and he had to stuff the napkin in his pocket to read later.

The following morning Van Dyck opened the napkin to discover what thought-provoking message his friend had left him. Sure enough, there scrawled in Descartes' hand was an expression of timeless insight: 'I think they're for 1 am.'

Graffiti

Examples from walls around the world:

A career is great, but you can't run your fingers through its hair.

ADVANCE TOWELMASTER – and be recognized.

After a year in therapy, my psychiatrist said to me, 'Maybe life isn't for everyone.'

All things are possible – except skiing through a revolving door.

And the angel said unto the shepherds: 'Shove off, this is cattle country.'

A nuclear war can ruin your whole day.

At the feast of ego, everyone leaves hungry.

Beer – it's not just for breakfast anymore.

Beethoven was so deaf he thought he was a painter.

Bigotry: one of the California redwoods.

Blow your mind – smoke gunpowder.

(above a condom machine) Buy two and be one jump ahead.

(above a condom machine) Buy 144 and be grossly oversexed.

Club sandwiches not seals.

Condoms aren't completely safe. My friend was wearing one and got hit by a bus.

Cunnilingus is a real tongue-twister.

Democracy is too good to share with just anybody.

Did you hear about the Irish abortion clinic? – There's a 12-month waiting list.

Dijon vu – the same mustard as before.

Does the lateral coital position mean having a bit on the side?

Don't be sexist – broads hate that.

Don't tell my mother I'm a lawyer – she thinks I'm a hooker.

Don't throw your fag ends in the loo,
    You know it isn't right.
    It makes them very soggy
    And impossible to light.
Drinking makes me see double and feel single.
Drink wet cement, and get completely stoned!
Eating plenty of fruit can help you live to a ripe old age.
Eating vegetables is crueller than eating animals; at least animals have a chance to run away.
Elitism: it's not for everyone.
Every day I beat my own previous record for the number of consecutive days I've stayed alive.
Exercise is a dirty word. Every time I hear it, I wash my mouth out with chocolate.
Fear is a little dark room where negatives are developed.
Fighting for peace is like screwing for virginity.
Flies spread disease – keep yours zipped.
Forget love – I'd rather fall in chocolate.
Free the Indianapolis 500.
Free the M62.
Freud put the 'anal' into psychoanalysis.
Gargling is a good way to see if your throat leaks.
Give a woman an inch, she'll park a car in it.
Give masochists a fair crack of the whip.
God is love, but Satan is 30 and two sets to one up.
God is not dead but alive and well and working on a much less ambitious project.
God made animals, great and small,
    Some that slither and some that crawl –
    And Chicago police employ them all.
Gripe: a ripe grape.
Gun control: Use both hands.
Have you ever wondered how much deeper the ocean would be without sponges?
Her legs are without equal – they know no parallel.
He who laughs last, thinks slowest.
Homosexuality is God's way of ensuring that the truly gifted aren't burdened with children.
How do I set a laser printer to stun?
How is being at a singles bar different from going to the circus? — At the circus the clowns don't talk.

Hypochondria is the one disease I haven't got.

I am in shape. Round is a shape.

I believe we should all pay our tax bill with a smile. I tried – but they wanted cash.

I can walk on water, but I stagger on alcohol.

I didn't claw my way to the top of the food chain just to eat leaves.

I'd kill for a Nobel Peace Prize.

I'd like to help the homeless, but they're never home.

I don't know if I want to change the world or just toilet train it.

I don't like to eat snails. I prefer fast food.

I don't mind dying. The trouble is you feel so stiff the next day.

I don't repeat gossip, so listen carefully.

I don't suffer from stress — I'm a carrier.

If at first you don't succeed, try management.

If dolphins are so smart, how come they always end up in tuna nets?

I feel like the whole world is a car wash and I'm riding a bike.

If flattery gets you nowhere, try bribery.

If God had intended for me to run around naked, he would have made my skin fit better.

If it weren't for stress, I'd have no energy at all.

If you can keep your head while those about you are losing theirs, have you considered becoming a guillotine operator?

If you leave alphabet soup on the stove and go out, it could spell disaster.

If you're not part of the solution, you're part of the precipitate.

If you woke up breathing, congratulations! You have another chance.

Ignorance can be cured. Stupid is for ever.

I got a sweater for Christmas, but what I really wanted was a screamer or a moaner.

I have a lot of issues with sex . . . mostly Playboy, Penthouse, and Hustler.

I have this theory that chocolate slows down the ageing process. It may not be true, but dare I take the chance?

I know that somewhere in the Universe exists my perfect soulmate – but looking for her is much more difficult than just staying home and ordering another pizza.

I like cats, too. Let's exchange recipes.

I live in my own little world, but it's OK, they know me here.

I lost my virginity, but I still have the box it came in.

I love my country. It's my government I fear.

I love my wife – for $30 you can too.

I'm enduring life's theatre in the hope of a good cast party.

I'm kind of lazy. I'm dating a pregnant woman.

I'm not a complete idiot – parts of me are missing.

I'm not cheap, but I am on special this week.

I'm out of my mind, but feel free to leave a message.

I'm so homophobic I can't even touch myself.

In a world without walls and fences, who needs Windows and Gates?

Incest: a game the whole family can play.

I never knew what happiness was until I got married. And by then it was too late.

IN GOD WE TRUST. All others we virus scan.

In the battle between you and the world, bet on the world.

In the beginning was the word. And the word was 'Aardvark'.

I once read a book about anti-gravity. I just couldn't put it down.

I put a dollar in a change machine. Nothing changed.

I tried sniffing Coke, but the ice cubes got stuck in my nose.

I tried to embrace my feminine side, but it filed a restraining order against me.

I try to take one day at a time, but sometimes several days attack me at once.

It's a small world so you gotta use your elbows a lot.

It's hard to be as fit as a fiddle when you're shaped like a cello.

It's not pretty being easy.

(in a men's toilet) It's no use looking for a joke. You've got one in your hand.

I used to watch golf on TV, but my doctor told me I needed more exercise. So now I watch tennis.

I used up all my sick days, so I'm calling in dead.

I've found Jesus. He was behind the sofa the whole time!

I've got a 12-inch willy, but I don't use it as a rule.

I've got Parkinson's disease. And he's got mine.

I've just had an operation for piles. All my troubles are behind me.

I've often wanted to drown my troubles, but I can't get my wife to go swimming.

I've taken a vow of poverty. To annoy me, send money.

I want patience – AND I WANT IT NOW!

I was high on life, but eventually I built up a tolerance.

I was stopped for doing 53 in a 35mph zone. I told the police I had dyslexia.

I wear the pants in my family – right under my apron.

I wish I could drink like a lady
  I can take one or two at the most.
  Three puts me under the table
  And four puts me under the host.
Jack is nimble
  Jack is quick
  But Jill prefers the candlestick.
JESUS LIVES! – does this mean we won't get an Easter holiday?
JESUS SAVES! But wouldn't it be better if he had invested?
Jesus was a typical man – they always say they'll come back but you never see them again.
  Join the army, meet interesting people, and kill them.
  Just hand over the chocolate and no one will get hurt.
  Keep America beautiful . . . dispose of your lawyer properly.
KEEP DEATH OFF THE ROADS – drive on the pavement.
Keep your city clean – eat a pigeon.
Little Mary from Boston, Mass.
  Stepped into water up to her ankles.
  It doesn't rhyme now, but wait till the tide comes in.
LET BUSES PULL OUT – and help reduce the minibus population.
Life is a test, and I didn't take very good notes.
Life is full of uncertainties. Of course, I could be wrong about that.
LIFT UNDER REPAIR: USE OTHER LIFT – this Otis regrets it's unable to lift today.
Little Red Riding Hood is a Russian contraceptive.
Love means never winning at tennis.
Monogamy leaves a lot to be desired.
My church accepts any denomination. But they prefer tens and twenties.
My computer goes down on me more often than my girlfriend.
My cousin is an agoraphobic homosexual, which makes it hard for him to come out of the closet.
My girlfriend used to kiss me on the lips. But now it's all over.
My greatest fear is there's no such thing as PMS and this is really your personality.
My take-no-prisoners attitude is starting to irritate my bosses at the marshal's office.
My wife and I had words, but I never got to use mine.
(in a men's toilet) Natalie, if you're reading this, we're through.
Never knock on Death's door – ring the doorbell and run (he hates that).

Never moon a werewolf.

No hand signals – the driver of this vehicle is a convicted Arab shoplifter.

Now is the winter of our discontent made glorious summer by central heating.

Old soldiers never die . . . just their privates.

On the other hand . . . you have different fingers.

Owing to lack of interest, tomorrow has been cancelled.

Palindromes date all the way back to Eve.

Paraplegics, stand up for your rights.

Pas de deux: father of twins.

(in an exam hall) Please don't ask me to relax. It's only the tension that's holding me together.

Pope Innocent is pious, OK.

Practise safe eating – always use condiments.

Prepare to meet thy God. (Evening dress optional)

Reality is an illusion produced by alcohol deficiency.

Religion: insurance in this world against fire in the next.

Repeal the law of gravity.

Richard Coeur de Lion – first heart transplant?

Rock is dead. Long live paper and scissors.

Rugby is a game played by gentlemen with odd-shaped balls.

Sado-masochism means never having to say you're sorry.

Save a tree; eat a beaver.

Save the whales. Collect the whole set.

Say it with flowers. Give her a triffid.

Scientists say there are over 3,000 spiders for every human being on earth. Does anybody want mine?

See no evil, hear no evil, date no evil.

Sex alleviates tension. Love causes it.

Sex discrimination hotline – switchboard manned 24 hours.

Sign at a deer crossing: The Buck Stops Here.

Sign at a nudist camp: Sorry – Clothed for Winter.

Since using your shampoo, my hair has come alive. Medusa.

Smoke dynamite and really blow your mind!

Some girls shrink from sex. Others get bigger . . . and bigger . . .

Sometimes I think I understand everything. Then I regain consciousness.

Stop inbreeding! Ban country music.

Support Women's Lib – make him sleep in the damp patch.

Take lettuce from top of stack, or heads will roll!

Take Milk of Amnesia – when you need to forget.

Take my advice – I don't use it anyway.

Tapeworms reach the parts that even Heineken cannot reach.

Teamwork means never having to take all the blame.

Teddy Kennedy. Good senator. Bad date.

The best things in life are duty-free.

The biggest drawback in the world – an elephant's foreskin.

(in dust on a Renault) The hatchback of Notre Dame.

The face is familiar, but I can't quite remember my name.

The only substitute for good manners is fast reflexes.

There is no substitute for a genuine lack of preparation.

There is nothing wrong with California that the San Andreas fault cannot cure.

Three of my fingers are willing to write, but my thumb and forefinger are opposed.

THE REV. CHARLES SPURGEON DEPARTED FOR HEAVEN AT 6.30 AM TODAY – 10.45am. Not yet arrived. Getting anxious, Peter.

To do is to be. – Descartes

    To be is to do. – Voltaire

    Do be do be do. – Frank Sinatra

Too many freaks. Not enough circuses.

Uncle Sid died of asbestosis. It took us three months to cremate him.

Under the English legal system you are innocent until proven to be Irish.

WARNING: PASSENGERS ARE REQUESTED NOT TO CROSS THE LINES – it takes hours to untangle them afterwards.

Was Handel a crank?

Wear short sleeves; support your right to bare arms!

What did the bra say to the top hat? — You go on ahead while I give these two a lift.

What do a beer bottle and a man have in common? – They're both empty from the neck up.

What does DNA stand for? National Dyslexics Association.

What has four legs and an arm? – A happy pit bull.

What should you give a man who has everything? – A woman to show him how to work it.

(in a ladies' washroom) What's so special about Christmas – the birth of a man who thinks he's a god isn't such a rare event?

What's the difference between a barrow-boy and a dachshund? — One bawls out his wares . . .

What's the difference between a battery and a woman? – A battery has a positive side.

What's the difference between beer nuts and deer nuts? — Beer nuts are $1.50 and deer nuts are under a buck.

What's the most popular pick-up line in Arkansas? – Nice tooth.

What's worse: ignorance or apathy? – I don't know and I don't care.

When does a woman want a man's company? — When he owns it.

Whenever I go near a bank, I get withdrawal symptoms.

When I'm not in my right mind, my left mind gets pretty crowded.

Where do you find a duck with no legs? – Where you left it.

Why don't men have mid-life crises? – They're stuck in adolescence.

Why experiment on animals with so many lawyers out there?

Why is American beer served cold? So you can tell it from urine.

Women: can't live with them, can't bury them in the back yard without the neighbours seeing.

Women's libbers should all be put behind bras.

Xerox and Wurlitzer are merging to market reproductive organs.

You can't go wrong with me, but you're welcome to try.

You should just say no to drugs. That will drive the prices down.

Home

While proudly showing off his new apartment to friends, a young businessman led them into the lounge.

'What's the big brass gong and hammer for?' asked one.

'Oh, that's the talking clock.'

'How does it work?'

'Like this,' said the flat-owner and he proceeded to whack the gong with the hammer.

Suddenly a voice screamed from the apartment next door: 'Cut that out, you idiot! Don't you know it's two o'clock in the morning!'

Have you heard about the new corduroy pillows? – They're making headlines.

A woman complained to her sister about the amount of housework she had to do.

'After a long day at work, I come home and there's always a mountain of household chores waiting for me. There are clothes to wash, dishes to wash, and at the weekend there are sheets to wash, floors to wash, and windows to wash.'

'But what about your husband?' asked her sister.

'No, he has to wash himself.'

A man called over to his neighbour one morning: 'Did you hear me thumping on the wall last night?'

'Oh, don't worry about it. We were making a fair bit of noise ourselves.'

Three men were reflecting upon their fortunes while enjoying a relaxing day's fishing off the Seychelles.

The first said: 'My house burnt down. I lost everything, but the insurance company paid up and that's why I'm here.'

The second said: 'My house burnt down too. I lost everything, but the insurance company paid up and that's why I'm here.'

The third guy said: 'My house was destroyed by an earthquake. I lost everything, but the insurance company paid up and that's why I'm here.'

The first two guys turned to him and said: 'Earthquake? How the hell do you start an earthquake?'

Dave turned up unannounced at a friend's house late one evening and asked whether he could stay the night. The friend said: 'Sure. You can either sleep on the floor in the living room, or you can sleep in the room with Baby.'

'I think I'll sleep on the floor in the living room,' said Dave.

The next morning he went to the bathroom and bumped into a beautiful blonde. 'Hi, who are you?' he asked.

'I'm Baby,' she said. 'Who are you?'

'I'm stupid.'

A vacuum cleaner salesman wormed his way into the home of a woman in a remote Welsh valley.

'This machine is amazing,' he enthused in his finest sales patter before tipping a bag of dirt over the lounge floor carpet. 'Watch this. If this machine doesn't remove every last speck of that dirt, I'll lick it off the carpet myself!'

'Do you want ketchup on it?' asked the woman. 'Only we're not connected for electricity!'

A woman rang up a pet shop and asked for three hundred cockroaches.

The shop owner said: 'If you don't mind me asking, what on earth do you want three hundred cockroaches for?'

The woman replied: 'Well, I'm moving today, and my lease says I must leave the place in the same condition I found it.'

A homeowner hired a decorator to paint his lounge and was so pleased with the end result that he decided to give the workman a bonus. 'Here's your cheque,' he said, 'plus an extra eighty dollars to take the missus out to dinner and a movie.'

'That's very thoughtful,' said the decorator as he loaded his equipment into the van.

Two hours later, the doorbell rang. It was the decorator.

'Oh, did you forget something?' asked the houseowner.

'No,' said the decorator. 'I'm here to take your missus out to dinner and a movie like you asked.'

A woman was having trouble with her neighbour's child throwing stones into her garden. So she ordered her husband to erect a boundary around the garden. The husband didn't want to upset the neighbours but bowed to his wife's pressure and spent the day fixing thirty posts into the ground.

Still the wife wasn't happy. 'Why haven't you attached the panels to the posts?' she raged.

The husband said: 'I didn't want to cause a fence.'

Bill Gates bought a new house . . .

Bill: There are a few issues we need to discuss.

Contractor: You have your basic support option. Calls are free for the first ninety days and seventy-five dollars a call thereafter. Okay?

Bill: Uh, yeah. The first issue is the living room. We think it's a little smaller than we anticipated.

Contractor: Yeah. Some compromises were made to have it out by the release date.

Bill: We won't be able to fit all our furniture in there.

Contractor: Well, you have two options. You can purchase a new, larger living room, or you can use a stacker.

Bill: A stacker?

Contractor: Yeah, it allows you to fit twice as much furniture into the room. By stacking it, of course, you put the entertainment centre on the couch, the chairs on the table, and so on. You leave an empty spot, so when you want to use some furniture you can unstack what you need and then put it back when you're done.

Bill: Uh. I don't know. Issue two: the light fixtures. The bulbs we brought with us from our old home won't fit. The threads run the wrong way.

Contractor: Oh, that's easy! Those bulbs aren't plug and play. You'll have to upgrade to the new bulbs.

Bill: And the electrical outlets? The holes are round, not rectangular. How do I fix that?

Contractor: Just uninstall and reinstall the electrical system.

Bill: You're kidding!

Contractor: Nope. It's the only way.

Bill: Well . . . I have one last problem. Sometimes when I have guests over, someone will flush the toilet and it won't stop. The water pressure drops so low that the showers don't work.

Contractor: That's a resource leakage problem. One fixture is failing to terminate and is hogging the resources preventing access from other fixtures.

Bill: And how do I fix that?

Contractor: Well, after each flush, you all need to exit the house, turn off the water at the street, turn it back on, re-enter the house and then you can get back to work.

Bill: That's the last straw. What kind of product are you selling me?

Contractor: Hey, nobody's making you buy it.

Bill: And when will this be fixed?

Contractor: Oh, in your next house, which will be ready to release some time near the end of next year. It was due out this year, but we've had some delays . . .

Fred was continually plagued by his next-door neighbour asking to borrow things. One morning he saw the neighbour approaching his front door and so he was ready for him.

'Can I borrow your power-saw this morning?' asked the neighbour.

'Afraid not,' replied Fred gleefully. 'I'll be using it all day.'

'In that case, you won't be using your golf clubs. Mind if I borrow them?'

For once in his life, the real estate agent decided to be honest with a prospective house-buyer. 'This property has its good and bad points. There is a chemical plant one block to the north and a slaughterhouse one block to the south.'

'Well, what are its good points?' asked the client.

'You can always tell which way the wind is blowing.'

Two women were discussing their most unusual items of furniture. One said: 'I learned from an antiques expert that the "W.C." carved on our dining room table may indicate that it once belonged to Winston Churchill.'

'Well,' said her friend, 'I bought a bureau once and twenty people fell out.'

'Really?'

'Yes. It turned out it was a missing persons' bureau.'

When a husband arrived home, his wife told him that the maid whom they had recently dismissed had stolen two of their towels as a parting gesture.

'How dare she!' stormed the husband.

'I know,' said his wife, 'and they were our two best towels – you know, the ones we got from the Hilton Hotel on holiday last year.'

Old college buddies Nat and Joey had not seen each other in years. When they finally got in touch, they had a lot of catching up to do, so Nat invited Joey to visit him in his new apartment. 'I have a wife and three kids and it would be great if you came to see us.'

'Sure. Why not?' said Joey. 'Where do you live?'

'The address is 68 Park Mansions,' said Nat. 'There's plenty of parking space behind the apartment. Park there and come round to the front door, kick it open with your foot, go to the elevator and press the button with your left elbow, then enter. When you reach the sixth floor, go down the hall until you see number 68. Then press the doorbell with your right elbow and I'll let you in.'

'Good,' said Joey. 'But tell me, what is all this business of kicking the front door open, then pressing elevator buttons with my right, then my left elbow?'

'Well, surely you're not coming empty-handed?'

When his computer printer began to print out faintly, a man called the repair shop.

The clerk said: 'From your description of the problem, the printer probably only needs cleaning. It will cost you fifty dollars to have it cleaned here so really you'd be better off reading the manual and doing the job yourself.'

Pleasantly surprised by the clerk's honesty, the man said: 'Does your boss know that you discourage business?'

'Actually,' replied the clerk sheepishly, 'it's my boss's idea. We usually make more money on repairs if we let people try to fix things themselves first.'

An elderly lady called the police to complain about the behaviour of her next-door neighbour. When the officer came out, she told him that the man next door kept wandering around naked with the curtains open.

The officer took a look through the window. 'But I can't even see into next door's house from here,' he said.

'No,' said the old lady. 'You have to climb on the dresser and look out of the skylight.'

Hotels

A guest checked in at a run-down hotel. 'The room is twenty dollars a night,' said the manager, 'but it's only ten if you make your own bed.'

'Okay,' said the guest. 'I'll make my own bed.'

'Stay there,' said the manager. 'I'll get you some nails and wood.'

A guest checked into a hotel. 'Would you like a room with a bath or a shower?' asked the receptionist.

'What's the difference?'

'You can sit down in a bath.'

A tourist staying at a top London hotel phoned down for room service one morning.

He said: 'I want three overdone fried eggs that are as hard as a rock, toast that is burnt to a cinder, and a cup of black coffee that tastes like mud.'

'I'm sorry, sir,' replied room service, 'we don't serve breakfast like that.'

The tourist said: 'Well, you did yesterday!'

A businessman travelling through rural England decided to stop for the night at a picturesque country pub, the George and Dragon.

Checking in at reception, he asked the lady co-owner whether meals were still being served in the bar.

'No,' she replied forcefully. 'Last meals are 8pm sharp. It is now 8.10pm.'

'Not even a sandwich?' he asked sheepishly.

'No, not even a sandwich. The chef has packed up, and I'm certainly not going to start slaving away in the kitchen at this time of night just because you haven't thought things out very well.'

'OK,' he said. 'Is there any chance of having breakfast in my room in the morning?'

'Certainly not,' she snapped. 'All breakfasts are served in the dining room at 7.30 prompt. Any more questions?'

'Yes,' he said. 'Do you think I might have a word with George?'

An elderly woman from the country was visiting the big city for the first time. She checked in at a smart hotel and let the porter take her bags. She followed him but as the door closed, her face fell.

'Young man,' she snapped. 'I may be old and straight from the country, but I'm not stupid. I paid good money for this room, and it simply won't do. It's nothing like the standard I expected. It's too small, there are no facilities and there's no air conditioning. For goodness sake, there's not even a bed!'

'Ma'am,' replied the porter. 'This isn't your room, this is the lift!'

As a guest checked into a cheap hotel, the receptionist said: 'I hope you have a good memory for faces.'

'Why?'

'Because there's no mirror in the bathroom.'

A drunk staggered down to hotel reception and demanded a change of room. He was so insistent that the receptionist was forced to call the manager.

'What seems to be the problem?' asked the manager.

'I want another room,' said the drunk.

'But I see you're in room 224. That's one of the best rooms in the hotel.'

'I don't care. I want another room.'

'Very well, sir. If you're absolutely adamant, we can move you from 224 to 260. But would you mind telling me what you don't like about your room?'

'Well,' said the drunk, 'for one thing, it's on fire.'

A man wrote to a small hotel asking whether he could bring his dog with him. 'The dog is well behaved,' he wrote, 'house-trained and does not bark unnecessarily. He will be no trouble.'

The hotel owner wrote back: 'I have been operating this hotel for many years. In all that time, I have never had a dog steal towels, bedclothes, silverware, or pictures off the walls. I have never had to evict a dog in the middle of the night for being drunk and disorderly.

And I have never had a dog run off without paying a bill. So, yes you dog is welcome at my hotel. And if your dog will vouch for you, you're welcome to stay here too.'

What Hotel Descriptions Really Mean:
 Olde worlde charm – Huge variety of insect life.
 Sea view — ... With a telescope.
 Secluded hideaway – Impossible to find.
 Some budget rooms – Sorry, already taken.
 Options galore – Nothing is included in the price.
 Explore on your own – At your own expense.
 No extra fees – No extras.
 Nominal fee – Outrageous charge.
 Standard – Sub-standard.
 Deluxe – Barely Standard.
 Superior accommodation – One complimentary chocolate, free shower cap.
 All the amenities – Two chocolates, two shower caps.
 Gentle breezes – In hurricane alley.
 Light and airy – No air conditioning.
 24-hour bar – Ice cubes at additional cost, when available.

A hotel guest marched down to reception to complain about the state of his room. 'Does the roof always leak?' he raged.
 'No,' said the receptionist. 'Only when it rains.'

Mary Poppins was travelling home but, because of deteriorating weather, she decided to stop at a hotel for the night. Having booked a room, she asked the receptionist whether the restaurant was still open.
 'Sorry, no,' came the reply, 'but room service is available all night. Would you care to select something from the menu?'
 Mary smiled, examined the menu and said: 'I would like some cauliflower cheese, please.'
 'Certainly, madam,' he replied.
 'And may I have breakfast in bed?' asked Mary politely.
 'Yes, we can arrange that, madam.'
 'Then I would love a couple of poached eggs, please.'
 And with that, Mary Poppins retired to her room.
 The following morning, she came down early to check out. The same receptionist was on the front desk.
 'Good morning, madam,' he said. 'Did you sleep well?'

'Yes, thank you,' replied Mary.

'Food to your liking?'

'Well, I have to say the cauliflower cheese was exceptional. I don't think I have ever tasted better. Shame about the eggs though. I'm afraid they were definitely not up to standard.'

'Oh,' said the receptionist. 'Well, perhaps you could put your thoughts in the Guest Comments Book. We are always looking to improve our service and would value your opinion.'

'Yes, I will,' said Mary who scribbled a note in the book before leaving the hotel and continuing with her journey home.

Curious, the receptionist looked in the book to see what Mary Poppins had written.

It read: 'Supercauliflowercheesebuteggswerequiteatrocious!'

A honeymoon couple stayed at the Watergate Hotel in Washington. The bride was worried in case the place was still bugged, so she asked her new husband to search the room thoroughly. He looked behind the curtains, under the bed, in the wardrobes, and finally under the rug. And there, beneath the rug, he found a mysterious disc with four screws. Using his Swiss army knife, he undid the screws and threw the disc out of the window.

The following morning as they checked out, the manager asked: 'How was your room? How was the service? How was your stay at the Watergate Hotel?'

'Why so many questions?' said the groom.

'Well,' said the manager, 'the room below you complained that the chandelier fell on them.'

Hotel Rules and Regulations:

Tipping is not only expected but demanded. Failure to so may result in your bags being sent to another country.

Don't eat the complimentary chocolate on the pillow – it's been stuck there for months.

Do not attempt to adjust the thermostat. If you even touch the dial, the temperature will either go up to 104 degrees or down to 32 degrees, depending on the season.

Please note that the small hole in the bathroom wall is designed to maximise ventilation. Do not cover this hole, as it will block our view.

We have designed the bathroom sink to help you sleep, with its soothing, metronome-like dripping sound. Enjoy.

Don't look under the couch.

Bringing pets into this room is strictly prohibited. Cats and dogs have been known to eat the mice that live here.

Don't eat the fuzzy grapes.

We recommend that you do not stick your head out of the window, as you may be struck by falling guests.

Checkout time is whenever we feel like kicking you out, so keep your bags packed and ready to go.

The management is not responsible for anything. Period.

Knock Knock

Knock knock.
Who's there?
Aaron.
Aaron who?
Aaron the side of caution.

Knock knock.
Who's there?
Abby.
Abby who?
Abby birthday to you, Abby birthday to you . . .

Knock knock.
Who's there?
Amanda.
Amanda who?
Amanda fix the television.

Knock knock.
Who's there?
Amos.
Amos who?
Amosquito.

Knock knock.
Who's there?
Anna.
Anna who?
Anna nother mosquito.

Knock knock.
Who's there?
Anita.
Anita who?
Anita tissue. Ah-choo! Too late!

Knock knock.
Who's there?
Cash.
Cash who?
You're nuts!

Knock knock.
Who's there?
Doris.
Doris who?
Doris locked – that's why I knocked.

Knock knock.
Who's there?
Earl.
Earl who?
Earl be glad to tell you when you open the door.

Knock knock.
Who's there?
Emma.
Emma who?
Emma bit cold out here, will you let me in?

Knock knock.
Who's there?
Harry.
Harry who?
Harry up and let me in.

Knock knock.
Who's there?
Howard.
Howard who?
Howard I know?

Knock knock.
Who's there?
Isabel.
Isabel who?
Isabel broken? I had to knock.

Knock knock.
Who's there?
Ivor.
Ivor who?
Ivor you let me in, or I'll knock the door down.

Knock knock.
Who's there?
Jesus.
Jesus who?
How many do you know?

Knock knock.
Who's there?
Justin.
Justin who?
Justin time for my dinner.

Knock knock.
Who's there?
Luke.
Luke who?
Luke through the keyhole and you'll see.

Knock knock.
Who's there?
Mahatma.
Mahatma who?
Mahatma coat, please.

Knock knock.
Who's there?
Minnie.
Minnie who?
Minnie people out here freezing. Open the door!

Knock knock.
Who's there?
Oscar.
Oscar who?
Oscar a stupid question, you get a stupid answer.

Knock knock.
Who's there?
Otto.
Otto who?
Otto remember, but I can't.

Knock knock.
Who's there?
Police.
Police who?
Police open the door cos I'm freezing out here.

Knock knock.
Who's there?
Sarah.
Sarah who?
Sarah doctor in the house?

Knock knock.
Who's there?
Shirley.
Shirley who?
Shirley I don't have to tell you.

Knock knock.
Who's there?
Toby.
Toby who?
Toby or not Toby, that is the question.

Knock knock.
Who's there?
Wendy.
Wendy who?
Wendy red red robin comes bob bob bobbin' along.

Knock knock.
Who's there?
Wilma.
Wilma who?
Wilma dinner be ready soon?

Knock knock
Who's there?
A little old lady.
A little lady who?
I didn't know you could yodel.

Law and Order

A young man had never been in trouble throughout his life but, faced with mounting debts, he decided he had no option but to turn to crime. He targeted a small, poorly protected country bank, which he hoped would provide easy pickings. He didn't feel up to armed robbery, but instead decided to break in at night and open the safe.

He had no trouble gaining entry to the bank but as he tried to pick the lock on the safe, the burglar alarm went off. Fortunately he had taken the precaution of bringing along a furniture dolly in case of emergencies and so he was able to load the small safe onto the dolly and roll it out to his van before the police arrived.

He then drove to a friend's house and explained his problem. In return for a share of the loot, he asked whether he could hide the safe in the friend's garage for a few days.

'Sure,' said his friend. 'And don't worry. Your safe is secret with me . . .'

The cross-eyed judge looked at the three defendants in the dock and said to the first one: 'How do you plead?'

'Not guilty,' said the second defendant.

'I wasn't talking to you,' boomed the judge.

'I never said a word,' replied the third defendant.

A doctor and a lawyer were talking at a party, but their conversation was constantly interrupted by people describing their ailments and asking the doctor free medical advice. After an hour of this, the exasperated doctor asked the lawyer: 'What do you do to stop people asking you for legal advice when you're out of the office?'

The lawyer said: 'I give it to them and then I send them a bill.'

Although shocked by this, the doctor agreed to give it a try.

The next day the doctor, acting on the lawyer's suggestion, was reluctantly putting a number of bills into his mailbox when he found a bill addressed to him. It was from the lawyer.

The defendant stood defiantly in the dock and said to the judge: 'I don't recognize this court.'

'Why?' rapped the judge.

'Because you've had it decorated since the last time I was here.'

A man who had been caught embezzling millions from his employer hired a lawyer in an attempt to stay out of jail. The lawyer promised: 'You'll never have to go to prison with all that money.'

The lawyer was right. By the time the case was over and the man had been sent to prison, he didn't have a dime!

Two new prisoners were shown to their cell.

'How long are you in for?' asked the first.

'Eighteen years,' replied the second. 'How about you?'

'Twenty-five years. So since you're getting out first, you'd better have the bed by the door.'

A lawyer's son graduated from university with honours and went straight into his father's firm. Eager to prove himself, he set about his work with boundless enthusiasm and had some great news to impart to his father at the end of his first day.

'Dad,' he announced proudly, 'in just one day I have cracked the Renshaw case that you have been working in for all this time.'

'You idiot!' said his father. 'We've been living on the funding of that case for the past ten years!'

Prosecutor: Did you kill the victim?

Defendant: No, I did not.

Prosecutor: Do you know what the penalties are for perjury?

Defendant: Yes, I do. And they're a lot less than the penalty for murder.

Taking his seat in his chambers, the judge faced the two lawyers in a high-profile murder trial.

'So,' he said ominously, 'you have both tried to bribe me.'

The lawyers squirmed uncomfortably.

'You, Harding, gave me fifteen thousand dollars. And you, Fanshawe, gave me ten thousand dollars.'

The judge reached into his pocket, pulled out a cheque and handed it to Harding. 'Right, I'm returning five thousand dollars and from now on, we're going to decide this case solely on its merits.'

Why did the escaped convict saw the legs off his bed? – He wanted to lie low.

A priest, a rabbi, a doctor and a lawyer were gathered at the graveside of a mutual friend to mourn his passing.

The priest said to the others: 'I think our good friend would have liked to take something with him to his next life.' He pulled a hundred-dollar bill from his wallet and dropped it on to the coffin.

The rabbi agreed: 'That's a fine idea,' and dropped his own hundred-dollar bill on the coffin.

The doctor, not to be outdone, did the same.

The lawyer murmured: 'What a wonderful gesture.' Whipping out his pen, he quickly wrote a cheque for four hundred dollars, dropped it into the grave and took the three hundred-dollar bills as change.

Tried in a hostile town, a guy didn't think he had a chance of getting off a murder charge, so shortly before the jury retired he bribed one of the jurors to find him guilty of the lesser crime of manslaughter.

The jury were out for over three days before eventually returning a verdict of manslaughter. The relieved defendant collared the bribed juror and said: 'Thanks. How ever did you manage it?'

'It wasn't easy,' admitted the juror. 'All the others wanted to acquit you.'

In prison for the first time, Dennis was puzzled by a strange ritual that was carried out at night immediately after the lights were turned off. Someone from another cell called out 'Thirty-seven' and the whole block burst out laughing. A few moments later another distant voice called out 'Sixty-one' and again everyone laughed.

'What do the numbers mean?' Dennis asked his cellmate.

'Down in the prison library there's a big joke book. We've memorised all the jokes. So now when anybody wants to tell a joke, they just have to shout out the page number from the book.'

Dennis was intrigued and the next day he studied the joke book in the prison library, writing down the numbers of a few good jokes so that he could join in the fun that evening.

That night, Dennis decided to take the initiative. Once the lights had gone off, he called out 'Fifty-five.' But instead of laughter there was silence. So he tried again. 'Eighty-seven.' Again there was an eerie silence.

He asked his cellmate: 'Why is it that when I call out the numbers, nobody laughs?'

His cellmate said: 'It's the way you tell them.'

A tough lawyer diagnosed with terminal illness was determined to disprove the saying 'You can't take it with you.' In order that he could take at least some of his money with him when he died, he ordered his wife to go to the bank and withdraw sufficient cash to fill two pillowcases. Hen then told her to take the bags of money up to the attic and leave them directly above his bed. His plan was that when he passed away, he would reach out and grab the bags on his way to heaven.

A couple of months after the funeral, his wife, while cleaning the attic, came across the two forgotten pillowcases stuffed with cash. 'Silly old fool,' she said. 'I knew he should have put the money in the basement.'

Judge: Is there any reason you could not serve as a juror in this case?
    Juror: I don't want to be away from my job that long.
    Judge: Can't they do without you at work?
    Juror: Yes, but I don't want them to realize it.

A man chosen for jury duty tried in vain to get out of serving. He pleaded sickness, prior commitments, pressure of work, the death of a distant cousin, but when all else had failed, he made one last desperate attempt just as the trial was about to begin. Having been granted permission to approach the bench, he told the judge: 'Your honour, I must be excused from this trial because I am prejudiced against the defendant. I took one look at the man in the blue suit with those beady eyes and that dishonest face, and I said straight away: "He's a crook. He's guilty." So you see, your honour, there is no way that I can be on that jury and guarantee a fair trial.'

    'Get back in the jury box,' barked the judge impatiently. 'That man is his lawyer!'

A robber burst into a bank brandishing a gun and yelled at the teller: 'Give me the money. One false move and you're geography!'

The teller said: 'Don't you mean history?'

The robber screamed: 'Don't change the subject!'

Signs That You Need a New Lawyer:

Whenever his objection is overruled, he tells the judge 'whatever'.

During the trial you catch him playing his Game Boy.

He keeps citing the legal case of Frankenstein vs The Mummy.

He begins closing arguments with 'As Ally McBeal once said . . .'

Just before the trial starts, he whispers: 'The judge is the one with the little hammer, right?'

He giggles every time he hears the word 'briefs'.

When the prosecutors see who your lawyer is, they high-five each other.

The District Attorney stared at the jury, unable to believe its verdict. Bitterly, he asked: 'What possible excuse could you have for acquitting this man of first-degree murder?'

'Insanity,' replied the foreman.

'What?' sneered the DA. 'All twelve of you?'

A judge grew tired of seeing the same town drunk in front of his bench week after week. One day he glared down at the intoxicated defendant and thundered: 'It is the sentence of this court that you be taken from here to a place of execution and there hanged by the neck until dead.'

The drunk immediately fainted and while the bailiff attempted to revive him, the judge simply shrugged and said: 'I've always wanted to do that.'

Did you hear about the psychic dwarf who escaped from prison? – The newspaper headline read: 'Small Medium At Large.'

Two small boys were talking about their fathers.

'What does yours do for a job?' asked one.

'It's kind of boring, but he's an accountant.'

'Mine's a lawyer.'

His friend was impressed. 'Honest?'

'No, just the regular kind.'

Five men held up a bank. They cleaned out the cash drawers, then herded the tellers and clerks into the vault. Just as they were about to make their getaway, one of the tellers whispered to the gang leader: 'Could you do me a favour, pal? Take the books, too. I'm five thousand short.'

The jurors in a multi-billion dollar lawsuit against the tobacco industry were ordered by a judge not to see a new movie called *Smoking Kills* in case it influenced their verdict. He also told them not to see *The House on Haunted Hill*.

The prosecutor was mystified. He said to the judge: 'I can understand why you have instructed the jurors not to watch *Smoking Kills*, but why have you told them not to watch *The House on Haunted Hill*?'

The judge leaned forward and said: 'Because I got it on video last night, and it stinks!'

Lawyer: Your honour, I wish to appeal my client's case on the basis of newly discovered evidence.

Judge: And what is the nature of this new evidence?

Lawyer: I discovered that my client still has five hundred dollars left.

Morris the burglar was caught leaving the scene of the crime with a bag of loot. Within a few days, he was appearing before the judge.

The judge asked: 'Did you have an accomplice or did you commit this crime by yourself?'

'I was alone, of course,' said Morris. 'Who can get honest and reliable help these days?'

Finding a window in his busy schedule, a prison governor agreed to listen to the pleas of a woman who was desperate for her husband to be released from jail.

'What was he convicted of?' asked the governor.

'Stealing bread,' said the woman.

'I see. And is he a good husband?'

The wife shifted awkwardly in her seat. 'To be honest, no, he's not a particularly good husband. He shouts at the kids, he hits me when he gets drunk, and he's been unfaithful on at least three occasions that I know of.'

'Well,' said the governor, 'it sounds to me as if you're better off without him. Why on earth do you want him out of jail?'

'We've run out of bread again.'

A wizened old prisoner was introduced to his new cellmate. 'Look at me,' said the old man, 'I'm way past it. You'd never believe that I used to lead the life of Riley. I wintered on the French Riviera, had a boat, four cars, a string of beautiful women, and ate at the finest restaurants.'

'So what went wrong?' asked the newcomer.

The old lag sighed: 'One day Riley reported his credit cards missing!'

A lady customer in a Post Office was puzzled to see a man spraying scent on a huge pile of Valentine's envelopes before posting them.

'What are you doing?' she asked.

He replied: 'I'm sending out a thousand Valentine's cards signed "Guess who?"'

'Why do you want to do that?' she queried.

'It's simple,' he replied. 'I'm a divorce lawyer.'

Judge: I thought I told you I never wanted to see you in here again.

Defendant: Your honour, that's what I tried to tell the police, but they wouldn't listen.

A woman celebrating her eightieth birthday was surprised to receive a notice for jury duty. So she called the clerk's office to remind them that she was exempt because of her age.

'You need to come in and fill out the exemption forms,' they said.

'I have done,' she protested. 'I did it last year.'

'You have to do it every year,' they insisted.

'Why? Do you think I'm going to get younger?'

Two burglars were robbing an apartment block when they heard the sound of police car sirens.

'Quick!' said one. 'Jump out of the window!'

'But we're on the thirteenth floor,' protested his accomplice.

The first burglar said: 'This is no time to be superstitious!'

A defendant was on trial for murder. There was strong evidence indicating guilt, but there was no corpse. In the defence's closing statement, the lawyer, knowing that his client would probably be convicted, resorted to a trick.

'Ladies and gentlemen of the jury, I have a surprise for you all,' he said as he looked down at his watch. 'Within one minute, the person presumed dead in this case will walk into this courtroom.' He looked towards the courtroom door. The jurors, somewhat stunned, all looked on eagerly. A minute passed, but nothing happened.

Finally the lawyer said: 'Actually I made up the previous statement. But you all looked on with anticipation. I therefore put it to you that you have a reasonable doubt in this case as to whether anyone was killed and insist that you return a verdict of not guilty.'

The jury, clearly confused, retired to deliberate. A few minutes later, the jury returned and the foreman announced a verdict of guilty.

'How could you come to that conclusion?' protested the lawyer. 'You must have had some doubt! I saw all of you stare at the door.'

The foreman replied: 'That's true – we did look. But your client didn't.'

Did you hear about the new sushi bar that caters exclusively for lawyers? – It's called Sosumi.

A bank had been robbed three times by the same bandit in the space of two months, and on each occasion he escaped with a substantial amount of cash. After the third raid, a senior detective was brought in to quiz the bank teller in the hope of unearthing some clues.

'Have you noticed anything distinctive about the robber?' he asked.

'There is one thing,' replied the teller. 'Each time he turns up, he's better dressed.'

A Mafia godfather, accompanied by his attorney, walked into a room to meet with his former accountant. The godfather asked the accountant: 'Where is the five million bucks you embezzled from me?' The accountant didn't answer.

So the godfather asked again: 'Where is the five million bucks you embezzled from me?'

The attorney interrupted. 'Sir, this man is a deaf mute and cannot understand you, but I can interpret for you.'

The godfather said: 'Well ask him where my money is!'

The attorney, using sign language, asked the accountant where the five million dollars was.

The accountant signed back: 'I don't know what you're talking about.' The attorney interpreted to the godfather: 'He doesn't know what you're talking about.'

Losing patience, the godfather produced a gun, put it to the temple of the accountant, cocked the trigger and snarled: 'Ask him again where my money is!'

The attorney signed to the accountant: 'He wants to know where it is!'

The accountant signed back: 'Okay! Okay! Okay! The money is hidden in a brown suitcase behind the shed in my backyard!'

The godfather said: 'So what did he say?'

The attorney interpreted to the godfather: 'He says that you don't have the guts to pull the trigger.'

Lawyer: Now would you mind telling the jury why you shot your husband with a bow and arrow?

Defendant: I didn't want to wake the children.

A man was in court on a charge of selling drugs. To determine the exact quantity of illegal substance allegedly sold, the judge asked the prosecutor how many grams there were in an ounce. While both attorneys checked their notes, the defendant, who had yet to enter a plea, announced helpfully: 'There are twenty-eight point three grams in an ounce, your honour.'

At this, his lawyer leaned over to him and said: 'I think you might as well plead guilty.'

A lawyer's closing speech was dragging on into its second hour when he suddenly stopped and told the judge: 'Your honour, a juror is asleep.'

The judge responded: 'You put him to sleep; you wake him up!'

A man's car was a total write-off and was covered with twigs, leaves, grass, mud and blood.

'What happened to your car?' asked a friend.

'I hit a lawyer.'

'That explains the blood, but what about the twigs, leaves, grass and mud?'

'I had to chase him all through the park.'

NASA was interviewing professionals to be sent to Mars. Only one could go, and it would be a one-way journey. Despite this stipulation, there were three applicants.

First up was a naturalist. Asked how much he wanted to be paid for going, he answered: 'A million dollars because I want to donate it to the World Wildlife Fund.'

Asked the same question, the next applicant, a doctor, replied: 'Two million dollars. I want to give a million to my family and leave the other million for the advancement of medical research.'

The last applicant was a lawyer. When asked how much money he wanted for going to Mars, he whispered in the interviewer's ear: 'Three million dollars.'

'Why so much more than the others?' queried the interviewer.

The lawyer replied: 'If you give me three million dollars, I'll give you one million, I'll keep one million, and we can send the naturalist!'

A driver caught speeding was brought before a judge. The judge said: 'What will you take, thirty days or a hundred dollars?'

The defendant said: 'I think I'll take the money.'

A dry cleaner was indicted with charges pressed for money laundering. A deal is being ironed out.

Before a highly publicized murder trial the slow process of jury selection took place. On this occasion, it was more painful than usual with both sides hotly contesting and dismissing potential jurors, usually on the grounds that they had already made up their minds about the case after reading the sensational pre-trial stories in the newspapers.

One man was called forward for his question session.

'Are you a property holder?' asked the judge.

'Yes, I am, your honour.'

'Married or single?'

'Married for twenty-two years, your honour.'

Then the judge said: 'Formed or expressed an opinion?'

The man replied: 'Not in twenty-two years, your honour.'

Two armed robbers tried to rob a lawyers' club, but the lawyers put up such a fight that the crooks were forced to flee prematurely. Once they had made their getaway, they counted their loot.

'There's good news and bad news,' said one robber to the other.

'How do you mean?' asked his accomplice.

'Well, the good news is we got away with sixty dollars; the bad is, we went in there with eighty.'

A lawyer's wife died. At her funeral, the mourners were appalled to see that the headstone read: 'Here lies Mary, wife of Spencer, L.L.D., Wills, Divorce, Malpractice, Personal Injury. Reasonable Rates.'

Suddenly Spencer burst into tears. His brother said: 'So you should be crying, pulling a disgraceful stunt like this!'

Spencer sobbed: 'No, you don't understand. They left off the phone number!'

A defence lawyer told his client: 'I've got good news and bad news. The bad news is your blood test came back and your DNA matches the blood found on the victim, the murder weapon and the getaway car.'

'Oh no!' said the client. 'I'm finished! What's the good news?'

'Your cholesterol levels are way down.'

A young lawyer defending a wealthy businessman in a complex lawsuit feared that the evidence was against his client. So he asked the senior partner of the law firm whether it would be appropriate to send the judge in the case a box of expensive cigars.

The partner was appalled by the suggestion. 'The judge is an honourable man, and I can guarantee that if you do that, you will lose the case.'

Six weeks later, the judge ruled in favour of the lawyer's client. Congratulating his colleague, the senior partner said: 'Aren't you glad you didn't send those cigars to the judge?'

'But I did send them. I just enclosed the plaintiff's lawyer's business card!'

When a car was involved in an accident, a large crowd immediately gathered round. An enterprising lawyer, eager to sign a new client, was unable to force his way through. Seeing the chance of rich pickings slipping away, he resorted to desperate measures and shouted: 'Let me through! I am the son of the victim.'

The crowd parted. Lying in front of the car was a donkey.

Two magistrates arrested for drunken driving agreed to try each other's cases the following morning. The first magistrate fined the second five dollars, but then when the first magistrate's case was heard, he received a hefty hundred-dollar fine and a two-month ban.

The first magistrate was furious. 'Why did you do that?' he asked his colleague. 'I only fined you five dollars!'

'I know,' said the second. 'But there's far too much of this type of thing going on these days. Yours is the second such case this morning!'

A husband and wife were walking down the main street of a city one night when the wife stopped at a jewellery shop.

'Oh, look at that beautiful gold watch, she said, peering in the window. 'I'd really love that watch.'

The husband coolly removed a brick from his jacket pocket, checked that there was nobody about, hurled the brick through the window, grabbed the watch and made his escape.

Ten minutes later on the next block, they saw another jewellery shop. 'Oh my!' exclaimed the wife. 'Look at that fabulous diamond ring. What I'd do for that ring!'

Without a word, the husband removed another brick from his jacket pocket, checked that there was nobody about, hurled the brick through the window, grabbed the ring and made his escape.

Two blocks on, the wife stopped at yet another jewellery shop. 'I don't believe it!' she exclaimed. 'That diamond necklace in the window is the one I've always wanted. That is a necklace to die for! If only that necklace was mine.'

The husband turned to her and growled: 'What do you think I am – made of bricks?'

Having drunk too much, a lawyer was involved in a car crash on his way home from the pub when he rear-ended the car in front at traffic lights. In his most pompous manner, he got out of the car, marched over to the innocent driver and sneered: 'Boy are you in trouble! I'm a lawyer!'

The other driver said: 'No, you're in trouble. I'm a judge.'

A judge was hearing a drink-driving case but the defendant, who had a history of driving under the influence, demanded a jury trial. It was nearly four o'clock in the afternoon and getting a jury would take some time, so the judge called an adjournment and went out in the hall looking to recruit anyone available for jury duty. In the main lobby he found a dozen lawyers and told them that they were a jury. The lawyers thought this would be a novel experience and followed the judge back into the courtroom.

The trial itself was over in about ten minutes and it was obvious that the defendant was guilty. The jurors retired to their room, and the judge, thinking that they would be back with their verdict in a matter of minutes, prepared to go home. But after three hours, the jury was still out. The judge was furious and sent the bailiff into the jury room to find out what was delaying the verdict.

When the bailiff returned, the judge said impatiently: 'Well, have they reached a verdict yet?'

The bailiff shook his head and said: 'Verdict? They're still arguing over who should be foreman!'

After being sentenced to five years in prison, Pete knew that the time would give him the opportunity to reflect upon his past mistakes. So he set out to be a model prisoner and soon impressed the prison staff who could see that he was basically a decent guy. He had simply taken one wrong turning in life. The governor encouraged him to learn a trade so that he could lead a fruitful life on his eventual release. Pete took up carpentry and became so adept that he was often given a weekend pass to odd jobs for local pensioners. Without fail, he reported back to prison on the Sunday evening.

The governor was thinking of rebuilding his own kitchen and had already done a lot of the work. But he lacked the skills to build a set of kitchen cupboards and the breakfast counter that he had promised his wife. So he called Pete into his office and asked him whether he could complete the job.

Pete had to decline the offer. He explained: 'I'd really like to help you but counter fitting is what got me into prison in the first place.'

After serving eighteen months of a twenty-year sentence, a man escaped from prison. His escape was the lead story on the early evening TV news and, knowing that there would be a big search party out looking for him, he took care to make his way home via a long cross-country route of fields and woodland. When he finally made it to his house, he checked to make sure the coast was clear before knocking on the door. His wife answered.

'You lousy rat!' she creamed. 'Where have you been? You escaped over six hours ago!'

A lawyer was talking to a client who had just been found guilty of murder.

'There's good news and bad news,' said the lawyer. 'The bad news is, you're getting the electric chair. The good news is, I got the voltage lowered.'

A rabbi, a Hindu and a lawyer were driving late at night in the country when their car broke down. Desperate to find somewhere to sleep, they walked to an isolated farmhouse and asked the farmer if they could stay the night. The farmer said they could, but pointed out that he had only two beds, so one of the three would have to sleep in the barn with the animals.

The rabbi said he didn't mind sleeping in the barn and went off to join the animals, leaving the Hindu and the lawyer to settle down in the bedroom. But five minutes later there was a knock on the bedroom door. It was the rabbi.

'I can't sleep in the barn,' he said. 'There's a pig in there, and it's against my religion to sleep in the same room as a pig.'

'Very well,' said the Hindu. 'I'll go and sleep in the barn.' And he set off to spend the night with the animals. But five minutes later there was another knock on the bedroom door. It was the Hindu.

'I can't sleep in the barn,' he said. 'There's a cow in there, and it's against my religion to sleep in the same room as a cow.'

The lawyer now realized that he had no choice but to volunteer to sleep in the barn. So he went off to get some much-needed rest. But five minutes later the bedroom door burst open. The pig and the cow were standing there . . .

A man was forced to take a day off work to appear in court on a minor charge. After hanging around all day waiting for his case to be heard, he was finally called before the judge late in the afternoon. But no sooner had he stood in the dock than the judge announced that the court would be adjourned until the following day.

'What for?' he raged at the judge.

Tired at the end of a long day, the judge rapped back: 'Twenty dollars contempt of court. That's what for!'

Then, noticing the man checking his wallet, the judge softened and said: 'It's all right. You don't have to pay right now.'

The man replied: 'I wasn't going to. I was just seeing if I'd got enough for two more words!'

Actual Courtroom Quotes:
Q: What is your date of birth?
A: July fifteenth.
Q: What year?
A: Every year.

Q: What gear were you in at the moment of the impact?
A: Gucci sweats and Reeboks.

Q: This myasthenia gravis, does it affect your memory at all?
A: Yes.
Q: And in what ways does it affect your memory?
A: I forget.
Q: You forget. Can you give us an example of something that you've forgotten?

Q: Trooper, when you stopped the defendant, were your red and blue lights flashing?
A: Yes.
Q: Did the defendant say anything when she got out of her car?
A: Yes, sir.
Q: What did she say?
A: What disco am I at?

Q: Is your appearance this morning pursuant to a deposition notice which I sent to your attorney?
A: No, this is how I dress when I go to work.

Q: What is your relationship with the plaintiff?
A: She is my daughter.
Q: Was she your daughter on February 13, 1979?

Q: Doctor, how many autopsies have you performed on dead people?
A: All my autopsies are performed on dead people.

Q: How old is your son – the one living with you?
A: Thirty-eight or thirty-five, I can't remember which.
Q: How long has he lived with you?
A: Forty-five years.

Q: You were not shot in the fracas?
A: No, I was shot midway between the fracas and the navel.

Q: Your first marriage was terminated by death?
A: Yes, by death.
Q: And by whose death was it terminated?

Q: You stated that the stairs went down to the basement, is that correct?
A: Yes.
Q: And these same stairs, did they also go up?

Q: All your responses must be oral, okay? What school did you go to?
A: Oral.

Q: Were you present when your picture was taken?

Q: How far apart were the vehicles at the time of the collision?

Q: Were you alone, or by yourself?

Q: You were there until the time you left, is that true?

Q: Did he kill you?

The judge told the witness: 'Do you understand that you have sworn to tell the truth?'
   'I do.'
   'And do you understand what will happen if you are not truthful?'
   'Sure. My side will win.'

A middle-aged woman was called to serve for jury duty, but asked to be excused because she didn't believe in capital punishment and feared that her personal views might prevent the trial from running its proper course. However the prosecution lawyer liked her thoughtfulness and quiet assurance, and tried to convince her that she would make an excellent juror.

   'Madam,' he explained, 'this is not a murder trial! It's a simple civil lawsuit. A wife is bringing this case against her husband because he gambled away the twelve thousand dollars with which he had promised to buy her a new kitchen.'

   'Well, OK,' agreed the woman, 'I'll serve. I guess I could be wrong about capital punishment after all.'

Judge: Have you anything to offer this court before I pass sentence?
   Defendant: No, your honour, my lawyer took every penny.

Judge: Is it true that you owe your neighbour a thousand dollars?

Defendant: Yes, it's true.

Judge: Then, why don't you simply pay him back?

Defendant: Because it wouldn't be true anymore.

Barrister: Please explain to the court how you came to stab your husband a hundred and twenty-two times?

Defendant: I couldn't turn off the electric knife.

Judge: You have been found not guilty of robbery and can leave this court without a stain on your character.

Defendant: Good. Does that mean I can keep the money?

A prosecuting attorney called his first witness, an elderly woman in a shawl, to the stand and asked: 'Mrs Penny, do you know me?'

'Sure I know you, Mr Bremmer. I've known you since you were this high. And frankly, you've been a big disappointment to me. You lie, you cheat on your wife, you manipulate people and talk about them behind their backs. You've got the principles of an alley cat. You might fool the people in this court into thinking that you're some big-shot attorney, but I know you don't have the brains to amount to anything more than a two-bit pen-pusher. Yes, I know you.'

Stunned by this outburst, the attorney was momentarily lost for words. All he could think of was to point across the room and ask: 'Mrs Penny, do you know the defence attorney?'

'You bet I do,' she said. 'I've known Mr Wiggins since he was a youngster too. And all I can say is, no wonder his mother has disowned him! He's lazy, bigoted and has a serious drinking problem. The man is incapable of building a normal relationship with anyone and visits seedy massage parlours in the dead of night. Yes, I know him.'

At this point, the judge rapped the laughing courtroom to silence and called both attorneys to the bench. Speaking quietly but firmly, he said: 'If either of you asks her if she knows me, you'll be jailed for contempt!'

Lists

Things You'll Never Hear a Dad Say:
  Well, fancy that . . . I'm lost. We'll have to stop and ask for directions.
  Your mother and I are going away for the weekend. Why don't you have a party?
  Some of your friends have a certain 'up yours' attitude. I like that.
  Father's Day? Don't worry about that, it's no big deal.
  Don't bother getting a job. I make enough money for you to spend.
  What do you mean you want to play football? Figure skating not good enough for you, son?
  Here's a credit card and the keys to my new car. Enjoy!
  That skirt's way too long. Show the boys some thigh.

Things You'll Never Hear a Mother Say:
  Just leave all the lights on – it makes the house look more cheery.
  Let me smell that shirt. Yeah, it looks good for another week.
  Go ahead and keep that stray dog, honey. I'll be glad to feed and walk him every day.
  Yeah, I used to skip school a lot, too.
  Of course I don't mind you criticizing my cooking.
  Just throw your old clothes on the floor of your room. I'll happily tidy them up.
  The curfew is just a general time to aim for. It's not like I'm running a prison.
  I don't have a tissue with me – just use your sleeve.
  Don't bother wearing a jacket – the wind-chill is bound to ease.

You Know You're a Mother When:
  Your feet stick to the kitchen floor . . . and you don't care.

When the kids are fighting, you threaten to lock them in a room together and not let them out until someone's bleeding.

Your idea of a good day is making it through without a child leaking bodily fluids over you.

Your favourite television show is a cartoon.

Spit is your number one cleaning agent.

The closest you get to gourmet cooking is making Rice Krispie bars.

You're so desperate for adult conversation that you pour your heart out to the telemarketer that calls, and HE hangs up on YOU!

Even though you spend all day rushing about the house doing chores and you have no time to eat or drink, you still manage to gain three pounds.

Would You Like To Join:
   The Yoko Club? Oh no.
   The Peter Pan Club? Never. Never.
   The Quarterback Club? I'll pass.
   The Anti-Perspirant Club? Sure.
   The Pregnancy Club? Conceivably.
   The Compulsive Rhymers' Club? Okey-dokey.
   The Co-Dependence Club? Can I bring a friend?

Sure Signs of Boredom:
   Your toothpick model of the Eiffel Tower is approaching life size.
   You actually start doing things on your 'to do' list.
   You invite Jehovah's Witnesses in for a chat.
   You start reading the dictionary to learn new words.
   You wear out your computer mouse playing solitaire.
   You start taking things apart just to see if you can rebuild them again.
   You master the art of sleeping with your eyes open.

Signs That Your Cat Is Overweight:
   It has a smaller cat in orbit around it.
   It needs a ramp to get into the cat litter box.
   It lands on its belly before it lands on its feet.
   Other neighbourhood cats point at it and snigger.
   You apply wax to its belly to polish the floor.
   It has a hula hoop for a collar.
   It uses Garfield comic strips as a diet guide.
   The vet always charges double.
   You can drill three holes in it and use it for a bowling ball.

A Cat's Guide to Political Correctness:
    I don't shed – I develop follicle abdication.
    I don't scratch – I cause temporary haemoglobin displacement.
    I don't purr – I am aurally appreciative.
    I am not indifferent – I am dispassionately neutral.
    I am not fat – I have a distended cat food storage facility.
    I am not asleep – I am temporarily inert.
    I don't chase mice – I am rodent defiant.
    I am not hungry – I suffer from craving derangement disorder.

Things Dogs Teach Us:
    When loved ones come home, always run to greet them.
    When it's in your best interest, practise obedience.
    Allow the experience of fresh air and the wind in your face to be sheer ecstasy.
    Let others know when they've invaded your territory.
    Take naps and stretch before rising.
    When someone is having a bad day, be silent, sit close by and nuzzle them gently.
    Avoid biting when a simple growl will do.
    Eat with gusto and enthusiasm. Stop when you have had enough.
    If what you want lies buried, dig until you find it.

You Know You're In Trouble When:
    Your accountant's letter of resignation is postmarked Panama.
    Your suggestion box starts ticking.
    Your secretary tells you the FBI is on line one, the DA is on line two, and CBS is on line three.
    You see your stockbroker hitchhiking out of town.
    A black cat crosses your path and drops dead.
    You take an assertiveness training course and are afraid to tell your wife.
    You see the cruise captain running towards you wearing a life jacket.
    They pay your wages out of petty cash.
    The pest exterminator crawls under your home and never comes out.
    Your pacemaker has only a thirty-day guarantee.

Things Not To Admit at a School Reunion:
    That school days were the best of your life.

That you're on the dole.

That you still like the Bay City Rollers.

That you used to have a crush on the janitor.

That you still live at home.

That you've brought your last piece of geography homework with you.

That this is the first time you've been invited out all year.

That you've still got your school uniform.

Famous Phrases:

Harlez-vous Francais? – Can you drive a French motorcycle?

Veni, Vipi, Vici – I came, I'm a very important person, I conquered.

Respondez S'Il Vous Plaid – Honk if you're Scottish.

Que Sera Serf – Life is feudal.

Haste Cuisine – French fast food.

Le Roi Est Mort, Jive Le Roi – The king is dead. No kidding.

Posh Mortem – Death styles of the rich and famous.

Monage a Trois – I am three years old.

Quip Pro Quo – A fast retort.

Après Moe Le Deluge – Curly and Larry got wet.

Visa La France – Don't leave your chateau without it.

Universal Truths:

Triangular sandwiches taste better than square ones.

One of the most awkward things that can happen in a pub is when your drink-to-toilet cycle gets synchronized with a complete stranger.

You're never quite sure if it's okay to eat green potato chips.

At the end of every party there is always a girl crying.

Reading when you're drunk is horrible.

You've turned into your dad the day you put aside a thin piece of wood specifically to stir paint with.

Sharpening a pencil with a knife makes you feel really manly.

You never know where to look when eating a banana.

Nobody ever dares make cup-a-soup in a bowl.

Try as you might, you can never run away from your knees.

It's impossible to describe the smell of a wet cat.

Old women with mobile phones look wrong.

A person with two first names cannot be trusted.

Despite constant warnings, you have never met anybody who has had their arm broken by a swan.

Despite the amount that you find, nobody ever recalls losing their plasters at the swimming baths.

When in somebody else's house you only realize that they have run out of toilet paper after you have used the toilet.

No matter what you feed it, a puppy's breath will always smell bad.

Bricks are horrible to carry.

Your computer will always crash one second before you remember to save.

People who don't drive slam car doors too hard.

Rummaging in an overgrown garden will always turn up an old ball.

You always feel a bit scared when stroking horses.

Intelligence is knowing that a tomato is a fruit; wisdom is not putting it in a fruit salad.

Everybody everywhere can always remember the day a dog ran into their school.

Every man has at some stage while taking a pee, flushed halfway through and then raced against the flush.

The most painful household incident is wearing socks and stepping on an upturned plug.

You can't respect a man who carries a dog.

It's impossible to look cool while picking up a Frisbee.

You never ever run out of salt.

Ketchup makes everything taste better, except ketchup.

Driving through a tunnel makes you feel excited.

The most embarrassing thing you can do as a schoolkid is to call your teacher 'mom' or 'dad'.

Old ladies can eat more than you think.

No one knows the origins of their metal coat hangers.

The smaller the monkey, the more it looks like it would kill you at the first given opportunity.

In every plate of fries there is a bad fry.

How To Maintain A Healthy Level of Insanity:

Every time someone asks you to do something, ask if they want fries with that.

Page yourself over the intercom without disguising your voice.

Put your garbage can on your desk and label it 'IN'.

Develop a phobia of staplers.

Dont use any punctuation

Ask people what sex they are. Laugh hysterically when they answer.

Sing along at the opera.

Go to a poetry recital and ask why the poems don't rhyme.

Call the psychic hotline and don't say anything.

Tell your children over dinner: 'Due to the state of the economy, we're going to have to let one of you go.'

Signs That You're Spending Too Much Time on Your Computer:

Your opening chat-up line is: 'So what's your home page address?'

You name your daughter Dotcom.

You see a beautiful sunset, and you half expect to see 'Enhanced for Netscape 1.1' on one of the clouds.

You are overcome with anger and depression when you encounter a web page with no links.

You know exactly how much free hard space drive you have but can't remember your spouse's birthday.

You're amazed to find spam is a food.

You introduce your wife as 'my lady@home.wife'.

Instead of calling you to dinner, your spouse sends e-mail.

When you read a magazine, you have an irresistible urge to click on the underlined passages.

Your phone bill comes to your doorstep in a box.

Your best friend is someone you've never met.

You Might Be Taking Scouting Too Seriously If:

You plan to serve foil meals at your next dinner party.

You enjoy lengthy power cuts to your house.

When driving south on holiday, you don't bother with a road map, preferring instead to rely on a compass or the direction in which the leaves are blowing.

Your plans for renovating the bathroom include digging the hole deeper.

Latrines at camp start becoming comfortable.

You think campaign hats are cool.

Your idea of a five-star hotel is no holes in the canvas.

You name one of your kids Baden.

You put a Monet in the loft in favour of a framed illustration of different types of knots.

You can't eat eggs anymore unless they are cooked in a zip-locked bag.

You took a chemistry course at the local college to help you develop a better fire starter.

You Know You're Too Stressed If:
 The sun is too loud.
 You say the same sentence over and over again, not realizing that you have said it before.
 Trees begin to chase you.
 You believe that if you think hard enough, you can fly.
 You and Reality file for divorce.
 You can skip without a rope.
 You say the same sentence over and over again, not realizing that you have said it before.
 Antacid tablets become your sole source of nutrition.
 You can travel without moving.
 You say the same sentence over and over again, not realizing that you have said it before.
 Losing your mind was okay, but when the voices in your head stopped, it was like losing your best friend.
 You say the same sentence over and over again, not realizing that you have said it before.

What Advertising Terms Really Mean:
 NEW – Different colour from previous design.
 ALL NEW – Parts are not interchangeable with previous design.
 EXCLUSIVE – Imported product.
 UNRIVALLED – Almost as good as the competition.
 FOOLPROOF OPERATION – No provision for adjustments.
 ADVANCED DESIGN – The advertising agency doesn't understand it.
 FIELD TESTED – Manufacturer lacks test equipment.
 ENERGY SAVING – When the power is off.
 FUTURISTIC – No other reason why it looks the way it does.
 REDESIGNED – Previous flaws fixed – we hope.
 DIRECT SALES ONLY – Factory had a big argument with distributor.
 YEARS OF DEVELOPMENT – We finally got one to work.
 BREAKTHROUGH – We finally figured out a use for it.
 MAINTENANCE FREE – Impossible to fix.
 HIGH RELIABILITY – We made it work long enough to ship it.
 MEETS ALL STANDARDS – Ours, not yours.

You Might Be a Geek If:
 You tend to save power cords from broken appliances.

You change your screen savers more than your car tyres.

Your IQ is a higher number than your weight.

You ran the sound system at the school dance.

Your wristwatch has more buttons than a telephone.

You can type seventy words a minute but can't read your own handwriting.

You own a slide rule, and you know how to use it.

You once took off the back of your television set to see what's inside.

You've used coat hangers and duct tape for something other than hanging coats and taping ducts.

You own one or more white short-sleeved dress shirts.

You can name six *Star Trek* episodes.

You think that people around you are yawning because they don't get enough sleep.

You know what 'http' stands for.

Symptoms of Being Over Twenty-Five:

You leave clubs before the end to 'beat the rush'.

You stop dreaming of being a professional footballer and start dreaming of having a son who might be instead.

Before throwing the paper away, you look through the property section.

Before going out anywhere, you ask what the parking is like.

Rather than throw an old pair of trainers out, you keep them because they might be all right for the garden.

You buy your first T-shirt without anything written on it.

Instead of laughing at the innovations catalogue that falls out of the newspaper, you suddenly see the benefits of a plastic winter cover for your bench or an electronic mole repellent for the lawn.

You get more excited about having a roast on a Sunday than going clubbing.

You start to worry about your parents' health.

All pop music begins to sound awful.

When sitting outside a pub, you become envious of their hanging baskets.

You become powerless to resist the lure of self-assembly furniture.

You always have enough milk in the house.

The benefits of a pension scheme become clear.

You wish you had a shed.

You have a shed.

Instead of tutting at old people who take ages to get off the bus, you tut at schoolchildren whose diction is poor.

You find yourself saying, 'Is it cold in here or is it just me?'

Little Johnny Jokes

Little Johnny was going to spend the weekend with his friend Timmy and had loaded all his favourite toys into a cart, which he then began pulling the mile or so to Timmy's house. He was doing fine until he reached a steep hill.

As he struggled with the cart up the hill, Johnny began swearing. 'This God damn thing is so heavy!' he moaned.

A passing priest ticked him off. 'You shouldn't be swearing, Johnny,' said the priest. 'God hears you. He is everywhere. He is in the church. He is on the sidewalk. He is everywhere.'

Johnny thought for a moment. 'Is he in my wagon?'

'Yes, Johnny, God is in your wagon.'

'Then tell him to get the hell out and start pulling!'

Little Johnny was overheard by his mother reciting his homework. 'Two plus two, the son of a bitch is four; four plus four, the son of a bitch is eight; eight plus eight, the son of a bitch . . .'

'Johnny!' shouted his mother. 'Watch your language! You're not allowed to swear.'

'But, Mum,' he protested, 'that's what the teacher taught us, and she said to recite it out loud till we learned it.'

The next day Johnny's mother went straight to the classroom to complain.

'No, no,' said the teacher, horrified. 'That's not what I taught them. They're supposed to say, "Two plus two, the sum of which is four . . ."'

Little Johnny's mother was becoming worried. She hadn't seen her elderly neighbour, Mrs Cohen, for days. Fearing that she may have had an accident, she sent Johnny next door to check up on her.

'Johnny, would you go next door and see how old Mrs Cohen is?'

'Sure, Mum,' he said, running out of the door. He returned a few minutes later.

'Well,' asked his mother, 'is Mrs Cohen all right?'

'She's fine,' said Johnny, 'except that she's mad at you.'

'At me? Whatever for?'

'She said it's none of your business how old she is.'

Little Johnny said: 'Mum, you know that lovely vase in the dining room that's been handed down from generation to generation?'

'Yes. What about it?'

'Well, the last generation just dropped it.'

The teacher called Little Johnny to her desk. She said: 'This essay you've written about your pet dog is word for word exactly the same essay as your brother has written.'

'Of course it is,' said Johnny. 'It's the same dog!'

Little Johnny's class were having an English lesson, and the teacher asked him to recite a sentence with a direct object. Johnny thought for a second and said: 'Teacher, everybody thinks you are very beautiful.'

'Why, thank you, Johnny,' she said, blushing. 'But what is the direct object?'

Johnny said: 'A good report card next month.'

His teacher was horrified to hear Little Johnny swearing in school.

'I never want to hear you using language like that again. Where on earth did you pick up such foul-mouthed talk?'

'From my Dad,' said Johnny.

'Well, he should be ashamed of himself,' said the teacher. 'And it's no reason for you to talk like that. Anyway, you don't even know what it means.'

'I do!' said Johnny. 'It means the car won't start.'

Teacher: Johnny, you know you can't sleep in my class.

Johnny: I know, miss. But maybe if you were a little quieter, I could.

Teacher: If you had one dollar and you asked your father for another, how many dollars would you have?

Johnny: One dollar.

Teacher: You don't know your arithmetic.

Johnny: And you don't know my father!

Teacher: If I had seven oranges in one hand and eight oranges in the other, what would I have?

Johnny: Big hands.

Teacher: Johnny, why weren't you at school yesterday?

Johnny: Our cow was on heat, so I had to take her to the bull.

Teacher: I'm sure your father could have done that.

Johnny: No, it has to be the bull.

Teacher: If you got ten dollars from ten people, what would you have?

Johnny: A new bike.

Teacher: Why have you got cotton wool in your ears? Do you have an infection?

Johnny: Well you keep saying things go in one ear and out the other, so I'm trying to keep them all in.

Teacher: There are two words I don't allow in my English class. One is gross, and the other is cool.

Johnny: So what are the words?

Teacher: An abstract noun is something you can think of, but you can't touch it. Can anyone give me an example?

Johnny: Sure. My dad's new car.

Teacher: Johnny, I told you to write this poem out ten times to improve your handwriting, but you've only done it seven times.

Johnny: Looks like my counting isn't too good either!

Teacher: Who invented fractions?

Johnny: Henry the Eighth.

Teacher: Does anyone know which month has twenty-eight days?

Johnny: All of them.

Teacher: Where's the English Channel?

Johnny: I don't know. My television doesn't pick it up!

Teacher: I told you to stand at the end of the line!

Johnny: I tried, but somebody was already there.

Teacher: Can anyone tell me what the Dog Star is?
  Johnny: Lassie.

Teacher: What do you want to be when you grow up, Johnny?
  Johnny: I want to follow in my father's footsteps and be a policeman.
  Teacher: I didn't know your father was a policeman.
  Johnny: He isn't. He's a burglar!

Teacher: If there are four birds on a fence and you shot one, how many would be left?
  Johnny: None.
  Teacher: No, Johnny. The correct answer is three.
  Johnny: But, miss, if you shot one, the other three would fly away.

Teacher: How can one person make so many stupid mistakes in one day?
  Johnny: I get up early.

Teacher: Didn't you promise to behave?
  Johnny: Yes, miss.
  Teacher: And didn't I promise to punish you if you didn't?
  Johnny: Yes, but since I broke my promise, you don't have to keep yours.

Teacher: In 1940, what were the Poles doing in Russia?
  Johnny: Holding up the telegraph lines.

Teacher: Let's test your counting. Johnny, how old were you on your last birthday?
  Johnny: Seven.
  Teacher: How old will you be on your next birthday?
  Johnny: Nine.
  Teacher: That's impossible.
  Johnny: No, miss, today's my eighth birthday.

Teacher: I hope I didn't see you looking at Tommy's test paper.
  Johnny: I hope you didn't see me either!

Teacher: I think you copied off Tommy in that test.
  Johnny: What makes you think that?

Teacher: Because when Tommy wrote 'I don't know' next to question five, you put 'Neither do I'.

Teacher: Where's your homework?
    Johnny: I couldn't do it. There was too much noise at home.
    Teacher: Noise? All evening? What kind of noise?
    Johnny: It was the television. It was too loud. I couldn't do my homework.
    Teacher: Surely you could have asked them to turn the sound down?
    Johnny: No, miss. There was no one else in the room.

Teacher: If coal is selling at six dollars a ton and you pay your dealer twenty-four dollars, how many tons will he bring you?
    Johnny: A little over three tons.
    Teacher: Johnny, that's not right.
    Johnny: I know, miss, but they all do it.

Teacher: Why are you standing on your head?
    Johnny: I'm just turning things over in my mind.

Teacher: Why are you late?
    Johnny: Because of the sign.
    Teacher: What sign?
    Johnny: The one that says 'School Ahead. Go Slow.' So I did!

Voice on phone: Little Johnny has a cold and can't come to school today.
    School secretary: Who is this?
    Voice: This is my dad.

Little Johnny came running into the house and asked: 'Mum, can little girls have babies?'
    'No,' said his mother, 'of course not.'
    Johnny then ran back outside and yelled to his friends: 'It's OK, we can play that game again!'

Little Johnny watched fascinated as his mother gently rubbed cold cream on her face.
    'Why are you rubbing cold cream on your face?' he asked.
    'To make myself beautiful,' replied his mother.

A few minutes later she began removing the cream with a tissue.
'What's the matter?' asked Johnny. 'Giving up?'

The teacher noticed that Little Johnny had arrived for school wearing only one glove.
'Why have you only got one glove?' she asked.
'Well, miss,' explained Johnny, 'I was watching the weather forecast on TV last night, and it said it was going to be sunny but on the other hand it could get quite cold.'

Little Johnny was late for school and apologized to the teacher. 'I'm sorry I'm late, miss, but I had to make my own breakfast this morning.'
'Very well, Johnny,' said the teacher, 'I'll accept your excuse, but now that you're here, perhaps you can take part in our geography test. So, Johnny, do you know where the Scottish border is?'
'Yes, miss, in bed with my mum. That's why I had to make my own breakfast.'

Mother: Why are you home from school so early?
  Johnny: I was the only one who could answer a question.
  Mother: Oh really? What was the question?
  Johnny: Who set Miss Walsh's dress on fire?

Little Johnny was called over by the lifeguard at the swimming pool.
'You're not allowed to pee in the pool,' said the lifeguard. 'You're going to have to leave.'
'But everyone pees in the pool,' protested Johnny.
'Maybe,' said the lifeguard. 'But not from the diving board.'

Little Johnny was asked by his mother what he had learned in Sunday School.
'Well, Mum, our teacher told us how God sent Moses behind enemy lines on a rescue mission to lead the Israelites out of Egypt. When he got to the Red Sea, he had his engineers build a pontoon bridge and all the people walked across safely. Then he used his walkie-talkie to radio headquarters for reinforcements. They sent bombers to blow up the bridge and saved the Israelites.'
'Is that really what your teacher taught you?'
'Well, no, Mum, but if I told it the way the teacher did, you'd never believe it.'

When his father brought home two colleagues from work one evening, it was such an unusual occurrence for the family to have dinner guests that Little Johnny offered to help his mother in the kitchen. Towards the end of the meal, Little Johnny proudly carried in the first piece of apple pie, giving it to his father who passed it to a guest. Then Little Johnny came in with a second piece of pie and gave it to his father who again passed it to a guest. This was too much for Little Johnny who said: 'Nice try, Dad, but the pieces are all the same size!'

The teacher was taking the class in basic maths. Turning to Little Johnny, she said: 'If I give you two cats and two cats and another two cats, how many cats have you got?'

'Seven,' replied Johnny confidently.

'No, Johnny,' explained the teacher. 'That's not the right answer. Listen, if I give you two oranges, then I add another two oranges and another two oranges after that, how many have you got?'

'Six,' answered Johnny.

'That's right,' said the teacher. 'So, let's try again. If I give you two cats and two cats and another two cats, how many have you got?'

'Seven,' replied Johnny.

'Seven!' wailed the teacher. 'How do you get seven?'

'Because I've already got one cat at home!'

The teacher asked the class to write an essay on what they would do if they had a million dollars. But Little Johnny handed in a sheet of blank paper.

The teacher said: 'Johnny, you've done nothing. Why?'

'Because,' he replied, 'that's exactly what I'd do if I had a million dollars.'

The teacher asked Little Johnny if he knew his numbers.

'Yes, I do,' he said. 'My Dad taught me.'

'Good. So what comes after four?'

'Five,' replied Johnny.

'And what comes after eight?'

'Nine.'

'And what comes after ten?'

'The jack.'

At the end of the school day, the teacher asked each child to bring one electrical appliance for 'show and tell' the following morning. So the next day everyone brought something electrical in to school.

'What did you bring, Wendy?' asked the teacher.

'I brought a Walkman.'

'And what is it for?'

'You can listen to music with it.'

'That's very good, Wendy,' said the teacher. 'Now Kenny, what have you brought for us?'

'I brought an electrical can opener,' said Kenny. 'It opens cans, miss.'

'Well done, Kenny, but I see that Johnny hasn't brought anything.'

'Yes I have, miss,' said Johnny. 'It's in the corridor.'

The whole class looked out into the corridor.

'What's that, Johnny?' asked the teacher.

'It's a heart/lung device,' replied Johnny. 'They use it in hospitals to keep your heart going.'

'I see. And what did your father say about it?'

'Aaaaaaaahhhhhhh!'

Little Johnny's father was disappointed that the boy scored such low marks in a spelling test.

'Why did you get such a bad mark?' he asked.

'Absence,' said Johnny.

'What, you were absent on the day of the test?'

'No, but the boy who sits next to me was!'

While staying with his grandma in the country, Little Johnny was asked to go down to the water hole to fetch some water for cooking dinner. As he waded in a few feet and lowered the bucket, he saw two big eyes looking back at him from across the pool. He immediately dropped the bucket and dashed back to grandma's kitchen.

'Where's my bucket and where's my water?' asked grandma.

'I can't get any water from that water hole, grandma,' blurted Johnny. 'There's a big old alligator down there!'

'Now don't you worry about that old alligator, boy. He's been there for a few years now, and he's never hurt no one. Why, he's probably as scared of you as you are of him!'

'Well, Grandma,' replied Johnny, 'if he's as scared as I am, then that water ain't fit to drink!'

Little Johnny was attending his new Catholic school. The nun asked him:
'Do you know where little boys and girls go when they do bad things?'

Johnny replied: 'Probably around the back of the bike sheds!'

Little Johnny's dog Benji was sick and the boy was afraid that his dad would come back from the vet with bad news.

As his dad stepped through the door with Benji in his carrier, Johnny rushed to find out what the vet had said.

'I'm afraid it's not good news, son,' said his father. 'The vet reckons Benji's only got another three weeks or so to live.'

Hearing this, Johnny burst into tears.

'But Benji wouldn't want you to be sad,' said the father, putting a comforting arm around Johnny's shoulder. 'He'd want you to remember all the good times you had together.'

Johnny rubbed his eyes. 'Can we give Benji a funeral?'

'Sure we can,' said his father.

'Can I invite all my friends?'

'Of course you can.'

'And can we have cake and ice-cream?'

'Sure, you can have whatever you want.'

'Dad,' said Johnny. 'Can we kill Benji today?'

The teacher asked her class what they all wanted to become when they grew up. Everyone yelled back their answers – 'a footballer', 'a model', 'a doctor', 'a racing driver', 'an astronaut', 'a fireman' and so on. Everyone that is, except Little Johnny.

The teacher noticed that he was sitting there quietly, so she asked: 'Johnny, what do you want to be when you grow up?'

'Possible,' replied Johnny.

'Possible?' queried the teacher.

'Yes,' said Johnny. 'My mum is always telling me I'm impossible. So when I get big, I want to be possible.'

The teacher set her class a maths problem to solve. 'A wealthy man dies,' she said, 'and leaves ten million dollars. One-fifth is to go to his wife, one-fifth to his son, one-fifth to his daughter and the rest to charity. So what does each family member get?'

Little Johnny shouted out: 'A lawyer!'

'Hey, Mom,' asked Little Johnny, 'can you give me ten dollars?'

'Certainly not!' answered his mother.

'If you do,' persisted Johnny, 'I'll tell you what Dad said to the maid while you were at the hairdresser's.'

His mother was intrigued and, grabbing her purse, handed over the money. 'Well? What did she say?'

'He said, "Carla, make sure you wash my socks tomorrow."'

Little Johnny spent ages studying the greeting cards in a stationer's shop. Eventually the assistant went over to him and said: 'What kind of card are you looking for? A birthday greeting, a get well message, a congratulations card, a good luck wish, an anniversary card?'

Little Johnny shook his head and said: 'Got anything like a blank report card?'

The children in class were asked to write a story with a moral. The next day, they read out their efforts to the teacher.

First to go was young Susan. She said: 'My daddy owns a farm and every Sunday we put the chicken eggs on the truck and drive to town to sell them at market. But one Sunday we hit a bump and all the eggs fell on the road and smashed. And the moral of the story is: don't put all your eggs in one basket.'

'That's very good, Susan,' said the teacher. 'Now it's your turn, Melissa.'

Melissa read out her story. 'My daddy also owns a farm. Every weekend we take the chicken eggs and put them in an incubator. Last weekend, only eight of the twelve eggs hatched. And the moral of the story is: don't count your chickens before they hatch.'

'Very nice, Melissa,' said the teacher. 'Now let's hear from you, Johnny.'

Little Johnny read out his story. 'My uncle Jim fought in the Vietnam War, but one day his plane was shot down. He parachuted out before it crashed but he could only take with him a case of beer, a machine gun and a machete. He drank the case of beer on the way down and landed in the middle of thousands of enemy soldiers. He shot seventy-five Viet Cong with the gun and when he ran out of bullets, he killed another twenty with his machete and throttled ten more with his bare hands.'

'That's very colourful, Johnny,' said the teacher, 'but what is the moral of the story?'

'Don't mess with my uncle Jim when he's drunk.'

The pastor was talking to a group of young children about being good and going to heaven. At the end of his talk, he asked: 'Where do you want to go?'

'Heaven!' called out Millie.

'And what do you have to be to get there?' asked the preacher.

'Six feet under!' yelled Little Johnny.

Little Johnny's father said: 'Let me see your school report.'

'I haven't got it,' said Johnny.

'Why not?'

'My friend just borrowed it. He wants to scare his parents.'

Because of an ear infection, Little Johnny had to go with his mother to the doctor's. When the doctor asked Little Johnny if there was anything he was allergic to, he nodded and whispered in the doctor's ear. Smiling, the doctor wrote out the prescription and handed it to Johnny's mother. She then put it in her purse without looking at it.

As the pharmacist filled the order, he remarked on the unusual food-drug interaction that Johnny had to have. The mother looked puzzled until the pharmacist showed her the label on the bottle. As per the doctor's instructions, it read: 'Do not take with broccoli.'

Little Johnny came home from school and said he got an F in maths.

'Why?' asked his father.

'The teacher asked me: "How much is two times three?" I said "six".'

'But that's right!'

'Then she asked me: "How much is three times two?"'

'What's the bloody difference?' asked the father.

'That's what I said!'

Little Johnny was sitting on a park bench munching on one candy bar after another. After the sixth, a man on the bench across from him said: 'Son, you know eating all that candy isn't good for you. It will give you acne, rot your teeth and make you fat.'

Little Johnny said: 'My grandfather lived to be a hundred and six years old.'

The man asked: 'Did your grandfather eat six candy bars at a time?'

'No,' replied Little Johnny. 'He minded his own business!'

Marriage

Harry, an elderly widower, was invited to his friend's house for dinner. Ernie, the host, preceded every request to his wife with a term of endearment, calling her darling, honey, pumpkin, sweetheart and so on. Harry was touched by this and when the wife was in the kitchen, he said to Ernie: 'I think it's really sweet that after more than fifty years of marriage you still have pet names for your wife.'

Ernie whispered: 'To tell the truth, I forget her name five years ago!'

A young man told his overbearing mother that he had finally fallen in love and was going to get married. He said: 'Just for fun, I'm going to bring three women over to the house tomorrow night and you have to try and guess which one I'm going to marry.'

'If I must,' muttered the mother miserably.

The following evening the son ushered three attractive women into the living room and asked them to sit down.

'Now,' he asked his mother, 'which one do you think is the woman I'm going to marry?'

'The one in the middle,' replied his mother immediately.

'That's right. How did you know?'

The mother said: 'Because I don't like her.'

The Invisible Man married an invisible woman. The kids were nothing to look at.

With their marriage in crisis, a young couple went to see a marriage counsellor. The male counsellor listened while the wife outlined her grievances, the main one being that her husband neglected her.

'We've only been married eighteen months, ' she said, 'but he never pays me any attention. He never takes me anywhere, never takes an interest in my appearance, and certainly never shows me any affection. He seems bored with me already.'

The husband merely shrugged his shoulders, so the counsellor decided to jolt him from his complacency. Jumping up from his chair, the counsellor walked over to the wife and kissed her passionately on the mouth.

As the wife slumped back into her seat in shock, the counsellor turned to the husband and said: 'Your wife needs that at least twice a week.'

The husband replied: 'Well, I can get her here Tuesdays and Fridays.'

Two strangers, Dan and Mike, had paired up together for a round of golf, but the afternoon was in danger of being spoiled by the slow play of two women in front. On the eighth hole, Dan had suffered enough and marched towards the women to ask if they would let him and his partner play through. He got halfway there and suddenly turned back.

'I'm sorry,' he explained to Mike. 'When I got closer, I realized that one of those women is my wife and the other is my mistress. Will you go and talk to them instead?'

So Mike walked towards the two women. But he stopped halfway before turning back.

'What's the problem?' asked Dan.

Mile said: 'It's a small world . . .'

If love is blind and marriage is an institution, does that mean marriage is an institution for the blind?

A newly married man came home from work to find his young wife stretched out on the sofa, wearing a sexy negligee.

'Guess what I've got planned for dinner?' she purred seductively. 'And don't you dare tell me you had it for lunch today!'

A husband and wife were chatting with friends when the subject of marriage counselling was raised. The husband said: 'Oh, we'll never need that. My wife and I have a great relationship. She has a communications degree and I have a degree in theatre arts. She communicates really well and I just act like I'm listening.'

When does a man know that he can count on his wife? – When she wears beads.

A man asked his wife what she would like for her birthday. 'I'd love to be eight again,' she said.

So he pulled out all the stops to make her dream come true. He whisked her off to Disneyland, made her go on all the scariest roller coasters, and force-fed her candyfloss and ice cream. Then he took her to McDonald's for a special kids' meal before rounding the day off with a trip to the cinema to see a two-hour cartoon carnival.

That night she slumped into bed, feeling exhausted and queasy.

'So what was it like being eight again?' asked her husband.

'Actually,' she said, 'I meant my dress size!'

If it weren't for marriage, men would go through life thinking they had no faults at all.

A husband was feeling sorry for himself and in a rare moment of candour, confessed to his wife: 'Sometimes I think I'm nothing but an idiot.'

His wife held his hand tenderly and said: 'Don't worry, darling. Lots of people feel like that. In fact, virtually everyone we know thinks you're an idiot.'

A little girl at a wedding asked: 'Why is the bride dressed in white?'

'Because,' explained her mother, 'white is the colour of happiness, and today is the happiest day of her life.'

The little girl thought about this for a moment, then said: 'So why is the groom wearing black?'

A guy on a date parked his car in a quiet street late at night and climbed in the back seat for sex. His partner was more than willing and asked him to do it four times. After a couple of hours of this, he was exhausted, but she was still up for more.

'Excuse me,' he said, 'but I must go for a pee.'

He climbed out of the car and noticed a man further down the street struggling to change a tyre. He went over to him and said: 'Look, I've got this woman in my car and I've given it to her four times but she still wants more. I don't think I can manage it. So if I change your tyre, will you take over from me?'

So the second guy took his place in the back seat and was just getting down to business when a police officer knocked on the window and shone a light on them.

'What are you doing in there?' asked the officer.

'I'm making love to my wife,' replied the man hesitantly.

'This is a public place. Can't you do that at home?'

'If you must know, officer, I didn't know it was my wife till you shined the light on her!'

Did you hear about the x-ray specialist who married one of his patients? – Everybody wondered what he saw in her.

Carl lamented to his friend Larry that all the excitement had gone out of his marriage.

'That often happens when people have been married for ten years, like you,' said Larry. 'Have you ever considered having an affair? That might put a bit of spark back into your relationship.'

'No, I couldn't,' said Carl, shocked.

'Get real,' said Larry. 'This is the 21st century. These things happen all the time.'

'But what if my wife found out?'

'No problem. Be upfront. Tell her about it in advance.'

Overcoming his initial misgivings, Carl plucked up the courage and broke the news to his wife the next morning.

'Honey,' he said hesitantly, 'I don't want you to take this the wrong way . . . and please remember that I'm only doing this because I love you, otherwise I would never dream of being unfaithful . . . but I think an affair might bring us closer to together.'

'Forget it,' said his wife. 'I've tried it, and it's never worked.'

A husband is someone who, after taking the trash out, gives the impression he just cleaned the whole house.

Once upon a time there was a prince who, through no fault of his own, was put under a spell by an evil witch. The curse was that the prince could speak only one word each year. However, he could save up the words from one year to the next so that if he did not speak for a whole year, he was allowed to speak two words the following year.

One day he met and fell madly in love with a beautiful princess who had golden hair, sapphire eyes and ruby lips. With the greatest diffi-culty he decided to refrain from speaking for two whole years so that he could look at her and say, 'My darling'. But at the end of the two years he wished to tell her that he loved her. Consequently, instead of speaking, he chose to remain silent for another three years, thus allowing himself the luxury of five words.

But at the end of those five years he was so madly in love with her that he wanted to ask her to marry him, so he decided to wait another four years without speaking.

Finally as the ninth year of silence ended, his joy knew no bounds. Leading the lovely princess to the most secluded and romantic spot he knew, the prince placed a hundred red roses on her lap, knelt before her, and, taking her hand in his, said huskily: 'My darling, I love you! Will you marry me?'

The princess tucked a strand of golden hair behind a dainty ear, opened her sapphire eyes in wonder, and, parting her ruby lips, said: 'Pardon?'

Two children were playing weddings. One was overheard saying: 'You have the right to remain silent, anything you say may be held against you, you have the right to an attorney, you may kiss the bride.'

Desperate to use a payphone, a visitor to a town searched high and low and when he eventually found one, it was already occupied. Hoping that the man inside the kiosk wouldn't be long, he waited impatiently outside, constantly looking at his watch. In an attempt to convey his sense of need, the visitor kept staring at the man on the phone but soon noticed that he wasn't actually saying anything. As the minutes passed, the visitor kept looking, nodding and pointing to his watch, but the guy inside paid no attention and just stood there with the phone in his hand, saying nothing into the receiver.

After fifteen minutes, the guy inside had still not said a word into the phone. Thinking that he was being deliberately obstructive and just wasting time, the visitor finally lost his cool. Opening the door of the box, he tried to snatch the phone from the other man's hand.

'Do you mind!' said the guy with the phone. 'I'm talking to my wife!'

A husband and wife were going through a rocky phase and were giving each other the silent treatment. One day, at the height of hostilities, he realized that he needed his wife to wake him at 5am so that he could catch an early morning business flight. Not wanting to be the first to break the silence, he wrote on a piece of paper: 'Please wake me at 5am.'

The next morning, he woke to discover that it was 9am and that he had missed his flight. Furious, he was about to confront his wife when he noticed a piece of paper on his pillow.

The paper read: 'It is 5am. Wake up.'

A mother travelled two thousand miles around the world to be with her only son on the day he received his Air Force Wings and also got married.

'Thank you for coming,' he said afterwards. 'It meant so much to me.'

'I wouldn't have missed it,' she said. 'After all, it's not every day a mother watches her son get his wings in the morning and have them clipped in the afternoon.'

Wife: Why don't you ever wear your wedding ring?

Husband: It cuts off my circulation.

Wife: It's supposed to.

A new neighbour said to the young woman next door: 'If you don't mind me saying so, you and your husband don't seem to have much in common. Why on earth did you get married?'

The young woman sighed: 'I suppose it was the old business of opposites attract – he wasn't pregnant and I was.'

A young couple returned from their honeymoon barely on speaking terms. The best man asked the groom what the problem was.

The groom explained: 'After making love on the first night, I got up to go to the bathroom and I put a fifty dollar bill on the pillow without thinking.'

'Don't worry,' said the groom reassuringly. 'She'll get over it. She surely didn't think you'd been saving yourself all these years?'

'Maybe,' said the groom. 'But I don't know if I'll get over it – she gave me twenty dollars change!'

A woman with fourteen children, aged between one and fourteen, decided to sue her husband for divorce on grounds of desertion.

'When did he desert you?' asked the judge.

'Thirteen years ago,' she answered.

The judge was baffled. 'If he left thirteen years ago, where did all the children come from?'

'He kept coming back to say he was sorry.'

John bought his new work colleague, Robert, home for dinner. As they arrived at the door, his wife rushed up, threw her arms around John and kissed him passionately.

'Wow!' said Robert. 'And how long have you two been married?'

'Twenty-four years,' replied John.

'You must have a terrific marriage if your wife greets you like that after all those years.'

'Don't be fooled,' said John. 'She only does it to make the dog jealous.'

When a young woman was getting married, she asked to wear her mother's wedding dress. Seeing her daughter walk into the room for the first time, the gown a perfect fit on her petite frame, made the mother burst into tears.

The daughter put a comforting arm around her. 'It's like they always say,' she said. 'You're not losing a daughter, you're gaining a son.'

'That's not why I'm crying,' said the mother. 'I used to fit into that dress!'

Deciding to wash his sweatshirt, a husband asked his wife: 'What setting do I use on the washing machine?'

'It depends,' she replied. 'What does it say on your shirt?'

'University of Oklahoma.'

A married couple were celebrating their fiftieth wedding anniversary. The husband asked his wife: 'Honey, have you ever cheated on me?'

'What a strange question to ask after all these years,' she said. 'But, if you really must know, yes, I have cheated on you. Three times.'

The husband was saddened by the confession but wanted to know the precise details.

She said: 'The first time was when you were thirty. Remember you wanted to start a business but no bank would give you a loan? And remember how the bank president came to our house in person and signed the papers? Well . . .'

The husband was touched. 'You mean, you slept with the president of the bank so that I could start up my business? That's the kindest thing anyone's ever done for me. When was the second occasion?'

'Remember when you were fifty-one you had a heart attack and no surgeon would operate on you? And then Dr Michaels came all the way up here to carry out the surgery himself, and after that you were in good shape again? Well . . .'

The husband was genuinely moved. 'So you slept with Dr Michaels to save my life? What a wonderful woman you are! I'm so lucky to have you as my wife. And when was the third time?'

'Remember how a few years ago you really wanted to be president of the golf club? But you were fifty-six votes short?'

Although only married for a short time, a husband and wife quickly realized that they weren't compatible and filed for a divorce.

At court, the judge asked the husband: 'What has brought you to this point? Why are you unable to keep this marriage together?'

The husband said: 'In the eight weeks that we've been together, we haven't been able to agree on a single thing.'

The judge turned to the wife: 'And what do you have to say?'

She said: 'It's been nine weeks, your honour.'

A friend asked a woman: 'What's in that locket, a memento of some sort?'

'Yes,' replied the woman. 'It's a lock of my husband's hair.'

'But your husband is still alive!'

'I know, but his hair's all gone.'

Enjoying a nice refreshing shower, a wife was interrupted when her husband poked his head in to ask: 'What shall I give Lucy for lunch?'

Although he was always very good with their baby daughter, there were times when the wife wanted him to think for himself without always bothering her. This was one such occasion. 'It's up to you,' she replied disinterested. 'There's plenty of food in the house. I'll tell you what, why don't you pretend that I'm not at home?'

'OK,' he said and went away.

A few minutes later, her mobile phone rang. Her husband's voice said: 'Hi, honey, how are you? What shall I give Lucy for lunch?'

As Carla was getting to know John and his family, she was particularly impressed by how much parents seemed to love each other. 'They're so thoughtful and considerate towards,' said Carla. 'Why, your dad even brings your mom a cup of hot coffee in bed every morning.'

Soon Carla and John became engaged, and then married. On the way from the wedding to the reception, Carla again remarked on

John's loving parents and his mother's morning coffee in bed. 'Tell me,' said Carla, 'does it run in the family?'

'It sure does,' said John. 'But I think you should know – I take after my mother.'

A man was lying in hospital close to death when he beckoned his wife to come nearer. 'You know,' he said, 'we've been through a lot together, and you've always been there for me in the bad times. I remember when my business collapsed, you were there. When I had that terrible car accident, you were right by my side. When I was fired from work, you were there to support me; when I was shot, once again, you were there at my side; and now that I'm dying, you're still here.' He thought for a moment and added: 'Actually, I reckon you bring me nothing but bad luck.'

At the height of an argument, the husband said: 'Admit it, Cheryl, the only reason you married me was because my grandfather left me ten million dollars.'

'Don't be ridiculous,' she said. 'I don't care who left it to you.'

A woman woke up one morning and said to her husband: 'I had the most vivid dream last night. I dreamed you bought me a really expensive diamond ring for my birthday. I've never had a dream like that before. What do you think it means?'

'You'll know tonight, darling,' he said.

Hardly able to contain her excitement all day, she eagerly awaited her husband's arrival home from work. Sure enough, he was carrying a small, beautifully wrapped package, which he then handed to her.

Thrilled, she opened it . . . and found a book entitled *The Meaning of Dreams*.

Marriage Names:
If Yoko Ono married Sonny Bono, she'd be Yoko Ono Bono.

If Olivia Newton-John married Wayne Newton, then divorced him to marry Elton John, she'd be Olivia Newton-John Newton John.

If Sondra Locke married Eliot Ness, then divorced him to marry Herman Munster, she'd become Sondra Locke Ness Munster.

If Bea Arthur married Sting, she'd be Bea Sting.

If Tuesday Weld married Hal March III, she'd be Tuesday March 3.

If Snoop Doggy Dogg married Winnie the Pooh, he'd be Snoop Doggy Dogg Pooh.

If David Broome married Irene Handl, he'd be David Broome Handl.

If Ella Fitzgerald married Darth Vader, she'd be Ella Vader.

If Bo Derek married Samuel Pepys, she'd be Bo Pepys.

If Dolly Parton married Salvador Dali, she'd be Dolly Dali.

If G. Gordon Liddy married Boutros-Boutros Ghali, then divorced him to marry Kenny G., he'd be G. Ghali G.

If Woody Allen married Natalie Wood, divorced her and married Gregory Peck, divorced him and married Ben Hur, he'd be Woody Wood Peck Hur.

A man asked his friend: 'How has marriage changed things for you?'

'Well,' said the friend sadly. 'Before we got married, I caught her in my arms. Now I catch her in my pockets!'

A man was sitting at a bar when a woman accidentally spilt her drink over him. As he dried himself off, they began chatting. After a while, she said: 'You look like my third husband.'

'Really?' he said. 'How many times have you been married?'

'Twice.'

Did you hear about the raisin who cheated on his wife? It was in the newspaper, in the current affairs section.

A bride stepped out of the shower on her wedding night wrapped in a robe. Her husband said: 'You don't have to be shy now – we're married.'

So she took off her robe to reveal her naked body.

'Wow,' said the husband. 'Let me take your picture.'

'Why?' said the wife, embarrassed.

'So I can carry your beauty next to my heart for ever.'

He took the photo and then went to have a shower himself. A few minutes later he emerged wrapped in a robe.

'Why are you wearing a robe, honey?' she asked. 'Remember, you don't have to be shy now – we're married.'

So he removed his robe to reveal his naked body.

'Let me take your picture,' she said.

'Why?' he asked, grinning.

'So I can get it enlarged.'

Two students – Steve and Paula — became involved in a debate as to whether men or women make the greater sacrifice when they get married. Naturally Steve thought men gave up much more and, to his surprise, Paula agreed. 'You're right, Steve,' she said. 'Men give up doing their cleaning, their cooking, their grocery shopping, their washing . . .'

Waking up after a restless night, a wife turned to her husband and said: 'I can't believe it! All night long you kept cursing me in your sleep!'
  The husband replied quietly: 'Who was sleeping!'

Deciding to throw a fortieth birthday party for his wife, a man ordered a huge cake from the bakery. Over the phone he said: 'The message I want is "You are not getting older, you are getting better."'
  The baker's assistant said: 'That's a lot of words. How should we arrange it?'
  After a moment's thought, the man said: 'Put "You are not getting older" at the top, "You are getting better" at the bottom.'
  'Okay,' said the assistant, making a note of the inscription to give to the baker.
  Come the day of the party, friends and family travelled from far and wide. At the height of the celebrations, the birthday cake was unveiled. The wife was greatly embarrassed to read the message on it: 'You are not getting older at the top, you are getting better at the bottom.'

A doctor and his wife were sunbathing on a beach when a beautiful young woman in a skimpy bikini strolled by. The near-naked woman looked at the doctor, smiled, and said in a sexy voice: 'Hi there, handsome. How are you doing?'
  She then wiggled her backside and walked off.
  'Who was that?' demanded the doctor's wife.
  'Er . . . just a woman I met professionally,' he replied.
  'Oh yeah?' snarled his wife. 'Whose profession? Yours or hers?'

Why did the polygamist cross the aisle? – To get to the other bride.

A man went up to a beautiful woman in a shopping mall. 'I seem to have lost my wife,' he said. 'Do you mind if I talk to you for a minute?'
  'Okay,' said the woman. 'But how's that going to help you find your wife?'

'Easy,' he said. 'She always turns up the moment I start chatting to attractive women.'

Three weeks after her wedding, a new bride called her priest in a state of great anxiety.

'Father,' she said, 'John and I had the most dreadful fight. It was really awful. I just don't know what to do next.'

'Calm down, my child,' said the priest. 'It's not as bad as you think. Every marriage has to have its first fight.'

'I know. I know,' she said. 'But what am I going to do with the body?'

A guy in an office revealed to his co-workers that, in a moment of tender romance, he had asked his girlfriend to marry him.

'What did she say?' asked one.

'I don't know. She hasn't e-mailed me back yet.'

A young couple went into the church office to fill out the pre-marriage questionnaire. Sensing that the young man was particularly nervous, the pastor guided him gently through the questions. When they reached the question, 'Are you entering this marriage of your own free will?' the groom-to-be hesitated for what seemed an eternity. Eventually the girl broke the silence by telling him firmly: 'Put down yes.'

Courtship is like looking at the beautiful photos in a seed catalogue. Marriage is what actually comes up in your garden.

A wife was lying in bed early one morning when she heard a commotion in the kitchen. She went downstairs to find her husband slumped at the table stinking of beer and with lipstick on his collar.

'I hope you've got a good reason for turning up here at seven o'clock in the morning!' she boomed.

'I have,' replied her husband. 'Breakfast.'

Wife: You're going to be really sorry. I'm going to leave you.
    Husband: Make up your mind. Which is it going to be?

On their first day at home after their honeymoon, the new bride said: 'If you make the toast and pour the juice, breakfast will be ready.'

'Great,' said the husband. 'What are we having?'

'Toast and juice.'

Two ladies were having coffee together. One lamented: 'I've been married four times and every one of my husbands has died.'

'How sad for you,' replied the other. 'What did they used to do for a living?'

'The first was a millionaire, the second was a magician, the third was an evangelist, and the fourth was a mortician.'

'Oh, I see: one for the money, two for the show, three to get ready and four to go . . .'

A man was talking to his best friend about married life. 'You know,' he said, 'I really trust my wife, and I'm pretty certain that she has always been faithful to me. But there's always that doubt.'

His friend said: 'Yeah, I know what you mean.'

A couple of weeks later, the man had to go out of town on business. Before leaving, he said to his friend: 'While I'm away, could you do me a big favour? Could you watch my house and see if there is anything fishy going on? I mean, I trust my wife, but there's always that doubt.'

The friend agreed to watch the house, and the man left town. Two weeks later, he turned and met up with his friend.

'So,' he said, 'did anything happen in my absence?'

'I've got bad news for you,' said the friend. 'The day after you left, I saw a strange car pull up in front of your house. The horn honked, your wife ran out, got into the car, and they drove off. After dark, they came back. I saw your wife and a strange man get out. They went into the house. I ran over and looked in the window, and saw your wife and the man kissing. Then they turned off the light.'

'Then what happened?'

'I don't know. It was too dark to see.'

'See what I mean? There's always that doubt.'

Two men were sitting in a bar, complaining about their wives. 'It really annoys me,' said one. 'Whenever we have a row, she gets historical.'

'Don't you mean "hysterical"'? queried his friend.

'No, I mean historical. Every time we argue, she says: "I still remember the time that you . . . "'

A business executive dialled his home phone number from work and was surprised when a strange woman answered.

'Who is this?' he asked.

'This is the maid,' replied the voice on the other end.

'But we don't have a maid,' he said.

'You do now. I was hired this morning by the lady of the house.'

'I see. Well, this is her husband. Is she there?'

There was a moment's silence before the maid answered: 'Er, well, actually, she's upstairs in the bedroom with someone I thought was her husband.'

The man couldn't believe what he was hearing, but decided to act swiftly and decisively. 'Would you like to make fifty thousand dollars?' he asked the maid.

'Sure would,' she said.

'Right. Now listen carefully. I want you to go into my study, look in the top drawer of my desk and take out my gun. Then I want you to go to the bedroom and shoot that bitch and the guy she's with. Do you understand?'

'Yes,' answered the maid and she put down the phone. The man listened and heard two shots ring out. The maid returned to the phone.

'What should I do with the bodies?' she asked.

'Dump them in the swimming pool,' said the man.

'What pool?'

'Er, this is 265-8844?'

A new bride was embarrassed at being known as a honeymooner. So when she and her husband pulled up to the hotel, she asked him if there was any way they could make it appear that they had been married a long time.

'Sure,' he said. 'You carry the suitcases.'

A couple had been married for forty-seven years during which time they had raised twelve children and been blessed with twenty-four grandchildren. When asked the secret of how they had managed to stay together for so long, they said: 'Years ago we made a promise to each other: the first one to pick up and leave had to take all the kids.'

A motorist was pulled over by a traffic cop. 'Excuse me, sir,' said the cop. 'Do you realize your wife fell out of the car two miles back?'

'Thank God,' he said. 'I thought I'd gone deaf!'

A man ran excitedly into his house one morning and yelled to his wife: 'Jane, pack up your stuff. I just won the lottery!'

'Shall I pack for warm weather or cold?' she asked.

'Whatever,' he said. 'Just so long as you're out of the house by noon.'

A couple went to see an illusionist. They were so impressed by his act that afterwards they went backstage to meet him.

'Tell me,' said the husband, 'how did you do that stunt with the swords? That was amazing.'

'I could tell you,' smiled the illusionist, 'but then I'd have to kill you.'

'OK,' said the man. 'Just tell my wife!'

A man was married to the worst cook in the world. One evening he came home from work to find her in floods of tears.

'It's a disaster,' she wailed. 'The cat's eaten your dinner!'

'Never mind,' said the husband. 'I'll buy you a new cat.'

Returning home a day early from an out-of-town business trip, a man caught a taxi from the airport shortly after midnight. On the cab journey, he confided to the driver that he thought his wife was having an affair. As they pulled up outside his house, the businessman asked the driver: 'Would you come inside with me and be a witness?'

The driver agreed, and they both tiptoed into the bedroom. The man then turned on the lights, pulled the blanket back and, sure enough, his wife was naked in bed with another man.

In a jealous rage, the businessman pulled out a gun and threatened to shoot his wife's lover. 'Don't do it,' she pleaded. 'This man has been very generous. Who do you think paid for the new car I bought you for your birthday? Who do you think paid for our new boat? Who do you think paid for the deposit on this house? He did!'

His mind in turmoil, the husband looked over at the cab driver and asked: 'What would you do in a case like this?'

The cabbie said: 'I think I'd cover him up before he catches cold.'

Convinced that his wife was having an affair, a husband came home to confront her.

'Was it my friend Ted?' he demanded.

'No.'

'Was it my friend Jim?'

'No.'

'Was it my friend Jake?'

'No,' she screamed. 'What is it – don't you think I have any friends of my own?'

After being engaged for twelve years, a man turned to his partner, held her hand tenderly and said: 'I'm going to make you the happiest woman in the world.'

She said: 'I'll miss you.'

On their silver wedding anniversary, a woman turned to her husband and said: 'Darling, will you still love me when my hair turns grey?'

'Why shouldn't I?' he replied. 'I stuck with you through the other six shades.'

A guy went into a bar and ordered a double shot of bourbon. He downed it, reached into his pocket and pulled out a photo. After staring at the picture for a few moments, he put it away and ordered another double. When he had finished that drink, he pulled out the photo again, looked at it for a moment, put it back and ordered another double. He repeated this behaviour for the next hour.

Finally the bartender's curiosity got the better of him. 'Excuse me,' he said, 'but after each drink, why do you keep taking out that picture and staring at it?'

'It's a picture of my wife,' explained the customer, 'and when she starts to look good, I'm going home!'

A man said to his friend: 'My wife's a peach.'

'Why? Because she's so soft and juicy?'

'No, because she has a heart of stone.'

What do you call a woman who knows where her husband is every night? – A widow.

A wife became increasingly annoyed by the fact that her shopkeeper husband was repeatedly late home from work. Every night he promised faithfully that he would be home in time for dinner but something always cropped up to keep him at the shop later than planned.

Eventually she got so mad that she issued him with an ultimatum. 'Tonight you get home at six o'clock sharp or it's the last meal I ever cook for you.'

Much as he hated the thought of losing business, he decided to appease his wife by finishing early. So he closed the shop an hour early and set off to catch the bus home. But as he crossed the street, he was hit by a car and rushed to hospital. Fortunately his injuries proved to be minor and he was discharged shortly afterwards. Nevertheless the delay meant that it was eight o'clock before he got home.

His wife was raging. 'What time do you call this?' she boomed. 'You promised me you'd be home by six!'

'Darling, I can explain. I know I'm two hours late, but I was run over by a car.'

'So what?' she said. 'It takes two hours to get run over?'

A husband said to his wife: 'Darling, let's go out and have some fun tonight.'

'OK then,' she said, 'but if you get home before I do, leave the hallway light on.'

On the way home from a party, a wife said to her husband: 'Have I ever told you how sexy and irresistible to women you are?'

'I don't believe you have,' he replied, flattered.

'Then what in hell's name gave you that idea at the party?'

Two husbands were drowning their sorrows in a bar. One said: 'Why do you and your wife fight all the time?'

The other replied: 'I don't know. She never tells me.'

Wife: When we got married, you said you had an ocean-going yacht.

Husband: Just shut up and row!

Three men were sitting at a bar. Two of them were boasting about how they controlled their wives. The third man was noticeably silent. Eventually they turned to him and said: 'What about you?'

'As a matter of fact,' he said, 'only the other night my wife came to me on her hands and knees.'

'Really?' they said, surprised. 'And what did she want?'

'She said: "Get out from under the bed and fight like a man!"'

Marriage is not a lottery – you get a chance in a lottery.

When her husband went missing, the wife and her sister reported his disappearance to the police.

The wife said: 'He's twenty-nine, six foot three inches tall, dark eyes, black wavy hair, athletic build, weighs a hundred and eighty pounds, softly spoken, generous, and good with the children.'

Her sister whispered: 'What do you mean? He's five foot two, fat, bald, has a big mouth, is tight-fisted and mean to your children!'

'I know,' said the wife, 'but who wants *him* back?'

Love: when your eyes meet across a crowded room
 Lust: when your tongues meet across a crowded room
 Marriage: when your belt won't meet around your waist

Love: when you argue over how many children to have
 Lust: when you argue over who gets the wet spot
 Marriage: when you argue over money

Love: when intercourse is called making love
 Lust: when intercourse is called sex
 Marriage: what's intercourse?

Love: when you phone each other just to say 'Hi'
 Lust: when you phone each other just to organize sex
 Marriage: when you phone each other to find out what time your son's game starts

Love: when you take a bubble bath together
 Lust: when you take a bath in Jell-O together
 Marriage: when you give the kids a bath

Love: when you write poems about your partner
 Lust: when all you write is your phone number
 Marriage: when all you write are cheques

Love: when you show concern for your partner's feelings
 Lust: when you show concern for your partner's sexual satisfaction
 Marriage: when you show concern for what's on TV

Love: when your farewell is 'Bye, darling, I love you.'
 Lust: when your farewell is 'Same time next week?'
 Marriage: when your farewell is silent

Love: when you are proud to be seen in public with your partner
   Lust: when you only ever see each other in the bedroom
   Marriage: when you never see each other awake

Love: when your heart flutters every time you see them
   Lust: when your groin twitches every time you see them
   Marriage: when your wallet empties every time you see them

Love: when a rainy day means more time to stay inside and talk
   Lust: when a rainy day means more time to stay inside and have sex
   Marriage: when a rainy day means it's time to clean the basement

Love: when breaking up is something you try not to think about
   Lust: when staying together is something you try not to think about
   Marriage: when just getting through the day is your only thought

Love: when you're interested in everything your partner does
   Lust: when you're only interested in one thing
   Marriage: when the only thing you're interested in is your golf
score

Love: a romantic candle-lit dinner for two
   Lust: 'do I have to buy you dinner first?'
   Marriage: 'four Happy Meals – to go'

A couple had been married for forty years and had just celebrated their sixtieth birthdays. At their anniversary party, a fairy appeared and, because they had been so devoted to each other for so long, granted each of them a wish.

   The wife said she wanted to travel the world, to visit exotic places, and POOF, the tickets appeared in her hand.

   Then it was the husband's turn to make a wish. Shyly he said: 'I'd like to have a woman thirty years younger than me.'

   POOF, and he was ninety.

Husband: I hear you've been telling everyone that I'm stupid.
   Wife: Sorry, I didn't realize it was a secret.

Two women were discussing their respective husbands. 'I don't know,' said one, 'it seems like all John and I do is fight. I've been so upset lately that I've lost eighteen pounds.'

'Why don't you leave him then?' asked her friend.

'Not yet. I want to lose at least another twelve pounds first.'

Lying on his deathbed, a man begged his wife: 'Grant me one last wish, my sweet. After I'm gone, marry Jack.'

'But I thought you hated Jack?' sneered the wife.

'I do.'

A jealous husband hired a private detective to check on his wife's movements. The husband demanded more than just a written report – he wanted a video of his wife's activities.

A week later, the detective returned with a tape and sat down to watch it with the husband. As the tape played, he saw his wife meeting another man. He saw the two of them laughing in the park. He saw them enjoying themselves at an outdoor café. He saw them having a playful fight in the street. He saw them dancing in a dimly lit nightclub.

When the tape ended, the distraught husband said: 'I can't believe this!'

'What's not to believe?' asked the detective. 'It's right up there on the screen. The camera never lies.'

The husband replied: 'What I mean is, I can't believe my wife is so much fun!'

Two old friends were chatting in a bar. 'What are you going to get your wife for your twentieth wedding anniversary?' asked one.

'I was thinking about a trip to New Zealand,' said the other. 'She'd love that.'

'A trip to New Zealand? That's pretty impressive. But how will you be able to top that for your twenty-fifth anniversary?'

'I don't know. Maybe I'll pay for her fare back.'

Two husbands were in a bar discussing the state of their marriages.

One said: 'My wife always complains that I don't help with the housework.'

The other said: 'Mine constantly complains that I never listen to her – or something like that.'

After a woman's barn burned down, she went to town to collect the insurance.

'We had that barn insured for fifty thousand dollars,' she said, 'and I want my money.'

The agent said: 'I'm afraid insurance doesn't work like that. We will ascertain the value of what was insured and provide you with a new one of comparable worth.'

'In that case,' said the woman firmly, 'I'd like to cancel the policy on my husband.'

A woman was taking a shortcut through a cemetery when she spotted a man sobbing uncontrollably beside a grave.

'Why did you have to go?' he cried. 'Why, oh why?'

The woman put a comforting hand on his shoulder. 'I don't wish to intrude on your grief, but I'm so sorry for your loss. Is this your wife's grave?'

'No,' sniffled the man. 'It's her first husband's.'

A man went to the police station to report that he suspected his wife was trying to poison him.

'Are you sure?' asked the officer.

'Absolutely,' said the man. 'I am convinced that she's poisoning me. The thing is, what should I do?'

The officer said: 'Don't do anything just yet, but stay vigilant. Watch what you eat and drink. In the meantime, I'll talk to her and try to find out whether your fears are justified. I'll get back to you.'

A week later, the police officer called the man and said: 'Well, I spoke to your wife. I talked to her on the phone for three hours. Then she came down to the station and we talked for another five hours. You want my advice?'

'Yes,' said the man anxiously.

'Take the poison.'

On their honeymoon night, the husband was surprised and a little disappointed to see his new wife gazing out of the window.

'Aren't you coming to bed, honey?' she asked.

'No,' she sighed dreamily. 'My mother told me this would be the most magical night of my life, and I don't want to miss a single minute of it.'

A woman arrived home to find her house had been ransacked, but she didn't report it until the following day. When a police officer came round to investigate, he asked her the reason for the delay.

She said: 'To tell you the truth, officer, I didn't know I'd been robbed. When I saw the place in such a state, I simply assumed my husband had been looking for some clean socks.'

After a furious row with his wife, a husband tried to make the peace.

'Why don't you meet me halfway on this?' he suggested. 'I'll admit you're wrong if you admit I'm right.'

Husband: Put your coat on, honey, I'm going to the bar.

Wife: Are you taking me out for a drink?

Husband: Don't be silly, woman. I'm turning the heating off!

A small boy came home from school and told his father excitedly: 'I've been given a part in the school play.'

'That's great, son. Who are you playing?'

'The husband.'

Dad frowned. 'Go back and tell your teacher you want a speaking part.'

If it weren't for marriage, women would have to spend most of their lives arguing with complete strangers.

An elderly couple were having their first row after thirty years of marriage.

She said: 'When we got married, you promised to love, honour and obey.'

'I know,' said the husband, 'but I didn't want to start an argument in front of all those people.'

Two brooms were hanging in the cupboard and after a while they got to know each other so well that they decided to get married. The bride broom looked very beautiful in her white dress and the groom broom looked handsome and suave in his tuxedo.

At the reception the bride broom was asked whether any baby brooms were on the horizon. 'It's far too soon to be talking about things like that,' she said. 'We haven't even swept together!'

Seven Ages of the Married Cold:

First year: Your husband says, 'Oh, my darling, you sound really poorly. I'll drive you straight to the hospital and insist that a doctor sees you straight away. And if they keep you overnight, I'll bring in your favourite takeaway because I know how bad hospital food can be. Don't worry about a thing.'

Second year: Your husband says, 'I don't like the sound of that cough. I've called the doctor. Now you go to bed and rest.'

Third year: Your husband says, 'You go and lie down, and I'll bring you something to eat. Is there any tinned soup in the house?'

Fourth year: 'No use wearing yourself out. When you finish those dishes and the kids' baths and get them to bed, why don't you go to bed yourself?'

Fifth year: Your husband says, 'Why don't you take some aspirin?'

Sixth year: Your husband says, 'You ought to gargle instead of going around barking like a dog!'

Seventh year: Your husband says, 'For Pete's sake, stop sneezing! It's so unhygienic and inconsiderate – I could end up catching it. You'd better pick up some tissues while you're at the store. And don't forget my shirt needs ironing for tomorrow!'

Medicine

When a patient came round after an operation, the surgeon told her: 'I'm afraid we're going to have to open you up again. You see, unfortunately, I left my rubber gloves inside you.'

The patient said: 'Well, if that's all it is, I'd prefer you to leave me alone and I'll buy you a new pair.'

A man went to see his doctor to see if he could prescribe something for a heavy cold. The doctor gave him some tablets, but they didn't work. On his next visit, the doctor gave him an injection, but that didn't work either.

On his third visit, the doctor told the man: 'Go home and take a hot bath. As soon as you finish, open all the windows and stand in the draught.'

'But doctor if I do that, I'll catch pneumonia.'

'I know,' said the doctor. 'But I can cure pneumonia.'

'How did it happen?' the doctor asked the farmhand as he set the man's broken leg.

'Well, doc, ten years ago . . .'

'Never mind the past,' the doctor interrupted. 'Tell me how you broke your leg this morning.'

'Like I was saying,' resumed the farmhand, 'ten years ago, when I first started working on the farm, that night, right after I'd gone to bed, the farmer's beautiful daughter came into my room. She asked me if there was anything I wanted.

'I said, "No, everything is fine."

'"Are you sure?" she asked.

'I said, "I'm sure."

'"Isn't there anything I can do for you?" she persisted.

'"I reckon not," I replied.

'Excuse me,' said the doctor, 'but what does this have to do with your broken leg?'

'Well, this morning when it suddenly dawned on me what she meant, I fell off the roof!'

A newly hired nurse listened while a hospital surgeon doing his rounds yelled: 'Typhoid! Tetanus! Measles!'

'Why does he keep doing that?' she asked a colleague.

'Oh, he just likes to call the shots around here.'

A doctor informed a middle-aged man that he had just six months to live. The man was understandably upset and the doctor could only suggest that he make the most of his remaining time.

After a few minutes' thought, the man said: 'I think I'll go and live with my mother-in-law.'

The doctor was dumbfounded. 'Why on earth would you want to spend your last six months with your mother-in-law?'

'Because,' replied the man, 'it will be the longest six months of my life!'

A man accidentally swallowed all the tiles from a Scrabble set. His doctor said the problem would eventually sort itself out, but not in so many words.

Old Doctor Morris went to see a woman patient at her home. 'Could you fetch me a hammer from the garage?' he asked the woman's husband.

The husband fetched the hammer.

'Right,' said the doctor a couple of minutes later. 'Now I'd like you to get me some pliers, a screwdriver and a hacksaw.'

The husband became alarmed at the last request. 'Just exactly what are you going to do to my wife?' he asked.

The doctor replied: 'Nothing until I can get my medical bag open.'

Feeling stressed out, a man decided to take a long hot bath, but just as he had made himself comfortable, the front doorbell rang. The man climbed out of the tub, wrapped a large towel around him, wrapped his head in a smaller towel, put on his slippers, and went to the door. It was a salesman trying to sell him brushes. Slamming the door, the man returned to his hot bath.

Two minutes later, the doorbell rang again. The man climbed out of the tub, wrapped a large towel around him, wrapped his head in a smaller towel, put on his slippers, and trudged downstairs to the door. It was an energy company trying to get him to change his power supply. Slamming the door, the man returned to his hot bath.

Five minutes later, the doorbell rang again. On went the slippers and towels, but as he made for the bathroom door, he slipped on a wet spot and hurt his back in falling against the hard porcelain of the tub.

Cursing under his breath, the man struggled into his street clothes and, with every move causing a stabbing pain, he drove to the doctor. After examining him, the doctor said: 'You know, you've been lucky. There are no bones broken. But you need to relax. Why don't you go home and take a long hot bath?'

Doctors were asked to contribute to the construction of a new wing at the hospital. What did they do?

The allergists voted to scratch it.

The cardiologists didn't have the heart to say no.

The dermatologists preferred no rash moves.

The gastroenterologists had a gut feeling about it.

The internists thought it was a hard pill to swallow.

The neurologists thought the administration had a nerve.

The obstetricians stated they were labouring under a misconception.

The ophthalmologists considered the idea short-sighted.

The orthopaedists issued a joint resolution.

The pathologists yelled, 'Over my dead body!'

The paediatricians said, 'Grow up!'

The plastic surgeons said, 'This puts a whole new face on the matter.'

The podiatrists thought it was a big step forward.

The proctologists said, 'We are in arrears.'

The psychiatrists thought it was madness.

The radiologists could see right through it.

The surgeons decided to wash their hands of the whole thing.

The urologists felt the scheme wouldn't hold water.

Having recently completed a first aid course, a woman was keen to try out what she had learned. One day at the shopping mall, she spotted a guy lying on the ground, surrounded by a crowd. Sensing this was her chance, she screamed: 'Get back! I have medical training!' She then ran over to him, loosened his clothing, and prepared to administer mouth-to-mouth resuscitation.

Just then a police officer tapped her on the shoulder and said: 'Madam, do you mind? I'm trying to arrest this man!'

A man walked into a doctor's office with a lettuce leaf sticking out of his ear.

The doctor said: 'Hmmm, that's strange.'

The man said: 'That's just the tip of the iceberg.'

A man went to the doctor and showed him cuts and bruises to his body.

'How did you get these?' asked the doctor.

'I was attacked in the street by a huge beetle. It kicked and punched me for about ten minutes.'

'Yes,' said the doctor, 'there is a nasty bug going around.'

'Doctor, doctor, please hurry. My son swallowed a razor-blade.'

'Don't panic, I'm coming immediately. Have you done anything yet?'

'Yes, I shaved with the electric razor.'

'Doctor, doctor, you've got to help me. My hands won't stop shaking.'

'Hmmm. Do you drink a lot?'

'Not really – I spill most of it.'

'Doctor, doctor, I've got amnesia.'

'Just go home and forget all about it.'

'Doctor, doctor, I feel like a ten-dollar bill.'

'Go shopping. The change will do you good.'

'Doctor, doctor, I can't stop stealing things.'

'Take these pills for a week and if they don't work, get me a digital camera.'

'Doctor, doctor, I have a ringing in my ears.'

'Don't answer.'

'Doctor, doctor, my wife thinks she's a lift.'

'Tell her to come in.'

'I can't. She doesn't stop at this floor!'

'Doctor, doctor, I think I may be suffering from déjà vu.'
  'Didn't I see you yesterday?'

'Doctor, doctor, I think I'm God.'
  'How did that start?'
  'Well, first I created the sun, then the Earth . . .'

'Doctor, doctor, you've got to help me. Some mornings I wake up and think I'm Donald Duck. Other times I think I'm Mickey Mouse.'
  'Hmmm. How long have you been having these disney spells?'

'Doctor, doctor, I've hurt my arm in several places.'
  'Well, don't go there any more.'

'Doctor, doctor, I keep thinking I'm a clock.'
  'Don't get so wound up.'

'Doctor, doctor, I can't pronounce my Fs, Ts or Hs.'
  'You can't say fairer than that.'

'Doctor, doctor, I keep thinking there are two of me.'
  'One at a time please.'

'Doctor, doctor, I keep thinking I'm a spoon.'
  'Sit there and don't stir.'

'Doctor, doctor, I feel awful.'
  'What are the symptoms?'
  'It's a cartoon show with yellow people.'

'Doctor, doctor, I keep thinking I'm a cat.'
  'How long have you felt like this?'
  'Ever since I was a kitten.'

'Doctor, doctor, I keep thinking I'm a packet of savoury biscuits.'
  'You must be crackers!'

'Doctor, doctor, I think I'm shrinking.'
  'Don't worry. You'll have to be a little patient.'

'Doctor, doctor, I can't stop singing "The Green Green Grass of Home."'
'That's what we doctors call Tom Jones Syndrome.'
'Really? Is it common?'
'It's not unusual.'

'Doctor, doctor, what does it mean if my feet smell and my nose runs?'
'You're built upside down.'

'Doctor, doctor, I've got a cricket ball stuck up my backside.'
'How's that?'
'Don't you start!'

'Doctor, doctor, I keep thinking I'm a bell.'
'Take these, and if they don't help, give me a ring.'

'Doctor, doctor, I feel like a needle.'
'Hmmm. I see your point.'

'Doctor, doctor, I think I'm a greyhound.'
'Take one of these every two laps.'

'Doctor, doctor, I keep thinking I'm a burglar.'
'Have you taken anything for it?'

'Doctor, doctor, I think I'm becoming a nymphomaniac.'
'Why don't you lie down and tell me about it?'

'Doctor, doctor, I keep thinking I'm a bee.'
'Buzz off, can't you see I'm busy?'

'Doctor, doctor, I think I'm a moth.'
'Get out of the way, you're in my light.'

'Doctor, doctor, everyone thinks I'm a liar.'
'I can't believe that.'

'Doctor, doctor, I can't get to sleep.'
'Sit on the edge of the bed. You'll soon drop off.'

'Doctor, doctor, I think I'm a snail.'
  'Don't worry, we'll soon bring you out of your shell.'

'Doctor, doctor, I think I'm a bridge.'
  'What's come over you?'
  'A bus, a taxi and three trucks.'

'Doctor, doctor, will I be able to play the violin after the operation?'
  'Yes, of course.'
  'Great! I never could before!'

'Doctor, doctor, I snore so loudly I keep myself awake.'
  'Hmm. Have you tried sleeping in another room?'

'Doctor, doctor, can you cure my sleepwalking?'
  'Try these.'
  'Are they sleeping pills?'
  'No, they're tintacks. Sprinkle them on the floor.'

'Doctor, doctor, you must help me. I'm under such a lot of stress.
I keep losing my temper with people.'
  'Tell me about your problem.'
  'I just did, you fool!'

'Doctor, doctor, I think I may need glasses.'
  'Quite possibly. This is the greengrocer's.'

'Doctor, doctor, my wife has lost her voice. What should I do to help
her get it back?'
  'Try coming home at three in the morning.'

A man went to see his doctor. 'Doctor,' he said, 'my arm keeps talking
to me.'
  'Don't be ridiculous,' said the doctor.
  'No, really it does. Listen.'
  So the doctor put his stethoscope to the man's arm and heard the
arm say: 'Lend me five bucks.'
  'It's okay,' said the doctor. 'It's just broke.'

A patient who had just undergone a very complicated operation kept
complaining that he could feel some sort of bump on his head and that

he had a terrible headache. Since the operation had been to his stomach, these were not the type of side effects that the nursing staff had anticipated. Fearing that he might be suffering from post-operative shock, one of the nurses mentioned the symptoms to the surgeon who had carried out the operation.

'Don't worry,' said the surgeon, 'he really does have a bump on his head. Halfway through the operation we ran out of anaesthetic.'

A woman went to the doctor's clutching the side of her face.

'What seems to be the problem?' asked the doctor.

'I don't know,' said the woman removing her hand. 'It's this pimple on my cheek. There's a small tree growing from it, and a table and chairs, and a picnic basket. What on earth can it be?'

'It's nothing to worry about,' said the doctor reassuringly. 'It's only a beauty spot.'

'Doctor,' said the woman as she bounced loudly into the room. 'I want you to tell me frankly what's wrong with me.'

He surveyed her from head to toe and said: 'Madam, I've just three things to tell you. First, you need to lose at least twenty pounds. Second, you should use about half as much rouge and lipstick. And third, I'm a chartered surveyor – the doctor's office is on the next floor!'

A middle-aged man went to the doctor for a routine medical. The nurse began with the basics.

'How much do you weigh?' she asked.

'Oh, about twelve stone,' he answered.

The nurse put him on the scale. 'Fourteen stone, ten pounds. And your height?'

'Oh, about six feet,' he said.

The nurse measured him. 'Five feet eight inches.'

Then she took his blood pressure. 'It's very high,' she said, concerned.

'High!' he exclaimed. 'Of course it's high! When I came in here, I was tall and slim. Now I'm short and fat!'

A young man was visiting a psychiatrist, hoping to cure his eating and sleeping disorder.

'Every thought I have turns to my mother,' he told the psychiatrist.

'As soon as I fall asleep and start to dream, everyone in my dreams turns into my mother. I wake up so upset that all I can do is go downstairs and eat a slice of toast.'

The psychiatrist replied: 'What, just one slice of toast for a growing boy like you?'

Over a round of golf, two surgeons began talking about work.

'I operated on Mr Goldberg the other day,' said one.

'What for?'

'About nineteen thousand dollars.'

'What did he have?'

'Oh, about nineteen thousand dollars.'

'Doctor,' said the patient. 'I seem to have lost my memory. I can't remember anything anymore. I can't remember my house number, I can't remember my kids' names, I can't remember where I work, I can't remember what car I drive. I don't even remember coming here.'

'How long have you been like this?'

'Like what?'

Crippled by indigestion, a man was told by his doctor to drink warm water one hour before breakfast. However there was no improvement in his condition – indeed when he went back to the doctor, he complained that he was actually feeling worse than ever.

The doctor said: 'Did you drink warm water an hour before breakfast each day?'

'No,' said the patient. 'All I could manage was twenty minutes.'

A woman had been having an affair with her dentist for six months, but the dentist was beginning to get worried about continuing the relationship.

'We're going to have to stop soon,' he said. 'Surely your husband must be getting suspicious about all these dental appointments you've been making?'

'No,' she argued. 'My husband doesn't suspect a thing.'

'But he's bound to find out sooner or later.'

'I don't see how.'

'And there's another thing.'

'What?'

'You're down to one tooth.'

A man walked into the doctor's office with a strawberry growing out of his head.

The doctor said: 'I'll give you some cream to put on it.'

What Doctors Say and What They Really Mean:

This should be taken care of right away . . . I'd planned a trip to Hawaii next month but this is so easy and profitable that I want to fix it before it cures itself.

Let's see how it develops . . . Maybe in a few days it will grow into something that can be cured.

Let me schedule you for some tests . . . I have a forty per cent interest in the lab.

I'd like to prescribe a new drug . . . I'm writing a paper and would like to use you as a guinea pig.

If it doesn't clear up in a week, give me a call . . . With any luck, whatever it is will go away by itself.

This may hurt a little . . . Last week two patients bit through their tongues.

If the symptoms persist, call for an appointment . . . I'm away for a month.

A man suffered a serious heart attack, as a result of which he had to undergo a triple bypass. He came round from the operation to find himself being cared for by nuns at a Catholic hospital. As the patient's condition improved, the hospital deemed it safe to raise the subject of how he intended paying for his care.

'Do you have health insurance?' asked one of the nuns.

'No, I don't,' said the man.

'Do you have any money in the bank?'

'Nothing worth speaking of.'

'Well, is there a relative who could help you out?'

'My only living relative is a spinster sister – she's a nun herself.'

The nun was indignant. 'Nuns are not spinsters!' she proclaimed. 'Nuns are married to God!'

'OK then,' said the patient, 'send the bill to my brother-in-law!'

How can you tell if your doctor's a quack? – By his large bill.

A woman went with her husband for his routine medical check-up. But afterwards the doctor took her to one side and said: 'I'm afraid I have some bad news. Unless you adhere to a strict routine, your husband will die. Every morning, you must give him a good healthy breakfast and you must cook him a nutritional meal at night. Furthermore, you must not burden him with household chores and you must keep the house spotless and germ-free. I know it places a great deal of work on your shoulders, but it really is the only way to keep him alive.'

On their way home, the husband asked his wife what the doctor had said to her. 'Oh,' she replied. 'He said you're going to die.'

The doctor knocked at the door of the examination room before entering, and the woman patient called out for him to come in. The doctor then told her to take all her clothes off. He proceeded to give her a thorough physical examination – from head to toe, front and back – leaving no part of her body untouched. When he had finished, he said that she appeared to be in good health and asked whether she had any questions.

'Just one, doctor,' she replied.

'And what's that?' he asked.

She said: 'Why did you bother to knock?'

Two young boys were discussing their respective ailments in the hospital children's ward.

'Are you medical or surgical?' asked one who had been in for several days.

'What do you mean?' said the other.

'It's simple. Were you sick when you came in here, or did they make you sick when you got here?'

A man was lying in hospital, covered with bandages from head to toe. The guy in the next bed said: 'What do you do for a living?'

'I'm a former window cleaner.'

'Oh, when did you give it up?'

'About halfway down.'

A woman phoned 911 to report that her sister had fallen down the stairs.

The emergency operator said: 'Do you know what caused the fall?'

'No,' said the woman. 'What?'

Taken ill while working in Africa, a missionary consulted the local witch doctor in the hope of finding a cure. The doctor cut him a long, thin strip from a leather hide and said: 'Chew on this. By the time it's all gone, you will feel better.'

The missionary took his advice but after following the course of treatment, he still felt unwell. So he returned to the witch doctor.

'Doctor, ' he said, 'my sickness is not cured.'

'And did you eat all of the leather strip, as I suggested?'

'Yes, I did. You see, doctor, the thong is ended, but the malady lingers on.'

A pioneering cardiologist was in such demand to talk about his breakthrough discovery that he was paid fifty thousand dollars to present it before a convention of his peers. After being asked to do several more presentations for a similar fee, he quickly realized that it was more lucrative to go on the medical lecture circuit than to continue as a working surgeon. So he decided to concentrate on the lectures full-time. To make the incessant touring more pleasurable, he bought a limousine and hired a chauffeur.

Six months into the new career, his chauffeur turned to him and said: 'It's not fair this . . .'

'What do you mean?' asked the surgeon.

'Well, you get fifty thousand dollars every time you give a lecture, and that's more than I get paid in a whole year.'

The surgeon tried to justify himself by explaining that the groundbreaking process he had discovered was extremely complex and that only he could deliver the lecture.

'That's nonsense,' said the driver. 'I could do your lecture. I've seen you give it so many times that I know it by heart.'

'All right then,' agreed the surgeon. 'I'll let you do the next lecture and you can keep the fifty thousand. Is that fair?'

The chauffeur said: 'Right. You're on.'

So on arrival at the lecture hall, the surgeon and the driver exchanged jackets. While the driver went up on stage to deliver the lecture, the surgeon, wearing the driver's cap, sat quietly at the rear of the hall.

The chauffeur was not only word perfect with the lecture but he also managed to field every question without the slightest problem. But just as he was about to wind the afternoon up, a medical geek in the audience stumped him with a really difficult question. Rather than admit not knowing the answer, the driver remained commendably calm. 'You know,' he said, 'I have done this lecture over two hundred and fifty times, and I have never been asked such a stupid question. As a matter of fact, that question is SO stupid that I am going to let my driver answer it.'

Concerned about the health of her aunt, a woman phoned her doctor. After consulting his case notes, the doctor said: 'There's no need for me to come out because your aunt isn't really ill at all – she just thinks she's sick.'

A week later, the doctor telephoned the house to check that his diagnosis was correct. 'And how's your aunt today?' he asked.

'Worse,' said the woman. 'Now she thinks she's dead!'

The psychiatrist told the patient that he was conducting a simple test to monitor normal human responses. 'So,' began the psychiatrist, 'what would happen if I cut off your left ear?'

'I wouldn't be able to hear,' answered the patient.

'Very good. And what would happen if I cut off your right ear?'

'I wouldn't be able to see.'

'That's interesting,' said the psychiatrist. 'Why do you say that?'

'Because my hat would fall over my eyes.'

A man went to the doctor complaining of insomnia.

The doctor said: 'You have to stop taking your troubles to bed with you.'

'I can't help it,' the man replied. 'My wife refuses to sleep alone.'

Two children were trying to figure out what game to play. One said: 'Let's play doctor.'

'Good idea,' said the other. 'You operate and I'll sue.'

In order to get to the valves, a mechanic carefully removed the engine parts from a car while the car owner – a surgeon – looked on. Afterwards the mechanic said to the surgeon: 'You know, I reckon my line of work is every but as difficult and skilled as yours.'

'Perhaps,' said the surgeon, 'but I'd like to see you do it while the engine is running.'

As he came round from the anaesthetic following an operation, a man saw his wife sitting patiently at his hospital bedside. Tenderly he murmured to her: 'You're beautiful.'

He then dozed off again but when he woke an hour later and saw her still sitting there, he said to her: 'You're cute.'

'What happened to beautiful?' she asked teasingly.

He said: 'The drugs are wearing off.'

A man went into the doctor's office for his annual check-up, and the doctor asked whether he had experienced any abnormalities over the past twelve months.

'Not really,' said the man, 'although I think my suit must have shrunk over the last year because it didn't fit when I went to put it on for a wedding three weeks ago.'

The doctor said: 'Suits don't shrink just hanging in a wardrobe. You've probably put on a few pounds.'

'That's just it, doctor, I know I haven't gained a single pound since the last time I wore it.'

'Well then,' said the doctor, 'you must have a case of furniture disease.'

'What in the world is furniture disease?'

'That's when your chest starts sliding down into your drawers.'

The condition of a man who had been in a mental home for some years finally seemed to have improved to the point where he was being considered for release. Before allowing him to go, however, the hospital chief wanted to find out how he was likely to adapt to the outside world.

'Tell me,' said the medic, 'if we release you – and all the reports indicate that you are now completely sane – what do you intend to do with your life?'

The inmate said: 'It would be wonderful to get back to real life and if I do, I will certainly refrain from making the same mistakes as before. I was a nuclear physicist, you know, and it was the stress of my work in weapons research that helped put me here. If I am released, I shall confine my work to pure theory, where I trust the situation will be less stressful.'

'Marvellous,' said the hospital chief.

'Or else,' continued the inmate, 'I might teach. There is something to be said for spending one's life bringing up a new generation of scientists.'

'Absolutely,' echoed the chief, enthusiastically.

'Then again, I might write. There is a considerable need for books on science for the general public. Or I might even write a novel based on my experiences in this fine institution.'

'An interesting possibility,' agreed the hospital chief.

'Or, if none of these things appeal to me,' mused the inmate, 'I can always carry on my life as a teapot.'

At a naval barracks the enlisted men were being given a series of injections prior to going overseas. Afterwards one lad asked for a glass of water.

'Not feeling too good?' asked the medical officer.

'No, I'm just making sure I'm still watertight.'

A mother worried so much about her unruly son that she became a bag of nerves, unable to sleep at night. Increasingly concerned about the effect his wayward behaviour was having on her health, she went to see a psychiatrist.

The psychiatrist advised: 'You are far too upset and worried about your son. It's making you ill. I'm going to put you on a course of tranquillizers. Come and see me again in two months.'

On her return visit, the psychiatrist asked: 'Have the tranquillizers calmed you down?'

'Oh yes. They do wonders for me.'

'And how is your son now?'

The mother said: 'Who cares?'

Fed up with her husband's persistent snoring, a woman called on the family doctor to ask him if there was anything he could do to relieve her suffering.

'Well,' said the doctor, 'there is one operation I can perform that will cure your husband, but it really is rather expensive. It will cost a thousand dollars down, followed by payments of fifteen hundred every month for twenty-four months.'

'What is it?'

'A new sports car.'

'A new sports car? How will that help cure my husband's snoring?'

'Well, he won't be able to sleep at night for worrying about how he's going to pay for it.'

A man went to the doctor's for his annual physical. He told the doctor: 'I'm getting really forgetful. I forget where I live, I forget where I've parked my car, and I go into shops and can't remember what it is that I want. And when I do get to the checkout, I find I've forgotten my wallet. It's getting pretty bad. What can I do?'

The doctor thought for a moment and said: 'Pay me in advance.'

After a routine medical, a guy confessed to the doctor that he was thinking about getting a vasectomy.

'That's a pretty big decision,' said the doctor. 'Have you talked it over with your family?'

'Yes, and they're in favour fifteen to two.'

When a wealthy businessman choked on a sharp fish bone in a restaurant, he was fortunate that a doctor was seated at a nearby table. Springing into action, the doctor skilfully removed the bone and saved the businessman's life.

Recovering slowly, he thanked the doctor profusely and offered to pay him. 'Just name your fee,' he croaked gratefully.

The doctor thought for a moment and said: 'Okay. How about half of what you would have offered when the bone was still stuck in your throat?'

A brown paper bag went to the doctor complaining of feeling unwell. The doctor took a blood sample and told the bag to come back the following week.

When the bag arrived for his follow-up appointment, the doctor said: 'I'm afraid I have some bad news. The results of your blood tests indicate that you have haemophilia.'

'How can I possibly have haemophilia? I'm a brown paper bag.'

'Yes,' replied the doctor, 'but it seems your mother was a carrier.'

A pharmacist was working in his room at the rear of the shop when there was suddenly a loud explosion. A minute or so later, he emerged into the shop, his white coat blackened and with sooty marks around his face. Handing a piece of scorched paper to a lady customer, he said: 'Would you ask your doctor to write your prescription again and this time print it?'

To test their ability to react to a genuine disaster, the emergency services staged a mock earthquake, using local Boy Scouts as victims. The 'wounded' scouts were ordered to lie still and wait to be collected by the first aid people. However after five hours of lying motionless on the ground, one young scout had still not been rescued. When the medical relief team finally arrived at the point where he was supposed to be, they found instead a note, which read: 'Have bled to death and gone home.'

A rat catcher told the doctor: 'I was putting down some poison when one of the little bastards bit me on the finger.'

'Which one?' asked the doctor.

'How should I know? Rats all look the same to me.'

A man went to the doctor to say he was feeling run down. The doctor gave him a thorough examination but could find nothing wrong.

'Do you smoke?' asked the doctor.

'No.'

'Do you drink to excess?'

'No.'

'What about your diet? What do you eat in an average day?'

'Snooker balls,' replied the patient. 'I have two reds for breakfast, three browns for lunch, and two yellows, two blues and a pink for dinner.'

'Well, that's the problem,' said the doctor. 'You're not eating enough greens.'

There are warnings of a new disease found in soft butter. Apparently it spreads very easily.

A man went to the doctor to complain that he was having trouble sleeping. 'It's the neighbourhood dogs,' he sighed. 'They bark all night, every night, and they're keeping me awake. I haven't had a proper night's sleep for weeks.'

'Take these sleeping pills,' advised the doctor. 'They should help.'

Ten days later the man was back, looking even more tired than before. 'The pills haven't worked,' he moaned. 'I'm still not getting any sleep. Those dogs are driving me mad.'

'I can't understand it,' said the doctor. 'These sleeping pills are the strongest on the market.'

'They may be,' said the man, 'but I'm up all night chasing those dogs and when I finally catch one, it's hell getting him to swallow the pill.'

A woman went to see a psychiatrist. 'Doctor, I want to talk to you about my husband. He thinks he's a refrigerator.'

'That's not so bad,' said the psychiatrist. 'It's a fairly harmless contraption.'

'Well maybe,' she said. 'But he sleeps with his mouth open and the light keeps me awake.'

A supermarket manager asked one of his young female cashiers why she was late for work.

'I'm so sorry,' she said, 'but on my way in, I witnessed a terrible car smash. This car swerved to avoid a child and somersaulted into a fence. The driver had a fractured skull and there was blood everywhere. It was awful, and I was first on the scene. But thank goodness I took that first aid course in the summer – all my training came back to me in a flash.'

'What did you do?'

'I sat down and put my head between my knees to stop myself from fainting.'

A God-fearing man was close to death in hospital, so his family called in the priest. As the priest stood by the bed, the man's condition seemed to deteriorate and he gestured frantically for something to write on. The priest handed him a pen and paper and the patient quickly scribbled a note. But no sooner had he finished writing than he died.

The priest left the note unread for three quarters of an hour while the family came to terms with their grief. But as he prepared to leave the hospital, he said: 'I think now would be an appropriate time to read John's last note. It was obviously something that meant a lot to him, something he felt the need to say.'

The priest opened the piece of paper and read aloud: 'Hey, you, you're standing on my oxygen tube!'

A man went to see a psychiatrist and listed all the things that were wrong with his life – how he had no job, no money, and no love life. After listening to the patient's story, the psychiatrist said: 'I think your problem is low self-esteem. It's very common among losers.'

A man went to the doctor's, complaining of feeling generally unwell. The doctor gave him a thorough examination and was amazed to find hundreds of dollar bills stuffed in the patient's ears.

When he had finished counting them, the doctor said: 'There was exactly one thousand, nine hundred and fifty dollars in there.'

'That figures,' said the patient. 'I knew I wasn't feeling two grand.'

A patient was waiting apprehensively in the examination room of a famous specialist. 'So who did you see before coming to me?' asked the specialist.

'My family doctor,' replied the patient.

'Your family doctor?' scoffed the specialist. 'What a waste of time! Tell me, what sort of useless advice did he give you?'

'He told me to come and see you.'

A grumpy grandmother was in hospital for the first time and hating every minute of it. Within two hours of her arrival, she had complained about everything – the food, the ward, the nurses, her bed, even her fellow patients.

On her first night there, she spotted a small button attached to a cord. 'What's that?' she demanded.

The intern explained: 'If you need anything in the middle of the night, just press that button.'

'What does it do? Ring a bell?'

'No, it turns on a light in the hall for the nurse on duty.'

'Look,' snapped granny, 'I'm the sick one around here. If the night nurse needs a light on in the hall, she can damn well get up and switch it on herself!'

A man walked into a psychiatrist's office with a pancake on his head, a fried egg on each shoulder and a piece of bacon over each ear.

'What seems to be the problem?' asked the psychiatrist.

The man said: 'I'm worried about my brother.'

Three nurses arrived at the Pearly Gates. St. Peter asked the first why he should admit her. She replied that she had been an emergency room nurse and had saved thousands of lives. St. Peter readily admitted her to heaven.

The second stated that she had worked in a children's ward and had helped improve the lives of thousands of sick youngsters. St. Peter immediately told her that she, too, could come into heaven.

The third nurse revealed that she had been a managed care nurse and had saved thousands of dollars for the insurance company.

St. Peter told her: 'Okay. Come on in. But you can only stay for three days.'

After losing his own ear in a car crash, a man was given a pig's ear as a replacement. Six weeks after the transplant, he returned to the hospital for a check-up.

'Any problems?' asked the surgeon.

'Not really,' said the patient, 'although I do get a bit of crackling.'

A distraught patient phoned her doctor. 'Is it true,' she said, 'that the medication you prescribed has to be taken for the rest of my life?'

'Yes, I'm afraid so,' said the doctor.

There was a moment's silence before the woman added: 'Then just exactly how serious is my condition, because the prescription is marked "No Refills".'

Patient: 'Can you recommend anything for yellow teeth?'

Dentist: 'A brown tie.'

A young doctor moved out to a rural community to replace an ageing medic. The older man suggested that the young doctor join him on his final round of house calls so that the villagers could get to know him. At the first house they visited, the younger doctor listened while the older doctor and an elderly lady discussed the weather, their grand-children and the forthcoming harvest festival. After a while, the senior doctor asked the patient what the problem was.

'I've been feeling really sick, doctor,' she replied.

'I think you've probably been eating too much fruit. Why don't you cut back on the amount of fresh fruit you eat and see if that helps?'

As they left the house, the younger doctor asked his older colleague how he had reached his diagnosis so quickly, and without even examining her.

'I didn't have to,' he explained. 'Did you notice that I dropped my stethoscope while I was in there? Well, when I bent down to pick it up, I looked around and noticed half a dozen banana peels in the trash can. That is probably what has been making her ill.'

The younger man was impressed by the detective work and asked whether he could try the same principle at the next house. Their next call was to an elderly widow. They spent several minutes with her discussing the weather, grandchildren and the forthcoming harvest festival. After several minutes, the younger doctor asked what the problem was.

'I've been feeling really run down,' she said. 'I simply don't seem to have as much energy as I used to.'

'You've probably been doing too much work for the church,' suggested the younger doctor without even examining her. 'Perhaps you should ease up a little and see if that helps.'

As they left, the senior physician said: 'Your diagnosis is probably right, but do you mind telling me how you came to that conclusion?'

'Sure,' replied the younger doctor. 'Just like you, I dropped my stethoscope on the floor. When I bent down to pick it up, I looked around and there was the preacher hiding under the bed!'

A man told a psychiatrist: 'I can't stop deep-frying things in batter. I've deep-fried my laptop, I've deep-fried my mobile phone, I've deep-fried my DVD player, and battered my jeans. What's wrong with me?'

The psychiatrist took a deep breath and said: 'It seems to me that you're frittering your life away.'

On her first visit to her handsome new doctor, a woman was given a thorough checkup.

'Right,' he said, 'I'm putting my hand on your back and I want you to say eighty-eight.'

She felt his gentle hand on her back and said, 'Eighty-eight.'

'Now, I'm going to put my hand on your neck, and again I want you to say eighty-eight.'

She felt his smooth hand on her neck and said, 'Eighty-eight.'

'And now I'm going to put my hand on your chest, and again could you please say eighty-eight?'

Feeling his hand on her chest, she said: 'One, two, three, four . . .'

The doctor told his patient: 'I have some good news and some bad news.'

The patient said: 'Give me the good news.'

The doctor said: 'They're going to name a disease after you.'

A mother took her young son to the doctor.

'Doctor,' she said, 'can an eight-year-old boy operate on himself and remove his own appendix?'

'Of course not,' said the doctor.

'See!' she said to the boy. 'Now put it back!'

A man had been seeing a psychiatrist for three years in an attempt to cure his fear that there were monsters lurking under his bed. But all the psychiatrist's efforts were in vain and the man was no nearer to being cured. Eventually the man decided that further sessions were a waste of time and money.

A few weeks later, the psychiatrist bumped into the man in a bar. The man was looking much happier.

'You look well,' remarked the psychiatrist.

'Yes,' beamed the man. 'That's because I'm cured. After all this time, I can finally go to sleep at night and not worry that there are monsters lurking under my bed.'

The psychiatrist was puzzled. 'How have you managed to get cured? Nothing I tried with you seemed to work.'

'I went to see a different doctor,' explained the man. 'He is a behaviourist and he cured me in one session.'

'In one session!' exclaimed the psychiatrist. 'How?'

'It was simple,' said the man. 'He told me to saw the legs off my bed.'

'I'm sorry, madam,' said the dentist, 'but I'm going to have to charge you a hundred dollars for pulling your boy's tooth.'

'A hundred dollars dollars! But I thought you only charged twenty!'

'I do,' said the dentist, 'but your son screamed so horribly that he scared four other patients out of the waiting room!'

An old woman went to see the doctor about her constipation.

She told him: 'I haven't moved my bowels in a week.'

The doctor said: 'Have you done anything about it?'

'Well, yes, I sit in the bathroom for half an hour in the morning and again at night.'

'No,' said the doctor. 'I mean, do you take anything?'

'Sure,' replied the old lady. 'I take a book.'

Actual Medical Records:

Patient has two teenage children, but no other abnormalities.

The baby was delivered, the cord clamped and cut and handed to the paediatrician, who breathed and cried immediately.

Exam of genitalia reveals that he is circus sized.

She stated that she had been constipated for most of her life until 1989 when she got a divorce.

Occasional, constant, infrequent headaches.

Coming from Detroit, this man has no children.

The patient had waffles for breakfast and anorexia for lunch.

While in the emergency room, she was examined, X-rated and sent home.

The lab test indicated abnormal lover function.

When she fainted, her eyes rolled around the room.

By the time he was admitted, his rapid heart had stopped, and he was feeling better.

The patient has no previous history of suicides.

The patient was to have a bowel resection. However he took a job as a stockbroker instead.

The patient was in his usual state of good health until his airplane ran out of gas and crashed.

The patient has been depressed since she began seeing me in 1993.

Bleeding started in the rectal area and continued all the way to Los Angeles.

She is numb from her toes down.

Discharge status: Alive but without my permission.

The patient lives at home with his mother, father, and pet turtle, who is presently enrolled in day care three times a week.

The patient refused autopsy.

She slipped on the ice and apparently her legs went in separate directions in early December.

Patient has chest pain if she lies on her left side for over a year.

The patient is tearful and crying constantly. She also appears to be depressed.

On the second day the knee was better, and on the third day it disappeared.

She has no rigours or shaking chills, but her husband states she was very hot in bed last night.

Two children were lying in adjacent beds in a hospital ward. The first kid leaned over and asked: 'What are you in here for?'

The second said: 'I'm in here to have my tonsils out and I'm a bit nervous.'

The first kid said: 'There's nothing to worry about. I had that done to me once. They put you to sleep and when you wake up, they give you lots of cake and ice cream. It's easy.'

The second kid then asked: 'What are you in here for?'

The first replied: 'I'm just here for a circumcision.'

'Whoa!' said the second boy. 'I had that done when I was born and I couldn't walk for a year!'

Why did the nurse always insist on using the rectal thermometer for taking temperatures? – Because nurses are always taught in nursing school to look for their patient's best side.

A man went to the doctor in a state of high agitation. 'I have this recurring dream, doctor, in which five women rush into my bedroom and start ripping off my clothes.'

'What do you do?' asked the doctor.

'I push them away.'

'I see. And how can I help you?'

'Please break my arms!'

A patient told his doctor: 'Those pills you gave me are great, but the only problem is, they make me walk like a crab.'

'Yes,' said the doctor. 'Those will be the side effects.'

A man walked into a doctor's surgery and the receptionist asked him what he had.

'Shingles,' he replied.

So she took down his name, address and medical insurance number, and told him to take a seat.

A few minutes later, a nursing assistant came out and asked him what he had.

'Shingles,' he answered.

So she took down his height, weight and complete medical history, and told him to wait in the examining room.

Ten minutes later a nurse came in and asked him what he had.

'Shingles,' he said.

So she gave him a blood test, a blood pressure test, an electrocardiogram, and told him to take off all his clothes and wait for the doctor.

Fifteen minutes later the doctor came in and asked him what he had.

'Shingles,' he replied.

'Where?' asked the doctor.

'Outside in the truck. Where do you want them?'

A Brief History of Medicine:

'Doctor, I have an ear ache.'

2000 BC – 'Here, eat this root.'

1000 BC – 'That root is heathen, say this prayer.'

1800 AD – 'That prayer is superstition, drink this potion.'

1940 AD – 'That potion is snake oil, swallow this pill.'

1985 AD – 'That pill is ineffective, take this antibiotic.'

2005 AD – 'That antibiotic is artificial. Here, eat this root!'

A woman called the hospital to inquire after a patient's health.

'I'd like to know if Hetty Goldblum in room 218 is getting better.'

'Yes, Mrs Goldblum is doing very well,' said the ward nurse. 'She's had two full meals, her blood pressure is fine, she's going to be taken off the heart monitor in a couple of hours and if she continues this improvement, Dr. Cohen is going to send her home on Wednesday.'

'Thank God!' said the caller. 'That's wonderful, wonderful news!'

The nurse said: 'From your reaction, I take it you must be a relative or a very close friend?'

'Actually,' said the caller, 'I'm Hetty Goldblum. Dr Cohen never tells me anything!'

The doctor told his patient: 'I want you to take one of these orange pills with a glass of water first thing in the morning; then I want you to take one of these yellow pills with a glass of water immediately after lunch; and I want you to take one of these green pills with a glass of water last thing at night.'

'What exactly is the matter with me?' asked the patient.

The doctor said: 'You're not drinking enough water.'

A doctor was driving his four-year-old daughter to preschool when she picked up a stethoscope that he had left on the back seat and began playing with it. Glancing in his mirror, he smiled at the thought that perhaps his daughter would eventually follow in his footsteps.

Then the child spoke into the instrument: 'Welcome to McDonald's. May I take your order?'

The doctor had some bad news to deliver to his patient. 'I'm sorry to have to tell you this, Mr Rogers, but you have only six months to live.'

Mr Rogers went ashen-faced. 'But I have no medical insurance,' he said. 'I can't possibly pay you in that time.'

'OK,' said the doctor, scribbling on his pad, 'let's make it nine months.'

A woman went to the doctor and said: 'Every time I go to the bathroom, dimes come out.'

'Go home and relax,' he advised. 'I'm sure it's nothing to worry about.'

A week later, she was back. 'It's got worse, doctor. Now every time I go to the bathroom, quarters come out.'

'Just go home and relax,' he said. 'It's nothing serious.'

A week later, she returned again. 'Things are no better. Now every time I go to the bathroom, half-dollars come out. What's happening to me, doctor?'

'Relax,' he said. 'You're just going through your change!'

Doctor: Did you take the patient's temperature?
   Nurse: No. Is it missing?

Three doctors – a general practitioner, a pathologist and a surgeon – were out on a duck shoot.
   Suddenly a bird flew overhead. The general practitioner stared at it and said: 'Looks like a duck, flies like a duck . . . it's probably a duck.' He then took aim but missed and the bird flew off.
   When the next bird flew overhead, the pathologist looked at it before flicking through the pages of a bird book. 'Hmmm. Green wings, yellow beak, quacking sound . . . might be a duck.' He raised his gun to shoot it, but the bird was long gone.
   A third bird then flew over. The surgeon raised his gun and, almost without looking, scored a direct hit. As the bird fell to the ground, the surgeon turned to the pathologist and said: 'Go see if that was a duck.'

Having failed to find a cure for persistent backache, a man went to a chiropractor as a last resort even though he didn't have any faith in their methods of treatment. Reluctantly he climbed on the examination table and allowed the chiropractor to work on his back and an hour later the problem was completely cured.
   'So,' said the chiropractor as the man got to his feet, 'how do you feel about chiropractors now?'
   The man said: 'I stand corrected.'

A respected doctor had just arrived home from work and was relaxing on his sofa when the phone rang. He calmly answered the call and heard the familiar voice of a colleague on the other end of the line.
   'We need a fourth for poker,' said the friend.
   'I'll be right over,' whispered the doctor.
   As he was putting on his coat, his wife asked: 'Is it serious?'
   'Yes, quite serious,' he replied gravely. 'In fact, three doctors are there already.'

What's the difference between a surgeon and a puppy? – If you put a puppy in a room by itself for an hour, it will probably stop whining.

Suffering from a bad case of flu, the outraged patient bellowed: 'Three weeks? The doctor can't see me for three weeks? I could well be dead by then!'

The receptionist calmly replied: 'If so, would you please have your wife call to cancel the appointment?'

A man was nervous about making an appointment with the dentist, but finally he plucked up courage and phoned the surgery.

'I'm sorry,' said the receptionist, 'but the dentist is out just now.'

'Thank you,' said the man, relieved. 'When will he be out again?'

Did you hear about the nurse who died and went to hell? – It was two weeks before she realized she wasn't at work anymore.

A doctor told his patient: 'There's good news and bad news.'

'Tell me the bad news first,' said the patient nervously.

'I've got the results of your tests and I'm afraid you've got less than a week to live.'

The patient's heart sank. 'So what's the good news?'

The doctor pointed to the door. 'See that sexy blonde on reception? I'm dating her.'

A doctor and his wife had a blazing row at breakfast about their sex life. It ended with him shouting, 'You're not so great in bed either!' and storming off to work.

By mid-morning, he was beginning to feel guilty so he phoned home to make the peace. After many rings, his wife finally picked up the phone.

'What took you so long to answer?' he asked.

'I was in bed.'

'What were you doing in bed this late?'

'Getting a second opinion.'

A man went into a drugstore and asked the pharmacist if he could give him something for hiccups. Without warning, the pharmacist reached across the counter and punched the man hard in the stomach.

'What did you do that for?' gasped the man.

'Well, you haven't got hiccups any more, have you?' said the pharmacist.

'No,' said the man, 'but my wife still has!'

While making his rounds, a doctor pointed out an X-ray to a group of medical students.

'As you can see,' she said, 'the patient limps because his left fibula and tibia are radically arched. Peter, what would you do in a case like this?'

'Well,' pondered the student, 'I suppose I'd limp too.'

An old man in hospital became increasingly irritated by the patronizing tone of one of the nurses. Every morning she would tuck in his sheets, pat him on the head and ask: 'And how are we today?'

He decided to take his revenge at breakfast. Having been given a urine bottle to fill, he instead emptied his apple juice into the container. When the nurse examined the supposed sample, she remarked: 'It seems we are a little cloudy today.'

To her horror, the old man snatched the bottle from her hand, drank the contents and said sarcastically: 'Well, I'll run it through the system again. Maybe I can filter it better this time!'

A man woke up in hospital after having a gangrenous leg amputated. The doctor told him: 'There's good news and bad news.'

'Okay, doc, give me the bad news first.'

'The bad news,' said the doctor, 'is that I'm afraid we've amputated the wrong leg.'

'The wrong leg! My God! How could you do that to me? What's the good news?'

The doctor said: 'I think we're going to be able to save the other leg.'

Two men were standing at the bus stop discussing their recent illnesses.

One said: 'My doctor promised he would have me on my feet in two weeks.'

'And did he?'

'Yes, I had to sell the car to pay his bill.'

A man went to an optician. The receptionist asked him why he was there.

The man said: 'I keep seeing spots in front of my eyes.'

'Have you seen a doctor?'

'No, just spots.'

A husband and wife entered the dentist's office. The husband said: 'I want a tooth pulled. I don't want gas or Novocain because I'm in a terrible hurry. Just pull the tooth as quickly as possible.'

'You're a brave man,' said the dentist. 'Now, show me which tooth it is.'

The husband turned to his wife and said: 'Open your mouth, dear, and show the dentist which tooth it is.'

What does the dentist of the year get? – A little plaque.

'Doctor, are you sure I'm suffering from pneumonia? I heard once about a doctor treating a patient for pneumonia but he ended up dying from typhoid.'

'Don't worry, you won't have that problem with me. If I treat someone for pneumonia, they'll die of pneumonia.'

Medical Dictionary

Artery: The study of paintings.
Bacteria: Back door to café.
Barium: What doctors do when patients die.
Benign: What you be after you be eight.
Catscan: Searching for kitty.
Cauterize: Made eye contact with her.
Colic: A sheep dog.
Coma: A punctuation mark.
Dilate: To live long.
Enema: Not a friend.
Fester: Quicker than someone else.
Fibula: A small lie.
Labour pain: Getting hurt at work.
Morbid: A higher offer.
Nitrates: Cheaper than day.
Node: Was aware of.
Outpatient: A person who has fainted.
Pap smear: A fatherhood test.
Post operative: A letter carrier.
Recovery room: Place to do upholstery.
Rectum: Darn near killed them.
Secretion: Hiding something.
Seizure: Roman emperor.

Tablet: A small table.
Terminal illness: Getting sick at the airport.
Varicose: Nearby.

Men

Three men won a contest, the prize for which was getting to spend a year in a room with anything they chose. The first man loved sex, so they put him in a room for a year with two hundred girls. The second man loved drink, so they put him in a room for a year with two thousand bottles of beer. The third man loved to smoke, so they put him in a room with every known brand of cigarette. Two hours later, the first two heard the man who loved to smoke banging on the door but they were so wrapped up in their own pursuits that they ignored him.

A year later all three came out of their rooms. The first man could barely walk because of the constant sex. The second man couldn't walk because he was so drunk. The third man came out crying.

'Why are you crying and why were you banging on the door?' asked the other two.

He sobbed: 'I forgot my lighter!'

The doctor told a man waiting in a surgery: 'I've got good news and bad news. The bad news is that you have an inoperable brain tumour. The good news is that our hospital has just been awarded a certificate to perform brain transplants and, by chance, there has been an accident right out front in which a young couple have been killed. You can have whichever brain you like. The man's brain is a hundred thousand dollars and the woman's brain is thirty thousand.'

The patient said: 'If you don't mind me asking, doctor, why is there such a large difference between the price of a male and female brain?'

The doctor explained: 'The female brain is used.'

A man came home from work sporting two black eyes.

His wife said: 'How did that happen?'

'I'll never understand women,' he explained. 'I was riding on the escalator behind this pretty young woman and I noticed her skirt was stuck in the crack of her ass. So I pulled it out, and she turned around and punched me in the eye!'

'Oh, right,' said the wife. 'And how did you get the second black eye?'

'Well,' he said, 'I figured she liked it that way, so I pushed it back in again!'

What's the difference between a boyfriend and a husband? – About thirty pounds.

What's the quickest way to a man's heart? – Straight through the ribcage.

What's a man's idea of doing housework? – Lifting his legs so you can vacuum.

Why are women called 'birds'? — Because they tend to pick up worms.

A bald man was neurotic about his lack of hair. He had tried all sorts of treatments, but without success. Then one day he passed a barber's shop with a sign in the window that read: 'Bald Men. Your Problems Solved Instantly. You Too Can Have a Head of Hair Like Mine For $1,000.' And beneath the sign was a photo of the barber with his flowing mane of hair.

So the bald man went into the shop and asked the barber: 'Can you guarantee that for a thousand dollars my hair will instantly look like yours?'

'Absolutely,' said the barber. 'It'll take just a few seconds for us to look exactly alike.'

'Right then,' said the bald man, handing over the money. 'Let's go for it.'

The barber took the money and shaved his own hair off.

What a woman wants in a man (original list):
   Handsome
   Charming
   Financially successful
   A caring listener
   Witty
   In good shape

Dresses with style
Appreciates the finer things in life
Full of thoughtful surprises
An imaginative, romantic lover

What a woman wants in a man (revised list):
Not too ugly
Doesn't belch or scratch his ass in public
Steady worker
Doesn't nod off during conversations
Can remember jokes from Christmas crackers
Is in good enough shape to rearrange the furniture
Usually wears matching socks
Knows not to buy champagne with crew-top lids
Remembers to put the toilet seat lid down
Shaves at weekends

One Monday morning an unmarried girl who worked in a busy office started handing out champagne and chocolates tied with blue ribbons. Asked what the happy occasion was, she flashed a diamond solitaire ring and announced: 'It's a boy, six foot tall and a hundred and ninety pounds!'

James Bond once slept through an earthquake. He was shaken, not stirred.

One day three men were walking along and came upon a wide, raging river. They needed to get to the other side, but had no idea how to do it.
    The first man prayed to God: 'Please, God, give me the strength to cross this river.' And POOF! God gave him big arms and strong legs and he was able to swim across the mighty river in two hours.
    Seeing this, the second man prayed: 'Please, God, give me the strength and ability to cross this river.' And POOF! God gave him a rowing boat and he was able to row across the river in an hour.
    The third man saw how this tactic worked for the other two, and so he prayed: 'Please, God, give me the strength, ability, and intelligence to cross this river.' And POOF! God turned him into a woman.
    She looked at a map, then walked across the bridge.

Did you hear about the man who fell into a lens-grinding machine? – He made a spectacle of himself.

What's the difference between a man and childbirth? – One can be really painful and almost unbearable while the other is just having a baby.

What's the one thing that all men in singles bars have in common? – They're married.

Everybody on Earth died and went to heaven. On their arrival, God announced that he wanted the men to form two lines – one for all the men who had dominated their women on Earth, the other for all the men who had been dominated by their women. Then he told the women to go with St. Peter. When God turned round, he saw that the men had indeed formed two lines. The line of men who had been dominated by their women stretched back a hundred miles whereas the line of men who had dominated their women consisted of just one person.

God was furious. 'You men should be ashamed of yourselves for having been so weak,' he boomed. 'Only one of my sons has been strong. He is the only man of whom I am truly proud.'

God turned to the man who was standing alone. 'Tell me, my son, how did you manage to be the only one in this line?'

'I'm not sure,' replied the man meekly. 'My wife told me to stand here.'

After a row with her husband, a woman went to her mother for moral support.

'Men are only good for one thing,' said the wife.

'Exactly,' said her mother. 'And how often do you have to double park?'

A man walked into a therapist's office, looking really depressed. 'Doctor, you've got to help me,' he said. 'I can't go on like this.'

'What's the problem?' asked the doctor.

'Well, I am thirty-five years old and I still have no luck with the ladies. No matter how hard I try, I just seem to scare them away.'

'My friend,' said the doctor, 'this is not a serious problem. You just need to work on your self-esteem. Each morning, I want you to get up and run to the bathroom mirror. Tell yourself that you are a good person, a fun person and an attractive person. But say it with real conviction. Within a week you'll have women buzzing all around you.'

The man seemed content with this advice and walked out intent on putting it into practice. Three weeks later he returned to the doctor's office wearing the same downtrodden expression on his face.

'Didn't my advice work?' inquired the doctor.

'It worked all right,' said the man. 'For the past three weeks I've enjoyed some of the best moments in my life with the most fabulous looking women.'

'So what's your problem?'

'I don't have a problem,' replied the man. 'My wife does.'

What can you tell about a well-dressed man? – His wife chooses his clothes.

One day in the Garden of Eden, Eve called out to God: 'Lord, I have a problem.'

'What's the problem, Eve?' asked God.

'Lord, I know you've created me and have provided this beautiful garden and all of these wonderful animals, but I'm just not happy.'

'Why is that, Eve?'

'I am lonely, Lord. And I'm sick to death of apples.'

'Well, Eve, in that case, I have a solution. I shall create a man for you.'

'What's a man, Lord?'

'This man,' said God, 'will be a flawed creature, with aggressive tendencies, an enormous ego and an inability to empathize or listen to you properly. All in all, he'll give you a hard time. But he'll be bigger and faster and more muscular than you. He'll be really good at fighting, kicking a ball about, and hunting fleet-footed ruminants, and he will help populate the Earth.'

'Sounds great,' said Eve, with an ironically raised eyebrow.

'Anyway, you can only have him on one condition.'

'What's that, Lord?'

'You'll have to let him believe that I made him first.'

Adam said to God: 'When you created Eve, why did you make her body so curvy and tender, unlike mine?'

God replied: 'I did that, Adam, so that you could love her.'

'And why,' asked Adam, 'did you give her long, shiny, beautiful hair, but not me?'

'So that you could love her,' answered God.

'Then why did you make her so stupid?' asked Adam. 'Certainly not so that I could love her?'

'No, Adam,' said God. 'I did that so that she could love you.'

The Different Qualities of Men and Women:

Women are honest, loyal and forgiving. They are smart, knowing that knowledge is power. But they still know how to use their softer side to make a point. Women want to do the best for their family, their friends, and themselves. Their hearts break when a friend dies. They have sorrow at the loss of a family member, yet they are strong when they think there is no strength left. A woman can make a romantic evening unforgettable. Women drive, fly, walk, run or e-mail you to show how much they care about you. Women do more than just give birth. They bring joy and hope. They give compassion and ideals. They give moral support to their family and friends. And all they want back is a hug and a smile. The heart of a woman is what makes the world spin.

Men are good at lifting heavy stuff and killing spiders.

Money

Once there was a millionaire who collected alligators, which he kept in the pool at the back of his mansion. He also had a beautiful daughter who was single.

One day the millionaire threw a lavish party, during which he issued a challenge to every male guest: 'My friends,' he said, 'I will give one million dollars, or my daughter, to the man who can swim across this pool full of alligators and emerge unharmed!'

No sooner had he finished than there was the sound of an almighty splash in the pool. A man was swimming across the pool as fast as he possibly could, cheered on by the crowd. Finally he reached the other side unharmed.

The millionaire walked over and shook him warmly by the hand. 'I'm truly impressed. That was amazing. I really didn't think anybody would do it. Now I must keep my side of the deal. Do you want my daughter or the million dollars?'

The man caught his breath, then said: 'Listen, I don't want your money. And I don't want your daughter. All I want is whoever pushed me in the pool!'

A Hollywood movie producer was lying by the pool at the Beverly Hills Hilton when his business partner arrived in a state of high excitement.

'How did the meeting go?' asked the first guy.

'Great,' said his associate. 'Tarantino will write and direct for eight million, Tom Hanks will star for nine, and we can bring in the whole picture for under fifty million.'

'Fantastic!' said the guy by the pool.

'There's just one snag,' warned his partner.

'What's that?'

'We have to put up five thousand in cash.'

A newly divorced man was in court to reach a settlement over his alimony payments. The judge said: 'After careful consideration, I have decided to give your wife a thousand dollars a month.'

'That's very generous of you, your honour,' said the man. 'And every now and then I'll try to send her a few bucks myself.'

Six men were playing poker when Norman lost five hundred dollars on a single hand. The shock was so great that he suffered a heart attack and dropped at the table. Showing respect for their fallen comrade, the other five counted their chips standing up.

Arthur looked around and said sombrely: 'Who is going to tell his wife?' They drew straws. Maurice picked the short one.

The others urged Maurice to be discreet and not to add to the poor woman's pain. Maurice promised that discretion was his middle name.

Arriving at Norman's house, Maurice composed himself and knocked on the door. Norman's wife answered and asked him what he wanted.

Maurice said: 'Your husband just lost five hundred dollars playing cards.'

The wife said: 'Well then, I hope he drops dead!'

Maurice said: 'I'll tell him.'

Why is a tax loophole like a good parking spot? – As soon as you see one, it's gone.

A small boy asked a wealthy old man how he had made his fortune. 'Well, son,' he replied, 'let me tell you a little story. It was back in the 1930s during the Great Depression. I was down to my last nickel and I invested that nickel in an apple. I spent the rest of the day polishing that apple so that it sparkled in the sun and at the end of the day I sold the apple for ten cents. The next morning, I invested those ten cents in two apples. I spent the entire day polishing them and then sold them for twenty cents. I carried on like that, and by the end of two weeks I had a dollar and twenty cents in my pocket. Then my aunt died and left me five million dollars . . .'

Tom was broke. His business had gone bust and in desperation he prayed to God to make him win the lottery. But he was out of luck and had to sell his car. The next week he again prayed to God to make him win the lottery, but once more he was out of luck and had to sell his house. With his wife about to leave him, Tom made one last plea to God to make him win the lottery. God came back to him and said: 'Listen, Tom, meet me halfway on this – buy a ticket.'

An antiques expert was strolling down the road when he spotted a mangy old cat in the doorway of a small store drinking milk from a saucer. As soon as he saw the delicate blue and white pattern on the saucer, he knew it was a valuable piece – one that he dearly wanted to acquire.

So he walked into the store and said to the owner: 'I'll give you five bucks for your cat.'

The owner replied: 'Sorry, but the cat isn't for sale.'

The antiques expert persisted. 'Look, I need a cat around the house to catch mice. I'll pay you thirty dollars for it.'

'Okay,' said the owner. 'Sold.' And he handed over the cat.

Disguising it as an afterthought, the expert added: 'Hey, for the thirty dollars, would you mind throwing in that old saucer? The cat's used to it and it would save me having to buy a dish.'

'Sorry, my friend,' said the store owner, 'I can't sell that. It's my lucky saucer. So far this week I've sold forty-seven cats!'

A window salesman phoned a customer. 'I'm calling, sir,' he said, 'because our company replaced all the windows in your house with our triple-glazed weather-tight windows over a year ago, and you still haven't sent us a single payment.'

The customer replied: 'But you said they'd pay for themselves in twelve months!'

Waiting in a long queue at the bank, a man had a sudden attack of hiccups. The hiccups were so powerful that the noise soon echoed around the bank and the poor man had to keep apologizing to the staff and fellow customers. When it was finally his turn to be served, he handed the teller a cheque and asked: 'Can you hic cash this hic please hic?'

The cashier tapped in his details on the computer but then said that she would be unable to cash it.

'Why?' he asked.

She explained: 'Our computer indicates that you have insufficient funds to cover this amount. In actual fact our records show that your account is overdrawn by five thousand dollars.'

'It can't be! You have to be kidding!'

'Yes, I am,' she smiled, counting out the cash. 'But it's cured your hiccups.'

Bidding at an auction was proceeding vigorously until the auctioneer suddenly announced: 'A gentleman in this room has lost a wallet containing ten thousand dollars. If it is returned, he will pay a reward of two thousand dollars.'

There was a moment's silence before a voice at the back of the room called out: 'Two thousand five hundred!'

A father came home from a long business trip to find his young son riding a brand new bicycle.

'How did you get the money to buy a new bike?' he asked.

'I earned it hiking,' replied the boy.

'Don't be silly. How can you earn that much money hiking?'

'Well,' explained the boy, 'every night while you were away Mr Brown from the bank came over to see Mom. He'd give me a twenty-dollar bill and tell me to take a hike.'

Several men were sitting around in the locker room of a private club after exercizing. Suddenly a mobile phone on one of the benches rang. One of the men picked it up.

'Hello?'

'Honey, it's me. Are you at the club?'

'Yes.'

'Great! I am at the mall two blocks from where you are. I just saw a beautiful mink coat. It's absolutely gorgeous. Can I buy it?'

'What's the price?'

'Only one thousand five hundred.'

'Well, okay, go ahead and get it if you like it that much.'

'Oh, and I also stopped by the Mercedes dealership and saw the 2005 models. There was one I really loved. I spoke with the salesman, and he gave me a really good price, and since we need to trade in the BMW that we bought last year . . .'

'What price did he quote you?'

'Only eighty thousand.'

'Okay, but for that price I want it with all the options.'

'Great! But before we hang up, something else.'

'What?'

'It might sound like a lot, but I was studying our bank balance and . . . I stopped by the real estate agent this morning and saw the house we looked at last year. Remember, the one with the pool, two acres of ground, beachfront property? Well, it's on sale again!'

'How much are they asking?'

'Only seven hundred fifty thousand – a terrific price, and we've got more than enough in the bank.'

'Okay then, go ahead and buy it, but just bid seven hundred fifty thousand, understand? No more.'

'Yeah, darling. Oh, thank you. See you later. I do love you.'

'Bye . . . I do too.'

The man hung up, closed the phone's flap, and, raising his hand while still holding the phone, asked all those present: 'Does anyone know who this phone belongs to?'

Don and Rick were enjoying a night on the town when they were approached by a beggar asking for money. Don refused point blank, but Rick was feeling in a generous mood and gave the beggar a few items of loose change before sending him on his way.

'You must be crazy,' said Don. 'You know he's only going to spend it on booze!'

Rick replied: 'And we weren't?'

A mother decided her daughter should have something practical for her tenth birthday and suggested opening a savings account. The girl thought this was an excellent idea and so they went along to the bank to fill in the necessary form.

'Since it's your account,' said the mother, 'and you're so grown up now, you can fill in the form. But if there's anything you don't understand, I'm right here.'

The girl did fine until she came to the space for 'Name of your previous bank' and, after a moment's hesitation, she put 'Piggy'.

Bill went up to his neighbour and said: 'I bet you a hundred dollars that I can jump higher than your house.'

The neighbour eyed him up carefully before concluding that with his short legs and beer belly, Bill appeared incapable of any astounding athletic feat. 'Okay,' he said. 'You're on.'

So Bill prepared himself mentally before jumping all of nine inches off the ground. The neighbour roared with laughter until Bill said: 'Right. It's your house's turn now.'

A young woman went into a bank to withdraw some cash.

'Can you identify yourself?' asked the teller.

The woman opened her handbag, took out a mirror, looked into it and said: 'Yes, it's definitely me.'

A regular theatregoer was dismayed to find that he had a seat near the rear of the house for the performance of an eagerly awaited mystery thriller. With half an hour to go before curtain up, he summoned an usher and said: 'Could you possibly help me? I have been looking forward to this play for weeks, but I am not happy with my seat. You see, my eyesight and hearing are not what they were and, in order to be able to follow the intricate plot and work out the clues, I need a seat nearer the front of the house. If you can get me a better seat, I'll give you a handsome tip.'

The usher promised to do what he could and after twenty-five minutes of delicate negotiations, he was finally able to offer the man a seat right in the middle of the front row. The man took his seat, thanked the usher, and handed him a quarter by way of a tip.

The deflated usher took one look at the quarter and then whispered in the man's ear: 'The butler did it with the candlestick in the ballroom.'

A blackjack dealer and a player with thirteen in his hand were arguing about whether or not it was appropriate to tip the dealer.

The player said: 'When I get bad cards, it's not the dealer's fault. And when I get good cards, the dealer obviously has nothing to do with it. So why should I tip him?'

The dealer countered: 'When you eat out, do you tip the waiter?'

'Of course.'

'Well then, he serves you food, and I'm serving you cards. So you should tip me.'

'I see your point,' said the player, 'but the waiter gives me what I ask for . . . I'll take an eight.'

A man was walking through a rough part of town when a beggar in threadbare clothes came over to him and asked him for two dollars.

'What do you want the money for?' asked the man. 'Is it to buy booze?'

'No.'

'Will you gamble it away?'

'No.'

'Then will you come home with me so I can show my wife what happens to a guy who doesn't drink or gamble?'

A man hired a taxi to take him to court for his bankruptcy trial. 'I'm in terrible debt,' he told the driver. 'I owe money to everyone – the taxman, my suppliers, the electric company, the gas company, the water company, a catering firm, two bookmakers, the council, and an office furnishing company.' As the taxi pulled up outside the court, he turned to the driver and added: 'Well, I suppose you might as well come in too.'

A stockbroker was 'cold calling' about a penny stock and found an interested client. 'I think this one will really move,' said the broker. 'It's only a dollar a share.'

'Buy me a thousand shares,' said the client.

The next day the stock was at two dollars, prompting the client to call the broker and say: 'You were right, give me five thousand more shares.'

The next day the client looked in the newspaper and saw that the stock had risen to four dollars. The client ran to the phone and called the broker. 'Get me ten thousand more shares.'

'Great,' said the broker.

The next day the client looked in the paper and the stock was standing at nine dollars. Seeing what a sizeable profit he had in just a few days, he phoned the broker and told him: 'Sell all my shares.'

The broker said: 'To whom? You were the only one buying that stock.'

A balding man went into a barber's shop and asked how much it would be for a haircut.

'Twenty-five dollars,' said the barber.

'Twenty-five dollars, that's outrageous!' said the man. 'I've hardly got any hair. How can it be that expensive?'

The barber explained: 'It's five dollars for the actual cut, and twenty dollars for the search fee.'

A woman was having a bad day at the casino. Down to her last fifty dollars, she exclaimed in exasperation: 'What lousy luck I've had today! What on earth am I going to do now? How can I turn it around?'

A man standing next to her at the roulette table suggested: 'I don't know. Why don't you play your age?' The man then wandered off.

But moments later his attention was grabbed by a great commotion at the roulette table. He rushed back and pushed his way through the crowd. The woman was lying limp on the floor with the table operator kneeling over her. The man was stunned.

'What happened?' he asked. 'Is she all right?'

The operator replied: 'I don't know. She put all her money on twenty-nine, and thirty-six came up. Then she just fainted!'

A building contractor was being paid weekly. As he opened his wage packet one week, he said to the site manager: 'But this is two hundred less than we agreed on.'

'I know,' said the manager, 'but last week I overpaid you by two hundred and you never complained.'

'Well,' explained the contractor, 'I don't mind an occasional mistake, but when it gets to be a habit, I feel I have to call it to your attention.'

A woman with a fifty dollar bill stuck in each ear went for a meeting with her bank manager.

'Mrs Smith is waiting outside,' the receptionist told the manager.

'Mrs Smith?' he said, looking through his files. 'Ah, yes. She's a hundred dollars in arrears.'

A one-dollar bill and a twenty-dollar bill met in a till. 'Where have you been?' asked the one-dollar bill. 'I haven't seen you around in ages.'

'I've been all over the world,' said the twenty-dollar bill. 'I've been hanging out at casinos, I went on a Mediterranean cruise and did the rounds of the ship, I came back to the US for a while, I went to a couple of baseball games, to the shopping mall, all kinds of places. What about you?'

The one-dollar bill said: 'Oh, you know, the same old stuff – church, church, church.'

A man complained to his friend: 'My wife is always asking me for more money. A month ago she asked me for a hundred dollars, two weeks ago she said she wanted two hundred dollars, and yesterday it was four hundred dollars.'

'What does she do with it all?' asked the friend.

'I don't know. I never give her any.'

The queue at the bank stretched right back to the door. A woman customer decided to save time by filling in a withdrawal slip while she was waiting, but she couldn't remember the date.

So she turned and asked the woman behind: 'What's the date

today?'

'It's the seventh.'

A man at the very back of the queue piped up: 'Don't write it in yet!'

A young woman told her father tearfully: 'Dad, you know you told me to put all my money in an account with that big bank? Well, that bank is now in trouble, and I don't know what I'm going to do!'

'That bank can't be in trouble,' said the father. 'It's one of the major players in the financial world. You must have got it wrong.'

'I don't think so,' she sobbed. 'They just returned one of my cheques with a note saying, "Insufficient Funds".'

A man, called to testify before the tax office, asked his accountant for advice as to what to wear for the hearing.

'Wear your scruffiest clothes,' said the accountant. 'Let them think you're a pauper.'

The man then asked his lawyer the same question, only to receive conflicting advice.

'Don't let them intimidate you,' said the lawyer. 'Wear your best suit.'

Confused, the man decided to consult his rabbi. 'Let me tell you a story,' said the rabbi. 'A girl who was about to be married asked her mother what to wear on her wedding night. The mother suggested: "Wear a heavy, long, flannel nightgown that goes right up to your neck." But the girl's best friend advised: "Wear your sexiest negligee."'

The man said: 'Yes, but what's all this got to do with my problem with the tax office?'

The rabbi replied: 'No matter what you wear, you are going to get screwed!'

On his first day with a finance company, a man was sent to try and sort out the firm's toughest client. To the amazement of his boss, he returned with the ten thousand dollars debt paid in full.

'How did you manage that?' asked the boss. 'We've been trying to get him to settle up for nine months.'

'It was easy. I simply told him that if he didn't pay us, I'd tell all his other creditors that he had!'

A man went into a bank and asked the cashier to check his balance. So the cashier pushed him over.

A shipping magnate decided to conduct a tour of his business to see how things were going. Going down to the docks, he noticed a young man leaning against the wall doing nothing.

Disgusted at this inactivity, the magnate walked up to the young man and said: 'How much do you make in a day, son?'

He replied: 'A hundred and fifty dollars.'

The magnate pulled out his wallet, gave him a hundred and fifty dollars and told him to clear off and never come back.

A few minutes later the shipping clerk came over to the magnate and asked: 'Have you seen that UPS driver? I asked him to wait here for me.'

A banker fell overboard while taking a cruise on a friend's yacht. The friend grabbed a lifebelt, held it up, and, not knowing if the banker could swim, shouted: 'Can you float alone?'

'Of course I can!' yelled the banker. 'But this is a heck of a time to talk business!'

A frog wanted to buy a new lily pond but had run out of money, so he went to the bank for a loan. He sat down at a desk and introduced himself as Kermit Jagger, son of Mick Jagger. He was interviewed by a bank official named Patty Whack who asked the frog what he could offer as collateral. The frog reached into his briefcase and produced a vase but Patty was unimpressed. 'I'm afraid we'll need something more than that,' she told the frog. 'It's just a cheap knick-knack.'

But just to cover herself, she decided to show the vase to the bank manager who claimed to know a thing or two about antiques. 'I've got this frog named Kermit Jagger,' she said, 'and he's brought this vase in as collateral. What do you think?'

The manager registered the name, took one look at the vase and said: 'It's a knick-knack, Patty Whack, but give the frog a loan. His old man's a Rolling Stone.'

Music

A tourist in Europe was walking through a graveyard when he suddenly heard music. With nobody around, he began searching for the source. He finally located the origin and discovered that it was coming from a grave with a headstone that read: Ludwig van Beethoven, 1770–1827. Then he realized that the music was the Ninth Symphony and that it was being played backwards. Puzzled, he left the graveyard and persuaded a friend to return with him.

By the time they arrived back at the grave, the music had changed. This time it was the Seventh Symphony but, like the previous piece, it was being played backwards. Curious, the men agreed to consult a music scholar. When they returned with the expert, the Fifth Symphony was playing, again backwards.

The expert noticed that the symphonies were being played in the reverse order to which they were composed – the Ninth, then the Seventh, then the Fifth. By the next day word of this strange phenomenon had spread, and a small crowd had gathered around Beethoven's grave. They were all listening to the Second Symphony being played backwards.

Just then the caretaker of the graveyard ambled up to the group. Someone in the crowd asked him if he had an explanation for the music.

'Oh, it's nothing to worry about,' said the caretaker. 'He's just decomposing.'

A Scotsman visited London on holiday but complained that the locals were unfriendly. He told his friends: 'At four o'clock every morning they hammered on the door of my hotel room, and on the walls, the floor and the ceiling. They hammered so loud I could hardly hear myself playing the bagpipes!'

Why do pipers march when they play? – To get as far away from the music as possible.

How are playing the bagpipes like throwing a javelin blindfold? – You don't have to be very good to get people's attention.

How can you tell if the bagpipes are out of tune? – Someone is blowing into them.

Following a late-night gig, an accordion player woke up in the morning and realized he had left his accordion on the back seat of his car, which was parked out in the street. Convinced that the instrument would have been stolen overnight, he dashed out in his pyjamas and, sure enough, saw that the side rear window of the car had been smashed. When he looked into the back seat, he saw that somebody had thrown in two more accordions.

If you drop an accordion, a set of bagpipes and a viola off a twenty-storey building, which one crashes to the ground first? – Who cares?

How can you tell that there's an accordionist at your front door? – He doesn't stop knocking even after you answer.

Why are an accordionist's fingers like lightning? – They rarely strike the same spot twice.

What is an accordion good for? – Learning how to fold a map.

A little boy thanked his grandfather for the recorder he bought him for his birthday. 'It's the best present I've ever had,' he said. 'It's already earned me sixty dollars.'

'Wow,' said the grandfather, 'you must have really learned to play it well.'

'No, I can't play a note,' said the boy. 'But Mom gives me five dollars not to play it during the day, and Dad gives me five dollars not to play it in the evening.'

Two intrepid explorers met in the heart of the Amazon jungle.

One said: 'I'm here to commune with nature in the raw, to contemplate the eternal truths and to widen my horizons. And what about you?'

The other said: 'I came because my daughter has started cello lessons.'

What's the range of a cello? – Twenty yards if you've got a good arm.

What's the difference between a cello and a chainsaw? – The grip.

An explorer in Indonesia was seeking out a remote tribe thought to be hostile to strangers. He sought the services of a local guide to act as translator and, if necessary, peacemaker.

At dusk on the first day the pair were sitting around a campfire when they heard the sound of tribal drums in the distance. The drums got louder. The guide admitted: 'I don't like the sound of those drums.'

As dusk turned to evening, the drums got even louder. The guide said: 'I really don't like the sound of those drums.'

Evening turned to dead of night and still the drums got louder. It was obvious that they were very close. The guide repeated: 'I really do not like the sound of those drums.'

Suddenly the drums stopped and a voice from the darkness cried out: 'Hey, man, he's not our regular drummer!'

Why are orchestra intermissions limited to twenty minutes? – So you don't have to retrain the drummers.

What's the difference between a drum kit and a lawnmower? – The neighbours are upset if you borrow a lawnmower and don't return it.

What's the difference between a pizza and a drummer? – A pizza can feed a family of four.

What's the difference between a drummer and a vacuum cleaner? – You have to plug one of them in before it sucks.

How is a drum solo like a sneeze? – You can tell it's coming, but you can't do anything about it.

If a drummer and a bass guitarist caught a cab, which one would be the musician? – The cab driver.

Why is a drum machine better than a drummer? – Because it can keep a steady beat and won't sleep with your girlfriend.

What's the last thing a drummer says in a band? – 'Hey, guys, why don't we try one of my songs?'

What did the drummer get on his IQ test? – Drool.

Fed up with drummer jokes, a drummer decided to take up the accordion. So he went to a music shop and asked to see the accordions.
   'Certainly,' said the clerk, 'they're over there.'
   'I'll have the big red one in the corner,' said the drummer.
   The clerk looked at him quizzically. 'You're a drummer, aren't you?'
   'Yes. How did you know?'
   'That "big red accordion" is a radiator!'

A man said to the bartender in a music bar: 'How late does the band play?'
   He replied: 'About a half-beat behind the drummer.'

You Might Be a Drummer If:
   You insist on spending an hour tuning your snare, even though no one can hear the difference.
   You tell a group of people singing and clapping 'Happy Birthday' at a restaurant that they are out of tempo.
   Your style of dancing involves slapping your thighs and pounding your feet.
   You play the drum part on a song and ask someone if they recognize the song.
   You've ever dropped a stick while playing and not noticed.
   While driving, you accidentally slam on the brake or accelerator, mistaking it for a bass drum pedal.
   You play soft rock songs on the steering wheel.
   Your drum kit costs more than your car.
   Your house constantly vibrates.
   You've ever tried to show your guitarist a riff using your drum kit.
   You were kicked out of your school band for always insisting on a solo.
   Twenty per cent of last year's income was spent on new cymbals.
   You've ever taken longer than thirty seconds to realize that the rest of your band has stopped playing.

You've ever set your pants on fire because a cigarette fell out of your mouth and you carried on playing anyway.

You've ever tried to play another instrument with drumsticks.

In a bid to keep his customers entertained, a bar owner hired a pianist and a drummer. However after discovering that the drummer had stolen some valuables from the upstairs accommodation, the owner was forced to call in the police.

Desperate for a replacement drummer, the bar owner then rang a friend who knew some musicians.

'What happened to the drummer you had?' asked the friend.

'I had him arrested.'

The friend said: 'How badly did he play?'

What's the difference between trombone players and government bonds? – Government bonds eventually mature and earn money.

What's the difference between a dead trombone player lying in the road and a dead squirrel lying in the road? – The squirrel might have been on his way to a gig.

How do you know when there's a trombonist at your door? – His hat says 'Domino's Pizza'.

What kind of calendar does a trombonist use for his gigs? – Year-at-a-glance.

A guy playing trombone in the opera was suddenly offered an unexpected gig at a prestigious jazz club on one of the days that he was supposed to be performing at the opera house. The gig was just too good to turn down, so he tried to find a fellow trombonist to replace him at the opera. Unable to find anyone, as a last resort he persuaded his accountant to stand in for him.

'I'll give you my other trombone,' he said. 'All you have to do is copy what the guy next to you is doing. It'll be fine.'

The next day he asked the accountant how it went.

'Terrible. Your colleague also sent his accountant to replace him!'

What's the definition of perfect pitch in a piccolo? – When you throw it in the toilet and it doesn't hit the rim.

Why are harps like elderly parents? – They're both unforgiving and hard to get in and out of cars.

An anthropologist visited a remote tropical island to investigate the natives. Accompanied by a guide, he travelled upriver to a clearing and pitched camp. Ominously in the distance he began to hear drums.
    'What are those drums?' he asked the guide.
    The guide turned to him and said: 'Drums okay, but when drums stop, very bad.'
    Three hours later the drumming suddenly stopped. Mindful of the guide's warning, the anthropologist began to panic. 'The drums have stopped,' he yelled. 'What happens now?'
    The guide crouched down, covered his head with his hands and said: 'Bass solo.'

What's the difference between a French horn and a '57 Chevy? – You can tune a '57 Chevy.

Two men were sentenced to die in the electric chair on the same day. The prison warden asked the first man: 'Do you have any last requests?'
    'Yes,' he said. 'Could you play me "The Birdie Song" one last time?'
    'Sure,' said the warden. Then he turned to the second man and said: 'And what's your final request?'
    'I'd like to go first.'

What's the definition of an optimist? – A folk musician with a mortgage.

A girl went on a date with a trumpet player. When she got home, her roommate wanted to know how it went.
    'Did his embouchure make him a great kisser?'
    'No, that dry, tiny, tight little pucker was no fun at all.'
    The next night she went out with a tuba player. When she got home, her roommate asked what he was like as a kisser.
    'Horrible. Those huge rubbery, slobbering lips were gross.'
    The following night she went out with a French horn player. When she got home, her roommate was eager to hear all the details.
    'Was he a good kisser?' she asked.
    'His kissing was so-so, but I just loved the way he held me!'

Why are conductor's hearts so coveted for transplants? – They've had so little use.

Why is a conductor like a condom? – It's safer with one, but more fun without.

A conductor was having a lot of trouble with one drummer. He talked and talked with the drummer, but his performance showed no sign of improving. Finally, in front of the whole orchestra, the conductor declared sarcastically: 'When a musician just can't handle his instrument and doesn't improve when given help, they take away the instrument, give him two sticks, and make him a drummer!'

A voice from the percussion section whispered loudly: 'And if he can't handle that, they take away one of his sticks and make him a conductor.'

Conductor: You should have taken up the viola earlier.

Viola student: Why, do you think the practice would have made me really good?

Conductor: No, but you might have given up by now.

A viola player came home late at night to find police cars and fire trucks outside his house. The chief of police intercepted him.

'I'm afraid I have some terrible news for you,' said the chief. 'While you were out, the conductor came to your house, killed your family and burned your house down.'

The viola player was stunned. 'You're kidding! The conductor came to my house?'

What do a lawsuit and a viola have in common? – Everyone is much happier when the case is closed.

What's the difference between a violin and a viola? – No difference. The violin just looks smaller because the violinist's head is bigger.

What's the difference between a violinist and a dog? – A dog knows when to stop scratching.

While a small boy was practising the violin in the living room, his father was desperately trying to read the paper. But as the boy scraped away tunelessly at the instrument, the family dog howled incessantly.

Finally the father lost patience and said to the boy: 'Can't you play something the dog doesn't know?'

What do you get when you drop a piano on an army base? – A flat major.

A woman answered the door to find a workman, complete with tool box, standing on the porch.
'I'm the piano tuner, madam,' he announced.
'But I didn't send for a piano tuner!'
'I know, but your neighbours did!'

Why is a bassoon better than an oboe? – A bassoon burns longer.

What is a burning oboe good for? – Setting a bassoon on fire.

How do you get a lead guitarist to stop playing? – Put sheet music in front of him.

How many baritones does it take to change a light bulb? – None. They can't get up that high.

What is the difference between a duet and a duel? – There is no difference.

How can you tell there's a singer at your front door? – She forgot the key and doesn't know when to come in.

What happens if you play country music backwards? – Your wife returns to you, your dog comes back to life, and you get out of prison.

Three men died and went up to heaven where they found themselves in a queue at the Pearly Gates. The angel responsible for admissions on this particular day warned that, because a few undesirables had managed to sneak in recently, the rules for entry had been tightened and she now had to ask each applicant their profession and annual salary.
    The first man in line announced: 'I made a hundred and fifty thousand last year as a bank manager.'
    'Very good,' said the angel. 'In you go.' And he was admitted to heaven.

The second man stated: 'I made ninety-five thousand last year as a head teacher.'

'Yes, that's fine,' said the angel. 'Through you go.'

The third man said: 'My annual salary last year was eight thousand.'

'Cool,' said the angel. 'Which instrument do you play?'

Tom had been drinking at the bar for four hours when a band of musicians began hauling their equipment onto the small pub stage. Tom swore to himself, cursing the fact that the landlord insisted on interrupting his quiet drink with a band every single Friday. He was in a foul mood anyway following a blazing row with his wife and by the time the band started playing, the combination of drink and anger made for a dangerous cocktail. Whereas others cheered the band's efforts, Tom simply jeered.

Eventually having exhausted their basic repertoire, the musicians asked if any of the audience had any requests. Half a dozen voices shouted out, including Tom who yelled: 'Play "Tiger Feet" or get off!'

The band conferred and played 'Tiger Feet.' Then the singer asked if there were any more requests. Tom shouted out: 'Play "Tiger Feet" again!' Since there were no other requests, they did a reprise of 'Tiger Feet', albeit a slightly shorter version. At the end of the song, the singer asked the dwindling audience: 'Has anyone got one last request?'

Tom bellowed drunkenly: 'Play "Tiger Feet" again!'

'Come on, mate,' said the singer. 'We've played it for you twice.'

'Sing bloody "Tiger Feet",' growled Tom menacingly.

'We just have – twice,' the singer pointed out.

'And you're gonna play it again!' demanded Tom, rising uneasily to his feet, 'or I'm gonna sort you out.' But as he lunged aggressively in the general direction of the stage, he stumbled over a stool, slipped on a pool of beer and fell, knocking his head on the corner of the stage, and cracking his skull. All of which only goes to demonstrate the wisdom of the old proverb . . . You should never fight the band that heeds you.

A movie director was testing Sylvester Stallone and Arnold Schwarzenegger for a new film about classical composers.

The director said to Stallone: 'Who do you fancy playing, Sly?'

Stallone looked down the list of characters and said: 'I'd like to play Mozart.'

Then the director turned to Schwarzenegger. Arnie said simply: 'I'll be Bach.'

Occupations

A man was flying in a hot air balloon when he became aware that he was lost. So he reduced height until he was able to call out to a man on the ground: 'Can you help me? I promised my friend I would meet him half an hour ago, but I don't know where I am.'

The man on the ground said: 'You are in a hot air balloon, hovering approximately twenty-five feet above this field. You are between latitude thirty-six and thirty-eight degrees north and between longitude forty and forty-five degrees east.'

'You must be an engineer,' said the balloonist.

'Yes. How did you know?'

'Well,' said the balloonist, 'everything you have told me is technically correct, but I have no idea what to make of you information, and the fact is I am still lost.'

The man on the ground said: 'And you must be a manager,'

'That's right,' said the balloonist. 'How did you know?'

'Because you don't know where you are or where you are going. You have made a promise that you cannot keep, and you expect me to solve your problem. The fact is that you are in the same position you were in before we met, but now it is somehow my fault.'

A social worker asked a colleague: 'What time is it?'

The other one answered: 'Sorry, I don't know, I'm not wearing a watch.'

'Never mind,' said the first. 'The main thing is that we talked about it.'

What is the difference between God and a social worker? – God doesn't pretend to be a social worker.

A social worker was walking home late at night when she was confronted by a mugger with a gun.

'Your money or your life!' snarled the mugger.

'I'm sorry,' she replied. 'I'm a social worker, so I have no money and no life.'

The Devil told a salesman: 'I can make you richer, more famous, and more successful than any salesman alive. In fact, I can make you the greatest salesman that ever lived.'

Intrigued, the salesman asked: 'What do I have to do in return?'

The Devil replied: 'You not only have to give me your soul, but you also have to give me the souls of your children, the souls of your children's children and indeed the souls of all your descendants throughout eternity.'

'Wait a minute,' said the salesman. 'What's the catch?'

A priest, a vicar and a consultant were travelling by plane when it suffered total engine failure. It was obvious that the plane was going to crash and all three would be killed. The priest began to pray and finger his rosary beads, the vicar began to pray and read the Bible, and the consultant began to organize a committee on air traffic safety.

A man trained in origami for eight years and opened a shop in London. But the business folded.

A tourist was browsing around a pet shop when a customer came in and said: 'Have you got a C monkey?'

The shopkeeper nodded, went over to a large cage at the side of the shop and took out a monkey. Fitting a collar and leash to the monkey, he told the customer: 'That will be five thousand dollars.' The customer paid and left with the monkey.

Startled, the tourist went over to the shopkeeper and said: 'That was a very expensive monkey – most of them are only priced at a few hundred dollars. What was so special about it?'

The shopkeeper replied: 'That monkey is invaluable to computer buffs. It can program in C with very fast, tight code, no bugs. Believe me, it's well worth the money.'

The tourist started to look at the other monkeys in the shop. Pointing at the same cage, he said to the shopkeeper: 'That monkey's even more expensive, ten thousand dollars. What does it do?'

'Oh,' said the shopkeeper, 'that one's a C ++ monkey. It can manage more complex programming, even some Java, all the really useful stuff.'

Then the tourist spotted a third monkey, in a cage of its own. The price tag around its neck said fifty thousand dollars. 'What on earth does that one do,' he asked, 'to justify that sort of price?'

The shopkeeper said: 'I don't know if it actually *does* anything. But it says it's a consultant.'

Insurance Agent Translations:

He says: I'll look into that.

He means: I want to see if you've paid your last premium before I spend any more time with you.

He says: Why don't I call you back tomorrow.

He means: I'm playing golf this afternoon.

He says: I really can't refer you to another person.

He means: I hate anyone muscling in on my commission.

He says: That's quite an extensive list of losses.

He means: I think I'm going to throw up.

He says: Everything looks in order with your policy.

He means: Damn!

He says: If I don't call you back by next week, give me a call.

He means: I don't know what the hell to do. Maybe you will forget until the policy runs out.

He says: This may take a little time.

He means: Last week two of my clients moved into retirement homes.

He says: I'd like to check with my supervisor on this first.

He means: I can't figure out what's wrong with these numbers. Maybe the new kid with the degree knows what to do.

He says: I have some good news and some bad news.

He means: The good news is that I'm going to buy that new BMW, and the bad news is that you're going to be paying for it.

A civil servant was sitting in his office when out of boredom he decided to see what was in an old filing cabinet. Poking through the dusty contents, he came across an old brass lamp and thought that it would look nice on his mantelpiece at home. So he took it home and while polishing it, a genie suddenly appeared from the lamp and granted him three wishes.

'I wish for an ice cold beer right now,' he began modestly, 'to help me with my next two wishes.'

He received his beer and drank it, then turned his thoughts to his second wish. 'I wish to be on an island inhabited only by beautiful women.'

As if by magic, he found himself on a tropical island surrounded by gorgeous women.

'And what is your third wish?' asked the genie.

The civil servant thought for a second and said: 'I wish I'd never have to work again.'

And POOF! He was back in his office.

At the construction site of a new church, the contractor stopped to chat with one of his workmen.

'Paddy,' he said, 'didn't you once tell me you had a brother who was a bishop?'

'That I did,' said Paddy.

'And yet you are a bricklayer. It sure is a funny old world. Things in life aren't divided equally, are they?'

'That they're not,' agreed Paddy as he proudly slapped the mortar along the line of bricks. 'My poor brother couldn't do this to save his life!'

Three engineers and three accountants were travelling by train. 'I can't get over how expensive my ticket was,' said one of the accountants. 'Forty dollars for such a short journey.'

'You should do what we do,' advised the chief engineer. 'We three always travel together but only ever buy one ticket. That way, we pay a third of the price each.'

The accountant was mystified. 'But how do you get away with only buying one ticket? The ticket collector always comes round.'

'It's easy,' said the engineer. 'Watch this.'

At the first sign of the ticket collector, the three engineers huddled into the train toilet and shut the door. When the collector knocked on the door and called 'Ticket please', a single arm held out one ticket. The collector stamped the ticket and went on his way.

The accountant was impressed and, knowing a thing or two about money, decided that he and his two colleagues should try the same trick the next time they travelled together. So the accountants bought just one ticket between them. The engineers happened to be on the same train and, to the accountants' surprise, hadn't even bought one ticket this time.

'You'll never get away with that,' warned the accountants.

'You wait and see,' replied the engineers.

When the ticket collector approached, both groups squeezed together in separate toilets and shut the doors. Then one of the engineers knocked on the door of the toilet in which the accountants were hiding and said: 'Ticket please.'

Jim was fired from his construction job.

'What happened?' asked his friend Ken.

'Well,' explained Jim. 'You know what a foreman is? The one who stands around watching the other men work?'

'Yes. What of it?'

'Well, he got jealous of me. Everyone thought I was the foreman!'

What kind of aftershave do genetic scientists wear? – Eau de clone.

A clerk in a drugstore was a hopeless salesman. He never seemed able to find the item that the customer wanted. His ineptitude reached the point where the owner warned him that the next missed sale would be his last.

Just then, a man came in coughing and asked the clerk for the best cough syrup. Try as he might, the clerk was unable to find the cough syrup, but, remembering his boss's warning, he sold the man a box of Ex-Lax and told him to take it all at once. The customer downed the contents as instructed before walking outside and leaning against a lamppost.

The shop owner came over to ask the clerk what had happened. The clerk explained: 'He wanted something for his cough but I couldn't find the cough syrup. So I substituted Ex-Lax and told him to take it all at once.'

'You fool!' yelled the owner. 'Ex-Lax won't cure a cough!'

'Sure it will,' said the clerk, pointing at the man leaning on the lamppost. 'Look at him. He's afraid to cough.'

A farmer received a visit from a government official over allegations that he was paying his staff less than the minimum wage. The official asked him for a list of his employees and details of their pay.

'All right,' said the farmer. 'I have a hired man, been with me for three years. I pay him six hundred a week, plus room and board. There's a cook – she's been here six months. She gets five hundred a week, plus room and board.'

'Anybody else?' asked the official as he scribbled on a pad.

'Yeah,' said the farmer. 'There's one guy here is none too bright. He works about eighteen hours a day. I pay him ten dollars a week and a bit of beer money.'

'Aha!' roared the official. 'That's the man I want to talk to!'

'Speaking,' said the farmer.

Preparing for the most important presentation of his life, a sales representative went to see a psychiatrist.

'I'll implant a hypnotic suggestion in your mind,' said the doctor. 'Just say "one-two-three" and you'll give your best-ever presentation. However, do not say "one-two-three-four" because it will cause you to freeze and make a complete fool of yourself.'

The sales rep was delighted. He tried it at home and gave a fabulous presentation. He tried it at work and received a standing ovation. Then came the big day. Everything was set up in the boardroom and the managing director signalled him to start.

The sales rep whispered under his breath: 'One-two-three.'

Then the managing director asked: 'What did you say "one-two-three" for?'

All through veterinary school, an aspiring vet made ends meet by working nights as a taxidermist. When he finally graduated, he decided to combine the two vocations in the hope not only of providing a more comprehensive service to his customers but also of doubling his income. So he opened his own offices with a sign on the door saying: 'Dr Brunskill: Veterinary Medicine and Taxidermy – Either Way You Get Your Dog Back!'

'Alec is so forgetful,' complained a sales manager to his secretary. 'It's a wonder he can sell anything. He's becoming a liability. I asked him to pick me up some sandwiches on his way back from lunch, but no doubt he'll have forgotten!'

A few minutes later Alec bounded in. 'Guess what?' he beamed. 'I was at lunch and who should I bump into but Clive Morris, an old

school friend. It turns out that he's head of a chain of stores that are
starting up next month on the south coast, and he's agreed to put a
huge order our way. It could be worth a couple of million over the next
twelve months. How about that!'

The sales manager turned to his secretary and said: 'See, I told you
he'd forget the sandwiches.'

Two nuclear physicists got married recently. The ceremony was
beautiful – she was absolutely radiant, and he was glowing too. Even
the bridesmaids shone.

The head of admissions at a school of agriculture asked a prospective
student: 'Why have you chosen this career?'

The student replied: 'I dream of making a million dollars from
farming, like my father.'

The head was impressed. 'Your father made a million dollars from
farming?'

'No, but he always dreamed of it.'

An engineer, a psychologist and a theologian were hunting in the
wilderness of northern Canada. Suddenly the temperature dropped and
a fierce snowstorm was upon them. Through the blizzard, they spotted
an isolated cabin and, having been told that the locals were hospitable,
they knocked on the door in the hope of obtaining respite from the
weather. Nobody answered their knocking but when they tried the
door, they found that it was unlocked and so they ventured inside.

The cabin was of basic layout, with nothing out of the ordinary
except for the stove. It was large, pot-bellied and made of cast iron but
what made it so unusual was its location – it was suspended in midair
by wires attached to the ceiling beams.

'Fascinating,' said the psychologist. 'It is obvious that this lonely
trapper, isolated from humanity, has elevated this stove so that he can
curl up under it and vicariously experience a return to the womb.'

'Nonsense!' replied the engineer. 'The man is practising the laws of
thermodynamics. By elevating his stove, he has discovered a way to
distribute heat more evenly throughout the cabin.'

'With all due respect,' interrupted the theologian, 'I'm sure that
hanging his stove from the ceiling has religious significance. Fire
lifted up has been a religious symbol for centuries.'

The three debated the point for several hours without resolving
the issue. When the cabin owner finally returned, they immediately

asked him why he had hung his heavy, pot-bellied stove from the ceiling.

He answered simply: 'Had plenty of wire, not much stove pipe.'

A man went to the dentist to have a tooth extracted.

'Don't worry,' said the dentist. 'This won't hurt much. What do you do for a living?'

'I'm a tax inspector.'

'Actually,' said the dentist, 'this might hurt a little more than I thought . . .'

A stockbroker's secretary answered the phone. 'I'm sorry, Mr Johnson is on another line.'

The caller said: 'This is Mr Stewart. I want to know if he's bullish or bearish right now.'

'He's talking to his wife,' said the secretary. 'Right now I'd say he was sheepish!'

Three boys were standing in the school playground bragging about their fathers.

One said: 'My dad scribbles a few words on a piece of paper, he calls it a poem, and they give him five hundred dollars.'

The second said: 'That's nothing. My dad scribbles a few words on a piece of paper, he calls it a song, and they give him a thousand dollars.'

The third said: 'I got you both beat. My dad scribbles a few words on a piece of paper, he calls it a sermon, and it takes eight people to collect all the money.'

The boss on a building site ordered one of his men to dig a hole six feet deep. After the job was done, the boss returned and explained that there had been a mistake and the hole wouldn't be needed after all. So he ordered the man to fill it in.

The worker did as he was told, but couldn't get all the soil packed back into the hole without leaving a mound on top. He went back to the office and explained his problem.

The boss snorted: 'Honestly! What sort of idiots do we employ these days? Obviously you didn't dig the hole deep enough!'

On his first day working part-time at the Post Office, a young man was given the job of sorting the mail. He sifted through the sacks of mail in record time, a feat which did not go unnoticed by his supervisor who said at the end of the day: 'Well done. You're one of the quickest workers we've ever had.'

The young man said: 'Thank you. And tomorrow I'll try to do even better.'

The supervisor was staggered. 'How could you possibly better what you have achieved today?'

The young man replied: 'Tomorrow I'm going to read the addresses.'

A doctor phoned a plumber in the middle of the night. 'What are you ringing me for at this hour?' asked the plumber.

'It's an emergency,' said the doctor. 'If it was the other way round, you'd expect me to come out, wouldn't you? So put yourself in my shoes.'

'Okay,' said the plumber. 'What's the problem?'

'The pipe under the kitchen sink is leaking.'

'All right,' said the plumber. 'Give it two aspirin and call me again in the morning if it's not better.'

Why don't actors stare out the window in the morning? – Because if they did, they'd have nothing to do in the afternoon.

On land by the Cheyenne River an enterprising Native American founded a business manufacturing crepe paper. Using modern equipment and Internet marketing techniques, he established a reputation for quality paper printed with traditional tribal designs.

As word of this unique product spread, it reached the ears of a New York gourmet who was planning a retirement party for a friend. Logging on to the Internet, he ordered what he thought was going to be twenty sets of designer-pattern crepe paper. However when the shipment arrived, it turned out that the order had been incorrectly entered as twenty *cases* of crepe paper.

Assuming his habitual restaurant demeanour, he bellowed at an assistant: 'Send this back. The Crepe Sioux Sets have been grossly overdone!'

A woman attending evening computer classes was relieved to find that she had a female teacher instead of the male head of department.

When she relayed this information to the teacher, the latter was flattered, if a little surprised. 'My colleague is far more experienced than me,' she admitted.

'Yes,' said the woman, 'but I feel much more comfortable with you – I get nervous around really smart people.'

A wealthy woman was throwing a lavish garden party attended by the cream of local society. While dignitaries and minor celebrities enjoyed themselves, two gardeners were busy weeding a flower border behind a low hedge.

As a guest watched, one gardener suddenly leaped high and did the splits in mid-air. Impressed by the spring in his heels and his obvious athleticism, the guest remarked to the host: 'That man is such a talented dancer. I'll pay him five hundred dollars to dance at my next party.'

When the host mentioned the suggestion to the other gardener, he called over to his colleague: 'Hey, Ted, do you think for five hundred dollars you could step on that rake again?'

An unemployed man was desperate to support his family. His wife did nothing but watch TV all day while his three teenage kids had dropped out of high school to hang around with the local troublemakers. His options limited, he applied for a janitor's job at a large company and easily passed the aptitude test.

The human resources manager told him: 'You will be hired at a minimum wage of five dollars an hour. Let me know your e-mail address so that we can get you in the loop. Our system will automatically e-mail you all the forms, and advise you when to start and where to report on your first day.'

But the man pointed out that he was too poor to afford a computer, and that therefore he didn't have an e-mail address. The manager replied icily: 'Surely you must realize that to a company like ours, not having an e-mail address means that you virtually cease to exist. Without e-mail you can hardly expect to be employed by a hi-tech firm. Good day.'

Stunned and dismayed, the man left. Not knowing which way to turn and with just ten dollars left in his wallet, he walked past a market wholesaler and saw a trader selling twenty-five-pound crates of beautiful red tomatoes. So he bought a crate, carried it to a busy street corner and began selling them. In less than two hours he sold all the tomatoes and made a hundred per cent profit. Repeating the process several more times that day, he finished up with nearly a hundred dollars and arrived home that night with several bags of groceries for his hungry family.

Not surprisingly, he decided to repeat the tomato business the next day, and by working long hours he quickly multiplied his profits. By the second week he had invested in a cart and two weeks later he bought a broken-down pickup truck. At the end of the year he owned three trucks. His two sons had left their neighbourhood gangs to help him with the tomato business, his wife was buying the tomatoes, and his daughter was taking night courses in accountancy at the local college so that she could keep his books.

After five years, he owned a fleet of trucks and a warehouse, which his wife supervized, plus two tomato farms managed by the boys. The tomato company's payroll gave work to hundreds of homeless and jobless people. His daughter reported that the business grossed a million dollars. Planning for the future, he decided to buy some life insurance and, with the help of an insurance adviser, he picked a plan that suited his newfound wealth. Then the adviser asked him for his e-mail address in order to send the final documents electronically.

When the man replied that he didn't have time to mess with a computer and had no e-mail address, the insurance advisor was stunned. 'What? No computer? No Internet? No e-mail? Just think where you would be today if you'd had all of that five years ago!'

'Ha!' snorted the man. 'If I'd had e-mail five years ago, I would be sweeping floors at a multinational computer company and making five dollars an hour.'

Two construction workers were toiling away on a swelteringly hot day. Pointing to the supervisor, Mick said to Dave: 'How come we do all the work while he sits in the shade under the tree and gets all the money?'

Dave replied: 'I don't know. Why don't you go and ask him?'

So Mick went over to the supervisor and said: 'Hey, how come we do all the work while you sit in the shade under the tree and get all the money?'

The supervisor answered simply: 'Intelligence.'

Mick looked bemused. 'What do you mean, intelligence?'

The supervisor said: 'I'll show you.' He put his hand on the bark of the tree and said: 'Hit my hand as hard as you can.'

Mick summoned up all his strength and pent-up frustration and prepared to land the hardest punch he could muster. But just before he made contact, the supervisor pulled his hand away, leaving Mick to crash his fist into the tree.

As Mick nursed his sore hand, the supervisor smiled: 'That's intelligence.'

Still smarting, Mick went back to Dave who asked: 'What did he say?'

With a wry grin, Mick promised to explain. He looked around for a tree but couldn't find one. So he put his hand on his face and said: 'Hit my hand as hard as you can . . .'

A team of archaeologists were excavating in Israel when they found a cave with the symbols of a woman, a donkey, a shovel, a fish, and a Star of David on the wall.

Pointing to the first drawing, the head of the team declared: 'This indicates that these people were family oriented and held women in high esteem. The donkey shows that they were intelligent enough to use animals to till the soil. The shovel means that they were able to forge tools. Even further proof of high intelligence is the fish: if famine hit the land, they would take to the sea for food. The last symbol is the Star of David, telling us they were Hebrews.'

However one of his fellow archaeologists begged to disagree. 'Hebrew is read from right to left,' he explained. 'The symbols say: "Holy Mackerel, Dig the Ass on that Chick!"'

You Know You Work For The Government When:
    The process becomes more important than the product.
    You don't see anything wrong with attending a meeting on a subject you know nothing about.
    You feel that you contributed to a meeting just by being there.
    You stop raising issue or problems because you know you will be the one having to address them.
    You and at least a dozen colleagues fly first-class to a foreign country and stay in a five-star hotel to attend a four-day conference to discuss how best to implement the latest economy drive.
    You work for an acronym, on an acronym, and jour job title is an acronym.
    You know that the location of a meeting is directly related to its importance.
    You don't laugh at phrases like 'think tank' or 'focus group'.
    You have sat at the same desk for three years, done the same thing for three years, but have had three different business cards.

Set in his ways, a man went to the same hairdresser every month, this despite the fact that the hairdresser had the annoying habit of belittling whatever his customers said. One month the customer said he had bought a new car.
    'What sort?' asked the hairdresser.

'A Mercedes,' replied the customer.

The hairdresser was quick to pour cold water on the purchase. 'You shouldn't have got a Mercedes,' he sneered. 'A Ferrari is much classier and with a more comfortable interior. No, you'd be better off with a Ferrari.'

The following month the customer revealed that he had bought an executive house on a new development on the outskirts of town. 'Oh, you don't want to move there,' said the hairdresser. 'It's in the middle of nowhere. There are no amenities nearby, and I've heard the land is liable to subsidence. You see, they'll be giving those houses away soon.'

At his next appointment, the customer said that he was going on holiday to Rome.

'What do you want to go to Rome for?' asked the hairdresser. 'There's nothing much there. It's all ruins. No, if you must go to Italy, go to Florence.'

'As a matter of fact,' said the customer, struggling to get a word in, 'it's always been my ambition to meet the Pope and, if possible, to get to speak to him.'

'You speak to the Pope?' mocked the hairdresser. 'You've got no chance. You won't get anywhere near him. I'll bet you two hundred dollars that the Pope doesn't talk to you.'

The customer was so fed up with the hairdresser's attitude that he accepted the bet. A month later he returned for his next haircut and was asked how he had got on in Rome.

'Don't forget our two hundred dollars bet,' crowed the hairdresser. 'You can pay by cheque.'

'No, actually you owe me two hundred dollars,' said the customer. 'The Pope did speak to me.'

'How did you manage that?' demanded the hairdresser indignantly.

'Well,' said the customer, 'I was wandering around St. Peter's Square one morning hoping to catch a glimpse of the Pope when, to my surprise, I saw him walking towards me. And then amazingly he stopped beside me and began talking to me.'

'What did he say?' asked the hairdresser.

'He said: "Where on earth did you get that terrible haircut?"'

A salesman was demonstrating an unbreakable comb in a department store. After twisting it and pulling it, he tried to show how amazingly flexible it was by bending it completely in half. Unfortunately the comb immediately snapped in two with a resounding crack. Without missing a beat, the salesman held up both halves of the supposedly unbreakable comb for everyone to see, and said bravely: 'And this, ladies and gentlemen, is what an unbreakable comb looks like on the inside . . .'

A guy was telling a friend about his time working at a large company. 'I tell you, it didn't matter if it was the managing director, the vice presidents or whatever, I always told those guys where to get off.'
'What was your job again?' asked the friend.
'I was the lift operator.'

A farmer was ploughing his field when his well-meaning but somewhat inept son came to help him.
'Dad, I'd like to do some ploughing.'
'I don't know, son. It takes a steady hand.'
'Please, I want to help.'
The farmer reluctantly agreed and handed the boy some tools but when he came to check the work an hour later, he found that the line was very erratic.
'Your line is as crooked as can be,' said the farmer.'
'But I was watching the plough to make sure that I kept straight,' said the son.
'That's the problem. Don't look at the plough. You have to watch where you're going. Look at the other end of the field, pick out one object, head straight for it and you'll cut a straight line every time. I'm going to get a drink of water, so can you handle it now?'
'Sure, dad.'
When the farmer returned, he saw to his horror that the son had cut the worst row he had ever seen. It went all over the field in curves and circles. The farmer ran up to his son and stopped him.
'What happened?' he yelled. 'I've never seen a worse looking field in my life. There's not one straight line!'
'But I did what you said,' insisted the son. 'I fixed my sights on that dog playing on the other side of the field.'

What is the definition of an extroverted accountant? – One who looks at your shoes while he's talking to you instead of his own.

A mechanical engineer, a chemical engineer, an electrical engineer and a computer engineer were travelling along the road when their car broke down.

The mechanical engineer said: 'Sounds to me like the pistons have seized. We'll have to strip down the engine before we can get the car working again.'

The chemical engineer begged to differ. 'It sounded to me as if the fuel might be contaminated. I think we should clear out the fuel system.'

'Well, I think it might be a grounding problem,' said the electrical engineer, 'or maybe a faulty plug lead.'

Having offered their opinions, the three turned to the computer engineer who was strangely silent on the matter. 'What do you think?' they asked.

'Hmmm,' said the computer engineer. 'Perhaps if we all get out of the car and get back in again?'

Ben and Aaron had started out with only five hundred dollars between them, but they had built up a computer business with sales in the millions. Their company employed over three hundred staff, and the two executives lived like princes.

But almost overnight things changed. Sales dropped alarmingly, major customers deserted them and the company plunged into freefall. Eventually personal debts forced both men into bankruptcy. Ben and Aaron each blamed the other for their predicament, and the parting of the ways was distinctly acrimonious.

Five years later, Ben drove up to a decrepit roadside diner and stopped for a cup of coffee. As he was discreetly wiping some crumbs from the table, a waiter approached. Ben looked up and gasped.

'Aaron!' he said, shaking his head in a patronizing manner. 'It's a terrible thing, seeing you working in a place as bad as this.'

'Yeah,' said Aaron, smiling thinly. 'But at least I don't eat here.'

Did you hear about the man who started writing poetry as soon as he got up in the morning? – He went from bed to verse.

Three former Post Office workers were out fishing on a lake one day when Jesus walked across the water and joined them in their boat. The three men were amazed.

The first said humbly: 'I've suffered from back pain ever since I lifted a heavy cabinet at work. Can you help me?'

'Of course, my son,' said Jesus, and when he touched the man's back, he felt relief for the first time in twelve years.

The second man, who wore thick glasses, said to Jesus: 'I haven't been able to see properly since some cleaning fluid sprayed into my face at work. Is there anything you can do to help?'

Jesus smiled, removed the man's glasses and tossed them into the lake. As soon as the glasses hit the water, the man's eyes cleared and he was able to see perfectly for the first time in ten years.

Then Jesus turned to the third man who immediately put up his arms defensively and cried: 'Don't touch me – I'm on a disability pension!'

A man was employed as a security guard at a factory where there had been a spate of thefts by workers on the night shift. Every morning when the night shift workers passed through his gate, it was his job to check their bags and pockets to make sure that nothing was being stolen.

On the first night, all was quiet until a man pushing a wheelbarrow full of newspapers came through his gate. The guard's suspicions were aroused at once. Convinced that the man was hiding something beneath the newspapers, he searched beneath them but found nothing. Nevertheless he still felt that the man was acting strangely, so he questioned him further about the cargo.

The man said: 'I get a little extra money from recycling newspapers, so I go into the canteen and pick up all the ones that people have discarded.'

The guard accepted the explanation for the time being, but resolved to keep a close eye on him in future.

The next night it was the same, and the night after that. Week after week it went on. The same guy would push the wheelbarrow of newspapers past the guard's checkpoint. The guard would always check the contents and find nothing. Then one night, about a year later, the guard reported for work only to find a message had been left ordering him to go straight to the supervisor's office. He walked into the office but before he could say a word, the supervisor shouted: 'You're fired!'

'Fired?' he asked, stunned. 'Why? What have I done wrong?'

'It was your job to make sure that no one stole anything from this plant, and you have failed miserably. So you're fired.'

'Hang on, what do you mean – failed? Nobody has stolen anything from this place while I've been on duty.'

'Oh, really?' said the supervisor. 'Then how do you account for the fact that there are three hundred and sixty-five missing wheelbarrows?'

Do bakers with a sense of humour make wry bread?

Two postmen were standing outside the sorting office at the end of their rounds when one spotted a snail crawling by. Suddenly he stamped on the snail, brutally squashing it into the ground.

'That was a bit cruel,' said his colleague.

'That snail had it coming. It's been following me around all day.'

An architect, an artist and an accountant were discussing whether it was better to spend time with a wife or a mistress. The architect said he enjoyed time with a wife, building a solid foundation for an enduring relationship. The artist said he enjoyed time with a mistress, because of the passion and mystery. The accountant said he liked both.

'Both?' chorused the others.

'Yes,' he explained. 'If you have a wife and a mistress, they will each assume you are spending time with the other woman, which means you can go to the office and get some work done.'

How do you drive an accountant insane? – Tie him to a chair, stand in front of him and fold up a road map the wrong way.

When the CIA lost track of one of their operatives, they called in one of their top spy hunters. The CIA boss said: 'All I can tell you is that his name is Jones and that he's in a small town somewhere in Wales. If you think you've located him, tell him the code words, "The forecast is for mist on the hills." And if you've got the right man, he will say, "But I hear it's sunny in the valleys."'

So the spy hunter set off for Wales and found himself in a small town. Reasoning that the local pub was the centre of the community, he gradually engaged the barman in conversation. Eventually he said: 'Maybe you can help me. I'm looking for a guy named Jones.'

The barman said: 'You're going to have to be more specific because around here there are hundreds of men named Jones. There's Jones the bread, who runs the baker's shop over the road; Jones the nail, who runs the hardware shop two doors down; not to mention Jones the bank, Jones the steam and Jones the fish. And as a matter of fact, my name is Jones, too.'

Hearing this, the spy hunter figured he might as well try the code words on the barman, so he leaned over the bar and whispered: 'The forecast is for mist on the hills.'

The barman replied: 'Oh, you're looking for Jones the spy. He lives at number forty-four, halfway up the hill.'

Did you hear about the bumper car operator who got fired? – He's suing his employer for funfair dismissal.

An accountant was walking along the street when he spotted a tramp begging for money.

'Spare some change, sir?' asked the tramp.

'And why should I do that?' replied the accountant.

'Because I'm completely broke without a penny to my name and I haven't had a proper meal in three months.'

'Hmm,' said the accountant, 'and how does this compare to your last quarter?'

An American animal orthodontist was called one day by a frantic farmer from Australia. 'Can you help me?' he pleaded. 'I just got braces and orthodontic equipment for a hundred of my sheep, but the local sheep orthodontist just died. I need a responsible animal dentist to come care for my flock.'

The orthodontist was moved, and a good price was offered, so he promptly flew to Australia for what he thought would be a week or two of work. However he found that he was entirely unfamiliar with the orthodontic equipment the sheep had been given and he spent six whole months in Australia trying to figure out the foreign braces. When he finally boarded a plane for home, after half a year of frustrating work, he was hugely relieved. 'At last,' he sighed happily, 'I'll be seeing ewes in all the old familiar braces . . .'

A muscular young man working on a construction site kept bragging that he was the strongest member of the gang. After a while his boasting began to irritate the older workers to the point that one issued him with a challenge.

'It's time to put your money where your mouth is,' said the older worker. 'I'll bet a week's wages that I can haul something in a wheelbarrow over to that outbuilding that you won't be able to wheel back.'

'You're on,' said the young man, already mentally counting his winnings.

So the older worker grabbed a wheelbarrow by the handles and said to the young man. 'Okay. Get in . . .'

Did you hear about the mathematician who turned off his heating because he wanted to be cold and calculating?

A Microsoft support technician went to a firing range and shot six bullets at a target thirty metres away. After checking the target, the scorers called out that all six shots had missed completely. Unable to believe that he had failed to register a single hit, the technician demanded that his score be checked again, but the answer was the same. So he fired a shot into the ground right by his feet. He then shouted to the scorers: 'It's working fine here. The problem must be at your end.'

After his wife walked out on him, a man became so depressed that he went to see a psychiatrist.

'My life isn't worth living,' he wailed. 'Everything is so empty without her.'

The psychiatrist said: 'The best thing I can suggest is for you to occupy your time fully so that you don't have time to dwell on your unhappiness. Try and submerge yourself in your work. What do you do for a living?'

'I clean out septic tanks.'

An engineer, an accountant, a pharmacist and a civil servant were arguing over whose dog was the smartest. To settle the argument, each dog was required to perform its best trick.

The engineer's dog used a compass to draw a perfect circle on a sheet of paper; the accountant's dog divided a pile of biscuits into four equal parts; and the pharmacist's dog poured exactly half a carton of milk into a measuring jug.

Finally it was the turn of the civil servant's dog. It sauntered over, peed all over the drawing paper, ate the biscuits, drank the milk, had sex with the other three dogs, claimed a back injury as a result and applied for compensation before going on sick leave.

How did the butcher introduce his wife? – Meat Patty.

A clergyman was walking along a country road when he saw a young farmer struggling to load a huge pile of hay back onto a cart after it had fallen off.

'It's a baking hot day,' said the clergyman, 'and the sweat's pouring off you. Why don't you rest for a while?'

'No, I can't,' said the farmer. 'My father wouldn't like it.'

And he continued re-loading the hay.

'But surely,' continued the clergyman, 'everyone is entitled to a break. Here, have a drink of water.'

'I'd better not,' said the farmer. 'My father wouldn't like it.'

And he continued re-loading the hay.

'Your father must be a real slave driver,' said the clergyman. 'Tell me where he is and I'll give him a piece of my mind!'

'He's under the load of hay.'

Why did the man clean shoes for a living? – Because he really took a shine to it.

A mathematician and a farmer were on a train journey. As they passed a flock of sheep in a field, the mathematician announced confidently: 'There are seven hundred and ninety-seven sheep out there.'

The farmer said: 'That's incredible! It so happens I know the owner and that figure is exactly right. But how did you count them so quickly?'

The mathematician said: 'Easy. I just counted the number of legs and divided by four.'

A bar was so convinced that its bartender was the strongest man in the town that the owner offered a thousand dollar bet that nobody could match his strength. The bartender would squeeze a lemon until all the juice ran into a glass and then hand the lemon to a customer. Anyone who could squeeze out another drop would win the money.

Dozens tried and failed. Lumberjacks, professional sportsmen, builders, farmers: all were unable to squeeze another drop out of the lemon. Then a skinny little man said he would like a go. The large crowd that had gathered roared with laughter at the prospect of this weedy fellow succeeding where the toughest guys in town had failed. But their jeers turned to cheers when he did indeed manage to squeeze one last drop out of the lemon.

The stunned bartender said: 'What on earth do you do for a living? Are you a lumberjack or a weightlifter?'

'No,' replied the little man, 'I'm a tax inspector.'

A moderately successful stockbroker dreamed of making big money someday. With a view to this, when he took a prospective client out for a drive he chose the route carefully in order to depict the brokerage business at its most impressive.

'Look at that yacht,' he said as they drove slowly past a marina. 'That beauty belongs to the senior partner at Merrill Lynch. And that one over there is owned by the head of Goldman Sachs. And that huge two hundred foot yacht out there. That's the pride and joy of the top seller at Prudential-Bache.'

'Yes, they're all very nice,' said the client. 'There's just one thing that concerns me slightly: why aren't there any customers' yachts?'

Two men were talking about their worst-ever jobs.

'I used to work in a liquorice factory,' said one.

'Well,' said the other, 'it takes all sorts.'

A tourist in Egypt met a man in a bar. 'What do you do for a living?' he asked.

'I'm a camel castrator.'

'That's an interesting job,' mused the tourist. 'Tell me, how do you castrate a camel?'

'You go behind him and spread his legs. Then you take a big rock in each hand and smack his testicles between the rocks.'

'Wow! That must really hurt.'

'No, you just have to keep your thumbs out of the way.'

At a banking convention, various branch managers were required to display their knowledge of figures. The first manager was called forward by the area boss and was asked: 'What is nineteen plus nineteen?'

'Twenty-seven,' he replied.

His answer was greeted with dismay by his fellow bankers who urged the boss: 'Give him another chance! Give him another chance!'

The boss thought it was a fair request and agreed to give the manager another chance. 'OK,' he said. 'What is twelve plus twelve?'

After careful deliberation, the manager answered: 'Twenty-one.'

His colleagues groaned but begged the boss: 'Give him another chance! Give him another chance!'

'All right,' conceded the boss, 'I'll give you one last chance. What is two plus two?'

The manager thought intensely and began counting slowly on his fingers. Eventually he announced hesitantly: 'Four.'

The other managers shouted: 'Give him another chance! Give him another chance!'

A plumber was called to a house to fix a leaking pipe. As he set to work, the attractive lady of the house began flirting with him. He needed no encouragement and soon they ended up in bed. He was really turned on by her but just as they were about to have sex, the phone rang.

'That was my husband,' said the woman. 'He's on his way home, but he's going out again at seven, so if you come back around seven-thirty, we can finish what we've started.'

The plumber looked at her in disbelief. 'What?' he said. 'In my own time?'

A man went into an electrical goods store and began looking around. He spotted a washing machine that he liked the look of and asked the salesman how much it was

'Five dollars,' said the salesman.

'You're joking, aren't you?' asked the customer.

'No,' insisted the salesman. 'That's the price. Do you want it or not?'

'Sure, I'll take it,' said the customer. His eye then caught a top-of-the-range stereo system.

'How much is that?' he asked the salesman.

'Eight dollars.'

'Is there something wrong with it?' inquired the customer incredulously.

'No, it's brand new and in perfect working order.'

'Right, I'll buy it.'

Next the customer saw a smart computer and printer.

'How much?' he asked.

'Hmmm, ten dollars,' said the salesman.

'Great! I'll have that too.'

As the salesman was ringing up the purchases, the customer asked: 'Tell me, why are your prices so cheap?'

The salesman replied: 'Well, the owner of this store is at my house right now with my wife. So I'm doing to his business what he's doing to her!'

An accountant was having difficulties sleeping at night, so he went to see his doctor.

The doctor said: 'Have you tried counting sheep?'

'That's the trouble,' said the accountant. 'I make a mistake and then spend three hours trying to find it!'

A statistician was walking along a corridor when he felt a sudden pain in his chest. Immediately he ran to the nearest staircase and threw himself down the stairs.

His friend came to visit him in hospital and asked him why he had thrown himself down the stairs.

The statistician replied: 'Because the chances of suffering a heart attack while falling downstairs are much lower than the chances of just having a heart attack.'

Experiencing teething troubles with their new computer, a couple called the Help Desk. But the guy there insisted on talking to the husband in complex computer jargon, none of which seemed to make much sense.

Eventually in frustration, the husband said: 'Look, you know what you're talking about but I don't. So can you treat me like a four-year-old and explain it to me that way?'

'Okay, son,' said the computer technician, 'put your mommy on the phone.'

A research scientist dropped a piece of buttered toast on the floor and was amazed to see that it landed butter-side up, thereby disproving the long-held theory that toast always lands butter-side down. Thinking that he might have made an important breakthrough that could lead to the rewriting of science textbooks, he took the slice of toast to a colleague for his observations.

'How could it be that when I dropped this slice of toast, it landed butter-side up when all previous knowledge suggests that the opposite should have occurred?'

'It's easy,' said the colleague. 'You must have buttered the wrong side.'

A farmer who grew watermelons was being plagued by local children who would sneak into his patch at night and eat the produce. After weeks of putting up with this, he devised what he thought was a foolproof plan to deter the trespassers. He put up a sign, which read: 'Warning! One of the watermelons in this field has been injected with cyanide.'

Sure enough, when the kids read the sign they headed straight home but instead of giving up altogether, they prepared a sign of their own, which they planted right next to the farmer's.

The following day when the farmer inspected the field, he was pleased to find that none of his watermelons were missing. But then he spotted the new sign next to his. It read: 'Now there are two.'

Albert Einstein died and went to heaven, only to be told that his room wasn't ready yet. Instead he was told that he would have to share a dormitory with four other men for the next few days.

As Einstein entered the dormitory, one of the men came over to greet him. 'It is an honour to have you with us, albeit temporarily,' he said. 'I myself have an IQ of a hundred and eighty.'

'Wonderful!' enthused Einstein. 'We can discuss mathematics.'

The second roommate came over and said: 'It is a pleasure to meet you. I have an IQ of a hundred and fifty.'

Einstein said: 'Marvellous! We can discuss physics.'

The third man then appeared and shook Einstein warmly by the hand. 'I have an IQ of one hundred,' he confided.

'Great!' exclaimed Einstein. 'We can discuss the latest theatre productions.'

Just then the fourth man joined the group. 'I am afraid my IQ is only eighty,' he confessed.

Einstein said: 'So where do you think interest rates are headed?'

In a slow news week, a local newspaper editor sent a young photographer to a reputedly haunted house on the edge of town in the hope of snapping some ghostly images to titillate the readership.

Any doubts the photographer might have had regarding the existence of the ghost were dispelled virtually as soon as he walked through the door of the rickety old house. For out of the darkness emerged a strange figure, complete with clanking chains.

Camera in hand, the terrified photographer spluttered: 'I'm not here to harm you – I just want to take your photo.'

To the young man's amazement, the ghost was only too happy to oblige and for the next ten minutes he posed for a succession of shots.

Back in his dark room at the office, the photographer waited excitedly to see what he had captured on film. It could be the scoop of the century. But as he began developing the photos, he saw to his dismay that each one was black and underexposed.

Just then, the editor passed by. 'How are the pictures?' he asked.

'Well,' replied the photographer dejectedly, 'the spirit was willing but the flash was weak.'

A pipe burst in a doctor's house, so he called a plumber. The plumber arrived, unpacked his tools, fiddled around for fifteen minutes, and then handed the doctor a bill for four hundred dollars.

The doctor said: 'This is ridiculous! I don't even make that much as a doctor!'

The plumber replied: 'Neither did I when I was a doctor.'

Three schoolboys were boasting about how fast their respective fathers could run.

The first, the son of an Olympic archer, said: 'My father can run the fastest. He can fire an arrow, start to run, and reach the target before the arrow!'

The second boy said: 'You think that's fast! My dad is a hunter. He can shoot his gun and be there before the bullet!'

'That's nothing,' said the third boy. 'My dad is a civil servant. He stops working at four thirty and he's home by three forty-five!'

In preparation for starting a new office job, a young accountant spent a week with the retiring accountant whom he was replacing. He hoped to pick up a few tips from the old master and studied his daily routine intently.

Every morning the experienced accountant began the day by opening his desk drawer, taking out a frayed envelope and removing a yellowing piece of paper. He then read it, nodded his head sagely, returned the envelope to the drawer and started his day's work.

After the old man retired, the new boy could hardly wait to read for himself the message in the drawer, particularly since he felt somewhat inadequate about stepping into such illustrious shoes. Surely, he thought to himself, the envelope must contain the secret to accounting success, a pearl of wisdom to be treasured forever. The anticipation was so great that his hands were actually trembling as he opened the drawer and took out the mysterious envelope. And there, inside, on that aged piece of paper he read the following message:

'Debits in the column nearest the potted plant; credits in the column towards the door.'

Work CV:

I once worked as a lumberjack but I couldn't hack it, so they gave me the axe.

I used to work in a shoe factory; I tried but I just didn't fit in.

I became a fisherman, but I couldn't live on my net income.

I got a job at the zoo feeding giraffes, but I wasn't up to it.

I found being an electrician interesting, but the work was shocking and I was discharged.

I worked at a coffee shop, but it was always the same old grind.

I became a writer, but I couldn't stand the paperwork.

I tried to be a deli worker, but I couldn't cut the mustard.

I worked as an elevator operator, but it had its ups and downs.

I got a job for a pool maintenance company, but the work was too draining.

I tried to become a tailor, but I just wasn't suited for it; it was a sew-sew job.

After many years of trying to find steady work, I finally got a job as a historian . . . until I realized there was no future in it.

An efficiency expert concluded his lecture with the warning: 'Don't try these techniques at home.'

'Why not?' asked a member of the audience.

'I watched my wife's routine at breakfast for twenty-two years,' he explained. 'She made up to ten trips between the fridge, the cooker, the toaster and the table, almost always carrying just a single item at a time. One day I told her: "You're wasting too much time. Why don't you try carrying several things at once?"'

'And did it save time?' asked the man in the audience,

'Yes it did,' replied the expert. 'It used to take her twenty minutes to make breakfast. Now I do it in ten.'

A woman applying for a job in a lemon grove seemed over-qualified. The foreman said to her: 'Have you any actual experience in picking lemons?'

'As a matter of fact, I have,' she answered. 'I've been divorced three times.'

A shepherd was patiently herding his flock in a remote field when a Jeep Cherokee pulled up in a cloud of dust. Out stepped a young man dripping in designer labels from his Ray-Ban sunglasses to his Gucci shoes.

'Hey, mister,' he called over to the shepherd, 'if I can tell you exactly how many sheep you have in your flock, will you let me have one?'

The shepherd was baffled by the proposition, but agreed to go along with it.

So the flash young man stopped out of his Jeep with his laptop under his arm. He hooked himself up to the Internet, consulted endless data and spreadsheets, before announcing: 'You have nine hundred and eighty-six sheep.'

'That's right,' said the shepherd. 'Fair enough. You can take one of my sheep.'

And he watched while the man made his selection and loaded it into the Jeep.

'Before you go,' said the shepherd, 'how about letting me have a go? If I can tell you exactly what your job is, will you give me my sheep back?'

'Sure,' said the young man.

'You're a consultant,' said the shepherd.

'That's right. How did you know that?'

'Easy,' said the shepherd. 'You turned up here uninvited. You wanted to be paid for telling me something I already knew. And you don't know anything about my business because you took my dog!'

A sales manager and an operations manager went bear hunting. While the operations manager remained in the cabin, the sales manager went looking for a bear. He eventually found one and took aim, but merely succeeded in wounding the animal, which proceeded to chase him back to the cabin. The bear was closing with every stride until just as he reached the cabin door, the sales manager tripped and fell flat on his face. Too close behind to stop, the bear vaulted over him and landed in the cabin.

The sales manager quickly jumped up, closed the cabin door and yelled to his friend inside: 'You skin this one while I go and get another!'

The chickens in a large hen house began to peck out each other's feathers. As the quarrelling escalated, a number died every day. The concerned farmer rushed to a consultant and asked for a solution to the problem.

'Add a little sugar to the hens' food,' he advised. 'It will keep them sweet and help them to calm down.'

A week later the farmer called on the consultant again. 'The sugar has had no effect. My chickens are still dying. What shall I do?'

'Add pear juice to their drinking water,' he suggested. 'That will help for sure.'

A week later the farmer was back once more. 'My chickens are still quarrelling,' he told the consultant. 'Do you have any more advice?'

'I can offer you more and more advice,' replied the consultant. 'The real question is whether you have any more chickens.'

A marketing manager married a woman who had previously been married nine times but still claimed to be a virgin. She explained her virginity thus:

'My first husband was a sales representative who spent our entire marriage telling me: "It's gonna be great!"

'My second husband worked in software services. He was never quite sure how it was supposed to function, but he said he would send me the instructions.

'My third husband was an accountant. He said he knew how to, but he just wasn't sure whether it was his job to.

'My fourth husband was a teacher. He simply remarked: "Those who can, do; those who can't, teach."

'My fifth husband was an engineer. He told me that he understood the basic process but needed three years to research, implement and design a new state-of-the-art method.

'My sixth husband was a psychiatrist, and all he ever wanted to do was talk about it.

'My seventh husband was a professional builder, but he never finished anything he started.

'My eighth husband was a help-desk coordinator, and he kept teaching me how to do it myself.

'My ninth husband was in technical support, and he kept saying, "Don't worry, it'll be up any minute now."

'And now I am married to you, my darling, a marketing manager.'

The husband looked at her and said nervously: 'I know I have the product, I'm just not sure how to position it.'

Due to poor annual profits, the management at an English crisp factory decided to introduce new working practices. Part of the manufacturing process involved the transportation of the crisps around the factory in purpose-made metal bins. Ever since anyone could remember, the materials for the bins had been supplied by a local sheet metal manufacturer, with final construction of the bins carried out by the workers within the factory. With their neatly soldered seams, the hand crafted bins were true works of art. Now as a cost cutting measure, management made the decision to replace the expensive hand crafted metal bins with cheaper, ready-made plastic bins. Not only would material costs be reduced but also staff levels within the factory could be cut.

This proposal angered the workers within the factory. A vote was taken and strike action unanimously agreed. As part of the action and in a bid to drum up national support, a local rally was organized, with a march taking place from the factory to the rally. To lift the workers' spirits as they marched with their banners, they sang: 'Onward crisp bin solderers . . .'

Old Age

Two old men – one a retired history professor, the other a retired professor of psychology – had been persuaded by their wives to take a holiday in Portugal. As they sat around on the hotel balcony watching the sunset, the history professor said to the psychology professor: 'Have you read Marx?'

To which the professor of psychology replied: 'Yes, I think it's the wicker chairs.'

Old age is when your doctor doesn't give you x-rays anymore but just holds you up to the light.

Two old men were sitting down to breakfast. One said to the other: 'Do you know you've got a suppository in your left ear?'

'Really?' said his friend, removing the suppository. 'I'm so glad you pointed that out. Now I think I know where I've put my hearing aid.'

After years of regular church attendance, a hundred-and-five-year-old man suddenly stopped attending. When the vicar happened to see him in the street, he asked why, after decades of never missing a Sunday service, he had given up going to church.

The old man whispered: 'When I got to ninety, I expected God to take me any day. But then I got to be ninety-five, a hundred, and now a hundred and five. So I thought God is obviously very busy and must have forgotten about me, and I don't really want to remind him.'

An elderly couple who had been courting for years finally decided to get married. While out making their plans, they stopped off at a drugstore.

The old man asked the sales assistant: 'Do you sell pills for arthritis?'

'Yes, we do,' replied the assistant.

'What about heart medication?'

'Yes, we stock that, too,' said the assistant.

'Got anything for constipation?'

'Naturally, sir.'

'How about Viagra?'

'Yes, we sell Viagra.'

'Sleeping pills?'

'Yes, we stock a large selection of sleeping tablets.'

'Do you sell denture cleaner?'

'Of course we do, sir.'

'That's great!' exclaimed the old man, nodding to his bride-to-be. 'We'd like to register here for our wedding gifts.'

Old age is when you can remember when the Dead Sea was only sick.

Two gas company employees were making house calls. The younger man decided to wind up his senior colleague by saying: 'My God, you're old!'

'Oh yeah?' said the older man. 'I may be getting on a bit, but I bet I can still outrun you.'

'Right. You're on,' said his colleague. 'How about a race around the block?'

With that, they began running at full speed around the block. The two men were neck and neck all the way but as they approached the last corner, they were amazed to see an elderly lady sprinting along-side them.

'What are you doing?' they panted.

The old lady replied: 'Well, you were at my home checking my gas meter, and when I saw you running away, I figured I'd better run too!'

Old age is when your friends compliment you on your new alligator shoes and you're not wearing any.

After living a wild life, an ageing gigolo finally found the years were catching up with him. So he went to the doctor for a medical.

'I've had a lifetime of wine, women and song,' he boasted proudly. 'And I don't think I could give it up.'

'Well, the good news,' said the doctor, 'is that you won't have to give up singing.'

A ninety-five-year-old woman at a nursing home received a visit from one of her fellow church members.

'How are you feeling, Doris?' asked the visitor.

'Oh,' said the old lady. 'I'm worried sick.'

'What are you worried about? You look like you're in good health. They are taking care of you here, aren't they?'

'Yes, they are taking very good care of me.'

'Are you in any pain?'

'No, I've never had a pain in my life.'

'Then what are you worried about?'

The old lady leaned back in her chair and explained: 'Every close friend I ever had has already died and gone to heaven. I'm afraid they're all wondering where I went!'

Three men with impaired hearing were walking down the street one day in March.

One said: 'Windy, ain't it?'

'No,' said the second, 'it's Thursday.'

The third man said: 'So am I. Let's have a Coke.'

An old man attended a school reunion but was dismayed to find that his surviving classmates just wanted to talk about their various ailments – heart conditions, kidney stones, liver complaints.

When he got home, his wife asked him how it went. 'It wasn't much of a reunion,' he sighed. 'It was more like an organ recital.'

An eighty-one-year-old gentleman was left all alone in the world after the death of his beloved wife. He longed for companionship and while walking in the park one day, he spotted an attractive, grey-haired lady sitting alone on a bench. Summoning courage, he approached her and asked graciously: 'Excuse me, madam, but would you mind if I sit here with you?'

Looking up to see such a distinguished gentleman, the lady replied: 'Of course not.' And she shuffled along to make room for him.

For the next two hours they sat and talked about everything under the sun. They found that they had so much in common – they liked the same sort of music, enjoyed the same kind of films, and shared the same taste in food. They even found that they originated from the same part of the country. Furthermore, their spouses had died in the same year following long and happy marriages. Finally the old gentleman cleared his throat and asked sheepishly: 'Madam, may I ask you two questions?'

'Certainly,' she replied, hopefully.

He then removed a handkerchief from his coat pocket and spread it out on the ground before her. Very gingerly he got down on one knee and looked her softly in the eyes: 'Eunice, I realize that we have only known each other for a couple of hours, but we have so much in common that I feel I have known you all my life. So would you do me the honour of becoming my wife?'

She reached out for his hands and said: 'Yes, I would be delighted to marry you.' With that, she leaned over and kissed him tenderly on the cheek. Then she added: 'You said you had two questions to ask me. What is the second question?'

He held his back and said: 'Will you help me get up?'

An old timer was sitting on his New England porch when a young man walked up holding a pen and clipboard.

'What are you selling, son?' asked the old man.

'I'm not selling anything. I'm the census taker.'

'The what?'

'The census taker. We're trying to find out how many people there are in the United States.'

'You're wasting your time with me,' said the old man. 'I have no idea.'

On his hundredth birthday, a man was asked the secret of his long life by a local newspaper reporter.

'My motto throughout life,' said the old man, 'has been to avoid arguments at all costs. I never argue with anyone.'

The reporter was sceptical. 'There must be some other reason – exercise, natural remedies, diet. I can't believe you have lived to a hundred simply by not arguing!'

The old man said: 'You know, you could be right.'

A group of pensioners in the lounge of a nursing home were exchanging complaints about their ailments.

One said: 'My arms are so weak I can hardly hold this cup.'

Another said: 'My cataracts are so bad I can't even see to pour my coffee.'

Another said: 'I can't turn my head because of the arthritis in my neck.'

Another said: 'My blood pressure pills make me feel dizzy all the time.'

Another said: 'I guess that's the price we pay for getting old.'

Another said: 'But it's not all bad. We should be grateful that we can all still drive.'

An old man had been virtually deaf for years until he was finally given a new hearing aid that allowed him to hear perfectly. Monitoring his patient's progress, the doctor said: 'Your family must be really pleased that you can hear again.'

The old man said: 'I haven't told them yet. I just sit around and listen to their conversations. I've changed my will three times in the last month!'

Two old age pensioners were talking about their husbands over a cup of coffee. One said: 'I do wish Fred would stop biting his nails. It's such a horrible habit.'

Her friend said: 'Albert used to do the same. But I cured him of the habit.'

'How did you do that?'

'I hid his teeth!'

An old man was running a fairground tent, which proclaimed: 'For fifty dollars I'll teach you to be a mind reader.'

Intrigued by the offer, a teenager entered the tent to try his luck.

'Okay,' said the old guy, handing him a garden hose, 'I want you to hold this hose and look in the end.'

'What for?' asked the teenager.

'It's all part of teaching you to become a mind reader.'

So the teenager, somewhat reluctantly, looked in the end of the hose and saw nothing – just darkness. Then suddenly the old man turned on the tap and water came gushing out all over the young man's face.

'I knew you were going to do something like that!' yelled the drenched teenager.

The old man said: 'Then that'll be fifty dollars.'

While writing at a Post Office desk, a young man was approached by an elderly man holding a postcard.

'Excuse me, young man,' he said. 'Could you possibly address this postcard for me? My arthritis is playing up today and I can't even hold a pen.'

'Certainly,' said the wrong man, and he wrote down the address given to him.

'Also,' added the old man, 'would you be so kind as to write a short message on the card and sign it for me?'

'No problem,' said the young man, and he patiently wrote the message that the old man dictated to him. 'Is there anything else I can help you with?'

'Yes,' said the old man. 'At the end, could you just add "PS, please excuse the sloppy handwriting."'

Two paramedics were sent to check on a ninety-two-year-old man who had become disorientated. They decided to take him to hospital for further examination. En route, with the sirens going, they questioned him to determine his level of awareness. Leaning close, one asked: 'Do you know what we're doing right now?'

The old man slowly looked up, stared out of the ambulance window and said: 'I'd say about fifty, maybe fifty-five.'

A wise old gentleman retired and bought a modest home near a junior high school. He spent the first few weeks of his retirement in peaceful contentment . . . until the new school year began. The very next afternoon three young boys, full of youthful, after-school enthusiasm, ran down his street, beating merrily on every trashcan they encountered. The crashing percussion continued day after day until finally the wise old man decided it was time to take action.

The next afternoon he walked out to meet the young percussionists as they banged their way down the street. Stopping them, he said: 'You kids are a lot of fun. I like to see you express your exuberance in that way. I used to do the same thing when I was your age. In fact, I'm so impressed that I'd like to give you a dollar each if you promise to come round every day and do your thing.'

The kids were delighted to take up the offer and for the next few days they joyously played the trashcans, creating a terrible racket right the way down the street. Then one afternoon the old man greeted the kids again, but this time he looked sad.

'Kids,' he said, 'the recession's really putting a big dent in my income. From now on, I'll only be able to pay you fifty cents to beat on the cans.'

The youngsters were obviously displeased, but they grudgingly accepted the reduced rate and continued their afternoon ruckus.

A few days later, the wily retiree approached them again as they drummed their way down the street. 'Look,' he said, 'I haven't received my Social Security cheque yet, so I'm not going to be able to give you more than twenty-five cents. Will that be okay?'

'A lousy quarter?' the drum leader exclaimed. 'If you think we're going to waste our time beating these cans around for a quarter, you're crazy! No way, mister. We quit!'

And the old man enjoyed peace and tranquillity for the rest of his days.

An old man boasted about his fitness to a group of youngsters. 'Every morning,' he said, 'I do fifty push-ups, fifty sit-ups and walk two miles. I'm as fit as a fiddle! And you want to know why? I don't smoke, I don't drink, I don't stay up late, and I don't chase after women. And tomorrow I'm going to celebrate my ninety-seventh birthday.'

'Oh really?' said one of the youngsters. 'How?'

An elderly lady walked into the bar on a cruise ship and ordered a scotch with two drops of water. As the bartender poured it, she revealed that it was her eightieth birthday.

Hearing this, a fellow passenger offered to buy her a drink. 'That's very kind of you,' she said. 'I'll have another scotch with two drops of water.'

As news of the celebration spread, four more passengers offered to buy her a drink. Each time she asked for a scotch with two drops of water.

The bartender was amazed at her drinking capacity but was puzzled why she always asked for two drops of water.

'Well,' she said, 'when you're my age, you learn how to hold your liquor. But water is a different matter!'

An old couple stopped at a roadside restaurant for lunch on their way to the coast. After returning to the car, they had driven about ten miles down the road when the woman suddenly remembered that she had left her glasses in the restaurant.

The old man was not happy about having to turn the car around and head back to the restaurant. 'How could you forget your glasses?' he moaned. 'This is a detour I could really have done without. By the time we get to the coast, it will be time to head back home again! What a waste of time!'

He was still complaining bitterly when they pulled up again outside the restaurant. As his wife got out of the car, he grumbled: 'While you're in there, you may as well get my hat, too.'

An elderly man went to the doctor for his annual physical. The doctor examined him and said: 'I'm afraid you have a serious heart murmur.'

The old man was shocked by the news.

'Tell me,' said the doctor. 'Do you smoke?'

'No.'

'Do you drink to excess?'

'No.'

'Do you still have a sex life?'

'Yes, I do.'

'Well, I'm sorry, but with your heart condition you'll have to give up half your sex life.'

'Which half?' asked the old man. 'The looking or the thinking?'

A daughter complimented her elderly father on his improved manners. 'After all these years, I notice that you have finally started putting your hand over your mouth whenever you cough.'

'I have to,' he said. 'How else can I catch my teeth?'

With a gale force wind blowing down the street, a policeman noticed an old woman standing on a corner. She was holding on tightly to her hat as her skirt blew up around her waist.

He went over to her and said: 'Look, lady, while you're holding on to your precious hat, everybody's getting a good look at everything you have!'

'Listen, sonny,' she replied. 'What they're looking at is eighty years old. But this hat is brand new!'

Birthday candles are for people who want to make light of their age.

An old man of ninety-one was sitting on a park bench crying. A passing police officer came over to ask him what was the matter.

'You see,' said the old man, 'I just got married to a twenty-five-year-old girl. Every morning she makes me a wonderful breakfast and then we make love. At dinner time she makes me a wonderful supper and then we make love.'

The policeman said: 'You shouldn't be crying! You should be the happiest man in the world!'

'I know!' said the old man. 'I'm crying because I can't remember where I live!'

A man went to the doctor to complain that his right knee was hurting. 'I don't think it's anything serious, doctor, but it keeps aching.'

'You're ninety-eight!' exclaimed the doctor. 'Are you surprised your knee hurts?'

'But my other knee is ninety-eight, too,' said the old man, 'and it doesn't hurt!'

Yes, I'm a Senior Citizen:

I'm the life of the party – even if it lasts until 8.30pm.

I'm smiling all the time because I can't hear a thing you're saying.

I'm usually interested in going home before I get to where I am going.

I'm very good at telling stories – over and over and over.

I'm aware that other people's grandchildren aren't as cute as mine.

I'm so cared for – eye care, dental care, long term care.

I'm sure everything I can't find is in a safe place, somewhere.

I'm a walking storeroom of facts, it's just that I've lost the key to the storeroom door.

I'm having trouble remembering simple words like . . .

An elderly couple were discussing their future plans. The husband asked: 'What will you do if I die before you?'

After some thought, she said: 'I will probably look for a house-sharing situation with three other single or widowed women. And since I'm active for my age, I'll go for roommates who are a little younger than me. What about you? What will you do if I die first?'

He replied: 'Probably the same.'

An old people's home was holding a special afternoon tea to celebrate the hundredth birthday of one of the residents. To mark the occasion, they asked the matron to arrange some form of entertainment. So she got in touch with a theatrical agent.

'What would you like?' asked the agent. 'A singer, a comedian, maybe a juggler?'

'No, none of those,' replied matron. 'We have them every year. The old people are tired of them. This is a special tea and I'm looking for something different, like an animal act.'

'An animal act?' queried the agent. 'Right, I'll see what I can do.'

He put down the phone and turned to his assistant. 'What animal acts do we have on the books?'

'There's Antonio and his tigers,' volunteered the assistant.

'They're a bit dangerous for an old people's home,' thought the agent.

'How about Pedro and his performing sea lions?'

'No,' said the agent. 'It takes weeks to get rid of the smell of fish.'

'There's always Charlie the Cheeky Chimp. He goes down well.'

'Hmmm. A monkey act. I like the sound of that,' enthused the agent. 'But not Charlie – he's got very bad-tempered in his old age. There's a risk that he might bite someone.'

'Well,' suggested the assistant, 'I do know someone who has a pet gibbon that does parties. And it's really tame, extremely calm.'

'Okay,' said the agent, 'let's try a mellow gibbon round the old folks' tea.'

Oxymorons

Postal service
Act naturally
Microsoft Works
Holy war
Military intelligence
Minor disaster
Auto pilot
Near miss
Never generalize
New classic
Phone sex
Fun run
Living dead
Taped live
Angry patient
Civil war
Genuine imitation
Athletic scholarship
Death benefits
Pretty ugly
Government organization
Peace force
Sweet sorrow
Diet ice cream
Alone together
Tight slacks
Legally drunk
Business ethics
Same difference

Healthy tan
Head butt
Affordable housing
Bankrupt millionaire
Airline food
Tax return
Virtual reality
Beginning Finnish
American beer
Art student
Soft rock
Original copies
Deafening silence
Great Depression
Good grief
Hot chilli
Free trade
Crash landing
Now then
Student teacher
Old news
Working holiday
Exact estimate
Religious tolerance
Singles club
Rap music

Pets

A woman saw an ad in the paper that read: 'Purebred Police Dog For Sale $25.' Thinking it a bargain, she rang the number and bought the dog. But when it was delivered, she found that she had bought nothing but a mangy-looking mongrel.

So she phoned the man who had placed the ad to complain. 'How can you possibly call that scruffy mutt a purebred police dog?'

The man said: 'Don't let his looks deceive you. He's working undercover.'

Two women were arguing over whose dog was the smarter.

The first woman said: 'My dog is so smart that every morning he waits for the paper boy to arrive, then he takes the paper from the letterbox and brings it to me.'

The second woman said: 'I know.'

'How do you know?' asked the first woman.

The second woman said: 'My dog told me.'

A lady customer walked into an exclusive pet store and said that she wanted to buy a red sweater for her dog. The sales assistant suggested it would be better to bring the dog in for a proper fit.

'I can't do that!' said the customer. 'The sweater is a surprise!'

Two dogs were walking down the street. One said: 'Wait here a minute, I'll be right back.' He then crossed the street, sniffed the lamp post for a while, then walked back across the street.

'What was that all about?' said the other dog.

'I was just checking my messages.'

A wealthy man went on safari to Africa, taking his faithful pet dog along for company. One day the dog started chasing butterflies and before long realized that he was hopelessly lost. As he wandered around in circles, he saw a leopard sizing him up for lunch. Just then he noticed some bones on the ground and immediately began chewing on the bones with his back to the approaching leopard. Just as the big cat was about to pounce, the dog announced loudly: 'Mmmm. That leopard was delicious! I wonder if there are any more around here?'

Hearing this, the leopard stopped his attack in mid-stride and slunk away into the trees. The dog, he reasoned, was not an animal to be messed with.

The incident had been watched from a nearby tree by a monkey who reckoned he could put his inside information to good use and trade it for protection from the leopard. So he headed off in pursuit of the leopard, closely watched by the dog who feared that his cunning ruse had been exposed. The monkey soon caught up with the leopard, spilled the beans and struck a deal for himself with the big cat. The leopard was furious at being fooled and said: 'Here, monkey, hop on my back and we'll sort out that conniving canine.'

Seeing the leopard approaching with the monkey on his back, the dog knew he had to think fast. Instead of running, the dog sat down with his back to the attackers, pretending that he hadn't yet seen them. And just as they got near enough to hear, the dog wondered aloud: 'Where's that monkey? I can never trust him. I sent him off half an hour ago to bring me another leopard, and he's still not back!'

In theory, housetraining your puppy may seem like a sensible idea, but it doesn't look good on paper.

Two dog owners were talking in the park. One said: 'I'm fed up with my dog – he'll chase anyone on a bike.'

'What are you going to do?' asked the other. 'Have him put down?'

'No. I think I'll just take his bike away.'

Did you hear about the dog that ate nothing but onions? – His bark was much worse than his bite.

A little man walked into a bar and asked politely: 'Does anyone own that Rottweiler outside?'

'Yeah, I do,' said a mean-looking biker, rising to his feet. 'What of it?'

'Well, I think my Chihuahua just killed him.'

'What are you talking about?' growled the biker. 'How could your puny little Chihuahua kill my mighty Rottweiler?'

'It seems she got stuck in your dog's throat.'

Why don't dogs make good dancers? – Because they've got two left feet.

A dog applied for a job as a high-powered secretary with a multi-national company. The advert stated that the successful applicant must have good keyboard skills, a command of shorthand, and be able to speak a second language.

The interviewer sat the dog at the computer and watched in wonder-ment as the animal successfully carried out the most complex functions, including spreadsheets and e-mail. Then he gave the dog dictation and was impressed by the hound's ability to write a hundred and twenty words a minute in immaculate shorthand.

'Well,' he said at the end of the interview, 'it looks as if the job's yours. There's just one thing though. What about the second language?'

To which the dog replied: 'Miaow!'

The citizens of Munich in the nineteenth century were faced with an unusual problem. The city's dog population was rising alarmingly, and not just little dachshunds, but really big, ferocious hounds. It reached the stage where people were afraid to venture out on to the streets for fear of being attacked by packs of marauding hounds. Eventually, with the help of the army and the police force, the people managed to drive the dogs out of the city and into the surrounding mountains.

But soon the dogs became hungry and descended in numbers into the neighbouring town of Lieblaten, Germany's leading paper manufacturer and a place where the paper mills were a major source of employment. When the dogs began breaking into shops for food, the people of Lieblaten fled to Munich to register their complaints. As all the townspeople evacuated their homes, they heard a strange noise coming from the paper mills. Who could be running them? Then an old man, blessed with the wisdom of age, explained: 'The mills are alive with the hounds of Munich.'

Dog's Reminder to Self:
   The garbage collector is not stealing our stuff.

I do not need to stand straight up suddenly when I'm lying under the coffee table.

I must not roll my toys behind the fridge, behind the sofa or under the bed.

I must shake the rainwater out of my fur before I enter the house.

I will not eat the cats' food, either before they eat it or after they throw it up.

I will stop trying to find the few remaining pieces of clean carpet in the house when I am about to be sick.

I will not roll on dead seagulls, fish, crabs, etc just because I like the way they smell.

The diaper bucket is not a cookie jar.

I will not chew my owner's toothbrush without telling him.

I will not chew crayons or pens, especially the red ones, or my owners will think I am haemorrhaging.

We do not have a doorbell. I will not bark each time I hear one on television.

I will not steal my owner's underwear and bury it in the garden.

The sofa is not a face towel. Nor is my owner's lap.

My head does not belong in the refrigerator.

I will not bite the officer's hand when he reaches in for my owner's driver's licence.

I will not run off with toilet rolls while people are using the bathroom.

I will not roll around in the mud just after being bathed.

Sticking my nose into someone's crotch is not an acceptable way of saying hello.

I will not hump on anybody's leg just because it seemed a good idea at the time.

I will not come in from outside and immediately drag my butt across the carpet.

The toilet bowl is not a drinking water supply and, just because the water is blue, it doesn't mean it is cleaner.

I will not sit in the middle of the living room and lick my crotch when there are visitors.

Suddenly turning around and smelling my butt can quickly clear a room.

The cat is not a squeaky toy, so when I play with him and he makes that noise, it's usually not a good thing.

My tail is simply not worth chasing, because even when I catch it, it hurts.

After forty-five years of dedicated service, a maid was stunned to learn that her employer was dismissing her in favour of someone younger. On hearing the news, the maid took a steak from the fridge and tossed it to the family dog.

'What on earth do you think you are doing?' snapped the employer.

The maid replied: 'That was for his help in cleaning the dishes all these years!'

Why didn't the dog speak to his foot? – Because it's not polite to answer back to your paw.

A man took his talking dog to a showbiz agent. The dog proceeded to tell ten jokes in a wide variety of accents, including American, French and Irish.

When the dog had finished his repertoire, his owner said excitedly: 'What do you think? We're going to make a fortune, right?'

The agent said: 'Well, his delivery's all right, but his material's a bit weak.'

A medieval castle had been under siege for three months. Supplies of food and water were virtually exhausted, leaving the occupants in dire straits. Unless aid arrived soon, everyone would perish.

Realising the gravity of the situation, one of the knights offered to break out of the castle and ride for help. Alas, all the horses had been killed so, in desperation, the knight suggested riding out on the back of a huge wolfhound.

'You can't,' said the keeper of the dogs, 'the wolfhound has injured its leg. The only dog available is this Chihuahua, and I wouldn't send a knight out on a dog like this!'

What's the difference between a businessman and a warm dog? – The businessman wears a suit, the dog just pants.

A man went to the vet to collect his sick dog. The vet came in carrying the dog and said: 'I'm really sorry, but I'm going to have to put your dog down.'

The man sobbed: 'Why?'

'Because he's too heavy.'

An avid duck hunter was in the market for a new bird dog. His search ended when he found a dog that could actually walk on water to retrieve a duck. Amazed by his discovery, he was sure none of his friends would ever believe him.

He decided to try and break the news to a friend of his, an eternal pessimist who steadfastly refused to be impressed by anything. In the hope that even he would be impressed by a dog that walked on water, he was invited to join the hunter and his dog on a trip into the country. However the hunter refrained from mentioning the dog's special talent – he wanted his pessimistic friend to see for himself.

The two men and the dog made their way to a good hunting lake and as they waited by the shore, a flock of ducks flew overhead. The men fired, and a duck fell. The dog responded and jumped into the water, but, instead of sinking, it walked across the water to retrieve the bird, never getting more than its paws wet. This continued throughout the day. Each time a duck fell, the dog walked across the surface of the water to retrieve it.

The pessimist watched carefully, observing everything, but did not say a single word. Then on the drive home, the hunter finally asked his friend: 'Did you notice anything unusual about my new dog?'

'Sure did,' responded the pessimist. 'He can't swim.'

How do you stop a dog smelling? – Put a clothes peg on its nose.

A man tried to sell his dog to a neighbour. 'This is a talking dog,' said the man, 'and he's yours for five bucks.'

'I don't believe you,' said the neighbour. 'There's no such thing as a talking dog.'

Just then, the dog looked up dolefully and said: 'Please buy me, sir. This man has been cruel to me. He never takes me for a walk, he buys me the cheapest, poorest quality dog food, and he makes me sleep in the garage without so much as a basket. He doesn't realize what a special dog I am. Two years ago, I climbed Everest and the year before that I swam the Atlantic.'

'You're right!' said the neighbour. 'This dog can talk! So why are you selling him so cheap?'

The owner replied: 'Because I'm sick of his lies.'

A man was walking his dog in the park when he bumped into an old work colleague.

'Do you want to pat my new dog?' he asked.

'He looks a bit vicious. Are you sure he won't bite?'

'I don't know. That's why I want you to pat him!'

A dog was sitting in a cinema with his owner. The dog never took his eyes off the screen, growling menacingly whenever the villain appeared and wagging his tail at the sight of the hero.

An elderly lady, who had been watching the dog's reactions from the seat behind, tapped the owner on the shoulder and said: 'That's amazing behaviour from a dog.'

'Yes, it is surprising,' said the owner, 'because he absolutely hated the book.'

A woman wanted to know whether she could take her new dog on board an airplane. The customer services assistant said it would be fine as long as she paid fifty dollars and provided her own kennel. The kennel, he added, needed to be large enough for the dog to stand up, sit down, turn around and roll over.

The woman said: 'Oh, I'll never be able to teach him all that by tomorrow!'

New Crossbreeds of Dog:

Collie and Lhaso Apso: Collapso, a dog that folds up for easy transport.

Deerhound and Terrier: Derriere, a dog that's true to the end.

Pointer and Setter: Poinsetter, a traditional Christmas pet.

Labrador Retriever and Curly Coated Retriever: Lab Coat Retriever, the choice of research scientists.

Bloodhound and Borzoi: Bloody Bore, a dog that's not much fun.

Terrier and Bulldog: Terribull, a dog that makes awful mistakes.

Collie and Malamute: Commute, a dog that travels to work.

Newfoundland and Basset Hound: Newfound Asset Hound, a dog for financial advisers.

Bloodhound and Labrador: Blabrador, a dog that barks incessantly.

Pekingese and Lhaso Apso: Peekasso, an abstract dog.

Malamute and Pointer: Moot Point, owned by – well, it doesn't matter anyway.

Jack saw Ray studying a chess board. Opposite him sat a dog.

'What's going on?' asked Jack.

'Just playing chess with my dog,' said Ray.

'You're kidding!' said Jack. 'Whoever heard of a dog that could play chess? That must be the smartest dog I've ever seen.'

'Oh, I don't know about that,' said Ray. 'I've beaten him three games out of four.'

When a woman's washing machine broke, she had to call out the repairman to fix it. Unfortunately he could only come to her house at a time when she was out at work, so she left him instructions.

'I'll leave the key under the mat,' she said. 'Don't worry about my Rottweiler, but, please, on no account talk to my parrot!'

The repairman let himself into the house as arranged and immediately spotted the biggest, meanest-looking Rottweiler he had ever seen. But just as the woman had said, the dog simply lay quietly on the carpet minding its own business.

The parrot was an altogether different proposition. From the moment the repairman arrived, the parrot did not stop squawking and chattering. Eventually the repairman was so fed up that he snapped: 'Shut up, you stupid bird!'

To which the parrot replied: 'Get him, Brutus!'

A man went into a pet shop and bought a talking parrot. He took the parrot home and tried to teach it to say a few things, but instead the parrot just swore at him. After a few hours of this, the man finally lost patience and told the bird: 'If you don't stop swearing, I'm going to put you in the freezer compartment as punishment.'

But the parrot carried on swearing, so the man carried out his threat and put the bird in the freezer. An hour later, the parrot begged the man to open the door. As the shivering parrot was brought out of the freezer, it said: 'I promise never to swear again. Just tell me what that turkey did!'

A man bought a budgie from a pet shop but was disappointed when it showed no signs of talking. So he went back to the pet shop.

'I've had this budgie for two months,' said the man, 'and he hasn't said a word. What should I do?'

'Try getting him a mirror,' suggested the owner. 'They love to look at their own reflections. You'll see, he won't stop talking.'

So the man bought a mirror, but still the budgie refused to talk. Two weeks later, the man returned to the pet shop.

'Try buying him a ladder,' advised the pet shop owner. 'They love climbing. You won't be able to shut him up once he's got a ladder.'

So the man bought a ladder, but the budgie remained silent. Two weeks later, the man was back at the pet shop.

'Try getting him a bell,' said the pet shop owner. 'That will definitely work. Music will bring out the talker in him.'

So the man bought a bell. Two weeks later, he returned to the pet shop.

'At last my budgie said something!' he exclaimed. 'He looked in his mirror, climbed up his ladder, rang his bell, said a few words, then dropped dead off his perch.'

'Oh no!' said the pet shop owner. 'What did he say?'

'He said: "Hasn't that shop got any bloody bird seed?"'

A couple shared their apartment with a parakeet. Since the exterminator was due to come, they put the parakeet in the bedroom and hung a sign on the door: 'Please skip this room. Do not open door. Pet flies.' The exterminator came, and on his receipt he wrote: 'Finished all of apartment except room with pet flies.'

His marriage becoming increasingly strained, a man decided that he wanted a pet as a companion he could relate to. So he went along to the pet shop in search of a new friend and there spotted a parrot with no legs or feet sitting on a perch.

'Goodness me!' said the man to the shop owner. 'What on earth happened to that parrot?'

'I was born this way,' squawked the parrot.

The man laughed to the owner. 'It was almost if the parrot understood me!'

'I did,' said the parrot. 'I understood every word. I'll have you know I'm a highly intelligent bird. I can speak three languages and can conduct a stimulating conversation on a whole range of subjects from nuclear physics to football. I would make a great companion.'

The man was impressed by the parrot's skills but one thing puzzled him. 'How do you hang on to your perch without any feet?'

'What I do,' replied the parrot quietly, 'is wrap my little parrot penis around the perch, rather like a hook. Nobody can see it because of my feathers.'

'How ingenious!' said the man. 'You're definitely the pet for me. How much are you?'

'The price tag says two hundred dollars,' replied the parrot.

'Two hundred dollars! I can't afford that!'

'Pssst,' hissed the parrot, beckoning the guy closer with one wing. 'Because I haven't got any feet nobody wants to buy me, so you can

get me for much less. I bet the shop owner would be willing to sell for
fifteen.'

So the man offered fifteen dollars and walked out with the parrot.

Over the ensuing weeks, the parrot proved the ideal companion. He
was witty, interesting, understanding and dished out excellent advice.
The man was delighted with him. Then one day the man arrived home
from work to find the parrot waiting eagerly for him.

'Here,' said the parrot, motioning him over to the cage. 'I don't
know if I should tell you this or not, but it's about your wife and the
window-cleaner.'

'What?' said the man.

'Well,' said the parrot, 'when he called round today, your wife
greeted him at the door in a skimpy nightdress and kissed him on the
mouth.'

'What happened then?' asked the man.

'The window-cleaner came into the house and lifted up her nightdress and began petting her all over,' reported the parrot.

'Oh no!' exclaimed the man. 'Then what?'

'Then he lifted up the nightdress, got down on his knees and began
fondling her body, starting with her breasts and slowly going lower
and lower . . .'

The parrot paused.

'What happened? What happened?' asked the man frantically.

'I don't know,' said the parrot. 'At that point I fell off my
perch.'

A woman bought a parrot with beautiful plumage but the only thing it
could say was 'Who is it?' After a few days she realized that the bird's
colour clashed with the rest of the living room, so she called a decorator
to give the room a new coat of paint. When he arrived to do the job, she
had just gone out to post a letter, leaving the parrot in charge.

The decorator knocked on the front door.

'Who is it?' squawked the parrot.

'It's the decorator.'

'Who is it?' repeated the parrot.

'It's the decorator.'

'Who is it?'

'It's the decorator!' yelled the man.

'Who is it?'

'It's the goddam decorator!'

'Who is it?'

'I said, it's the decorator!'

And with that, the man suffered a fatal heart attack and collapsed on the doorstep.

A few minutes later, the woman returned home. Seeing the body on the step, she said: 'My God! Who is it?'

The parrot replied: 'It's the decorator!'

Attending an auction, a man started bidding for a parrot. He thought it would cost him about ninety dollars, but just when the sale was about to be confirmed, another bidder stepped in at the last minute. This happened repeatedly, pushing the price up to over a hundred and fifty dollars and way past what the man had intending spending. Although by now he was determined to purchase the bird, he had set himself an absolute limit of two hundred and twenty-five dollars. If he couldn't buy the parrot for that, he was going to pull out. Prompted by the mystery bidder, the price continued to soar and the man put in his final bid of two hundred and twenty-five dollars.

The auctioneer said: 'Going once . . .'

The man waited with baited breath.

'Going twice . . .'

No sound of the mystery bidder.

'Sold.' The man breathed a huge sigh of relief.

As he was paying for the bird, he said to the auctioneer: 'I hope this parrot can talk. I would hate to have paid so much money for him if he can't talk.'

'Don't worry, he can talk,' said the auctioneer. 'Who do you think was bidding against you?'

A vicar new to the area visited a little old lady who owned a pet parrot. He noticed that the bird had a ribbon tied to each leg.

'What are the ribbons for?' he inquired.

The old lady said: 'If I pull the left ribbon, he sings "Clementine", and if I pull the right ribbon, he sings "We'll Meet Again".'

'And what happens if you pull both ribbons at the same time?' asked the vicar.

'I fall off the bloody perch!' said the parrot.

A man went into a pet shop and saw a duck tap dancing on an up-turned flowerpot. Impressed, he offered the shop owner twenty dollars for the duck and took it home.

The next day he went back to the shop and complained: 'That duck has been sitting on my kitchen table for hours and it hasn't danced a step. I want my money back.'

The shop owner said: 'Did you remember to light the candle under the flowerpot?'

A little boy was distraught when his new hamster died. Seeing his obvious distress, his father went to the pet shop to buy a replacement. While there, he said to the shopkeeper: 'Have you any suggestions as to what I can do with the old one? I don't want to bury it in case the cat digs it up and I don't want to throw it away for fear that my son sees it in the bin.'

The pet shop owner said: 'What I do is mix a strong sugar solution, bring it to the boil, add the dead hamster and simmer for about two hours, stirring occasionally. It makes quite a nice jam.'

So the father decided to prepare this bizarre jam recipe, but when he put it on a slice of bread, it tasted so disgusting that he promptly threw the rest of the mixture on to the garden. A few days later he noticed daffodils springing up where he had dumped the jam, which was especially puzzling because he had never had daffodils in his garden before. When calling in at the pet shop to buy food for the replacement hamster, he mentioned this strange occurrence to the shopkeeper.

'You remember that recipe you gave me?'

'Yes.'

'Well, it tasted so foul that I threw it out of the window. But the funny thing is, where it landed, I've now got daffodils growing.'

'That is odd,' agreed the shopkeeper. 'You usually get tulips from hamster jam.'

A game warden spotted a man leaving a lake carrying two buckets of fish. 'Excuse me,' he asked. 'Do you have a licence to catch those fish?'

The man said: 'No, but you don't understand, sir. These are my pet fish.'

'Pet fish?' replied the warden incredulously.

'Yes, sir. Every night I take these fish down to the lake and let them swim around for a while. Then I whistle and they jump back into their buckets, and I take them home.'

'I've never heard such nonsense,' said the warden. 'Fish can't do that!'

The man thought for a second before suggesting: 'If you don't believe me, I'll show you.'

'I can't wait to see this!' said the warden mockingly.

So the man poured the fish into the lake and stood and waited. After several minutes, the game warden turned to him and said: 'Well?'

'Well what?' asked the man.

'When are you going to call them back?'

'Call who back?'

'The fish!' snapped the warden.

'What fish?'

A man was passing a pet shop when he saw a talking monkey advertised for sale. He was so impressed by its vocabulary that he bought it on the spot.

That evening he took it to his local bar and bet everyone ten dollars that the monkey could talk. A dozen people accepted the challenge but, despite his new owner's coaxing, the monkey refused to say a word and the man had to pay up. When he got it home, the man was puzzled to hear the monkey chatting away merrily.

The next evening, the man returned to the bar and bet everyone twenty dollars that the monkey could talk. Again there were plenty of takers but, to the man's anger, the monkey remained silent. After paying up, the man took the monkey outside.

'I'm taking you back to the shop,' he stormed. 'You're a complete waste of money!'

'Chill out,' said the monkey. 'Think of the odds we'll get tomorrow.'

A man went into a pet shop and told the owner that he wanted to buy a pet that could do everything. The shop owner suggested a faithful dog.

'No,' said the customer. 'A dog can't do everything. When was the last time you saw a dog doing the ironing?'

'How about a cat?' said the shop owner.

'No, cats are too independent. Even if they could do everything, they wouldn't.'

The shop owner thought for a minute, then said: 'I've got it! A centipede!'

The man said: 'A centipede? I can't imagine a centipede being able to do everything. But it's certainly different. Go on then, I'll have a centipede.'

So the man took the centipede home and said to it: 'Clean the kitchen.'

Half an hour later he walked into the kitchen and it was spotless. All the dishes and cutlery had been washed, dried and put away. The counter tops were sparkling clean, the floor was waxed, everything looked immaculate. The man was amazed. So he said to the centipede: 'Go clean the living room.'

Twenty minutes later he walked into the living room. The carpet had been vacuumed, the furniture dusted and polished, the cushions on the sofa plumped, even the pot plants watered. The man was truly impressed and said to himself: 'This really is a pet that can do everything.'

Next he asked the centipede: 'Run down to the corner shop and get me a newspaper.'

The centipede walked out the door. Ten minutes, later it still wasn't back with the newspaper . . . twenty minutes, no centipede . . . thirty minutes, still no centipede. Wondering what was causing the delay, the man opened the front door and found the centipede sitting right outside.

'Hey!' said the man. 'I sent you down to the corner shop forty minutes ago to get me a newspaper. What's the matter?'

The centipede said: 'I'm going, I'm going! Give me a chance to put my shoes on!'

Did you hear about the cat that swallowed a ball of wool? – She had mittens.

What's the difference between a cat and a comma? – One has the paws before the claws and the other has the clause before the paws.

How did a cat take first prize at the bird show? – By reaching into the cage.

Why did the litter of Communist kittens become capitalists? – Because they finally opened their eyes.

If there are ten cats on a boat and one jumps off, how many cats are left on the boat? – None. They were copy cats.

How do cats end a fight? – They hiss and make up.

What happened when the cat went to the flea circus? – He stole the whole show.

How many cats can you put into an empty box? – Only one. After that the box isn't empty.

A man hated his wife's cat so much that he decided to get rid of it by driving it twenty blocks from home and dumping it. But as he got back home, he saw the cat wandering up the driveway. So he drove the cat forty blocks away and dumped it. But when he arrived back home, there was the cat waiting for him at the front door. In desperation, he drove the cat fifty miles out into the country and dumped it in the middle of a wood.

Four hours later his wife got a phone call at home. 'Darling,' said her husband. 'Is the cat there?'

'Yes,' said the wife. 'Why?'

'Just put him on the line will you? I need directions.'

While a little boy was away at school, his cat died. Worried about how he would take the news when he got home, his mother consoled him and said: 'Don't worry, darling. Tiger is in heaven with God now.' The boy said: 'What's God gonna do with a dead cat?'

How To Give Your Cat A Pill:

Pick up cat and cradle it in the crook of your left arm as if holding a baby. Position right forefinger and thumb on either side of cat's mouth and gently apply pressure to cheeks while holding pill in right hand. As cat opens mouth, pop pill into mouth. Allow cat to close mouth and swallow.

Retrieve pill from floor and cat from behind sofa. Cradle cat in left arm and repeat process.

Retrieve cat from bedroom, and throw soggy pill away.

Take new pill from foil wrap, cradle cat in left arm holding paws tightly with left hand. Force jaws open and push pill to back of mouth with right forefinger. Hold mouth shut for a count of ten.

Retrieve pill from goldfish bowl and cat from top of wardrobe. Call spouse from garden.

Kneel on floor with cat wedged firmly between knees, hold front and rear paws. Ignore low growls emitted by cat. Get spouse to hold head firmly with one hand while forcing wooden ruler into mouth. Drop pill down ruler and rub cat's throat vigorously.

Retrieve cat from curtain rail, get another pill from foil wrap. Make note to buy new ruler and repair curtains. Carefully sweep shattered Doulton figures from hearth and set to one side for gluing later.

Wrap cat in large towel and get spouse to lie on cat with head just visible from below armpit. Put pill in end of drinking straw, force mouth open with pencil and blow down drinking straw.

Check label to make sure pill not harmful to humans, drink glass of water to take taste away. Apply band-aid to spouse's forearm and remove blood from carpet with cold water and soap.

Retrieve cat from neighbour's shed. Get another pill. Place cat in cupboard and close door onto neck to leave head showing. Force mouth open with dessert spoon. Flick pill down throat with elastic band.

Fetch screwdriver from garage and put door back on hinges. Apply cold compress to cheek and check records for date of last tetanus shot. Throw ripped T-shirt away and fetch new one from bedroom.

Call fire department to retrieve cat from tree across the road. Apologize to neighbour who crashed into fence while swerving to avoid cat. Take last pill from foil-wrap.

Tie cat's front paws to rear paws with garden twine and bind tightly to leg of dining table. Find heavy duty pruning gloves from shed. Force cat's mouth open with small wrench. Push pill into mouth followed by large piece of fillet steak. Hold head vertically and pour half a pint of water down throat to wish pill down.

Get spouse to drive you to casualty department, sit quietly while doctor stitches fingers and forearm, and removes pill remnants from right eye. Stop at furniture shop on way home to order new table.

Arrange for your nearest animal shelter to collect cat, and call local pet shop to see if they have any hamsters.

A mother told her little boy: 'Stop pulling the cat's tail!'

'I'm not,' he protested. 'I'm just holding it. The cat's doing the pulling.'

An old lady's two cats died within a few weeks of each other. Unable to bear the thought of being parted from her beloved pets, she decided to take them to a taxidermist and have them put on display in her living room.

'These are my two cats,' said the old lady. 'They used to get on so well together.'

'Oh, that's nice,' said the taxidermist. 'Tell me, do you want them mounted?'

'No,' replied the old lady. 'Just holding hands.'

A little girl was in the garden filling in a hole when her neighbour peered over the fence. 'What are you doing?' he inquired politely.

'My goldfish died,' replied the little girl tearfully, 'and I've just buried him.'

'That's an awfully big hole for a goldfish,' remarked the neighbour.

Patting down the last heap of earth, the little girl said: 'That's because he's inside your cat.'

A man was being driven mad by his neighbour's cat. It kept him awake at night, left a mess on his drive and dug up his plants. But worst of all, it peed on his prize tomatoes the night before the local garden show. The man burst into tears at the sight of his shrivelled specimens and vowed revenge on the cat.

So the next day, he killed it, cooked it and had it for dinner. But that evening he suffered such bad indigestion that he had to call out the doctor.

The doctor said: 'It's nothing serious. I think you've just eaten something that's upset you.'

What happened when the cat swallowed a coin? – There was some money in the kitty.

What's the difference between cats and dogs? – Dogs have owners, cats have staff.

Why was the cat so small? – It only drank condensed milk.

What do you get if you cross a cat with a gorilla? – An animal that puts you out at night.

Why do you always find the cat in the last place you look? – Because you stop looking after you find it.

A man was driving along the road when a cat darted out in front of his car. Unable to stop in time, he ran over the cat and killed it. Feeling really guilty, he looked at the address on the cat's collar and went to relay the sad news to the animal's owner.

A little white-haired old lady opened the door.

'I'm so sorry,' said the man, 'but I'm afraid I've run over your cat. I'd like to replace it.'

'Sure,' said the old lady. 'How are you at catching mice?'

Roy had invited a friend round for a beer and a chat. They talked about football, women, and cars and then Roy happened to mention the trouble he was having with his cat.

'I don't know what's wrong with it,' Roy said. 'Just lately it has started biting and chewing all of my shoes. Only last week I bought a new pair of shoes to replace the ones that the cat had destroyed, but this morning I found that the cat had got those too.'

Just then the cat walked through the living room.

The friend interrupted, saying: 'Pardon me, Roy, is that the cat who chewed your new shoes?'

Similarities Between Teenagers and Cats:

Neither teenagers nor cats turn their heads when you call their name.

Cats and teenagers can lie on the sofa for hours on end without moving.

Just as you rarely see a cat out walking with a human being, no teenager ever wants to be seen in public with his or her parents.

Cats and teenagers yawn in exactly the same manner, communicating a sense of complete and utter boredom.

No cat or teenager shares your taste in music.

No matter what you do for a cat or a teenager, it is never enough. You are just there to feed them.

No matter how well you tell a joke, no cat or teenager will ever crack a smile.

Cats and teenagers wreck furniture.

Given the chance, cats and teenagers like to wander off at night in search of action.

Cats have nine lives; teenagers carry on as if they did.

A tomcat and a female tabby were courting on the back fence one night. He leaned over to her and purred seductively: 'I'd die for you.' She looked up coyly and said: 'How many times?'

A newly discovered chapter in the Book of Genesis has finally provided the answer to the eternal question: 'Where do pets come from?'

Adam said: 'Lord, when I was in the garden, you walked with me every day. Now I no longer see you. I am lonely here and it is difficult for me to remember how much you love me.'

And God said: 'No problem! I will create a companion for you that will be with you forever and who will be a reflection of my love for you, so that you will love me even when you cannot see me. Regardless of how selfish, childish or unlovable you may be, this new companion will accept you as you are and will love you as I do, in spite of yourself.'

And God created a new animal to be a companion for Adam. And it was a good animal. And God was pleased. And the new animal was pleased to be with Adam and he wagged his tail. And Adam said, 'Lord, I have already named all the animals in the Kingdom and I cannot think of a new name for this animal.'

And God said: 'No problem, because I have created this new animal to be a reflection of my love for you. Therefore his name will be a reflection of my own name, and will call him Dog.'

And Dog lived with Adam and was a companion to him and loved him.

And Adam was comforted.

And God was pleased.

And Dog was content and wagged his tail.

Soon it came to pass that Adam's guardian angel came to the Lord and said: 'Lord, Adam has become filled with pride. He struts and preens like a peacock and believes he is worthy of adoration. Dog has indeed taught him that he is loved, but perhaps too well.'

And the Lord said: 'No problem! I will create for him a companion who will be with him forever and who will see him as he is. The companion will remind him of his limitations, so he will know that he is not always worthy of adoration.'

And God created Cat to be a companion to Adam. And Cat would not obey Adam.

And when Adam gazed into Cat's eyes, he was reminded that he was not the Supreme Being. And Adam learned humility.

And God was pleased.

And Adam was pleased.

And the Dog was pleased.

And the Cat didn't give a damn one way or the other.

Police

Don was driving along a country road when a police officer pulled him over. He rolled down his window and said: 'Is there a problem, officer?'

'No problem at all. I just observed your safe driving and am pleased to award you a five-thousand dollar Safe Driver Award sponsored by the state. Congratulations. What do you think you'll do with the money?'

Don thought for a minute and said: 'I guess I'll get my driving licence.'

Hearing this, Carla, sitting in the passenger seat, said to the officer: 'Oh, don't pay attention to him – he's a bit of a smartass when he's drunk and stoned.'

Aaron from the back seat said: 'I told you guys we wouldn't get far in a stolen car!'

Just then, there was a knock from the trunk and a muffled voice said: 'Are we over the border yet?'

A young boy ran down the street in search of a police officer. Finding one, he begged: 'Please, officer, come back to the bar with me. My dad is in a fight.'

The policeman accompanied the boy back to the bar where he found three men involved in a fistfight. 'Okay, son,' he said to the boy. 'Now which one is your father?'

'I don't know, officer,' replied the boy. 'That's what they're fighting about!'

An infant school party went on a day trip to a police station to learn a little about how the law worked. There they saw pictures, tacked to a notice board, of the country's ten most wanted criminals. One of the boys pointed to a picture and asked if it really was the photo of a wanted person.

'Yes,' replied the officer. 'He's extremely dangerous. We desperately want to capture him.'

The boy asked: 'Why didn't you keep him when you took his photo?'

Did you hear about the thief who stole a calendar? – He got twelve months.

A rookie cop was teamed up in a patrol car with a veteran of thirty-five years' service. On his first day out on the road, the eager youngster spotted a crowd gathered on a street corner and prepared to spring into action.

'I'm going to disperse that crowd,' he announced to his partner. 'Watch this!'

Before his colleague could answer, the rookie had jumped out of the car and was marching over towards the assembled throng.

'Come along,' he said. 'Whatever the show was, it's over now, so it's time to move on.'

The people shuffled awkwardly but appeared reluctant to move.

Producing his baton, the rookie snapped: 'Listen, I don't want have to get rough. Move along now, folks! I'm sure none of you want a night in the cells.'

Intimidated by his threats, the crowd slowly dispersed.

Proud of his work, the rookie jumped back into the car and asked his partner: 'Well, how did I do?'

'Pretty good,' said the veteran, 'especially since this is a bus stop!'

Two police officers responded to a crime scene behind a grocery store. The murder detective was already there.

'What happened?' asked the first officer.

'Male, about twenty-five, covered in Rice Krispies and dead as a doornail.'

'My God!' said the second officer. 'Didn't we have one covered in Crunchy Nut Cornflakes yesterday? And Coco Pops last week?'

'You're right,' said the detective. 'I'm afraid this is the work of a cereal killer.'

A traffic cop pulled over a driver who had been weaving erratically in and out of lanes. Approaching the car, he said: 'Sir, I need you to blow into this breathalyser.'

'Sorry, officer, I can't do that. I'm an asthmatic. If I do that, I'll have a really bad asthma attack.'

'Okay, fine. I need you to come down to the station to give me a blood sample.'

'I can't do that either, officer. I'm a haemophiliac. If I do that, I'll bleed to death.'

'Well, then, we need a urine sample.'

'Sorry, officer, I can't do that either. I'm also a diabetic. If I do that, I'll get really low blood sugar.'

'Okay then, I need you to come out here and walk along this white line.'

'I can't do that, officer.'

'Why not?'

'Because I'm drunk.'

A police recruit was asked during his exam: 'What would you do if you had to arrest your own mother?'

He answered: 'Call for backup!'

A workman was killed at a construction site and the police began questioning a number of the other workers. Based on their previous records, many of these workers were considered prime suspects.

The electrician was suspected of wiretapping once but was never charged.

The carpenter was once arrested for getting hammered, but was never nailed.

The cement mixer was a hard case but there was nothing concrete to link him with the crime.

The window glazier went to great panes to conceal his past.

The painter had a brush with the law several years ago.

The mason got stoned regularly but his alibi was rock solid and they couldn't pin anything on him.

So who did it?

The window glazier. But he claimed he was framed.

A persistent offender was arrested yet again. Leafing through his file, the detective said: 'Hmm, this is quite a criminal record. Shoplifting, hit and run, forgery, fraud, burglary, armed robbery, car theft, burglary, burglary, burglary.'

'Yeah, I know,' said the suspect. 'It took me quite a while to figure out what I was good at.'

Two teenagers arrested for breaking into a school were taken to the local police station. The desk sergeant advised them that they were entitled to one phone call.

Half an hour later, a man entered the station.

'I assume you're the kids' lawyer?' said the sergeant.

'No way,' said the man. 'I'm here to deliver a pizza.'

A fail little old lady walked up to a police officer and said: 'I was attacked! I was attacked!'

The officer reached for his notebook. 'When did this happen, ma'am?'

'Seventy-one years ago.'

'Seventy-one years ago! What are you telling me for now?'

She said: 'I just like to talk about it once in a while.'

A country gentleman was at the police station explaining to the officer why his cousin had shot him. 'We'd had a few drinks over lunch when my cousin picked up his rifle and asked us if we wanted to go hunting.'

'Okay,' said the officer. 'Then what happened?'

'Well, that's when I stood up and said, "Yes, I'm game!"'

Police are searching for a thief who robs his victims by threatening them with a lighted match. They want to catch him before he strikes again.

A traffic cop in a small town stopped a motorist for speeding. 'But, officer,' pleaded the driver. 'I can explain . . .'

'Save your excuses,' said the cop. 'You can cool your heels in a cell till the chief gets back.'

'But, officer . . .'

'Be quiet!' snapped the cop. 'You're going in a cell. The chief will deal with you when he gets back.'

A few hours later the officer looked in on the prisoner. 'Lucky for you that the chief's at his daughter's wedding. It means he's sure to be in a good mood when he gets back.'

'Don't count on it,' said the prisoner. 'I'm the groom.'

A police officer pulled over a guy for weaving across two lanes of traffic. He walked up to the driver's window and asked: 'You drinkin'?'

The driver said: 'You buyin'?'

A police patrol car driver out of his normal area was amazed to spot an inspector on traffic duty.

'It's Inspector Jones, isn't it?' said the patrol car driver.

'Not now, I'm afraid. It's just plain old Constable Jones these days.'

'What happened? I didn't know you had been demoted.'

'My downfall,' sighed Jones wearily, 'was arresting a judge on his way to a fancy dress party. How was I to know that his convict suit was only a costume?'

'I guess that's a lesson for us all,' said the patrol car driver. 'Never book a judge by his cover.'

Alerted by a noise in the garden, a man looked out of his bedroom window late one night and saw a gang of thieves breaking into his shed. He immediately phoned the police who informed him that no officers were available at present.

'Okay,' he said, and put the phone down.

A couple of minutes later, he called the police again. 'Don't worry about sending anyone round to Woodbridge Avenue to arrest the burglars,' he said. 'I've just shot them.'

Within five minutes half a dozen police cars came screeching down the street and, naturally enough, caught the burglars.

The officer in charge was furious. He said to the houseowner: 'I thought you said you'd shot them!'

The man replied: 'I thought you said there was nobody available . . .'

A woman reported the disappearance of her husband to the police. The officer in charge looked at the photograph she handed him, questioned her, and then asked if she wished to give her husband any message if they found him.

'Yes,' she replied readily. 'Tell him mother didn't come after all.'

Once upon a time there was a US sheriff who, no matter what the situation, always said, 'It could have been worse' after viewing the scene of a crime. It drove his two deputies absolutely crazy.

One day, the two deputies in the sheriff's office answered an emergency call at a farmhouse. When they walked in, they found the naked bodies of a man and a woman in the bedroom. Both had been shot dead. When the deputies went into the living room, they found the body of a man with a gun at his side.

'No doubt about it,' said one deputy to the other. 'This was a double murder and suicide. This guy came home, found his wife in bed with somebody else and shot them both. Then he shot himself.'

'You're right,' agreed the other deputy. 'Double murder and suicide. But I'll bet you when the sheriff gets here, he'll say "It could have been worse," just like he always does.'

'No way!' said the first deputy. 'How could it be worse? There are three people in the house, and all of them have been shot to death. It couldn't possibly be any worse.'

'I'm just telling you what he'll say, that's all.'

'No, not this time, so yeah, I'll take up your bet. Ten dollars?'

'You're on.'

Just then, the old sheriff arrived on the scene. He walked into the bedroom and saw the two naked bodies on the bed. He then walked into the living room and saw the man on the floor with the gun by his side. 'No doubt about it,' said the sheriff, shaking his head. 'It was a double murder and suicide. This guy came home, found his wife in bed with somebody else and shot them both. Then he shot himself.' After pausing for a moment, the sheriff looked his deputies squarely in the eyes and said solemnly: 'But you know, it could have been worse.'

The deputy who had lost his bet jumped up and shouted indignantly: 'Sheriff, how could it have been worse? There are three people in this farmhouse, and all three of them are dead. It couldn't have been worse!'

'Yes, it could,' the sheriff retorted. 'You see that guy on the floor? If he had come home yesterday, that would be me in there on that bed!'

A man fell out of a tenth-storey window. He was lying on the ground with a small crowd gathered around him when a police officer walked over and asked: 'What happened?'

'I don't know,' gasped the man. 'I just got here.'

Did you hear about the cannibal policeman who was arrested? – He was caught grilling his suspects.

When a farmer was sent to jail, his wife struggled to keep the farm going until his release. It was no easy task for she knew nothing about farming and had to write frequent letters to her incarcerated spouse seeking his advice. One day he received a letter from her, which read: 'My dearest darling, I want to plant the potatoes. When is the best time to do it?'

The farmer wrote back: 'Honey, don't go near that field. That's where the proceeds from the robbery are buried.'

But because he was in jail, all of his mail was censored. So when the sheriff and his deputies read the letter, they rushed out to the farm and dug up the entire potato field looking for the buried loot. After two days of solid digging, they didn't find anything.

The farmer then wrote back to his wife: 'Now is the time to plant your potatoes!'

A crook tried to hijack a bus full of Japanese tourists. Fortunately the police had five hundred photos of the suspect.

A police officer pulled a man over for speeding. As the officer approached the car, he could see that the man was very anxious about something.

'Good afternoon, sir. Do you know why I stopped you?'

'Yes, officer, I know I was speeding. But it's a matter of life and death.'

'Oh, really?' said the officer, unconvinced. 'How's that?'

'There's a naked woman waiting for me at home.'

'I don't see how that is a matter of life and death.'

'You're joking,' said the man. 'If I don't get home before my wife does, I'm a dead man!'

A highly agitated young woman phoned the local police and said: 'I have a sex maniac in my apartment.'

'Okay, ma'am, we'll be right over.'

'Oh,' she said. 'Can you wait until morning?'

A farmer was stopped by a police officer for going five miles an hour over the speed limit on a straight country road. The officer's attitude was heavy-handed as he began to lecture the farmer about his speed and generally belittle him. When the officer finally got around to writing out the ticket, he had to swat some flies that were buzzing around his head.

'Having some problems with them circle flies are you?' inquired the farmer.

'Well, yeah,' said the officer, 'if that's what they're called. But I've never heard of circle flies.'

The farmer explained: 'Circle flies are common on farms. They're called circle flies because they're almost always found circling around the back end of a horse.'

'Oh,' said the officer as he continued writing out the ticket. Then it dawned on him what the farmer was implying. 'Wait a minute, are you trying to call me a horse's rear end?'

'Oh, no, officer,' said the farmer. 'I have too much respect for law enforcement to consider calling you such a thing.'

'That's all right, then.'

After a pause, the farmer added: 'Hard to fool them flies though.'

Policeman: I'm afraid that I'm going to have to lock you up for the night.

Man: What's the charge?

Policeman: Oh, there's no charge. It's all part of the service.

A police officer came upon a terrible car smash in which the driver and passenger had both been badly injured. As he studied the wreckage, a dog came out of the bushes and hopped around the crashed car. The officer looked down at the dog and said: 'I wish you could talk.'

The dog looked up at the officer and shook his head up and down.

'You can understand what I'm saying?' asked the officer incredulously.

Again, the dog shook his head up and down.

'Well, did you see this accident?'

'Yes,' motioned the dog.

'What happened?'

The dog pretended to have a can in his hand and raised it to his mouth.

'They were drinking?' asked the officer.

'Yes,' nodded the dog.

'What else?'

The dog pinched his fingers together, held them to his mouth and adopted a dreamy expression.

'They were smoking marijuana?'

'Yes,' motioned the dog.

'Now wait,' continued the officer. 'You're saying your owners were drinking and smoking before they had the accident?

'Yes,' nodded the dog.

'And what were you doing during all this?'

'Driving,' motioned the dog.

A hole has appeared in the ladies' changing rooms at a local sports club. Police are looking into it.

During a training exercise at police academy, a student was asked: 'What steps would you take if someone came at you with a large, sharp knife?'

The student replied: 'Big ones.'

A police dog handler parked his van at the station at the end of the day. As he gathered his equipment, his dog started barking.

A small boy passing by asked: 'Is that a dog you've got in the back of the van?'

'Sure is,' replied the cop.

'Gee!' said the boy. 'What did he do?'

Hurtling along the road, the driver of a high-sided lorry saw a sign, which read 'Low bridge ahead'. Before he could react and take avoiding action, it was too late. His vehicle was stuck fast under the bridge, with a line of traffic forming behind.

Eventually a police patrol car arrived on the scene. One of the officers came over to the lorry driver and said: 'Got stuck, huh?'

The lorry driver replied innocently: 'No, I was delivering this bridge and ran out of gas.'

A van load of wigs was stolen yesterday. Police are combing the area looking for clues.

Two men found three hand grenades and decided that they ought to take them to the police station.

'What if one of them explodes before we get there?' asked one.

The other replied: 'Don't worry. We'll just lie and tell them we only found two.'

A woman was driving down the highway at seventy-five miles an hour when she noticed that she was being followed by a motorcycle police officer. Instead of slowing down, however, she picked up speed. When she looked back again, there were two police bikes. So she put her foot right down, doing over a hundred miles an hour, and the next time she looked around, there were three police bikes. Then suddenly up ahead, she spotted a gas station, screeched to a halt and ran into the ladies' toilet. When she emerged from the toilet a few minutes later, the three officers were standing there waiting for her. She said coyly: 'I bet none of you thought I'd make it . . .'

A persistent thief who stole ladies' underwear from washing lines escaped capture yesterday. He gave police the slip.

A tourist asked a man in uniform: 'Are you a policeman?'
   'No, I'm an undercover detective.'
   'So why are you in uniform?'
   'Today is my day off.'

A man went to the police station demanding to speak to the burglar who had broken into his house the previous night.
   'You'll get your chance in court,' said the desk sergeant.
   'No, you don't understand,' said the man. 'I just want to know how he got into the house without waking my wife. I've been trying to do that for years!'

Driving to work, a guy had to swerve to avoid a box that fell out of a truck in front. Seconds later, a police patrol car stopped him for reckless driving. Fortunately another officer had seen the carton in the road and when he picked up the box, he found that it contained large upholstery tacks.
   'I'm sorry, sir,' said the first officer, 'but I'm still going to have to write you a ticket.'
   'What for?' asked the driver.
   'Tacks evasion.'

A basketball player and a jockey just robbed a bank. Police are looking high and low.

A man was speeding down the highway, feeling secure in a gaggle of cars all travelling at the same speed. However, as they passed a speed trap, he was nailed by a speed detector and was pulled over.
   As the officer took his details, the man complained: 'Officer, I know I was speeding, but I don't think it's fair. There were plenty of other cars around me going just as fast, so why did I get the ticket?'
   'Ever go fishing?' asked the officer.
   'Uh . . . yeah. So?'
   The officer grinned and added: 'Ever catch *all* the fish?'

Although scheduled for all-night duty at the station, a police officer was relieved of duty early and arrived home at 2am – four hours earlier than expected. Not wanting to wake his wife, he undressed in the dark, crept into the bedroom and began to climb into bed.

But just as he pulled back the covers, his wife sat up sleepily and said: 'Tom, would you go down to the all-night drug store on the next block and fetch me some aspirin? I've got a splitting headache.'

'Certainly, honey,' he said, and feeling his way across the room, he got dressed and walked to the drug store.

As he entered, the pharmacist looked up in surprise. 'Hey,' said the druggist, 'aren't you Officer Renton of the 8th District?'

'Yes, I am,' said the officer.

'Then why are you wearing the fire chief's uniform?'

Police are investigating an accident in which two trucks loaded with copies of Roget's Thesaurus collided as they left a London publishing house. Witnesses were stunned, startled, aghast, taken aback, shocked, stupefied . . .

A murder suspect was holed up in his house, surrounded by armed police officers. With no end to the siege in sight, the officer in charge yelled: 'Come on out, or I'll come in there myself and drag you out!'

The suspect shouted back: 'I'm warning you. If you don't wipe your feet when you come in, my wife will kill us both.'

A middle-aged man was driving his Mercedes along the motorway at night when he decided to put his foot down. As the speedometer touched eighty miles per hour, he suddenly he saw a police car behind him, blue light flashing. Instead of pulling over, he decided, in a moment of uncharacteristic recklessness, to try and outrace the patrol car. Accelerating away, he touched a hundred miles per hour before finally coming to his senses and pulling over.

The police car stopped. The officer got out and asked the driver for the relevant documents. Finding them to be in order, he said: 'It's been a long day and I'm at the end of my shift, and the last thing I want is to have to go back to the station and complete more paperwork. So if you can come up with a satisfactory reason for why you were speeding, I'll let you go.'

The man quickly explained: 'Last week my wife ran off with a cop and I was afraid you were trying to give her back.'

Politics

A vicar walked into a barber's shop and after getting a haircut, he asked how much it would be. The barber said: 'No charge. I consider it a service to the Lord.' The next morning the barber came to work and there were twelve Bibles and a thank you note from the vicar at the front door.

Later that day a police officer came in and got his hair cut. He then asked how much it was. The barber said: 'No charge. I consider it a service to the community.' The next morning the barber came to work and there were a dozen doughnuts and a thank you note from the police officer at the front door.

Then a politician came in for a haircut. Afterwards he asked how much it was. The barber said: 'No charge. I consider it a service to the country.' The next morning the barber came to work and there were twelve politicians at the front door.

A lifelong Republican supporter suddenly announced that he was switching to the Democrats on his deathbed.

'I can't believe you're doing this,' said his friend. 'For your entire life you've been a staunch Republican. Why would you now want to become a Democrat?'

'Because I'd rather it was one of them that died than one of us.'

Albert Einstein died and went to heaven. St. Peter said: 'You certainly look like Einstein, but you have no idea the lengths some people will go to in order to sneak into heaven. Can you prove who you really are?'

Einstein thought for a second and asked: 'Could I have a blackboard and some chalk?'

St. Peter had them fetched and Einstein proceeded to outline his theory of relativity.

St. Peter was suitably impressed. 'You really are Einstein. Welcome to heaven!'

Next to arrive was Pablo Picasso. Once again St. Peter wanted to check his credentials.

Picasso asked: 'Mind if I use that blackboard and chalk?'

St. Peter said: 'Be my guest.'

Picasso erased Einstein's equations and sketched a brilliant drawing in a matter of minutes.

St. Peter applauded. 'You must be the great artist you claim to be. Come on in!'

Then St. Peter looked up and saw George W. Bush.

'I'm the former President of the United States and I demand entry,' said Bush.

'Sorry,' said St. Peter, 'you'll have to prove it to me first. Einstein and Picasso both had to prove their identity.'

Bush looked puzzled. 'Who are Einstein and Picasso?'

St. Peter sighed: 'Come on in, George.'

When politicians get the flu, you never know which way they're going to vote. Sometimes the eyes have it, and sometimes the nose.

A politician was guest speaker at a golf club dinner. As the politician stood up to speak, a few of the men saw it as an opportunity to sneak off to the bar. An hour later, with the politician still in full flow, another man joined them.

'Is he still speaking?' they asked.

'Yes,' answered the newcomer.

'What on earth's he talking about?'

'I don't know. He hasn't got that far yet.'

Once upon a time the US government had a vast scrap yard in the middle of a desert.

Congress said: 'Someone may steal from it at night.' So they created a night watchman position and hired a person for the job.

Then Congress said: 'How does the watchman do his job without instruction?' So they created a planning department and hired two people – one person to write the instructions, and one person to carry out time studies.

Then Congress said: 'How will we know the night watchman is doing his job properly?' So they created a quality control department and hired two people – one to do the studies and the other to write the reports.

Then Congress said: 'How are these people going to get paid?' So they created positions for a timekeeper and a payroll officer, then hired two people.

Then Congress said: 'Who will be accountable for all these people?' So they created an administrative section and hired three people – an administrative officer, an assistant administrative officer, and a legal secretary.

Then Congress said: 'We have had this command in operation for one year and we are sixteen thousand dollars over budget. We must cut back on the overall cost.' So they laid off the night watchman.

Three men were sitting in an Albanian café. One man looked at the newspaper headlines, shook his head and sighed. Then the second man looked at his newspaper, shook his head and sighed. The third man reached for his hat and said: 'If you two are going to discuss politics, I'm off.'

A son in his late twenties was still living with his parents who worried that he seemed unable to decide on a career. Even they didn't know what he was best suited for, so, in the hope that they might be able to offer some valuable advice, they set up a secret test. They took a ten dollar bill, a Bible, and a bottle of whiskey and put them on the hall table. The couple then hid from view in the nearby closet. The father explained to his wife: 'If our son takes the money, he will be a businessman; if he takes the Bible, he will be a priest; but if he takes the bottle of whiskey, I am afraid he will end up a drunkard.'

Peeping through the closet keyhole, they saw their son arrive home and look at the items on the table. First, he took the ten dollar bill, held it up to the light, and slipped it into his pocket. Next he picked up the Bible, leafed through the pages, and put it in another pocket. Then he grabbed the bottle of whiskey, had a quick swig, and took it with him. Thus he headed up to his room carrying all three items. The watching father said: 'Damn! Our son is going to be a politician!'

A busload of politicians was speeding along a country road when it crashed into a tree and overturned. There was blood and glass everywhere. An old farmer saw the accident and was first on the scene. Within two hours, he had dug a huge hole and buried all the politicians.

A few days later, the local sheriff was passing through when he saw the wreckage of the bus. The farmer explained what had happened.

'Were they *all* dead?' inquired the sheriff.

'Well,' said the farmer, 'some of them said they weren't, but you know how them politicians lie!'

A local council debate was becoming increasingly heated with politicians from both major parties locking horns. As tempers became frayed, one councillor sneered at an opponent: 'Have you actually heard of John Westlake?'

'No,' admitted the other.

'Well,' said the first triumphantly, 'if you had bothered to attend a few more council meetings, you would know that he is the man who is planning to open a new strip club in the town.'

Stung into retaliation, the opponent responded: 'Have you ever heard of Alfie Johnson?'

'No,' said the first councillor. 'Who is he?'

'Well,' said the second, 'if you had attended fewer council meetings, you would know that he is the man who has been sleeping with your wife!'

When the band began playing at an embassy function, a drunken politician asked: 'Beautiful lady in red, will you waltz with me?'

'Certainly not. First, you are drunk. Second, it is not a waltz but the Venezuelan national anthem. And third, I am not a beautiful lady in red, but the papal nuncio.'

Religion

A man lived alone in the countryside with only his dog for company. One day the dog died, and the man went to his parish priest and said: 'Father, my dear dog is dead. Could you possibly say a Mass for the poor creature?'

The priest replied: 'I'm afraid not. We cannot have a church service for an animal. But there is a new denomination down the lane, and there's no telling what they believe. Maybe they'll do something for your dog.'

'Thank you, Father,' said the man. 'I'll go right away. Do you think five thousand dollars is enough to donate for the service?'

The priest exclaimed: 'Sweet Mary, Mother of Jesus! Why didn't you tell me the dog was Catholic?'

Christ was up high on the cross while Peter and the disciples watched in anguish from below. Suddenly Jesus called out: 'Peter . . . Peter . . . Peter.'

Peter rushed forward and attempted to climb the hill to reach Christ, but a centurion sliced off Peter's left arm and he fell back down the hill.

A few minutes later, Jesus again called out: 'Peter . . . Peter . . . Peter.'

Peter tried to break through once more but a centurion sliced off his other arm and he stumbled back down the hill.

Shortly afterwards, Jesus again shouted: 'Peter . . . Peter . . . Peter.'

Peter made another desperate attempt to reach Christ, but a centurion sliced off Peter's left leg and he collapsed down the hill in a heap.

A few minutes after, Jesus yelled plaintively: 'Peter . . . Peter . . . Peter.'

Peter hopped defiantly towards Christ, but a centurion sliced off Peter's other leg and he rolled back down the hill.

Moments later, Jesus screamed: 'Peter . . . Peter . . . Peter.'

Even though he had no arms or legs, Peter managed to propel himself forward. Touched by such devotion, the head centurion finally allowed him through to talk to Christ. Peter lay on the ground writhing in agony at the foot of the cross and, looking up at Jesus, gasped weakly: 'Yes, Lord. What is it?'

Jesus said: 'Peter . . . Peter . . . Peter, I can see your house from up here.'

Who is the greatest babysitter in the Bible? – David. He rocked Goliath to sleep.

One day a Catholic, a Baptist and a Methodist were going fishing. No sooner had they set up their rods and nets in the middle of the lake than the Catholic remembered that he had left the food provisions on the shore. So he got out of the boat, walked on the water, picked up his supplies, walked back on the water and climbed into the boat.

Then the Baptist realized that they did not have enough bait. So he got out of the boat, walked on the water, bought a packet of bait, walked back on the water and climbed into the boat.

Then the Methodist realized that his watch wasn't working and wanted to buy a new one. So he took it off, got out of the boat . . . but sunk all the way down to the bottom of the lake.

The Catholic turned to the Baptist and said: 'I guess we should have told him where the rocks are!'

A Christian fundamentalist couple felt it important to own a pet with similar leanings, so they visited a kennels that specialized in Christian fundamentalist dogs. One particular dog caught their eye. When they asked the dog to fetch the Bible, he did it immediately. When they instructed him to look up Psalm 23, he used his paws with great dexterity to locate the exact page.

They were so impressed that they bought the dog and took him home. That night they had friends over and took the opportunity to show off their new fundamentalist dog. The friends were equally impressed and asked whether the dog could perform any of the usual doggie tricks as well. This momentarily stumped the couple who had not given any thought to ordinary dog tricks.

'We don't really know,' they said. 'We've only seen him perform religious tricks. I suppose there's only one way to find out. Let's give it a try.'

So they called the dog and clearly pronounced the command, 'Heel!'

The dog immediately jumped up, put his paw on the man's forehead, closed his eyes in concentration, and bowed his head.

A priest was celebrating the twenty-fifth anniversary of his arrival in the parish. To mark the occasion, the church had laid on a special evening at the town hall, to be attended by various local dignitaries.

Invited to make a little speech of his own, the priest admitted: 'When I first came here, all those years ago, my immediate thoughts were what an awful town this was. For example, although obviously I cannot reveal his identity, the very first chap who entered my confessional told me how he had stolen money from the school charity box, vandalized the park greenhouse, and had been having an affair with the wife of the factory owner. But thankfully I soon discovered that he was an isolated case and that this town has many warm-hearted souls.'

As others then paid tribute to the priest's unstinting service to the community, the mayor, who was making the main speech, apologized for arriving late. Taking to the stage, the mayor then began his speech. 'I well remember Father Sullivan's arrival in this town twenty-five years ago. As a matter of fact, I had the honour of being the first person to go to him in confession . . .'

Each day at sunrise it was the tradition at a monastery for the monks to sing out the solitary word 'Morning' from their windows. On this particular day it was business as usual with a chorus of 'Morning' ringing out across the monastery until, quite unexpectedly, the word 'Evening' was heard from one window.

Two monks were strolling in the courtyard below. 'Did you hear that, Brother Timothy?' asked one.

'Hear what, Brother Michael?'

Brother Michael burst into song. 'Someone chanted evening . . .'

Did you hear about the man who told religious jokes? – He got put on the Sects Offenders List.

A woman was trying to get the ketchup to come out of the bottle. During her struggle the phone rang so she asked her four-year-old daughter to answer it.

'Mum, it's the vicar,' said the little girl.

'Tell him I won't be a moment,' called out the mother.

So the little girl said: 'Mommy can't come to the phone right now. She's hitting the bottle.'

A vicar, notorious for his lengthy sermons, watched as a man got up and left halfway through his message. The same man returned just before the end.

Afterwards the vicar asked him where he had gone.

'I went to get a haircut,' said the man.

'Why didn't you do that before the service?' asked the vicar.

'I didn't need one then!'

Four Catholic women were enjoying a coffee morning.

The first told her friends: 'My son is a priest. When he walks into a room, everyone calls him "Father".'

The second said proudly: 'My son is a bishop. Whenever he walks into a room, people say "Your Grace".'

The third said smugly: 'Well, my son is a cardinal. Whenever he walks into a room, everyone says "Your Eminence".'

The fourth woman sipped her coffee in silence until the other three turned to her.

'Well . . . ?' they chorused.

Putting her cup down, she said: 'My son is a gorgeous six foot tall male stripper. Whenever he walks into a room, everyone says "Oh my God!"'

A bartender was tending the bar one Tuesday when two nuns walked in. 'Sisters,' he said, 'I'm surprised to see you here.'

'Why is that?' asked one of the nuns.

The bartender said: 'Well, to be honest, we don't get many nuns in here.'

The nun said: 'We minister to fallen souls, and thought that this would be a good place to find them.'

'Fair enough,' said the bartender, and he fetched them two iced waters.

The next day, the bartender was going about his duties when two rabbis walked in. 'Well,' he said, 'I'm really surprised to see you two here.'

'Why is that?' asked one of the rabbis.

'Because, to tell the truth, we don't get a lot of rabbis in this bar.'

'The synagogue is closed for repairs,' explained the rabbi, 'and we needed somewhere quiet to debate rabbinical law.'

'Fair enough,' said the bartender, and he set them up with two orange juices.

The next day, the bartender was tending the bar when two Irish priests walked in. He said: 'Fathers, I must say I'm really surprised to see you two in here.'

One priest replied: 'And why is that, my son?'

The bartender said: 'Because you usually don't come in until the weekend.'

At a church harvest festival, the vicar put a sign in front of a pile of freshly baked cakes, reading 'Please take one cake only – God is watching.'

At the other end of the table sat a display of newly picked pears. A small boy put a sign in front of it, reading 'Take all the pears you want – God's watching the cakes.'

Which area of Palestine was especially wealthy? – The area around the Jordan because the banks were always overflowing.

A four-year-old boy was asked to return thanks before Christmas dinner. He began his prayer by thanking his family – his mother, his father, his sister, his uncle, his aunt, his grandpa and his grandma, even his dog – and then he thanked God for the food. He thanked God for the turkey, the sausage, the potatoes, the cranberry sauce, the fruit salad, the pies and the cakes. Then he paused. Everyone waited. Eventually he looked up at his mother and said: 'If I thank God for the broccoli, won't he know I'm lying?'

Unable to remember the names of the couples who were due to be married next week, the vicar asked the congregation: 'Would all those who want to get married please step forward.'

He was almost knocked over in the rush as eight spinsters and four widows battled their way to the front.

An old lady well known for her faith loved to shout 'Praise the Lord!' at the top of her voice. This particularly irritated her next-door neighbour, a confirmed atheist, who would insist: 'There ain't no Lord!'

The old lady struggled to make ends meet on her meagre pension and, with no food in the pantry, she decided to pray to God for help. 'Praise the Lord!' she exclaimed from her front porch. 'God, I need food. Please send me some groceries.'

The next morning she found a large bag of groceries on her front porch. She shouted: 'Praise the Lord! God has delivered for me!'

'Aha!' said the neighbour, emerging from behind a bush. 'That's where you're wrong. I bought those groceries, not God. Like I keep telling you, there ain't no Lord!'

The old woman threw her hands in the air in delight. 'Praise the Lord! He not only sent me groceries, but he made the devil pay for them!'

A young boy arrived late for Sunday School. Knowing that he was usually very prompt, the teacher asked him whether anything was wrong.

'No,' replied the boy. 'I was going fishing but my Dad told me I needed to go to church.'

The teacher was impressed and asked whether his father had explained to him why it was more important to go to church than to go fishing.

'Yes, he did,' said the boy. 'Dad said he didn't have enough bait for both of us.'

Having left the area some years ago, a teenage girl went to confession in the church she had attended as a child. The priest recognized her and asked her what she had been doing with her life.

'I'm an acrobatic dancer, father,' she replied.

'And what does that entail?'

'I can show if you like, father.'

'Please do.'

With that, the girl performed an impressive series of cartwheels, somersaults, handstands and backflips across the church.

Waiting their turn near the confessional were two middle-aged women. One said to the other: 'Will you just look at the penance Father O'Reilly is giving out tonight, and me with no bloomers on!'

When a priest was pulled over for speeding, the police officer noticed an empty wine bottle in his car and could smell alcohol on his breath.

'Father, have you been drinking?' asked the officer.

'Only water, my son,' replied the priest.

'Then why can I smell wine?'

The priest looked at the wine bottle and exclaimed: 'Oh my Lord! He's gone and done it again!'

In hospital recovering from a heart bypass operation, a man received a visit from a member of his church's council.

The council member said: 'I bring greetings from the entire church council along with their wishes that you recover soon and go on to lead a long and healthy life.'

'Thank you. That's nice.'

'It was more than nice! It was an official resolution passed by a vote of twelve to nine.'

Who was the greatest financier in the Bible? – Noah. He was floating his stock while everyone else was in liquidation.

One Sunday morning, a New York priest spotted a small boy gazing intently at the large plaque that hung in the church foyer. The plaque was covered with names, and small American flags adorned either side of it.

After observing the boy for a few minutes, the priest walked over to him and said: 'Good morning, Tim.'

'Good morning, Father,' replied the boy, still focused on the plaque. 'What exactly is this? What do all those names mean?'

'Well, Tim,' explained the priest, 'it's a memorial to all the young men and women who died in the service.'

The boy nodded silently and together they stared at it in awe until he whispered: 'Which service, Father, the 9.45 or the 11.15?'

What did St. Patrick say to the snakes when he was driving them out of Ireland? – Are ye all right in the back there, lads?

After creating Heaven and Earth, God was faced with a lawsuit for failure to secure planning permission. At the hearing he was asked why he began his earthly project in the first place. He replied that he just liked to be creative.

Then God said 'Let there be light', and immediately the officials demanded to know how the light would be made. Would there be strip mining? What about thermal pollution? God explained that the light would come from a huge ball of fire. He was granted provisional permission to make light, on condition that no environmentally damaging smoke would result from the ball of fire; that he would obtain a building permit; and that, in order to conserve energy, he would have the light out half the time. God agreed and said he would call the light 'day' and the darkness 'night'. The officials replied that they were not interested in semantics.

God said: 'Let the earth bring forth green herb and such as many seed.' The officials agreed so long as native seed was used.

Then God said: 'Let waters bring forth creeping creatures having life; and the fowl that may fly over the earth.' The officials pointed out that this would require approval from other authorities, such as the Department of Game and the Heavenly Wildlife Federation.

But everything looked on course until God said he wanted to complete the project in six days. Officials said that it would take at least six months to review the application, and after that there would need to be a public hearing, which could take another year to arrange.

At that point God created Hell.

Ducking into confession with a turkey in his arms, Brendan said: 'Forgive me, Father, for I have sinned. I stole this turkey to feed my family. Would you take it and ease my guilt?'

'Certainly not,' said the priest. 'As penance, you must return it to the one from whom you stole it.'

'I tried,' sobbed Brendan, 'but he refused. Oh, Father, what should I do?'

'If what you say is true, then it is all right for you to keep it for your family.'

Thanking the priest, Brendan hurried off.

When confession was over, the priest returned to his house. Walking into the kitchen, he saw that someone had stolen his turkey.

Three women were talking about the declining numbers in church attendance.

One said: 'The congregation at my church is down to around forty.'

The second said: 'You're lucky. Most Sundays we consider ourselves fortunate if there are more than twenty people in the congregation at our church.'

The third said: 'That's nothing. It is so bad in our church that when the minister says "dearly beloved", I blush!'

A vicar was sitting on a train doing a crossword but was shaking his head in frustration. 'One of these answers must be wrong,' he said. 'But which?'

'Can I help?' said the man in the seat opposite.

'Perhaps you could,' replied the vicar. 'Try this one. Found on the bottom of a budgie's cage, four letters, ends in I-T.'

'Grit?' suggested the man.

'Yes, of course it is!' exclaimed the vicar joyously. 'Do you have an eraser?'

A little boy was spending the weekend with his grandmother who decided to take him to the park. Admiring the beautiful landscape, she remarked: 'Doesn't it look like an artist painted this scenery? Did you know God painted this just for you?'

The boy said: 'Yes, God did it and he did it left-handed.'

His grandmother was confused. 'What makes you say God did this with his left hand?'

'Well,' said the boy, 'we learned at Sunday School last week that Jesus sits on God's right hand!'

A Sunday School teacher was struggling to open the four-digit combination lock on the church cabinet. She had been told the combination, but couldn't remember it. In the end, she asked the vicar for help. After the first three numbers, the vicar paused, stared blankly for a moment and then looked heavenward as if for divine inspiration. Immediately he came up with the fourth number and opened the cabinet.

The teacher gushed: 'I'm so impressed by your faith.'

The vicar said: 'It's nothing really. You see, I can never remember the combination either. That's why I wrote the number on a piece of paper and stuck it to the ceiling.'

A priest was speeding along on a motorbike when he was stopped by a cop. The officer said: 'I can't help noticing you've got L plates, Father. For someone who has yet to pass his test, you were going dangerously fast.'

'Don't worry, my son,' said the priest. 'Jesus is with me.'

'In that case,' said the officer, 'I'm going to have to book you. You're not allowed a pillion passenger.'

The Pope had just arrived in New York on a special papal visit. While his luggage was being loaded into the limo, he waited hesitantly on the pavement.

'Excuse me, your holiness,' said his driver. 'Would you please take your seat so that we can leave?'

The Pope looked wistfully at the car. 'They never let me drive at the Vatican, and to tell you the truth, I'd really like to drive today.'

'I'm afraid I can't let you do that,' said the chauffeur. 'I'll lose my job! And what if you had an accident?'

But the Pope was becoming insistent. 'I'll make sure you are hand-somely rewarded if you let me drive. Please. Just for this one day.'

Reluctantly, the chauffeur climbed into the back while the Pope positioned himself behind the wheel. No sooner had they left the airport than the Pope put his foot down and soon had the Popemobile doing a hundred and ten miles per hour.

'Slow down, please, your holiness!' begged the driver, but the Pope kept the pedal to the metal until he heard the sound of police car sirens.

'Oh great!' wailed the suffering chauffeur. 'Now I really will lose my licence!'

As the patrolman approached, the Pope pulled over and rolled down the window. Taking one look at him, the patrolman beat a hasty retreat back to his motorcycle and got straight on the radio. 'I need to talk to the chief,' he said urgently.

The chief of police got on the radio and the patrolman told him that he had stopped a limo that was doing over a hundred and ten miles per hour.

'So bust him,' said the chief.

'I don't think we want to do that,' said the cop. 'He's really important.'

'All the more reason.'

'No, I mean *really* important,' repeated the cop.

'Who've you got there, the mayor?'

'Bigger.'

'The governor?'

'Bigger.'

'Well,' said the chief, 'who is it?'

'I think it must be God,' replied the flustered cop.

'What on earth makes you think it's God?'

'Well, he's got the Pope driving for him!'

An atheist was spending a quiet day fishing in Scotland when suddenly his boat was attacked by the Loch Ness Monster. In one easy flip, the beast tossed him and his boat high into the air. Then it opened its mouth to swallow both.

As the man flew head over heels, he yelled out: 'Oh, my God! Help me!'

Immediately this terrifying scenario was frozen in time, and as the atheist hung in mid-air, a booming voice came down from the clouds: 'I thought you didn't believe in me!'

'Come on, God, give me a break!' pleaded the man. 'Two minutes ago I didn't believe in the Loch Ness Monster either!'

A Sunday School teacher asked her class why Joseph and Mary took Jesus with them to Jerusalem. A little girl answered: 'Because they couldn't get a babysitter.'

It was the height of summer and a fearful drought threatened the crops throughout the land. One hot, dry Sunday, the village clergyman told his congregation: 'The only thing that will save us is to pray for rain. Go home, pray, believe, and come back next Sunday ready to thank God for the rain he will send.'

The people did as they were told and returned to church the following Sunday. But as soon as the clergyman saw them, he was furious.

'We can't worship,' he raged. 'You do not yet believe that God will send us rain, perhaps this very day.'

They protested: 'We prayed and we do believe.'

'Believe?' he responded. 'Then where are your umbrellas?'

A vicar was walking near a school wearing his clerical clothes when a group of boys aged about three asked him: 'Why do you dress funny?'

'This is the uniform that vicars wear in church,' he replied.

'Can I see your collar?' asked one.

The kindly vicar took it off and handed it to the boy. On the back were letters giving the name of the manufacturer. As the little boy looked at the letters. The vicar asked: 'Do you know what those words say?'

'Yes, I do,' said the boy, who was not old enough to read. Peering intently at the letters, he said: 'Kills ticks and fleas for up to six months.'

Two nuns who worked in a hospital were out driving in the country when they ran out of petrol. As they stood beside their car on the hard shoulder, a truck approached them. Noticing the nuns in distress, the truck driver stopped and offered to help. When the nuns explained that they had run out of petrol, he said he would be more than happy to drain some from his tank, but he didn't have a bucket or a can.

Hearing this, one of the nuns produced a clean bedpan from the boot of their car and asked the truck driver if it would do. He said it would and proceeded to drain a couple of quarts of petrol into the pan. He then handed the pan to the sisters, got back into his truck and waved goodbye.

While the nuns were carefully pouring the precious fuel into their petrol tank, a police officer happened to be passing by. He stopped and watched them tipping in the contents of the bedpan before remarking: 'Sisters, somehow I don't think that's going to work, but I admire your faith!'

Exiting church one Sunday, a middle-aged woman said to her husband: 'Do you think that Nicholson girl is tinting her hair?'

'I didn't even see her,' admitted the husband.

'And that skirt Mrs Rogers was wearing,' continued the woman. 'Don't tell me you thought that was suitable attire for a mother of two?'

'I'm afraid I didn't notice that either,' said the husband.

'Huh,' said the woman. 'A lot of good it does you going to church!'

A clergyman was walking down the street when he came upon a group of young boys who were crowded around a dog. Concerned that the boys might be mistreating the animal, he went over and asked them what they were doing.

One of the boys replied: 'The dog is an old neighbourhood stray. We take him home with us sometimes, but since only one of us can take him home, we're having a contest: whichever one of us tells the biggest lie can take him home today.'

The clergyman was horrified. 'You boys shouldn't be having a contest about telling lies! Don't you know it's a sin to lie?' He then launched into a ten-minute sermon against lying, concluding with the words: 'Why, when I was your age, I never told a lie.'

Stunned into silence, the boys lowered their heads. Just as the clergyman thought he had got through to them, the smallest boy gave a deep sigh and handed him the leash: 'All right, reverend,' he said. 'You win. You can take him home.'

A deeply religious man lived in a house by the river, but one day the banks burst and the house was flooded. As the water level rose alarmingly, the man climbed on to the roof of the house. A boat came by.

'Climb aboard,' called the captain.

'No, I shall stay here,' said the man. 'God will take care of me.'

Twenty minutes later, with the waters still rising, the man climbed on to the chimney. Another boat came past.

'Jump aboard,' said the captain.

'No, I shall stay here,' said the man. 'God will take care of me.'

With the water now up to the man's waist, a helicopter suddenly swooped down.

'Quick!' shouted the pilot. 'Climb aboard!'

'No, I shall stay here,' insisted the man. 'God will take care of me.'

The water level continued to rise and soon the man was swept from the chimney and drowned. Up in heaven, he sought out God. 'I thought you said you would take care of me,' he complained.

God said: 'I sent you two boats and a helicopter. What more do you want?'

Did you hear about the man who used to pick fluff out of his belly button but gave it up for lint?

The vicar shocked the congregation when he announced that he was resigning from the church and moving to Spain.

After the service, a distraught lady came up to him and wailed: 'Oh, vicar, we are going to miss you. We really don't want you to leave.'

The vicar patted her hand reassuringly and said: 'It's very kind of you to say that but you never know, the next vicar might be even better than me.'

'Yes,' she sighed, her voice tinged with disappointment. 'That's what they said the last time too . . .'

Sean went into confessional and told the priest: 'Bless me, father, for I have sinned. I have been with a loose woman.'

The priest said: 'Oh dear. Who was it? Was it Niamh O'Connell?'

'No, father,' said Sean.

'Was it Colleen Murphy?'

'No, father.'

'Was it Siobhan Kelleher?'

'No, father.'

'Was it Mary O'Reilly?'

'No, father.'

'Was it Angela O'Byrne?'

'No, father.'

'Was it Bernadette O'Casey?'

'No, father.'

A few moments later, Sean emerged from the confessional box to be greeted by his friend Patrick.

'What did you get?' asked Patrick.

'Four Our Fathers, five Hail Marys, and six good leads.'

At a gathering to celebrate the church centenary, several former vicars and the bishop were in attendance. Prior to the formalities, the vicar gathered the children at the altar to talk about the importance of the day. He began by asking: 'Does anyone know what the bishop does?'

There was a moment's silence until one small boy said: 'He's the one you can move diagonally.'

Jesus came upon a woman being stoned by a mob. Running over to protect her, he yelled: 'Let he who is without sin cast the next stone!'

There was silence for a few moments until a rock was thrown, hitting Jesus on the side of the head. Clutching his head, Jesus shouted: 'Damn it, mother, I wish you'd just stay out of this!'

A woman was getting a homemade apple pie ready to put into the oven when the phone rang. It was the school nurse. The woman's son had come down with a high fever and needed collecting from school. The mother calculated how long it would take to drive to school and back, and how long the pie should bake for, and reckoned she would be back before the pie needed lifting out of the oven. So he popped the pie into the oven and left for school. However when she arrived, her son's fever was worse and the nurse urged her to take him to the doctor.

She drove to the clinic as fast as she dared, her nerves beginning to fray. After examining the boy, the doctor told her to get him to bed immediately and gave her a prescription for some medicine. By the time she got her son home and in bed and headed out again for the shopping mall, she was not only frayed, but frazzled and frantic as well. And she had forgotten all about the pie in the oven.

At the shopping mall she found a pharmacy, collected the prescription, and rushed back to the car, only to find it locked. In her haste, she had forgotten to remove her keys from the ignition switch. And now they were locked inside the car.

She began searching the mall for a wire coat hanger so that she could break into the car, but all of the shops seemed to stock wooden or plastic hangers. Eventually, at the fifteenth store she tried, she found a wire hanger. It was only when she hurried out of the mall towards the car park that it dawned on her that she had no idea how to pick the lock with the hanger. Then she remembered the pie in the oven. All of the frustrations of the past hour suddenly came flooding over her and she sank to her knees, bursting into tears. Looking up to the heavens, she prayed: 'Dear Lord, my boy is sick and he needs the medicine, and my pie is in the oven, and the keys are locked in the car, and I don't know what to do with this coat-hanger! Dear Lord, send somebody who knows what to do with it, and I really need that person NOW.'

As she wiped away her tears, she saw a young man climb out of a beaten-up old banger. Seizing the moment, she ran over to him, held out the wire coat hanger and gabbled: 'Do you know how to get into a locked car with one of these?'

He gawped at her for a moment, took the hanger from her hand and asked: 'Where's the car?'

Within a matter of seconds he had used the hanger to force his way into her car. All it took was a couple of twists. She was so grateful that she threw her arms around him and said: 'The Lord sent you! You're such a good boy.'

He stepped back and said: 'Actually no, ma'am, I'm not a good boy. I just got of prison yesterday.'

With this, the woman hugged him even tighter. 'Bless the Lord!' she cried. 'He sent me a professional!'

The new priest was nervous about hearing confessions, so he asked an older priest to sit in on his sessions. After the young man had heard several confessions, the older priest asked him to step out of the confessional so that he could give him a few suggestions.

The older priest advised: 'Cross your arms over your chest and rub your chin with one hand.'

The new priest tried out the gesture.

'That's good,' said the old priest. 'Now try saying things like, "I see, yes, go on" and "I understand, how did you feel about that?"'

The new priest repeated what his colleague said and nodded sagely.

The old priest concluded: 'Now, don't you think that's a little better than slapping your knee and saying, "You're kidding! What happened next?"'

After a painfully long church service, a lady parishioner went round to greet some new members of the congregation. Spotting a sleepy-looking man, she decided to rouse him from his slumbers by intro-ducing herself.

'Hello,' she said. 'I'm Gladys Dunn.'

The man opened his eyes and said: 'You're not the only one!'

A man was struck by a bus on a busy city street. As he lay dying, a crowd gathered around.

'A priest. Somebody get me a priest!' the dying man gasped. A policeman checked the crowd, but there was no priest, no vicar, no man of God of any kind.

'A priest, please!' the dying man repeated.

Then out of the crowd stepped a little old man. 'Mr policeman,' said the old man. 'I'm not a priest, I'm not even a Catholic. But for the past fifty years I've lived behind St. Mary's Catholic Church on Market Street, and every night I overhear the Catholic litany. Maybe I can be of some comfort to this man.'

The policeman agreed and brought the old fellow over to where the man lay dying. The pensioner knelt down gingerly, leant over the man and said in a solemn voice: 'One little duck, number two; doctor's orders, number nine; two fat ladies, eighty-eight . . .'

A drunk staggered in to a Catholic church, sat down in the confession box and said nothing. The bewildered priest coughed to attract his attention, but still the drunk remained silent. The priest then knocked on the wall three times in a final attempt to get the man to speak.

The drunk said: 'No use knocking, mate. There's no paper in this one either.'

Several elderly nuns were in a second floor convent when fire broke out. Thinking quickly, they took their habits off, tied them together to make a rope and climbed out of the window. After they made it safely to the ground, a news reporter quizzed one of the nuns about her ordeal.

'Weren't you afraid,' he asked, 'that the habits could have ripped or fallen apart since they are so worn?'

'No, no,' replied the nun. 'Old habits are hard to break.'

An elderly priest invited a young priest over for dinner. The younger man couldn't help noticing that his colleague employed an extremely attractive housekeeper and was highly suspicious as to whether the relationship was purely platonic. When the subject was raised, the elderly priest insisted that it was all quite innocent.

A week later, the housekeeper said that she couldn't find a silver gravy ladle and hadn't seen it since the young priest had come to the house.

'You don't think he could have taken it, do you?' she said. The elderly priest said he would write to him.

His letter began: 'Dear Father, I am not saying you "did" take my silver gravy ladle and I am not saying you "did not" take my silver gravy ladle, but it has been missing since you came to my house.'

Two days later, the younger priest wrote back: 'Dear Father, I am not saying you "do" sleep with your housekeeper and I am not saying you "do not" sleep with your housekeeper, but if you were sleeping in your own bed, you would have found your silver gravy ladle by now.'

Three wise men arrived to visit the child lying in the manger. One of the wise men was exceptionally tall and bumped his head on the low doorway as he entered the stable. 'Jesus Christ!' he exclaimed.

Joseph said: 'Write that down, Mary. It's better than Wayne.'

How do you know when you're living in a really bad neighbourhood?
– The church has a bouncer.

A minister conducting missionary work in Africa was suddenly confronted by a lion. The minister tried to escape but the lion chased him for two miles, finally cornering him against a rock face. Fearing that his life was about to end, the minister sank to his knees and prayed to God for salvation. To his amazement, the lion also began to pray.

'It's truly a miracle,' said the missionary, 'you a killer lion joining me in prayer just when I thought my time was up.'

'Ssshh!' said the lion. 'I'm saying grace.'

Where is the first tennis match mentioned in the Bible? – When Joseph served in Pharaoh's court.

An over-zealous young preacher came across a farmer working in a field. Being concerned about the farmer's soul, he asked: 'Are you labouring in the vineyard of the Lord, my good man?'

Without even pausing to look at the preacher, the farmer replied: 'Naw, these are soybeans.'

'You don't understand,' said the preacher. 'Are you a Christian?'

The farmer answered disinterestedly: 'Nope, my name is Miller. You must be looking for Jim Christian. He lives a mile south of here.'

The preacher tried again: 'Are you lost?'

'Naw. I've lived here all my life.'

Becoming increasingly frustrated with the lack of response, the preacher asked: 'Are you prepared for the resurrection?'

This finally caught the farmer's attention and he replied: 'When's it going to be?'

Thinking he had achieved the breakthrough, the preacher said: 'It could be today, tomorrow, or the next day.'

Wiping his brow, the farmer said: 'Well, don't mention it to my wife. She don't get out much and she'll wanna go all three days.'

A man went to confession and told the priest that he had been having affairs with women from five neighbouring villages.

'How could you do that?' asked the priest.

'It's easy,' said the man. 'I've got a bicycle.'

A hat was passed around a church congregation to take up a collection for a visiting vicar. But when the hat was returned to him, it was embarrassingly empty. After shaking the hat in vain to see if any coins were trapped in the lining, the vicar raised his eyes heavenward and said: 'I thank you, Lord, that I got my hat back from this congregation.'

Moses was sent by the Israelites to the top of Mount Sinai to negotiate with God over the Commandments. After two weeks of intense discussion, an exhausted Moses came down with a list of two hundred and fifty Commandments. The Israelites were not happy with this and sent him back to see if he could negotiate a better deal. Four days later, a haggard-looking Moses returned from his mission.

'I have some good news and some bad news,' he told the Israelites. 'The good news is, I've got the list down to ten. The bad news is, adultery is still in.'

How was a car mentioned in the Bible? – When David's Triumph was heard throughout the land.

A child was watching his mother sift through and delete a long list of junk e-mail on the computer screen.

'This reminds me of the Lord's Prayer,' said the child.

'What do you mean?' asked the mother.

'You know. That part about "deliver us from e-mail."'

Just before the start of a Sunday service, the townspeople were chatting away happily to each other when Satan suddenly appeared at the front of the church. There was a mass stampede for the exit as the parishioners almost trampled each other underfoot in a frantic effort to get away from evil incarnate. Soon the church was deserted except for one old man who sat calmly in his pew without moving, seemingly oblivious to the fact that God's ultimate enemy was in his presence.

Irked by this affront to his reputation, Satan walked up to the old man and said: 'Don't you know who I am?'

'Sure do,' replied the old man.

'Aren't you afraid of me?' demanded Satan.

'Nope, sure ain't.'

'Don't you realize I could kill you with a word?'

'Don't doubt it for a minute,' returned the old man, still displaying marked indifference.

'Did you know,' persisted Satan, 'that I could cause you profound, horrifying, physical agony for all eternity?'

'Yup, I guess you could.'

'And you're still not afraid?'

'Nope.'

By now, Satan was worried that he was losing his powers of intimidation. 'Well, why aren't you afraid of me?' he roared.

The old man said: 'Been married to your sister for forty-four years!'

Having invited some friends round to dinner, a couple asked their young son to say grace.

The boy was reluctant. 'I wouldn't know what to say,' he protested.

'Just say what you've heard your father say,' advised his mother.

So the boy bowed his head and began: 'Dear Lord. Why the hell did we invite these people round when there's a match on television?'

One afternoon a new pastor in town was doing the rounds of meeting his parishioners. All went well until he came to a cottage on the outskirts. Someone was obviously home, but, even though the pastor knocked on the door several times, nobody answered. Finally he took out his card and wrote on the back: 'Revelation 3:20.'

The next day as he was counting the collection, the pastor noticed that his card had been left in the plate. Below his message was written: 'Genesis 3:10.'

Revelation 3:20 reads: 'Behold, I stand at the door and knock. If any man hears my voice, and opens the door, I will come in to his house and eat with him, and he will eat with me.' Genesis 3:10 reads: 'And he answered, I heard you in the garden; I was afraid and hid from you because I was naked.'

At Sunday School the children were being taught about how God created everything, including human beings. One boy was especially interested when he heard that Eve was created out of Adam's ribs.

Later in the week his mother noticed him lying down as though he were ill, and asked: 'What's the matter?'

The little boy said: 'I've got a pain in my side. I think I'm going to have a wife.'

A man called on the vicar's wife, a woman well known for her charitable deeds. 'Madam,' he said, close to tears, 'I feel I must draw your attention to the awful plight of an impoverished family in this district. The father is dead, the mother is too ill to work, and the nine children are starving. They are about to be turned out onto the cold, empty streets unless someone pays their rent, which amounts to five hundred dollars.'

'How terrible!' exclaimed the vicar's wife. 'May I ask who you are?'

The sympathetic visitor dabbed his handkerchief to his eyes. 'I'm the landlord.'

Jesus and Satan were having an ongoing argument about who was better on the computer. They had been niggling away at each other for days until God became tired of all the bickering. Finally God said: 'Enough. I am going to set up a two-hour test, with me as judge, to determine who is better on the computer.'

So Jesus and Satan sat at their respective keyboards and typed away. They did spreadsheets, they wrote reports, they sent faxes, they sent e-mail, they sent out e-mail with attachments, they downloaded, they did genealogy reports, they made cards. In fact, they did just about every known job.

But ten minutes before their time was up, lightning suddenly flashed across the sky, thunder rolled, and the electricity went off. Satan stared at his blank screen and screamed every curse word known to the underworld.

Jesus simply sighed. The electricity finally flickered back on, and both restarted their computers. Satan began searching frantically for his work. 'It's gone! It's gone!' he screamed. 'I lost everything when the power went off!'

Meanwhile Jesus quietly started printing out all of his files from the past two hours. Seeing this, Satan became furious.

'He must have cheated!' raged Satan. 'How did he do it?'

God shrugged and said: 'Jesus saves.'

Two youngsters were walking home from Sunday School, each deep in his own thoughts. Finally one said: 'What do you think about all this devil business we studied today?'

The other boy replied thoughtfully: 'Well, you know how Santa Claus turned out. This is probably just your Dad, too.'

The minister explained to the congregation that church funds were running low and that as an incentive scheme, he would allow whoever put most in the collection plate that morning to pick three hymns. After the plate was passed around, the minister noticed that someone had generously put in a cheque for a thousand dollars. He was so touched by the warm gesture that he immediately shared his joy with the congregation and declared that he would personally like to thank whoever it was that put the thousand-dollar cheque in the plate.

At this, a shy, elderly spinster raised her hand. The minister asked her to come to the front, and she slowly made her way forward. He then thanked her again for her generosity and asked her to pick out three hymns.

Glancing around the congregation with a gleam in her eyes, she pointed to the three most handsome men in the church and said: 'I'll take him and him and him!'

Before performing a baptism, the priest approached the young father and said solemnly: 'Baptism is a serious step. Are you prepared for it?'

'I think so,' replied the man. 'My wife has been baking cakes all week, and her mother is going to lay on a nice spread – you know sandwiches and the like.'

'I don't mean that,' said the priest. 'I mean, are you prepared spiritually?'

'Oh that! Silly me! Yes, don't worry. I also got a keg of beer and a case of whiskey.'

A priest was walking down the street one day when he noticed a small boy trying to press the doorbell on a house. However despite standing on tiptoe, the boy was unable to reach. Sympathizing with his predicament, the kindly priest wandered over and pressed the doorbell for him. Then, crouching down to the child's level, the priest smiled benevolently and asked: 'And now what, my little man?'

The boy replied: 'Now we run like hell!'

Adam and his son Abel were walking past the Garden of Eden.

'Who owns that place?' asked Abel.

'That's where we used to live,' said Adam. 'Before your mother ate us out of house and home.'

A new young priest was keen to bring the church into the twenty-first century and wanted to introduce a number of modern innovations. One that proved particularly popular was his drive-through confessional.

When the bishop visited, he was greatly impressed by the new service. 'The drive-through confessional is a wonderful idea,' he said. 'It is so convenient for our church members. However I am afraid that we will have to do away with the bright neon sign that says 'TOOT and TELL or GO to HELL'.

Arriving at church one Monday morning, a preacher discovered a dead donkey in the churchyard. He called the police, but since there was no indication of foul play, the police referred him to the public health department. They said that as there was no obvious health threat, he should call the sanitation department. The manager there said he could not collect the dead donkey without authorization from the mayor. The preacher was reluctant to call the mayor, who had a reputation for being impatient and bad tempered, but he realized that in this instance he had little choice.

The mayor was every bit as cantankerous as the preacher had feared. 'What are you calling me for?' he raged. 'I've got better things to do with my time than worry about donkeys. Anyway I thought it was your job to bury the dead.'

Unable to resist the temptation to retaliate, the preacher replied calmly: 'Yes, mayor, it is my job to bury the dead, but I always like to notify the next of kin first!'

A priest and pastor from the local parishes were standing by the side of the road holding up a sign that read: 'The End Is Near! Turn Yourself Around Now Before It's Too Late!' They planned to hold up the sign to each passing car.

'Leave us alone, you religious nuts!' yelled the first driver as he sped by. From around the corner they then heard screeching tyres and a big splash.

'Do you think,' said the priest to the pastor, 'that maybe we should change the wording on our sign to "Bridge Out"?'

Moses was praying to God to free his people when the voice of God was heard from the heavens.

'Moses,' he said, 'I have good news and bad news.'

'What's the good news?' asked Moses.

God said: 'If Pharaoh will not let my people go, I will send down a rain of frogs, a plague of locusts and a plague of flies, and I will turn rivers to blood. And if Pharaoh pursues you, I shall open a path for you in the Red Sea but close it again to drown his army.'

'That would be so helpful,' enthused Moses. 'But tell me, what's the bad news?'

God said: 'Before I can do all this, you have to prepare an environmental impact statement.'

The minister was concerned about how to raise the two thousand dollars still needed to repair the church roof. Before Sunday service, he asked the organist to play some inspirational music to get the congregation into a giving mood.

'But I'm afraid I haven't any bright ideas as to what precisely you could play,' said the minister.

'Don't worry,' said the organist, 'I'll think of something.'

During the service, the minister made an appeal from the pulpit. 'As you know, we have so far raised eight thousand dollars to repair the church roof. But we still need another two. Many of you have already made generous donations, but if you were able to dig just a little deeper into your pockets, it would mean so much to the community. So, if any of you can pledge another hundred dollars, perhaps you would be so kind as to stand up.'

At that point the organist started playing the National Anthem.

One day in Sunday School, the teacher was talking to the children about Jesus.

'Alex, where is Jesus?' asked the teacher.

'Jesus is in heaven,' answered Alex.

'Very good,' said the teacher.

The teacher then asked a little girl: 'Where is Jesus, Philippa?'

'Jesus is in my heart,' said Philippa sweetly.

The teacher beamed at Philippa and said: 'That's very nice.'

The teacher then asked William: 'Where is Jesus?'

'Jesus is in my bathroom,' replied William confidently.

'How do you mean?' asked the teacher, puzzled.

'Well, every morning my dad gets up, bangs on the bathroom door and yells: "Jesus Christ, are you still in there!"'

While the preacher delivered his most robust fire and brimstone message, two little old ladies sat in their usual place in the front row, taking snuff.

'Those that fornicate are going to hell!' he bellowed.

'Amen brother!' responded the two women in unison.

'. . . And those that drink alcohol are going to hell!'

'Amen brother!' the pair sang out enthusiastically.

'. . . And those that take snuff . . .' he began, only to be interrupted by one of the old ladies, jumping to her feet.

'Hold it right there, brother! You're about to quit preachin' and start meddlin'!'

A passenger aircraft was being bounced around by severe turbulence in a thunderstorm. Things got so bad that a young woman turned to a minister sitting next to her and, with a nervous laugh, asked: 'Reverend, you're a man of God. Can't you do something about this storm?'

The minister replied: 'Madam, I'm in sales, not management.'

Three couples – an elderly couple, a middle-aged couple and a pair of young newlyweds – wanted to join a church. The priest informed them: 'We have special requirements for new parishioners: you must abstain from having sex for two weeks.' The couples agreed to the condition and returned two weeks later.

The priest began with the elderly couple and asked them: 'Were you able to abstain from sex for the two weeks?'

'No problem at all, father,' replied the old man.

'Congratulations!' said the priest. 'Welcome to the church!'

Then he moved on to the middle-aged couple and asked: 'Were you able to abstain from sex for the two weeks?'

The middle-aged man replied: 'The first week was easy enough, but the second week was tough going and I had to sleep on the sofa for a few nights, but, yes, we made it.'

'Congratulations!' said the priest. 'Welcome to the church!'

Finally he moved on to the young newlyweds and asked: 'Were you able to abstain from sex for the two weeks?'

The young man replied sadly: 'No, father, I'm afraid we were not able to go without sex for the two weeks.'

'What went wrong?' inquired the priest.

'Well, my wife was bending over the freezer to fetch out a packet of frozen peas, and I was overcome with sheer lust and took her right there.'

The priest shook his head in despair. 'You do understand that this means you will not be welcome in our church?'

'We know,' said the young man. 'We're not welcome back at the supermarket either.'

Three vicars were discussing their problems with cockroaches in their respective churches.

The first vicar said: 'I've tried putting down poison, but nothing seems to get rid of them.'

The second vicar said: 'I called in the council exterminator, but even he couldn't destroy them.'

The third vicar said: 'I managed to get rid of all mine. I simply baptised them all and I haven't seen them since.'

A man trying to understand the nature of God asked him: 'God, how long is a million years to you?'

God replied: 'A million years is like a minute to me.'

Then the man asked: 'God, how much is a million dollars to you?'

'A million dollars is like a penny.'

'God, could you give me a penny?'

'In a minute.'

There were two Catholic boys, Declan Murphy and Antonio Secola, whose lives paralleled each other in a number of amazing ways. In the same year that Declan was born in Ireland, Antonio was born in Italy. Both took their vows to enter the priesthood early in college and upon graduation became priests. Both rose through the ranks to bishop, archbishop and eventually cardinal at an astounding rate and the entire Catholic world knew that when the Pope died, the choice for his successor would rest between Declan and Antonio.

However it was generally accepted that for all Declan's virtues, Antonio was the outstanding candidate, and although it was officially a two-horse race, he was a very hot favourite to become the next pontiff. So when the Pope died, Antonio was confident of being appointed to the highest office, only to learn that the cardinals had decided to choose Declan instead.

Antonio was so upset at being overlooked that he demanded a

private meeting with the cardinals so that they could explain their shock choice. They told him: 'We are terribly sorry for your disappointment. We knew that you were the better candidate but, in our heart of hearts, we could not bear the thought of the leader of the Roman Catholic Church being called Pope Secola.'

A man joined an order of the priesthood which stipulated that he could not speak for six years, and even then he was only permitted to say two words.

After the first six years of silence, he was led into a small room. His two words were 'too cold.'

Following another six years of silence, he was taken into the same room and his two words were 'poor food'.

The next six years passed, and he was taken back to the room. This time his two words were 'I quit.'

'Good,' said a fellow priest. 'All you have done since you've been here is complain!'

Various religious leaders attended a conference in an attempt to answer the vexing question: 'Where does life begin?'

'At conception,' said the Catholic firmly.

'No, at birth,' said the Presbyterian.

'It's in between,' stated the Baptist. 'Life begins at twelve weeks when the foetus develops a functional heartbeat.'

'I disagree with all of you,' said the rabbi. 'Life begins when your last child leaves home and takes the dog with him.'

A small boy was flicking through the pages of a dusty old edition of the Bible when something fell out. It was a leaf that had been pressed between the pages.

'Look what I've found, Mum,' he called out.

'What have you got there?' asked his mother.

The boy said: 'I think it's Adam's underwear!'

Noah went to see God in order to ask him for a new, improved ark.

'OK,' said God, 'what sort of design had you in mind?'

'Well,' said Noah, 'I want it to have plenty of floors. At least five, maybe even six.'

'Right,' said God, taking notes. 'Five or six floors.'

'And naturally I'll want some animals.'

'Naturally. Any particular sort?'

'Fish, I think,' replied Noah.

'What type of fish?' inquired God.

'Carp would be nice. Yes, definitely. Carp.'

After going through the other details – door and window positions, colour schemes etc – they came up with an overall ark design that they were both happy with.

'So,' said God, 'what are you going to call it?'

'I was thinking along the lines of Noah's Multi-Storey Carp Ark.'

A man was driving down the road when his car broke down near a monastery. He went to the monastery, knocked on the door and said: 'My car has broken down. Could I possibly stay the night?'

The monks graciously accepted him, fed him dinner, and even fixed his car. But as the man was drifting off to sleep, he heard a strange sound. The next morning he asked the monks what the sound was, but they said: 'We can't tell you. You're not a monk.'

The man was mystified but thanked them anyway and went on his way.

Some years later the same man broke down again in front of the same monastery. Once more, the monks fed him, fixed his car and allowed him to stay the night. Just as he was falling asleep, he heard the same strange noise that he had heard years earlier. The next morning he asked what it was, but the monks replied: 'We can't tell you. You're not a monk.'

The man was so frustrated that he said: 'Look, I'm dying to know. If the only way I can find out what that noise was, is to become a monk, how do I become a monk?'

The monks said: 'You must travel the earth and tell us how many blades of grass there are and the exact number of grains of sand. When you find these numbers, you will become a monk.'

The man set about this daunting task. For the next fifty years he travelled the length and breadth of the globe, counting blades of grass and grains of sand until his work was finally complete. Armed with this information, he returned to the monastery and announced: 'I have travelled the earth and have found what you asked for. There are 347, 498, 675, 212, 031 blades of grass and 664, 981, 732, 434, 109, 597, 436, 501 grains of sand on this earth.'

The monks replied: 'Congratulations. You are a monk. We will now show you the way to the sound.'

The monks led him to a large wooden door and told him: 'The sound is right behind that door.'

They gave him the key to the door and he opened it. Behind the wooden door was another door made of stone. The monks gave him the key and he opened it, only to find another door made of silver. He demanded the key to that door from the monks and was given it. As he opened the door, it revealed yet another door, this time made of copper. He asked for the key to the copper door, certain that this would reveal the answer to the secret that had troubled him for over half a century, but behind it he merely found another door, this time made of iron. On and on he went – through doors made of emerald, ruby and gold – until finally the monks said: 'This is the key to the last door.'

The man was hugely relieved. He unlocked the door, turned the knob, and behind that door he was amazed to discover the source of that strange sound.

But I can't tell you what it was because you're not a monk.

Riddles

How do you turn a duck into a soul singer? – Put him in the microwave until his bill withers.

Why did the boa constrictors get married? – Because they had a crush on each other.

What happened when the glassblower inhaled? – He got a pane in the stomach.

What do you call the drivers in an Egyptian traffic jam? – Tootin-car-men.

What is a myth? – A female moth.

How can you get in touch with a fish? – Drop him a line.

If Ireland sank into the sea, which county wouldn't sink? – Cork.

Which side of a bird has the most feathers? – The outside.

What do you call Santa's helpers? – Subordinate Clauses.

How can you tell if there is an elephant under your bed? – Your nose touches the ceiling.

Why wouldn't the butterfly go to the dance? – It was a moth-ball.

What did the fish say when he hit a concrete wall? – Dam!

How can you get four suits for a dollar? – Buy a pack of cards.

How did the belt break the law? – It held up some trousers.

Why did the man stamp on his watch? – Because he had time to kill.

What do Eskimos get from sitting on the ice too long? – Polaroids.

How did vampires come over from Europe? – On blood vessels.

What happened when the bicycle salesman broke his ankle? – He was unable to peddle his wares.

Why is it hard for a ghost to tell a lie? – Because you can see right through him.

How do we know the ocean is friendly? – It waves.

What do you get if you cross a Frisbee with a cow? – Skimmed milk.

What's black and white and makes a lot of noise? – A zebra with a drumkit.

Which is faster – hot or cold? – Hot: you can catch a cold.

What happened to the man caught hanging around a circus? – He was arrested for loitering within tent.

What do you call two spiders who just got married? – Newlywebs.

What happened when the waltzers broke down at an amusement park? – They had to hire a spin doctor.

What's the most popular Christmas wine? – 'I don't like Brussels sprouts.'

How can you tell if a ghost is flat? – Use a spirit level.

Who invented King Arthur's round table? – Sir Cumference.

How do you get a mouse to smile? – Say cheese.

What is never built to scale? – Prison walls.

What happened when the ladies' panties fell in the vat at a beer-maker's? – A scandal was brewing.

What do you call a polite snake? – A civil serpent.

Why is a maths book sad? – Because it has so many problems.

What lies on the ground, a hundred feet in the air? – A dead centipede.

How many successful jumps must a skydiver make before he gradu-ates? – All of them.

Why do people become bakers? – Because they knead the dough.

Why was the guitar player nervous? – He was always fretting about something.

What do you get if you pour boiling water down a rabbit hole? – Hot cross bunnies.

What do you call an ice cream van man? – Sundae driver.

Why don't prawns give to charity? – Because they're shellfish.

What did the log say to the lumberjack? – You give me a splitting headache.

Why did the fitness instructor cross the road? – Because someone on the other side could still walk.

What's the difference between a fitness instructor and a dentist? – A dentist lets you sit down while he's hurting you.

What do you get when two strawberries meet? – A strawberry shake.

How do you make a cigarette lighter? – Take out all the tobacco.

Why were the early years of history called the Dark Ages? – Because there were so many knights.

Why is Santa so jolly? – Because he knows where all the bad girls live.

What is a five-letter word that if you take out the first, third, and last letter, it's still the same word? – Empty.

What's black, white, black, white, black, white, black, white? – A penguin rolling down the stairs.

Why don't skeletons like parties? – They have no body to dance with.

What's the difference between a jeweller and a jailer? – A jeweller sells watches, a jailer watches cells.

How are false teeth like stars? – They come out at night.

What do astronauts get when they're far apart? – Spaced out.

Why was the electrician disqualified from the race? – Because he made a short circuit.

What do you call a parrot wearing a raincoat? – Polyunsaturated.

How did the teenager know he had bad acne? – His dog called him Spot.

Why do elephants have corrugated feet? – To give ants a fifty-fifty chance.

Where do ships go when they're ill? – To the docs.

If a girl falls down a well, why can't her brother help her out? – Because he can't be a brother and assist her too.

What's the best way to kill a circus act? – Go for the juggler.

How do you keep flies out of the kitchen? – Put a pile of manure in the living room.

What subject did the witch pass in school? – Spelling.

What did the skeleton have for supper? – Ribs.

What's grey? – A melted penguin.

What's orange and sounds like a parrot? – A carrot.

What's brown and sticky? – A stick.

What do you call a fly with no wings? – A walk.

Why don't witches like to ride their brooms when they're angry? – Because they're afraid of flying off the handle.

What grows down when it grows up? – A goose.

Why did the tomato blush? – Because he saw the salad dressing.

What do John the Baptist and Winnie the Pooh have in common? – Their middle name.

Why was the refrigerator afraid? – The milk went bad and turned rotten.

When doesn't it matter if a sailor can't swim? – When he's not in the water.

When is a car not a car? – When it turns into a driveway.

How do you know when you've passed an elephant? – You can't get the toilet seat down.

Riddles

How could a cowboy ride into town on Friday, stay two nights, and ride out on Friday? – Friday is the name of his horse.

When is it dangerous to be hit on the head by a tomato? – When it's still in the can.

What do you get if you put a budgie in a blender? – Shredded tweet.

Where does a sheep get a haircut? – At the baa-baa shop.

Where does success come before work? – In the dictionary.

Where was the Magna Carta signed? – On the bottom.

What's got horns and a beard and walks through walls? – Casper the friendly goat.

What gets smaller the more you put in it? – A hole in the ground.

How did Darth Vader know what Luke was getting for Christmas? – He felt his presents.

What is so fragile that even saying its name can break it? – Silence.

Why are elephants wrinkled? – Have you ever tried to iron one?

Why did the baby strawberry cry? – Because his mother was in a jam.

Why did Henry VIII put skittles on his lawn? – So he could take Anne Boleyn.

Why did the traffic light turn red? – You would too if you had to change in the middle of the street!

What is E.T. short for? – Because he's got little legs.

What has two humps and is found at the North Pole? – A lost camel.

What's the red stuff between an elephant's toes? – Slow pygmies.

What is the difference between a hill and a pill? – One is hard to get up; the other is hard to get down.

Why didn't anyone play cards on Noah's Ark? – Because Noah sat on the deck.

Why didn't the horse draw a cart? – Because it couldn't hold the pencil.

What do you call bears with no ears? – B.

Why is getting up at four o'clock in the morning like a pig's tail? – It's twirly.

Why do lions eat raw meat? – They don't know how to cook.

What bird can lift the most weight? – A crane.

What's long, yellow, and fruity? – An apple in disguise.

What can you put in a box that will actually make it lighter? – Holes.

Why did E.T. have such big eyes? – He saw his phone bill.

What do you call an unemployed jester? – Nobody's fool.

Why was six unhappy? – Because seven eight nine.

What has two grey legs and two brown legs? – An elephant with diarrhoea.

What do you do if you see a spaceman? – Park your car in it man.

Why do ghouls and demons hang out together? – Because demons are a ghoul's best friend.

What do you call a sleepwalking nun? – A Roamin' Catholic.

What time is it when an elephant sits on the fence? – Time to get a new fence.

How many birthdays does the average man have? – Just one!

What do you do with a dog that has no legs? – Take him out for a drag.

Why was the theatre crying? – The seats were all in tiers.

What's the quickest way to make anti-freeze? – Hide her clothes.

What does a penguin have that nothing else has? – Baby penguins.

What do you call a missing parrot? – A polygon.

What do you get if you cross a snowflake with a crocodile? – Frostbite.

What do you call an underground train full of professors? – A tube of smarties.

What did the bald man say when he got a comb for his birthday? – 'Thanks, I'll never part with it.'

What is half of infinity? – Nity.

How do Eskimos stop their mouths from freezing up? – They grit their teeth.

What did Batman say to Robin before they got in the car? – 'Get in the car, Robin.'

What do you get if you cross an elephant with a fish? – Swimming trunks.

What do you call something that runs around your garden all day and never stops? – The fence.

Why couldn't Dracula's wife get to sleep? – Because of his coffin.

What do elephants have for lunch? – An hour, like everyone else.

What dog keeps the best time? – A watch dog.

What do you call an igloo without a toilet? – An ig.

Which fish is very musical? – A tuna fish.

What word is always pronounced incorrectly? – Incorrectly.

What gets wetter the more it dries? – A towel.

What has eighteen legs and catches flies? – A baseball team.

What has four legs but only one foot? – A bed.

What is as sharp as a vampire's fang? – His other fang.

What has teeth but doesn't bite? – A comb.

What do you call a fish on a motorcycle? – A motor pike.

What do you call a sheep with no legs? – A cloud.

What has tracks that arrive before it gets there? – A train.

What's green and fuzzy and would kill you if it fell out of a tree? – A pool table.

How can you tell if an elephant is sitting behind you in the bathtub? – You can smell the peanuts on his breath.

What is a volcano? – A mountain with hiccups.

What is black and white and has sixteen wheels? – A zebra on roller skates.

What is dark but made out of light? – A shadow.

What is Dracula's favourite soup? – Scream of tomato.

What is grey, has large ears, a trunk, and squeaks? – An elephant wearing new shoes.

What happened to the guy who couldn't keep up his payments to the exorcist? – He was repossessed.

What is worse than raining cats and dogs? – Hailing taxis.

What kind of clothing lasts the longest? – Underwear: it's never worn out.

What two words have the most letters? – Post Office.

What do you call a centipede crossed with a parrot? – A walkie-talkie.

What do you call a female magician? – Trixie.

What do you call a man with a government subsidy? – Grant.

What do you call a man with a seagull on his head? – Cliff.

What do you call a man who wears a coat? – Mac.

What do you call a man who wears two coats? – Max.

What do you call a man with sports equipment on his head? – Jim.

What do you call a woman with a boat on her head? – Maude.

What do you call a woman with a roulette wheel on her head? — Bette.

What do you call a man in debt? – Owen.

What do you call a woman lying in the middle of a tennis court? – Annette.

What do you call a Brazilian with a rubber toe? – Roberto.

Royalty

Shortly after Queen Victoria visited the city in British Columbia named in her honour, she was asked if a housing development could also be named after her – Victoria Mews. She replied loftily: 'We can be a city in Canada and we can be a falls in Africa, but we are not a mews.'

Prince Charles arrived in Iran on a state visit and asked the President: 'Where's the Shah?'

The President looked puzzled. 'What do you mean? There is no Shah. We got rid of the Shah years ago.'

'Very well,' said Prince Charles. 'In that case I'll take a bath.'

A humble crab fell in love with a beautiful lobster princess, but her father, the king, forbade the relationship on the grounds that the crab was of lowly stock. The unsuitable suitor was a crushed crustacean.

'Why, oh, why does your father disapprove of me?' he wailed.

The equally tearful princess replied: 'Daddy says you're not a well-dressed crab, but in truth, he doesn't like crabs anyway. He says they're common and, above all, they have that silly sideways walk. I'm so sorry, my darling, but it seems that we can never be together.'

The crab was determined to prove the king wrong and win the claw of his fair daughter. The ideal opportunity to prove his worth was the forthcoming Grand Lobster Ball, an occasion that attracted lobsters from far and wide to feast, drink and dance. While the king sat on his throne, the lobster princess sat at his side, her heart longing for her absent lover.

Suddenly the door flew open and in walked the crab. The music stopped and all eyes focused on him as he painstakingly made his way up the red carpet towards the throne, walking dead straight, one claw after another. Nobody had ever seen a crab walk straight before. Even the king was impressed.

Finally after twenty long minutes of straight walking, the crab reached the throne. There, he stopped, looked up at the king and said: 'Man, I'm drunk!'

Once upon a time there was an old man who lived in a house made entirely of grass. It had a grass floor, grass walls and a grass roof. The old man never troubled anyone but he did have a strange phobia – he couldn't help stealing the seats of kings and queens. Whenever he went to Spain, Scandinavia or Britain, he would return with a royal throne so that eventually he amassed a collection of over a dozen. He kept them all hidden away in his house, hoping that his secret would never be discovered.

Then one day the police arrived and led the old man away.

'What have I done wrong?' he protested.

'You know the law,' said the chief of police. 'People in grass houses shouldn't stow thrones.'

Sex

A man complained to his doctor that his sex life had become boring. The doctor told him he needed to spice it up, to introduce some excitement, some unexpected passion. The man thought about what the doctor had said and came up with a plan.

The following week he returned to the doctor and said: 'I did everything you suggested. The boss let me leave work an hour early. I sped home as fast as I could, roared up the driveway, slammed the door, charged into the house and found my wife in the living room. Then I stripped her naked and made wild, passionate love to her on the coffee table.'

'And did you enjoy it?' asked the doctor enthusiastically.

'Kind of, but the Bible group thought it was really cool!'

A couple had been married for thirty-five years. Then one day the husband suddenly announced that he was planning to throw himself off a bridge.

'Why, honey?' asked his shocked wife. 'What's wrong?'

'We're in terrible debt. All my investments have failed, I'm in trouble with loan sharks, and I've lost a small fortune gambling on the horses. I can't see any way out.'

'Don't worry,' she said reassuringly. 'I've never told you this, but ever since we got married, I've been putting aside two dollars from every time we had sex. And now our savings have grown to over a hundred thousasnd dollars.'

The husband sighed: 'And to think, I didn't give you all my business!'

Two guys – Jerry and Carl – were discussing the glamorous new office secretary over lunch.

Jerry whispered to Carl: 'I dated her last Tuesday and we had fantastic sex. I know I shouldn't say this, but she's a lot better in bed than my wife.'

Two days later, Carl sidled up to Jerry at work and said: 'I dated the secretary last night and we had sex too. But I still think your wife is better in bed.'

A guy asked his girlfriend what he was like as a lover.

'Warm,' she said. 'Yes, that's the word I'd use: warm.'

He was flattered until he went home and, just out of interest, looked up the meaning of the word 'warm' in the dictionary.

It said: 'warm: not so hot.'

A salesman was testifying in divorce proceedings against his wife. His lawyer said: 'Please describe the incident that first caused you to suspect your wife's infidelity.'

The husband began: 'I'm on the road all week, so naturally when I'm home I'm very attentive to my wife. One Sunday morning we were in the middle of a really heavy session of lovemaking when the old lady in the apartment next door pounded on the wall and yelled: "Can't you at least stop all that racket at weekends?"'

A father asked his ten-year-old son if he knew about the birds and the bees.

'I don't want to know!' shouted the child, bursting into tears and fleeing the room.

Confused, the father went looking for the boy. He finally found him in the garden, still crying. 'What's wrong, son?' he asked.

'Oh, Dad,' he sobbed. 'When I was six, I got the "there's no Santa" speech. At seven, I got the "there's no Easter bunny" speech. Then at eight, you hit me with the "there's no tooth fairy" speech. If you're going to tell me now that grown-ups don't really have sex, I've got nothing left to live for!'

A woman went to the doctor complaining of exhaustion. After tests revealed nothing obvious, the doctor asked her how often she had sex.

'Every Monday, Wednesday and Saturday,' she answered.

The doctor advised: 'Cut out Wednesday.'

'I can't,' she said. 'That's the only night I'm home with my husband.'

A middle-aged man was told at the hospital that he had only twenty-four hours to live. He went home in a state of shock and fell into his wife's arms.

'I've been told I've only got twenty-four hours to live,' he said. 'Can we have sex one last time?'

'Of course, honey,' she said, and they went to bed.

Four hours later, he turned to her and said: 'Could we have sex again? I've only got twenty hours to live. It will probably be our last chance.'

'Sure, honey,' replied his wife, and they had sex.

Eight hours later, he asked her: 'Do you think we could have sex one more time? After all, I've only got twelve hours to live.'

'OK,' said the wife, and they had sex.

Four hours later, he nudged her in bed. 'I just realized I've only got eight hours to live. Could we have sex one last time?'

'Very well,' she sighed. 'It's the least I can do in the circumstances.'

So they had sex. Four hours later, he woke her again. 'I've only got four hours to live,' he said. 'Would you mind if we had sex just one more time – our final act of love?'

This was too much for the wife. 'Listen,' she snapped, 'you might not have to get up in the morning, but I have!'

Following a succession of complaints about her shortcomings as a cook and housekeeper, a maid was dismissed by her wealthy female employer.

Refusing to accept such criticism, the maid answered back. 'Your husband considers me a better cook and housekeeper than you, madam. He has told me himself. And furthermore, I am better in bed than you!'

'And I suppose my husband told you that, too?' said the rich woman angrily.

'No, madam. The postman.'

A man walked into the bedroom to find his wife in bed with another man.

'Who is this man?' demanded the husband.

'That's a fair question,' said the wife, turning to her lover. 'What is your name?'

A fireman and his wife had become bored with their sex life, so he tried to liven it up by incorporating the bell system that was used at work. At the fire station when the first bell rings, everyone runs to the engines; on the second bell, they gear up; and on the third bell they jump on the engines and head for the fire. So he went home and told his wife: 'I've got this fabulous idea to spice up our sex life. We're gonna use the bell system. When I shout "bell one", you run into the bedroom; when I shout "bell two", you take off your clothes; and when I call "bell three", you jump on the bed and we make passionate love. Got it?'

The next evening he returned home from work and immediately shouted 'bell one'. His wife ran into the bedroom. Then he called out 'bell two' and she took off her clothes. Then he yelled 'bell three' and the pair leaped on the bed together and started making love. But no sooner had they started than she suddenly cried: 'Bell four, bell four!'

'What the hell's bell four?' he gasped.

'More hose! More hose! You're nowhere near the fire!'

An old man complained to the doctor of feeling tired. The doctor asked him whether he had done anything unusual lately.

'Well,' said the old man, 'Wednesday night I did pick up a twenty-year-old secretary and nailed her three times. Then Thursday night I hooked up with a nineteen-year-old waitress, and we ended up in bed at her place. On Friday night I met an eighteen-year-old nurse and we finished up in the back of her car out at lovers' lane. Then Saturday night I was lured to a motel room by seventeen-year-old twins.'

The doctor was impressed by such stamina at his age but warned: 'I hope you took precautions.'

'Of course I did,' said the old man. 'I gave them all phoney names.'

A businessman packing for a trip glanced in his briefcase and called to his wife: 'Honey.'

'Yes, darling?' she answered.

'Honey,' he said mildly exasperated, 'why do you persist in putting a condom in my briefcase every time I go on a trip? You know I only have eyes for you. I'd never be unfaithful.'

'I know, darling,' she said, 'and I trust you implicitly. It's just that, well, you know, with all those terrible diseases out there, it would make me feel better to know that if anything did happen, you'd be protected. So please, darling, take it with you, won't you? For my sake?'

'Oh, all right, if you put it like that,' he relented. 'I'll do it for you. But for heaven's sake, give me more than one!'

A nervous young man was pacing up and down the waiting room at a maternity hospital. Meanwhile a middle-aged man was relaxing reading a magazine. Sensing that the older man obviously had considerable experience of these matters, the young man asked him tentatively: 'How long after the baby is born can you have sex with the mother?'

The man raised his head from his magazine and replied: 'It depends if she's in a public ward or a private ward.'

A guy wandered over to a beautiful woman in a bar and started chatting her up. Soon he said: 'Do you mind if I ask you a personal question?'

'That depends on how personal it is,' she replied icily.

'Okay,' he said, going for broke. 'How many men have you slept with?'

'I'm certainly not going to tell you that!' she snapped. 'That's my business!'

'Sorry,' he said. 'I didn't realize you made a living out of it.'

A man was prescribed Viagra by his doctor who told him to take it one hour before sex. The man collected his prescription and went home to wait for his wife to get in from work. An hour before she was due home, he took the Viagra pill. But just as he was expecting her, she phoned to say that she wouldn't be home for another two and a half hours.

In a panic, he phoned the doctor. 'What should I do?' he asked. 'I've taken the pill, but the effects will have worn off by the time my wife gets home.'

'I see,' said the doctor. 'It's a pity to waste it. Do you have a maid?'

'Yes.'

'Well, could you not occupy yourself with her instead?'

'But I don't need Viagra with the maid.'

Sharon: I had that gorgeous man we've all been trying to date banging on my door last night for nearly an hour and a half.

Tracey: Why didn't you open it?

Sharon: I didn't want to let him out!

A woman went to consult a psychiatrist over problems she was having with her sex life. The psychiatrist asked her a series of questions but did not appear to be getting a clearer picture of her problems. Finally he asked: 'Do you ever look at your husband's face while you are having sex?'

'Well, yes,' she said. 'I did once.'

'And how did he look?'

'Really angry.'

'Now this is very interesting. We must delve deeper into this. Tell me, you say that you have only seen your husband's face once during sex; that seems somewhat unusual. How did it occur that you saw his face that one time?'

'He was looking through the window at us.'

A circus owner advertised for a new lion tamer and two young people showed up for an audition. One was a good-looking lad; the other was a beautiful blonde girl.

The circus owner told them: 'I'm going to give it to you straight. This is one ferocious lion. He ate my last tamer, so you guys had better be good or you're history. Here's your equipment: a chair, a whip and a gun. Who wants to try out first?'

The girl said: 'I'll go first.' She walked past the chair, the whip and the gun and walked straight into the lion's cage. The lion began to snarl and pant and began to charge her. But about halfway there, she threw open her coat to reveal her gorgeous naked body. The lion stopped dead in his tracks, sheepishly crawled up to her and started licking her ankles. Then he started licking her calves and kissing them tenderly before resting his head at her feet.

The circus owner was stunned. 'I've never seen a display like that in my life.' Then he turned to the young man and asked: 'Can you top that?'

The young man replied: 'No problem. But first, get that lion out of the way.'

Having announced that he was going to marry a woman of twenty-five, a ninety-year-old man was persuaded by his friends and family to undergo a medical examination to see whether he was still sexually fit.

The doctor said: 'Let me see your sex organs.'

The old man stuck out his tongue and his middle finger.

George went on a golfing holiday with his pal Bill, but after driving for a couple of hours they got caught up in a terrible storm. With the road ahead flooded, they realized that there was no chance of reaching their hotel and so they pulled into a nearby farmhouse and asked the attractive lady of the house whether they could possibly stay the night.

'I'm recently widowed,' she explained, 'and I'm afraid the neighbours will talk if I let you stay in my house.'

'That's no problem,' said George. 'We'll sleep in the barn.'

Ten months later, George received a letter from the widow's lawyer. George immediately phoned Bill and said: 'Bill, do you remember that good looking widow at the farm where we stayed over last March?'

'Yes, I do.'

'Did you happen to get up in the middle of the night, go up to the house and have sex with her?'

'Yes, I have to confess that I did.'

'And did you happen to use my name instead of telling her yours?'

Bill said sheepishly: 'Yes, I'm afraid I did.'

'Well, thanks pal,' said George. 'She just died and left me her farm!'

Two men were having a drink together. One said: 'I had sex with my wife before we were married. What about you?'

'I don't know,' said the other. 'What was her maiden name?'

Arriving home from school, a boy asked his mother: 'What is sex?'

Dreading the day that she would have to explain all this, she spent the next hour telling him about the birds and the bees and where babies come from.

When she had finished, her son smiled, pulled a school questionnaire from his pocket and pointed to the word 'sex'. 'That's cool, mom, but how am I supposed to get it all in this little box next to the F and the M?'

According to popular belief, when God was creating the world, he called Man aside and bestowed upon him twenty years of normal sex life. Man was horrified and demanded more, but God refused to reconsider.

Then God called the monkey aside and awarded him twenty years of sex life.

'But I don't need twenty years,' said the monkey. 'All I need is ten.'

Hearing this, Man spoke up and said: 'Can't I have the other ten?' The monkey agreed to let Man have the other ten years.

Then God called the lion aside and gave him twenty years of sex life. The lion said that ten would be sufficient, whereupon Man asked for the other ten and the lion agreed.

Then God called the donkey aside and awarded him twenty years.

'I don't need twenty years,' said the donkey. 'Ten is plenty.' Once again Man asked for the other ten years and was duly given them.

All of this explains why Man has twenty years of normal sex life, ten years of monkeying around, ten years of lion about it, and ten years of making an ass of himself.

'I have a confession to make,' a young man told his girlfriend. 'While we've been dating, I've been secretly seeing a psychiatrist.'

'Don't worry,' she said. 'I've been secretly seeing a footballer and a car salesman.'

Shopping

It was the day of the big sale at the city's leading department store. Determined bargain-hunters had been queuing all night so that by 8.30 in the morning the line stretched right around the block. Amid the anticipation and impatience, a small man pushed his way to the front of the queue, only to be shoved back by the irate shoppers. When he tried again to barge his way forward, he was punched in the face for his trouble and thrown back to the end of the line. As he got to his feet for the second time, he said to one of the shoppers: 'I've had enough! If they hit me one more time, I'm not going to open the damn store!'

A customer walked into a small hardware store and asked the manager: 'Do you have any brackets?'
 'No, sorry.'
 'Well, do you have any screwdrivers?'
 'No, we're out of those, too.'
 'How about hammers? Have you got any hammers?'
 'No.'
 'Garden forks?'
 'No.'
 'Shears?'
 'No.'
 'Door handles?'
 'No.'
 'This is a complete waste of time!' raged the customer. 'If you haven't got anything in stock, you might as well lock up the damn shop!'
 The manager shrugged his shoulders and said: 'I haven't got a key.'

A wife asked her husband to buy organic vegetables. He went to the supermarket but couldn't find any. So he asked an elderly male employee for some help.

'These vegetables are for my wife. Have they been sprayed with poisonous chemicals?'

'No,' said the old man. 'You'll have to do that yourself.'

The owner of a small town shoe shop was horrified when a new shoe shop opened right next door and put up a huge sign promising 'Cheapest Prices in Town'. He was even more appalled when a week later another shoe shop opened, this time on the other side of his, and displayed a huge sign promising 'Fantastic Bargains'. The small shopkeeper feared he would be ruined until, in a moment of inspiration, he put up a huge sign of his own. It read: 'Main Entrance'.

A customer went into a hardware store and asked for some nails.

'How long do you want them?' asked the assistant.

'Oh,' said the customer, 'I was rather hoping to keep them.'

One lunchtime, with money to waste and time to kill, a man decided to investigate a recently opened magic shop.

Inside, he told the shop owner: 'I'm looking for a fun present for myself —money no object as long as it amuses me.'

The shop owner surveyed shelves of numbered boxes before reaching into one and producing a pair of glasses. 'These are not any ordinary glasses,' he said, handing them to the customer. 'They're magic glasses. They cost a thousand dollars, but believe me, they're worth it, because whenever you wear them, you can see people naked!'

Intrigued, the customer tried them on and, sure enough, the shop owner appeared naked. And when his pretty female assistant walked through, she was naked too. But when he removed the glasses, everyone was fully clothed.

'They're amazing,' he said. 'I'll buy them.'

He left the shop, wearing the glasses, and headed back towards his office. Everyone he passed was naked – pretty girls, old women, men with beer bellies, even traffic wardens. He was absolutely delighted with his new toy. Indeed such was his excitement that he thought it would be fun to surprise his wife, so before going back to work, he dropped in at home. He was still wearing the glasses when he walked into the living room. There were his wife and his best friend sitting on the sofa completely naked.

'Hi, surprise!' he said, removing the glasses, but they were still naked.

'Look at that,' he moaned. 'A thousand dollars for a pair of magic glasses and after half an hour they're broken!'

Walking into a gift shop that sold religious items, a woman spotted a display of caps with WWJD printed on them. Puzzled by what the letters meant, she asked the sales assistant who said they stood for 'What Would Jesus Do'. The assistant added that the slogan was meant to inspire people not to make rash decisions but instead to imagine what Jesus would do in the same situation.

'Well,' said the woman, 'I'm not very religious, but I know one thing – Jesus wouldn't pay nineteen dollars ninety-five for one of these caps.'

A man went to the perfume counter of a big department store and said he would like a bottle of Chanel No. 5 gift wrapped for his wife's birthday.

'A little surprise, is it?' asked the sales assistant.

'Yeah. She's expecting a cruise!'

After a ladder was stolen from a store, the manager warned that further steps would be taken.

Having popped into the supermarket to pick up a bag of crisps on the way to the match, the young man was impatient to get through the checkout as quickly as possible. He headed for the six-item express lane, only to see an elderly woman push in front of him at the last minute, her trolley piled high with groceries. He was fuming at her flagrant disregard for the 'six items or less' rule, but was left utterly speechless when the cashier beckoned the old lady forward and asked sweetly: 'Now, Gladys, which six items would you like to buy?'

A man bought his middle-aged wife a new line of expensive cosmetics guaranteed to make her look years younger. After painstakingly applying them over a period of hours, she said: 'Darling, tell me honestly, what age would you say I am?'

He studied her carefully before replying: 'Judging from your skin, twenty; your hair, eighteen; and your figure, twenty-four.'

'Oh, you flatterer!' she gushed.

'Hey, wait a minute!' he said. 'I haven't added them up yet.'

A woman was going round the supermarket with a three-year-old girl in her shopping trolley. As they passed the chocolate section, the little girl asked for some chocolate, but her mother said 'No.' The child immediately began to whine, and the mother said quietly: 'Now, Alice, we've only got two more aisles to go. Don't get upset. It won't be long now.'

Soon they came to the biscuit section, and the child began to shout for biscuits. When told she couldn't have any, she started to cry. The mother said quietly: 'No tears, Alice. We've only got one aisle to go. We'll soon be at the checkout.'

When they reached the checkout, the little girl threw a tantrum when she realized that they hadn't bought any doughnuts. She screamed her head off and began kicking her mother. Quietly but firmly, the mother said: 'Alice, we'll be through this checkout in a couple of minutes and then you can go home and have a nice nap.'

A male shopper who had observed all this caught them up in the parking lot and stopped the woman to compliment her.

He said: 'I couldn't help noticing how patient you were with little Alice.'

The mother said: 'I'm Alice – my little girl's name is Charlotte!'

Visiting a shopping mall, a couple agreed to go their separate ways and rendezvous in an hour. So while he visited the sports shop, she hit the major clothes store. When he met up with her as arranged outside the clothes store, she was carrying a dozen bags full of items.

'Have you bought all that?' he asked incredulously.

'Well, yes,' she said. Then waving towards the interior of the shop, she added: 'But look at all the stuff I'm leaving behind.'

A store manager overheard a sales assistant saying to a customer: 'No, madam, we haven't had any for some weeks now, and it doesn't look as if we'll be getting any soon.'

Alarmed, the manager rushed over to the customer as she was walking out the door and said: 'That isn't true, madam. Of course, we'll have some soon. In fact, we placed an order for it a couple of weeks ago.'

Then the manager pulled the sales assistant to one side and growled: 'Never, ever say we don't have something. If we haven't got it, say we ordered it and we're expecting it any day. Understand? Now what was it that she wanted?'

'Rain.'

A man went to a hardware store and bought a chainsaw that was guaranteed to cut through six trees in an hour. The following day he took it back to the store and complained: 'That chainsaw is useless! It took me all day to cut down one tree.'

To find out what the problem was, the sales assistant took the chainsaw and started it up.

The man looked startled and said: 'What's that noise?'

A guy in a supermarket noticed an old lady following him around. Whenever he stopped, she stopped. Furthermore, she kept staring at him. She finally overtook him just before the checkout where she turned to him and said: 'I hope I haven't made you feel uncomfortable – it's just that you look so much like my late son.'

'That's OK,' he said.

'I know it's silly,' she continued, 'but if you'd call out "Goodbye, Mother" as I leave, it would make me so happy.'

The old lady went through the cash desk and as she left the supermarket, the man called out 'Goodbye, Mother.' The old lady waved back and smiled warmly.

Pleased that he had brought a little sunshine into someone's day, the man went to pay for his groceries.

'That comes to a hundred and twenty-one dollars, eighty-five cents,' said the clerk.

'How come?' said the man. 'I've only bought five things.'

'Yeah, but your mother said you'd pay for her things, too.'

A husband and wife were out shopping when the husband eyed up a shapely young woman in a short, tight skirt. Without looking up from the item she was examining, the wife said: 'Was it worth the trouble you're in?'

A man bought his wife a lovely looking diamond ring for Christmas.

A friend said: 'I thought she wanted one of those four-wheel drive vehicles?'

'She did,' said the husband. 'But where in the world was I going to find a fake jeep?'

A man parked his car at a supermarket and was walking past an empty trolley when he heard a woman ask: 'Excuse me, did you want that trolley?'

'No, I'm only after one thing.'

'Huh,' she muttered. 'Typical man!'

A man went into a newsagent's and asked the sales assistant: 'Do you keep stationery here?'

'No,' she said, 'I have to move about to keep warm.'

A man stopped off at a toy store to buy a baseball bat for his son. At the cash desk, the clerk asked: 'Cash or charge?'

'Cash,' snapped the customer before apologizing. 'I'm really sorry, I've just spent the whole afternoon at the car pound after my van had been clamped. It's been so frustrating.'

The clerk said: 'Shall I giftwrap the bat or are you going back there?'

A scruffy couple were looking at a new kitchen. After a while, the man said to the salesman: 'Yeah, we really like it, but I don't think we can afford it.'

The salesman said: 'You just make a small down payment, then you don't make another payment for twelve months.'

The woman growled: 'Who told you about us?'

A woman was examining an expensive jumper in a department store. She wanted to buy it but was put off by the price tag.

Sensing that she could be persuaded into a purchase, the assistant wandered over ready to deliver her sales patter.

'Can I help you, madam?' she inquired.

'Yes, this jumper's a bit overpriced, isn't it? I've seen similar garments in other shops for around sixty dollars, yet this one's priced at a hundred and ninety.'

'Well, you see,' began the assistant, 'there's a reason for that. This jumper is of vastly superior quality. Feel the texture. The wool actually comes from a rare breed of albino sheep confined to a tiny mountainous area in Mongolia. It's a beautiful yarn.'

'Yes,' replied the woman. 'And you tell it so well!'

'Sorry,' said the florist. 'We don't have any potted geraniums. Would African violets do instead?'

'No,' said the customer, 'it was definitely geraniums my wife told me to water while she was away at her sister's.'

Arriving home from the supermarket, a mother handed her son the box of animal crackers that he had been eagerly waiting for. He then tipped them out all over the work surface.

'Why have you done that?' she asked.

'Because the box says you can't eat them if the seal is broken. So I'm looking for the seal.'

A man walked into a bookshop and said: 'Can I have a book by Shakespeare?'

'Certainly, sir,' replied the salesman. 'Which one?'

'William, of course.'

A new mother took her baby daughter to the supermarket for the first time, with the little girl dressed in pink from head to toe. At the grocery store, the mother placed the baby's seat in the shopping trolley and placed her purchases around the seat.

When she reached the checkout, there was a small boy and his mother ahead of her in the line. The little boy was crying and begging his mum for a special treat. The new mum listened, thinking the little boy probably wanted some candy or gum, and that his mum was refusing.

Suddenly the boy's mother turned and looked at the baby in the shopping trolley. 'No, Billy,' she said, looking at the new mother and grinning. 'You may not have a baby sister today. That lady got the last one!'

Actual Instructions On Product Packaging:

On a pushchair: Remove child before folding.

On a carpet cleaner: Safe for carpets, too.

On a bottle of hand lotion: Warning: Starts healing skin on contact.

On a curling iron: Do not insert curling iron into any bodily orifice.

On a bar of soap: Directions – use like regular soap.

On bottom of Coca-Cola bottle: Do not open here.

On a bottle of Nytol (a sleep aid): Warning – May cause drowsiness.

On the box of a clockwork toy made in Hong Kong: Guaranteed to work throughout its useful life.

On a child's Superman costume: Wearing of this garment does not enable the wearer to fly.

On a 6x10 inch inflatable picture frame: Not to be used as a personal flotation device.

On a shower cap box: Fits one head.

On a Japanese food processor: Not to be used for the other use.

On a bottle of Chinese medicine: Known to cure itching, colds, stomachs, brains, and other diseases.

On the packaging for a muffin: Remove wrapper, open mouth, insert muffin, eat.

On German headphones: Do not increase volume past threshold of pain.

On a Korean kitchen knife: Warning – Keep out of children.

On the back of a cardboard windshield used to keep a car cool: Please remove before driving.

On Styrofoam packing: Do not eat.

On a string of Chinese-made Christmas lights: For indoor or outdoor use only.

On a puzzle toy made in Taiwan: Let's decompose and enjoy assembling.

On a Japanese medicine bottle: Adults: one tablet three times a day until passing away.

On the packaging for a wristwatch: Warning! This is not underwear! Do not attempt to put in pants.

On a Swedish chainsaw: Do not attempt to stop chain with your hands.

On the back of a can of de-icing windshield fluid: Cannot be made non-poisonous.

On a Boeing 747: Fragile: Do not drop.

On Boots' children's cough medicine: Do not drive car or operate machinery.

On a box of rat poison: Warning — has been found to cause cancer in laboratory mice.

On a bottle of dog shampoo: Caution — The contents of this bottle should not be fed to fish.

On curling iron instructions: Do not put into eyes.

On a container of salt: Warning — high in sodium.

In a computer manual: Do not dangle the mouse by its cable or throw the mouse at co-workers.

On instructions for a hairdryer: Do not use while sleeping.

On packaging from a Rowenta iron: Do not iron clothes on body.

On a coffee cup: Caution — hot beverages are hot.

On Sainsbury's peanuts: Warning – contains nuts.

On a sweet wrapper: Remove plastic before eating.

On a frozen dinner package: Serving suggestion – defrost.

Printed on the bottom of a box of Tesco's tirimisu dessert: Do not turn upside down.

On an American Airlines packet of nuts: Instructions – open package, eat nuts.

On a shipment of hammers: May be harmful if swallowed.

On a toilet bowl cleaning brush: Do not use orally.

On instructions for an electric thermometer: Do not use orally after using rectally.

A farmer who lived in a remote part of the country never ventured into the city until one day he was persuaded by his wife to take the family to a shopping mall. It was their first taste of city life. While the wife was in the toilet, the man and his young son looked around the mall. They were amazed by everything they saw, especially the two shiny silver walls that could move apart and then slide back together again.

'What is it?' asked the boy.

The father, never having seen an elevator, said: 'I don't know, son.'

They watched enthralled as an elderly lady went over to the moving walls and pressed a button. The walls then opened and she shuffled into a small room. The walls closed behind her, and the boy and his father gazed in awe as the small numbers above the walls lit up in sequence. They continued to watch until the last number was reached and then the numbers began to light up in reverse order. Finally the walls opened again and out stepped a beautiful young woman.

Without taking his eyes off her, the father quietly said to the boy: 'Go get your mother.'

Two tigers were walking down the aisle of a supermarket. One turned to the other and said: 'Quiet in here today, isn't it?'

One day Snow White was shopping in town when she stopped to look in a photography shop. She thought to herself: 'Wouldn't it be great to have a camera so that I can take photos of the Seven Dwarfs?'

So she bought a camera and rushed home to tell Dopey, Bashful, Doc and co. That afternoon she used up the whole film, taking photographs of her vertically challenged friends – in the woods, by the lake, and in their home. Snow White was so excited that she couldn't wait to get the photos developed.

The next day she took the film in to the store and asked when her photos would be ready for collection.

'Thursday,' said the clerk.

Come Thursday and Snow White could hardly contain herself. First thing in the morning she went into town to collect the pictures, only to be told by the clerk that they hadn't come in yet.

'Try again Saturday,' he suggested.

Barely concealing her disappointment, Snow White trudged home and counted the hours till Saturday. First thing Saturday morning she returned to the store.

'Are my photos ready yet?' she asked the clerk.

'Sorry, they're not. Try again Tuesday.'

Snow White was mortified by the latest setback but consoled herself with the thought that it wasn't long till Tuesday. First thing Tuesday morning, she went back to the camera shop.

Before she could even speak, the clerk said sympathetically: 'I'm really sorry, they're still not in.'

A tear began to trickle down Snow White's face. Seeing her obvious distress, the clerk stepped from behind the counter, put a comforting arm around her and said: 'Don't worry. Some day your prints will come.'

Sport

Did you hear who won the Bangkok marathon? – I heard it was a Thai.

God and the Devil arranged a football match between Heaven and Hell. God had a small wager on the outcome, but the Devil was supremely confident and bet five hundred dollars on a win for Hell.

'You're crazy,' said God. 'I've got all the best players in the history of the game in my team.'

'I know,' said the Devil. 'But I've got all the referees.'

A man went into a barber's shop advertising David Beckham-style haircuts. Twenty minutes later he glanced in the mirror and saw his head half bald and covered in cuts.

'That's not how David Beckham has his hair,' complained the man.

The barber said: 'It would be if he came here.'

A soccer goalkeeper was walking along the street one day when he heard screams from a nearby building. He looked up to see smoke billowing from a fourth-floor window and a woman leaning out holding a baby.

'Help! Help!' screamed the woman. 'I need someone to catch my baby!'

A crowd of onlookers had gathered, but none was confident about catching a baby dropped from such a great height. Then the goalkeeper stepped forward. 'I'm a professional goalkeeper,' he called to the woman. 'I'm renowned for my safe hands and sense of positioning. Drop the baby and I will catch it. For me, it will be just like catching a ball.'

The woman agreed: 'OK, then. When I drop my baby, treat it as if you were catching a ball.'

On a count of three, the woman dropped the baby. Everyone held their breath as the goalkeeper lined himself up to catch it. There was a huge sigh of relief, followed by wild cheering as the goalkeeper caught the baby safely in his arms. Then he bounced it twice on the ground and kicked it fifty yards down the street.

A soccer fan had a lousy seat at the stadium, right behind a pillar. But he spotted an empty seat with a much better view a few rows along, and so he made his way there. When he got there, he asked the man sitting in the next seat whether the empty seat was taken.

'This is my wife's seat,' he replied solemnly. 'She passed away. She was a big United fan.'

'I'm terribly sorry to hear of your sad loss. May I ask why you didn't give the ticket to a friend or a relative?'

'They're all at the funeral.'

Reading through a magazine, a woman suddenly started laughing. She turned to her husband and said: 'There's a classified ad here where a guy is offering to swap his wife for season tickets. You wouldn't swap me for season tickets, would you?'

'Of course not, honey,' he replied.

'Ah, that's sweet.'

'The season's half over.'

An under-elevens soccer team were preparing for a match one Saturday morning. Just before kick-off, the coach went over to one of his young players and said: 'You do understand that you mustn't swear at the referee if he gives you a card, and that you mustn't hit an opponent if he fouls you?'

'Yes, I understand,' said the boy.

'Good,' said the coach. 'Now go and explain it to your mother.'

A wife was having an affair with the television repairman. She complained: 'My husband never pays the slightest attention to me – all he's ever bothered about is watching the football game on television. That's why we've got the biggest set in the neighbourhood – so he can watch the game.'

Just then, she heard a key in the front door. Her husband had arrived home unexpectedly. She said to her lover: 'Quick, hide in the back of the television!'

So the lover hid in the television while the husband sat down to watch the football game. After ten minutes, it became so hot and uncomfortable in the back of the television set that the lover climbed out, walked straight past the husband and out of the front door.

The husband turned to his long-suffering wife and said: 'Hey, honey, I didn't see the referee send that guy off, did you?'

Bill challenged Tom to a game of darts.
    Tom said: 'OK.'
    Bill said: 'Nearest to a bull starts.'
    Tom said: 'Baaaa.'
    Bill said: 'Moooo.'
    Tom said: 'You're closest.'

Riding in the Grand National, a jockey was leading at Becher's Brook the second time around when he was suddenly hit on the head by a chicken drumstick and a pork pie. Although he lost several places, he managed to keep control of his horse and by the Canal Turn, had fought his way back to the front, only to be hit by a smoked salmon sandwich and a half bottle of champagne. Again, he lost valuable ground but, showing commendable bravery and agility, battled back into the lead over the final fence. With victory in sight, he was struck on the head yet again, this time by a tin of caviar and half a dozen Scotch eggs. As a result, he lost control of his mount for a few vital strides, enabling another horse to pass and win the race. Highly aggrieved at finishing only second, the jockey marched straight into the stewards' room to complain that he had been hampered.

A champion jockey was about to ride a new horse in a big race. The horse's trainer met him before the race and said: 'All you have to remember with this horse is that every time you approach a jump, you have to shout, "ALLLEEE OOOP" really loudly in the horse's ear. Providing you do that, you'll be fine.'

The jockey thought the trainer was mad but promised to shout the command. The race began and they approached the first fence. But the jockey was too embarrassed to shout out the order in front of his weighing room colleagues, so he said nothing and the horse ploughed through the fence, barely managing to stay on its feet. Approaching the second fence, the jockey thought he had better do something, so he whispered 'Allleee Ooop' in the horse's ear. Again the horse hit the fence hard and lost valuable ground. At the third fence, the jockey realized he would have to do as the trainer said and shouted

'ALLLEEE OOOP' in the horse's ear. The horse responded with a magnificent jump and, with the correct command given at each fence, continued to jump brilliantly for the rest of the race. However the two early mistakes meant that the partnership could only finish third.

The trainer was fuming and demanded to know what went wrong. 'I didn't do anything wrong,' insisted the jockey. 'It's this horse. What is he – deaf or something?'

Incandescent with rage, the trainer replied: 'Deaf? Deaf? He's not deaf – he's blind!'

At a race meeting, a punter saw a priest blessing a horse before the first race and, thinking it was a good omen, decided to bet on that particular horse. To the punter's delight, it won. He then watched the priest do the same for the next four races and continued to win. The first five horses that the priest had blessed had come in first, earning the punter a small fortune.

Certain that he had come up with an infallible formula, he decided to bet all his winnings on the priest's chosen horse in the last race. Once again he watched as the priest went through his familiar pre-race ritual, after which the punter put every last dime on that horse. But this time the horse dropped dead two furlongs before the finish.

The furious punter sought out the priest and demanded an explanation. The priest smiled: 'That's one of the problems with you Protestants: you don't know the difference between a blessing and the last rites.'

A boxer went to a doctor complaining of insomnia.

'Have you tried counting sheep?' asked the doctor.

'It doesn't work,' replied the boxer. 'Whenever I get to nine, I stand up!'

Two country boys went away for a long weekend's fishing. They spent a fortune on renting all the equipment – reels, rods, wading suits, rowboat, car, even a cabin in the woods – but figured that it would be worth it. They found the best spot on the lake but on the first day they caught absolutely nothing. It was the same story on the second day. Not a single bite. Finally on the third day they struck lucky, but even then it was just one small fish.

As they were driving home, the brighter of the pair said: 'Do you realise that this one lousy fish we caught cost us one thousand, five hundred bucks?'

'Wow!' said his friend. 'Then it's a good thing we didn't catch any more!'

A fisherman turned to a guy and said: 'Excuse me, pal. You've been standing there watching me fish for three and a half hours. Why don't you get a rod and reel and do some fishing yourself?'

'No, I don't have the patience for it.'

It was a bitterly cold winter's day. A man went fishing and cut a hole in the ice, but didn't catch a thing. Then a young boy came along, cut a hole in the ice nearby and proceeded to catch fish after fish.

Eventually the man went over to the boy and said: 'I've been here six hours and haven't caught a single fish. Yet you've been here barely half an hour and you've caught at least ten. What's your secret?'

The boy replied: 'Roo raf roo reep ra rurms rarm.'

'Sorry,' said the man. 'I didn't get that.'

The boy repeated: 'Roo raf roo reep ra rurms rarm.'

'I'm sorry. I can't understand a word you're saying.'

The boy spat a wad of ugly brown slime into his hand and said: 'You have to keep the worms warm!'

Two friends were recounting their dreams.

'I dreamed I was on holiday,' said one man fondly. 'It was just me and my fishing rod and this big beautiful lake. What a dream.'

'I had a great dream too,' recalled the other. 'I dreamed I was on a date with two gorgeous women and having the time of my life.'

'Hey!' cried his friend, hurt. 'You dreamed you were with two women, and you didn't call me?'

'I did,' said the other. 'But your wife said you'd gone fishing.'

A drunk decided to go ice fishing, so he gathered his gear and scoured the neighbourhood until he found a big patch of ice. Then he headed into the centre of the ice and began to saw a hole. All of a sudden, a loud voice came booming out of the sky: 'You will find no fish under that ice.'

The drunk looked around, but couldn't see anyone, so he started sawing again. Once more, the voice spoke: 'As I said before, there are no fish under the ice.'

The drunk looked all around, high and low, but couldn't see a single soul. He picked up the saw and tried to complete the hole, but before he could even begin cutting, the huge voice interrupted: 'I have warned you three times now. There are no fish!'

The drunk was starting to feel uneasy and asked the mysterious voice: 'How do you know there are no fish? Are you God trying to warn me?'

'No,' replied the voice. 'I am the manager of this hockey rink.'

A small boy was looking after his baby sister while his parents went shopping in town. He decided to go fishing, so he took her with him.

'I'm never taking her fishing again!' he told his mother that evening. 'I didn't catch a thing.'

'Oh,' said his mother, 'next time I'm sure she'll be quiet and not scare the fish away.'

'It wasn't that,' said the boy: 'She ate all the bait!'

A shivering wife turned to her husband while they were ice fishing and said: 'Tell me again how much fun we're having – I keep forgetting.'

Two young men were out fishing in their favourite secluded location when a Game Warden suddenly emerged from the bushes. One of them immediately ran for it. The Game Warden gave chase. Hotly pursued every yard of the way, the fisherman dashed through thickets, over hillocks and across streams until, after three quarters of a mile, he finally pulled up exhausted, enabling the Game Warden to collar him.

'Right,' said the warden. 'Let's see your fishing licence.'

The young man reached into the pocket of his jacket and produced a perfectly valid fishing licence.

The warden said: 'You must be real dumb! You don't have to run from me if you have a valid licence.'

'I know,' said the fisherman. 'But the thing is, my friend back there, he ain't got a valid licence.'

Many years ago, a fisherman's wife blessed her husband with twin sons. Although they loved the children dearly, the fisherman and his wife were unable to think of any names they liked for the boys. After several days of fruitless deliberation, the fisherman suggested: 'Let's not decide on names right now. If we wait a little while, I'm sure the right names will suddenly occur to us.'

By the time the boys were two months old, the fisherman and his wife had noticed a peculiar trait. When left alone, one of the boys would turn towards the sea while the other would face inland. No matter how the parents positioned the children, the same child always faced the same direction. So the fisherman said: 'Let's call the boys Towards and Away.' His wife agreed, and from then on, the boys were known as Towards and Away.

The years passed and the lads grew tall and strong. The day came when the ageing fisherman said to his sons: 'Boys, it is time that you learned how to make a living from the sea.' So the two sons and the father provisioned their ship, said their farewells, and set sail on a three-month voyage.

The fisherman's wife was used to her husband being away at sea for long periods, but found it difficult to cope with the absence of her sons too. She eagerly awaited their return, ticking off each passing day, but at the end of the three months, there was no sign of them. Another three months went by, but still no ship. Indeed three whole years passed without so much as a word. By now, she had given up her beloved family for dead. Then one morning she saw a bedraggled man shuffling up the path towards her house and recognized him as her husband. But he was alone.

'Where are my darling boys?' she wailed.

The fisherman began to tell his story: 'We were barely a day out to sea when Towards hooked into a giant of a fish. Towards fought long and hard, but the fish was more than his equal. For a whole week they wrestled upon the waves without either of them giving way. Sadly, the great fish eventually started to win the struggle, and Towards was pulled over the side of our ship. He was swallowed whole.'

'Oh!' gasped the wife in shock. 'How terrible! What a huge fish that must have been!'

'Yes, it was,' said the fisherman, 'but you should have seen the one that got Away.'

Two sardines were big tennis fans. 'Let's go to Wimbledon this year,' said one.

'How would we get there?' asked the other.

'On the London Underground, of course.'

'What, and get packed in like commuters?'

One day a man decided to try out some new sports and went on the Internet to find out what was available. After a few months, he invited his friends to watch him test his new pastimes.

With no idea of what they were about to witness, they all followed him to the top of a local cliff.

'Why have you brought us up here?' they asked.

'Just watch,' he said, producing a small green bird from a cage. He held the bird by the feet, and proceeded to jump off the cliff.

His friends were worried, but he eventually returned to the top of the cliff, bruised but otherwise okay. 'Well,' he said, 'I don't think much of this budgie-jumping.'

Then he revealed that he had brought a chicken with him. He held the chicken by the feet and jumped off the cliff. Once more, he hit the sand at the bottom of the cliff, trudged back to the top, and, battered and bruised, said to his friends: 'Hen-gliding doesn't seem to work for me either.'

He had one last trick up his sleeve. This time it involved a parrot. Holding the parrot by the feet, he launched himself off the top of the cliff. This time, however, as he jumped, he pulled out a handgun and shot the bird as he fell. The end result was pretty much the same though, and he arrived back at the top of the cliff with even more bruises than from his previous attempts.

His friends waited expectantly to hear what he would say this time. He paused, scratched his head, took a deep breath and said: 'And that's the last time I try parrot-shooting too!'

A skydiver jumped from a plane, only to discover that his parachute was broken. As he plunged towards the ground, frantically trying to fix the chute, he passed another man on the way up.

'Do you know anything about parachutes?' he cried.

'No,' replied the other man. 'Do you know anything about gas cookers?'

While performing a routine physical, a doctor noticed that his patient's shins were covered in hideous bruises.

'Tell me,' said the doctor, 'do you play soccer or rugby?'

'No,' said the man. 'But my wife and I play bridge.'

Two men were engaged in an animated conversation about the best way to ski down a particular hill. To solve the dispute, they asked the advice of a man pulling his sledge.

'Sorry,' he said. 'There's not much point asking me. I'm a tobogganist.'

'Oh,' said one of the skiers, 'in that case can I have twenty Benson and Hedges?'

A business executive injured his leg skiing one weekend. By the time he got home on the Saturday night, the leg was badly swollen and he was experiencing difficulty walking, so he called his doctor at home. The doctor advised soaking it in hot water but this caused the leg to swell up even more.

Seeing him limping in agony, the businessman's maid said: 'It's probably not my place, because I'm only a maid, but I always thought it was better to use cold water, not hot, for swelling.' So he took her advice, switched to cold water, and the swelling rapidly subsided.

The following afternoon he called his doctor again to complain. 'What kind of doctor are you? You told me to soak my leg in hot water, and it got worse. My maid told me to use cold water, and it got better!'

'Really?' said the doctor. 'I don't understand it; my maid said hot water.'

A business executive who had retired the previous year admitted to friends that he had been forced to give up skiing, a sport which he had enjoyed for many years.

'Afraid of injuries?' asked one.

'Now I am. Before, I could drag a cast into work and still do my job, but now I'd be messing up my golf game.'

While scuba diving in the sea at a depth of twenty feet, a man noticed another guy at the same depth, but without any diving gear whatsoever. The diver plunged twenty feet deeper, but the other guy joined him minutes later. The diver went down another twenty feet, but within a few minutes, the same guy was beside him again.

Confused, the diver took out a waterproof chalk and board set, and wrote: 'How are you able to stay under this deep without equipment?'

The guy grabbed the board and chalk, erased what the diver had written, and wrote: 'I'M DROWNING, YOU IDIOT!!!'

A middle-aged married couple were attending the World Snooker Championships when, in the darkness, they spotted a pair of young lovers locked in a passionate embrace, their hands all over each other.

'I don't know whether to watch them or the game,' remarked the husband.

'Watch them,' said the wife. 'You already know how to play snooker.'

Fred and George were playing golf when Fred sliced his ball into a deep wooded gully. Taking his eight-iron, he clambered down the embankment in search of his ball. After spending ten minutes hacking at the undergrowth, he suddenly spotted something glistening among the leaves. As he got closer, he could see that it was an eight-iron in the hands of a skeleton.

Fred immediately called up to George: 'Hey, George, I've made a shocking discovery!'

'What's up?' shouted George.

'Bring me my wedge,' yelled Fred. 'You can't get out of here with an eight-iron.'

A man and a woman were standing at the altar about to be married when the bride-to-be spotted that the prospective groom had a set of golf clubs with him.

'What on earth are you doing with those golf clubs in church?' she snarled.

'Well,' he said, 'this isn't going to take all afternoon, is it?'

A golf fanatic met the Pope on a trip to Rome. 'Your Holiness,' he said, 'I'm crazy about golf. I play every day of the year. But tell me, is there a golf course in heaven?'

'I'm not sure,' said the Pope. 'I'll have to ask God.'

A few days later, the man bumped into the Pope again and asked: 'Any news from God about the golf course in heaven?'

'Yes,' replied the Pope. 'Apparently there is a beautiful course in heaven with velvet-smooth greens and lush fairways. The bad news is, you have a tee time for tomorrow morning.'

Having been given a set of clubs as a retirement present, a guy in his sixties decided to take up golf. Explaining that he knew nothing whatsoever about the game, he asked the local professional for lessons. The pro showed him the proper stance and swing, then said: 'Just hit the ball towards the flag on the first green.'

The novice teed up and smacked the ball straight down the middle of the fairway and onto the green where it stopped inches from the hole. 'Now what?' he asked.

The pro was rendered almost speechless. 'Well, er, you're supposed to hit the ball into the cup.'

'Oh great!' exclaimed the newcomer. '*Now* you tell me!'

After a wayward shot landed in a group of players, two golfers came to blows. One started lashing out with a six-iron, repeatedly hitting his adversary on the back with the club. Soon the police arrived to break up the fracas.

'How many times did you hit the other man with that golf club?' asked the police officer.

'Eight,' he replied. 'But you can put me down for five.'

An elderly golfer harboured a lifelong ambition to play one hole at a seaside course the same way as the professionals. They drive the ball out over the sea and onto a tiny green situated on a spit of land that juts out off the coast. It was a shot that he had tried hundreds of times without success, his ball always falling short and ending up in the sea. As a result whenever he played that hole, he always used an old ball – one with a cut or a nick.

Last year he visited the course in another attempt to fulfil his dream. At his age, who knows how many more chances he would have? When he reached the fateful hole, he teed up an old cut ball and said a silent prayer.

As he prepared to address the ball, a powerful voice from above suddenly boomed out: 'Wait. Replace that old ball with a brand new ball.'

Interpreting this vocal intervention as a sign that God was finally going to let him achieve his ambition, he duly placed a new ball on the tee. But as he stepped up in readiness for the crucial drive, the voice came down again: 'Wait. Step back. Take a practice swing.' So the golfer stepped back and took a practice swing.

The voice boomed out again: 'Take another practice swing.' Obeying God's every instruction, the old man took another practice swing.

Then there was a moment of silence before the voice spoke out again. 'Put back the old ball.'

A man went to see his doctor, suffering from exhaustion.

'Yes, I see your problem,' said the doctor. 'You're completely worn out. I think you've been playing too much golf.'

'Too much golf? What should I do?'

'You need to take some time off and relax. Try spending some time at the office.'

Two guys were playing golf on a Saturday, just as they had every week for the past nine years. Just as the first man was about to tee off, a woman in a wedding dress ran over to him, screaming: 'You bum!

You lousy bum! You promised!'

The golfer replied calmly: 'Honey, I said only if it rains today . . .'

At a golf course, the eleventh fairway was bordered to the left by a cycle path and a road, both out of bounds. One day, a club member hooked his tee shot so violently that his ball sailed over the fence that rang alongside the course, bounced off the cycle path onto the road where it hit the tyre of a passing bus and rebounded back on to the fairway.

Flabbergasted by such luck, his playing partner asked: 'How did you do that?'

The member said: 'You have to know the bus timetable.'

Watched by the club professional, a golfer enjoyed a torrid start to his first-ever game. His tee shot flew into the woods, his second ball landed in a lake and his third buried itself in a bunker. And with each passing shot, his swing grew wilder, so that by the time he had attempted to extricate himself from the bunker for the fifth time, he was brutally hacking away at the ball. With the ball still deep in the sand, he belatedly sought the advice of the professional.

'What club should I use on this shot?' he asked.

'I don't know,' replied the pro. 'What game are you playing?'

A golfer stumbled into the clubhouse and ordered a double scotch.

'What's up with you?' said the steward behind the bar. 'You look as if you've been to hell and back!'

'You'll never believe this,' he said. 'I've just lost a game to Donaldson.'

'What? Donaldson's the worst player in the club. How on earth could you lose to him?'

'He tricked me. On the first tee, he asked for a handicap and, since I've been playing pretty well lately, I told him he could have ten, twenty, thirty strokes – any handicap he wanted. He said, "Just give me two gotchas."'

'What's a gotcha?' asked the steward.

'That's what I wanted to know. But Donaldson just said, "You'll see." Then, as I was teeing off, and just at the top of my backswing, he screamed out "Gotcha!" Well, inevitably I missed the ball completely.'

'Understandably,' said the steward sympathetically. 'But still, that's only one swing. How did he manage to win the game?'

'You try swinging at a golf ball all afternoon while waiting for that second "Gotcha!"'

An old man spent most afternoons at the local golf course, always playing by himself. Whenever he returned to the clubhouse, the course professional would inquire about his score. And every time the old man would reply: 'Another perfect par.'

The pro was highly suspicious that a man of such advanced years could shoot straight par every time, but he was too sensible to accuse a club member of lying. Finally the opportunity arose for him to accompany the old man on his daily round. On the first tee, the veteran sliced his drive horribly into the rough. His second landed in a bunker and he ended up taking eight strokes on a par-four hole. The golf pro thought to himself: 'I knew it. He's been lying all along. There's no way he's going to shoot anywhere near par.'

The old man's form continued in that vein, never once getting a par on any hole. As they teed off on the twelfth, he hit his best drive of the day – straight down the middle. He promptly walked along the fairway, picked up his ball and headed back towards the clubhouse.

The pro was confused. 'Hey, that was a great shot. Why are you packing up?'

'Oh, I'm done,' smiled the old man. 'That shot was number seventy-two – another perfect par!'

After hitting six balls into a lake, a frustrated golfer hurled his clubs into the water and began to walk off the course. Then suddenly he turned around and jumped in the lake. His playing partners thought he must have had a change of heart about dumping such valuable golfing equipment but he emerged moments later without the clubs and headed off the course once more.

'Why did you jump into the lake?' they asked.

He replied: 'I left my car keys in the bag.'

A golfer was in a close match with a friend, who was leading by a couple of strokes. The golfer said to himself: 'I'd give anything to sink this next putt.'

At that moment, a complete stranger walked up to him and whispered: 'Would you give up a quarter of your sex life to sink this putt?'

The golfer immediately thought the man was crazy, and that whatever he answered would be irrelevant. But then, sensing that perhaps it was a good omen and that it might put him in the right frame of mind to sink the difficult putt, he replied: 'Okay, I would give up a quarter of my sex life in return for sinking this putt.' And he promptly sank the putt.

Two holes later, he mumbled to himself: 'Boy, if I could only get this bunker shot in the hole.'

The same stranger appeared at his side and said: 'Would it be worth another quarter of your sex life?'

'Sure,' shrugged the golfer, and he duly holed the bunker shot.

It was all down to the final hole. The golfer needed to sink a sixty-foot putt to win – an almost impossible task. Although he said nothing, the stranger appeared at his side and said: 'Would you be willing to give up the rest of your sex life to win this match?'

'Certainly,' said the golfer, and he sank the putt.

As the golfer walked to the clubhouse, the stranger appeared alongside and said: 'You know, I've not really been fair with you because you don't know who I am. I'm the devil, and from now on you will have no sex life.'

The golfer just smiled and said: 'And I haven't been fair to you. You see, my name is Brother Benedict.'

Bill and Bob, longtime golfing friends, were involved in a match-play competition, with the score all-square on the eighteenth tee. But while Bob then smashed his drive straight down the middle, Bill sliced his tee shot way right, the ball finally coming to rest on a concrete path.

'Oh well,' said Bill optimistically, 'I should get a free drop from there.'

'No way,' said Bob who was always ultra-competitive. 'We play the ball as it lies.'

So while Bob looked on confidently, a disgruntled Bill selected a club and made a few aggressive practice swings from the path, each one producing a shower of sparks as the metal from the club head came into contact with the concrete. Eventually Bill hit the ball off the path and played a miraculous shot right to the heart of the green, leaving himself with no more than a three-foot putt.

Even Bob grudgingly admitted that it was a great shot from such a terrible lie. 'Well done,' he said. 'What club did you use?'

Bill replied: 'Your six-iron.'

A regular golfer approached the club professional for advice. 'You've seen me play. What do you think I'm doing wrong?'

The pro said: 'Your main problem is that you stand too close to the ball – after you've hit it.'

Ken and Steve went for a game of golf one Saturday afternoon, but Ken was under strict instructions from his wife to be back by four o'clock because she wanted him to take her shopping. Four o'clock passed, so did five o'clock and six o'clock. Eventually Ken arrived home at seven.

'Where on earth have you been?' screamed his wife.

'Honey,' said Ken, 'a terrible thing happened. We made it to the third green when Steve suddenly dropped dead of a heart attack.'

The wife felt guilty. 'That's awful,' she said.

'You're telling me,' said Ken. 'The rest of the round it was, hit the ball, drag Steve, hit the ball, drag Steve . . .'

Two golfers were talking. 'Guess what!' said one. 'I got a set of golf clubs for my wife.'

The other nodded: 'Great swap!'

Golfer: Do you think it's a sin to play on a Sunday?

Caddie: The way you play, it's a sin any day.

After a long evening drinking in the golf club bar, a man set off for home but half a mile down the road his car was pulled over by a police officer.

The officer did not need a breathalyser to see what the problem was. 'You're too drunk to drive,' he said.

'Too drunk to drive?' repeated the golfer. 'I'm too drunk to putt!'

Golfer: This is the worst course I've ever played on.

Caddie: This isn't the golf course. We left that an hour ago!

A hack golfer was enduring a particularly torrid round. His tee shot on the first hole sailed out of bounds, his fourth shot ended up in the woods, and his sixth in the lake. In total, he lost three brand new golf balls on that hole.

Teeing off at the second hole, he hooked his drive wildly into a plantation. 'Damn!' he cursed. 'There goes another new ball!'

His next shot fared no better, flying into a field. 'I don't believe it! That's yet another new ball I've lost! This round is costing me a fortune!'

Watching his struggles, a player in the group behind advised:

'Seeing how you lose so many balls, why don't you play with an old ball?'

'Because,' said the hack golfer caustically, 'I've never had one!'

Wife: You think so much of golf that you don't even remember when we got married!

Husband: Of course I do, honey. It was the day after I sank that forty-foot putt.

A preacher was an avid golfer and couldn't help sneaking off to play a round one Sunday. An angel watching him from above was furious and told God: 'Look at that preacher down there, abandoning his duties to play golf on a Sunday. He should be punished.'

God agreed and promised to act. A few minutes later, the preacher hit a superb hole-in-one on a two hundred and ninety-five-yard hole.

The angel rounded on God: 'I thought you were going to punish him! Instead he's just hit a brilliant hole-in-one.'

God smiled: 'Think about it – who can he tell?'

Golfer: Please stop checking your watch all the time – it's a distraction.

Caddie: It's not a watch – it's a compass.

Jim and Harry headed out of their weekly round of golf. Jim suggested: 'To make it more interesting, why don't we have five dollars on the lowest score for the day?'

Harry agreed, and they enjoyed a great game. With one hole to play, Harry led by a single stroke, but then on the eighteenth, he cut his ball into the rough.

'Help me find my ball,' he called to Jim. 'You search over there, I'll look around here.'

After five minutes of fruitless searching, Harry, knowing only too well that he was facing a disastrous penalty for a lost ball, sneakily pulled a ball from his pocket, dropped it on the ground and called out triumphantly: 'Hey, I've found my ball!'

Jim looked across at him despairingly. 'After all the years we've been friends, how could you cheat on me at golf for a measly five bucks?'

'What do you mean cheat?' protested Harry. 'I found my ball sitting right there!'

'And a liar too!' exclaimed Jim in disbelief. 'I'll have you know

I've been standing on your ball for the last five minutes!'

After a long, hard day on the golf course, the exasperated player turned to his caddie and said: 'You must be the worst caddie in the world!'

'No, I don't think so,' replied the caddie. 'That would be too much of a coincidence.'

A man in his eighties moved to a new town and joined the local golf club. When he went there hoping to play his first round, he was told that all the tee times were booked for that day. Seeing his disappointment, the assistant professional offered to let the old man join him on his round and suggested a twelve-stroke handicap.

The old man said: 'I really don't need a handicap. The only real problem I have is getting out of bunkers.'

Both men played well and coming to the final hole, a short par-three, the scores were even. The pro landed his tee shot on the edge of the green, but the old man put his drive into a greenside bunker. Steadying himself in the sand, the octogenarian then played a superb bunker shot that ended with the ball in the hole.

The assistant pro was stunned. 'Great shot, but I thought you said you have a problem getting out of bunkers.'

'I do,' replied the old man. 'Give me a hand.'

Golfer: That can't be my ball. It looks much too old.
    Caddie: Well, it's a long time since we started.

A golfer hit his drive on the first hole three hundred yards right down the middle. When it landed, however, it hit a sprinkler and ricocheted sideways into the woods. Seething with anger, he marched into the woods and hit a two-iron with such force that it smacked into a tree and rebounded onto his head, killing him instantly.

He duly arrived at the Pearly Gates and St. Peter, consulting his big book, said: 'I see you were a golfer. Is that correct?'

'Yes, that's right.'

'Do you hit the ball a long way?' asked St. Peter.

The golfer replied: 'Well, I got here in two, didn't I?'

Golfer: I think I'm going to drown myself in the lake.
    Caddie: Think you can keep your head down that long?

A man had been stranded on a desert island for ten years and in that time hadn't seen another living person. Then one day, a gorgeous blonde woman suddenly stepped out of the sea wearing a wet suit and scuba diving gear. She walked over to him and began caressing his beard.

'How long is it since you last had a cigarette?' she asked.

'Ten years,' he gasped.

She slowly unzipped a waterproof pocket on her left sleeve and produced a packet of cigarettes and a box of matches. He lit the cigarette and sighed: 'I've been desperate for a cigarette. This is fantastic.'

When he had finished the first cigarette, she said: 'And how long is it since you last tasted whiskey?'

'Ten years,' he answered.

And she slowly unzipped the waterproof pocket on her right sleeve and brought out a bottle of whiskey.

'This is great!' he said, drinking half of the bottle. 'I'd forgotten how good whiskey tasted.'

Then she began to unzip the long fastening at the front of her wet suit and purred seductively: 'How long is it since you had some *real* fun?'

The man could hardly believe his luck. 'Don't tell me you've got a set of golf clubs in there!'

Why do golfers carry a spare sock? – Because they might get a hole in one.

A husband and wife were both keen golfers. The wife was feeling neglected and wanted to know how much he loved her.

'If I were to die tomorrow,' she said, 'and you remarried, would you give your new wife my jewellery?'

'What an awful thing to ask!' exclaimed the husband. 'But no, of course not.'

'And would you give her any of my clothes?'

'No, honey, of course I wouldn't. I can't believe you're even asking me that.'

'What about my golf clubs?'

'No. She's left-handed.'

The Pope met with the College of Cardinals to discuss a proposal from Shimon Peres, the former leader of Israel.

'Your holiness,' said one of the cardinals, 'Mr Peres wants to determine whether Jews or Catholics are superior by challenging you to a golf match.'

The Pope was greatly disturbed, as he had never held a golf club in his life. 'Don't worry,' said the cardinal. 'We'll call America and talk to Jack Nicklaus. We'll make him a cardinal. He can play Shimon Peres. We can't lose!'

Everyone agreed it was a good idea. The call was made, and Jack Nicklaus was honoured to play.

The day after the match, Nicklaus reported to the Vatican to inform the Pope of the result. 'I came second, your Holiness,' he said.

'Second?' exclaimed the Pope, surprised. 'You came second to Shimon Peres?'

'No,' said Nicklaus, 'second to Rabbi Woods.'

'How was your golf game, honey?' asked Tom's wife.

'Well, I was hitting pretty well, but my eyesight's now so bad that I couldn't see where the ball went. I ended up losing four balls!'

'But you're seventy-five years old, Tom!' admonished his wife. 'Next time you play, you don't you take my brother Ken along?'

'But he's eighty-eight and doesn't even play golf anymore,' protested Tom.

'I know he hasn't got all his faculties, but he has got perfect eyesight. He could watch your ball.'

So Tom took his wife's advice and the next day he teed off with Ken looking on. Tom swung and the ball disappeared down the middle of the fairway.

'Did you see it?' asked Tom.

'Yup,' said Ken.

As they set off down the fairway, Tom peered ahead: 'Well, where is it?' he yelled.

Ken said: 'I forget.'

A guy was lining up his drive when a voice from the clubhouse called out: 'Will the gentleman on the ladies' tee please move back to the men's tee!'

The golfer ignored the request and continued with his practice swings. The voice called out again: 'Sir, will you please move back to the men's tee now!'

The golfer carried on regardless and was just addressing the ball when the voice called out for a third time: 'You are violating club rules! Move back to the men's tee immediately or I will have you thrown off the course!'

   The golfer turned angrily in the direction of the clubhouse and
shouted back: 'Do you mind shutting up while I play my second shot!'

Unwritten Laws of Golf:
No matter how bad your last shot was, the worst is yet to come.
Your best round of golf will be followed almost immediately by your
worst round ever. The possibility of the latter increases with the
number of people you tell about the former.
The more expensive the golf ball, the greater its attraction to water.
The higher a golfer's handicap, the more qualified he deems himself
as an instructor.
Trees eat golf balls.
Sand is alive. If it isn't, how do you explain the way it works against
you?
Golf carts always run out of juice at the farthest point from the
clubhouse.
Every par-three hole in the world has a secret desire to humiliate
golfers.
Topping a three-iron is the most painful torture known to man.
A golfer hitting into your group will always be bigger than anyone in
your group. Likewise, a group you accidentally hit into will consist of
a football player, a professional wrestler, a convicted murderer and an
IRS agent – or some similar combination.
All three-woods are demon-possessed.
Golf should be given up at least twice a month.
A severe slice is a thing of awesome power and beauty.
The last three holes of a round will automatically adjust your score to
what it really should be.
All vows taken on a golf course shall be valid only until the sunset.

Travel

A man was walking down the street when he stopped to look in a travel agent's window. Seeing a cheap cruise advertised for eighty dollars, he went into the agency and handed over the money. The travel agent then whacked him over the head with a baseball bat and threw him into the river.

A few minutes later another man was walking down the street when he noticed the same advert. He went into the agency and paid his eighty dollars. The travel agent then whacked him in the ribs with the baseball bat and hurled him into the river.

Soon afterwards the two men were floating down the river together.

The first man said: 'Do you think they'll serve any food on this cruise?'

'I don't think so,' said the second man. 'They didn't last year.'

Like all pilots, Santa Claus receives regular visits from the Federal Aviation Administration, and the FAA examiner duly arrived on 19 December last year for the pre-Christmas flight check.

In preparation, Santa had the elves wash the sled and bathe all the reindeer. He got his logbook out and made sure that all his paperwork was in order. He knew that the examiner would examine the sleigh and all his other equipment and truly put his flying skills to the test.

On arrival, the examiner walked slowly around the sleigh. He checked the reindeer harnesses, the landing gear, and Rudolph's nose. He painstakingly reviewed Santa's weight and balance calculations for the sleigh's enormous cargo. Finally they were ready for the test ride. Santa got in, fastened his seatbelt and shoulder harness, and checked the compass. Then the examiner hopped in, carrying, to Santa's surprise, a shotgun.

'What's that for?' asked Santa incredulously.

The examiner winked and whispered in Santa's ear: 'I'm not supposed to tell you this in advance of the test, but you're going to lose an engine on takeoff.'

When a taxi passenger tapped the driver on the shoulder to ask a question, the driver screamed, lost control of the vehicle, nearly hit a bus, mounted the pavement and stopped just short of a shop window.

As he came to his senses, the driver shouted at the passenger: 'Don't ever do that again! You scared the living daylights out of me!'

The passenger apologized and said that he hadn't realised a little tap would scare him so much.

'No, I'm sorry,' said the driver, calming down. 'It's not really your fault. Today is my first day as a cab driver – I've been driving hearses for the last twenty-five years!'

Lost in the Sahara Desert, a traveller became increasingly thirsty. As the hours passed and the sun continued to beat down on him, he realised that if he didn't find water in a few hours, he would not survive. Desperately he staggered on in the hope of encountering some form of civilization. Feeling fainter by the minute, he was on the verge of passing out when he spotted a tent in the distance. Barely conscious, he staggered towards the tent and called out: 'Water . . .'

A Bedouin appeared in the tent doorway and said: 'I am sorry, sir, But I have no water. However, would you like to buy a tie?' With this, he produced a collection of exquisite silken neckwear.

'What do I want with a tie, you idiot!' gasped the traveller. 'I'm dying! I need water!'

'Well, sir,' said the Bedouin helpfully, 'if you really need water, there is a tent about two miles west of here where you can get some.'

Somehow the traveller managed to summon sufficient strength to drag his body through the desert and reach the second tent. On his knees, he tugged at the door of the tent.

Another Bedouin, wearing an expensive tuxedo, appeared at the door and inquired: 'May I help you, sir?'

'Water . . .' replied the traveller feebly.

'Sorry, sir,' said the Bedouin, 'but you can't come in here without a tie.'

At a plane crash site, the lone survivor sat with his back against a tree, chewing on a bone. As he tossed the bone onto a huge pile of bones, he noticed the rescue team. 'Thank heavens!' he cried out in relief. 'I am saved!'

Seeing the pile of human bones beside the lone survivor, the rescue team were too stunned to speak. He had obviously eaten his comrades. The survivor detected the look of horror on their faces and hung his head in shame.

'You can't judge me for this,' he pleaded. 'I had to survive. Is it so wrong to want to live?'

The leader of the rescue team stepped forward, shaking his head in disbelief. 'I won't judge you for doing what was necessary to survive,' he said, 'but for goodness sake, your plane only went down yesterday!'

A man on holiday in Spain thought he would e-mail his sister back in England to tell her what a great time he was having. Unfortunately instead of sending it to Joan Foster, he made a mistake with the address, as a result of which it went to Jean Foster, a recently widowed vicar's wife. When she looked at the e-mail, she promptly fainted. It read: 'Arrived safely, but it sure is hot down here.'

Tony had never been on a fishing boat before, and he was now thinking it was the dumbest thing he had ever done in his life. He was stricken with violent seasickness and with every pitch and roll, he wondered how he was going to survive the remaining two hours of the trip.

One of the deckhands came over to him and said: 'Don't worry, young fella. Nobody ever died of seasickness.'

'Great!' said Tony. 'You've just taken away my last hope of relief!'

A tourist was being led through the swamps of Florida. 'Is it true,' he asked the guide, 'that an alligator won't attack you if you carry a flash-light?'

'That depends,' replied the guide, 'on how fast you carry the flash-light!'

A coach load of tourists arrived at Runnymede. They gathered around the guide who said: 'This is the spot where the barons forced King John to sign Magna Carta.'

One of the tourists asked: 'When did that happen?'

'1215,' said the guide.

'Damn!' said the tourist, looking at his watch. 'Missed it by half an hour.'

A doctor and a minister were seated next to one another on an airplane. After take-off had been delayed due to technical problems, the captain announced that the airline staff would be serving free drinks to the passengers.

The pretty flight attendant came round with the trolley and the doctor ordered a gin and tonic. She then asked the minister what he would like to drink.

'Thank you, but no,' said the minister gravely. 'I would rather commit adultery than drink alcohol.'

The doctor said: 'Oh, I didn't know there was a choice.'

A photographer wanted to take some aerial shots of the countryside and so he booked a flight with the local aerodrome. On arrival, he was directed to the runway and told that the plane was waiting for him. Seeing a light aircraft with its engine running, he climbed in and told the pilot: 'Let's go.'

Shortly after take-off, the photographer said: 'Now, if you can come in low over that lake, I'll be able to take some nice pictures.'

'Why do you want to do that?' asked the pilot.

'It's my job. I'm a photographer.'

'Oh,' said the pilot, ashen-faced. 'So you're not the flight instructor?'

Signs That You've Chosen a 'No Frills' Airline:
   You can't board the plane unless you have the exact change.
   Before the flight, the passengers get together and elect a pilot.
   The captain asks all the passengers to chip in for a little gas.
   Before you take off, the stewardess tells you to fasten your Velcro.
   When they pull the steps away, the plane starts rocking.
   The captain yells at the ground crew to get the cows off the runway.
   The plane has both a toilet and a chapel.
   There is no movie – you don't need one because your life keeps flashing before your eyes.

Two anthropologists flew to a pair of adjacent South Sea Islands to study the natives. A few months later one of them paddled a canoe over to the other island to see how his colleague was doing. On arrival, he found the other anthropologist surrounded by a group of natives.

'How's it going?' said the visiting anthropologist.

'Amazingly well,' enthused the other. 'I have discovered an important fact about the local language. Just watch this.'

And he pointed at a palm tree and asked the natives: 'What is that?'

In unison they answered: 'Umpeta.'

Then he pointed at a rock and asked them: 'What is that?'

Together the natives replied: 'Umpeta.'

'You see!' said the anthropologist excitedly, 'they use the same word for palm tree and rock!'

'That's incredible!' said the visitor. 'On the other island, the same word means "index finger".'

The flight attendant listened patiently to the man's tirade. 'You bring me cold coffee, you feed me lousy food. I can't see the movie, not that it matters anyway because you didn't bring me any headphones, and my window doesn't have a shade so that I can close it and go to sleep.'

When he had finally finished, she said: 'Just shut up and land the plane!'

Doing the rounds of his barns in a remote country area, a farmer came across a parachutist who had landed in a bale of hay.

'What happened?' asked the farmer.

'My chute failed to open.'

'Ah well, if you'd asked the locals before making your jump, they'd have told you that nothing round here opens on a Sunday.'

A big train was meandering its way across the country. After a while the first engine broke down. The driver continued at half-power but then the other engine failed and the train came to a standstill. Speaking over the intercom, the driver told the passengers: 'I have good news and bad news. The bad news is that both engines have failed and we will be stuck here for some time. The good news is that you decided to take the train instead of an airplane.'

When a passenger aircraft flew into some turbulence, it started juddering and rocking noticeably from side to side. In a bid to keep the passengers calm, the flight attendant wheeled out the drinks trolley.

'Would you like a drink?' she asked a businessman.

'Why not?' he said caustically. 'I'll have whatever the pilot's been having.'

A tourist was admiring a necklace worn by a local Indian. 'What is it made of?' she asked.

'Alligator's teeth,' replied the Indian.

'I suppose,' said the tourist patronizingly, 'that they mean as much to you as pearls do to us?'

'No,' said the Indian. 'Anybody can open an oyster.'

A little old lady was on a National Express coach travelling north out of London. After just a few minutes of the journey, she asked the driver: 'Are we at Sheffield yet?'

'No,' said the driver. 'I'll let you know when we are.'

Ten minutes later, she asked him again: 'Are we at Sheffield yet?'

'No,' he answered, struggling to keep his patience. 'Like I say, I'll let you know when we are.'

She kept this up for the next four hours. Every ten minutes or so, she would ask the driver whether they were at Sheffield yet and each time he would tell her no. Finally, with his nerves almost in shreds, Sheffield coach station came into view and the relieved driver announced: 'Right, madam, this is Sheffield. Off you get.'

'Oh, no, driver,' she said. 'I'm going all the way to Edinburgh. It's just that my daughter told me that when I got to Sheffield I should take my blood pressure tablet.'

As a crowded airplane was about to take off, a small boy decided to throw a temper tantrum. His mother tried desperately to calm him down but he continued to kick seats and scream at the top of his voice. From the rear of the plane, a man wearing the uniform of an Air Force General walked slowly up the aisle. Reaching the boy's seat, he bent down and whispered something into his ear. Immediately the child calmed down and sat quietly, allowing his mother to fasten his seat belt. The old airman returned to his seat and the other passengers breathed a collective sigh of relief.

A few minutes later, one of the flight attendants went up to the General and asked him: 'Could I ask what magic words you used on that little boy?'

The old man smiled serenely and confided: 'I showed him my pilot's wings, service stars and battle ribbons, and explained that they entitle me to throw one passenger out the door on any flight.'

A woman boarded the bus with her young son and tried to get away with paying only one fare. The driver wasn't having any of it and insisted that she pay for the boy, too.

'But children under six ride free,' she protested.

'He doesn't look a day under thirteen,' said the driver.

The woman said: 'Can I help it if he worries a lot?'

An airplane was already virtually full and in danger of exceeding its baggage allowance when a last-minute passenger asked for the one remaining ticket.

The clerk was unsure whether to give him the ticket. 'Do you mind me asking how much you weigh?'

'With or without clothes?' queried the passenger.

'Well,' said the clerk, 'how do you intend to travel?'

A mother was anxiously awaiting her twenty-something daughter's return from a year of overseas travel. As the passengers stepped off the plane, the mother noticed that standing right behind her daughter was a man dressed in feathers with exotic markings all over his body, and carrying a shrunken head. As they came through the barrier, the girl introduced him as her new husband.

The mother threw up her hands in horror. 'You never listen to me, darling!' she shrieked. 'I said for you to marry a RICH doctor. A RICH doctor.'

After crawling along at a pitifully slow pace for miles, a passenger train finally came to a complete halt. Seeing the guard walking alongside the track, a passenger leaned out of the window and asked: 'What's going on?'

'There's a cow on the track,' replied the guard.

Ten minutes later, the train moved off and resumed its slow pace, but within five minutes it had stopped again.

The passenger saw the same guard walking past outside once more and inquired: 'What happened? Did we catch up with the cow again?'

A group of holidaymakers were trapped by an avalanche in Switzerland. After three hours, a St Bernard arrived with a keg of brandy tied under its chin.

'Hooray!' cried one of the tourists. 'Here comes man's best friend!'

'Yes,' said another. 'And look at the size of the dog that's bringing it!'

Following a particularly bumpy landing, the plane cabin crew stood at the door while the passengers exited, thanking each person for flying with the airline. The last person to leave was an old lady who, still recovering from the jolts and jerks, said falteringly: 'Do you mind if I ask a question?'

'Sure,' replied the flight attendant.

'Did we land or were we shot down?'

As a coachload of tourists drove through Wiltshire, the guide was pointing out places of interest. When they approached Stonehenge, the guide announced: 'This is Stonehenge, a megalithic monument dating from about 2800BC. It consisted originally of thirty upright stones, their tops linked by lintel stones to form a continuous circle about a hundred feet across. The uprights were built from local sandstone and each stone weighs around twenty-six tons.'

At the back of the coach one tourist turned to his wife and said: 'Pretty impressive, huh?'

'Yes,' she agreed. 'But wouldn't you think they'd have built it further back from the main road?'

Making his first-ever night-time approach to a small airfield, a cocky young pilot wanted to sound cool on the aviation frequencies. So instead of making any official landing request to the tower, he said simply: 'Guess who?'

Irritated by such arrogance, the controller responded by switching off the runway lights and saying: 'Guess where?'

A holidaymaker phoned a seaside hotel to check on its precise location. The proprietor said: 'It's only a stone's throw from the beach.'

'But how will I recognize it?'

'It's the one with all the broken windows.'

When a skinny bus driver pulled up at the stop, a giant of a man climbed on board. 'Big John doesn't pay,' said the passenger and marched straight to a seat. In view of the difference in physique between the two men, the driver realized that he was in no position to argue.

The same thing happened the following day. The man mountain got on the bus, glared at the driver, said 'Big John doesn't pay', and went to a seat.

This went on for several days, by the end of which the driver was starting to resent Big John's attitude. Why should he get away with paying the fare when everyone else had to? It seemed so unfair. The driver was fed up with having metaphorical sand kicked in his face. So he went to the gym and embarked on an intensive course of bodybuilding in the hope that he would be able to stand up and face Big John like a man.

Two weeks later and with rippling muscles where once there was skin and bone, the driver eagerly anticipated his daily encounter. At his usual stop, the huge passenger got on and announced in familiar tones: 'Big John doesn't pay.'

But this time the driver wasn't going to take it lying down. He rose to his feet and said: 'Oh yeah. And why doesn't Big John pay?'

The man reached into his inside pocket. The driver momentarily feared the worst. Then the man said: 'Because Big John got bus pass.'

A British zoo decided to send a consignment of ten small tortoises to another zoo by train. They were neatly packed in a solid wooden crate with straw and airholes and sent on their way.

When the train arrived at its destination, the station porters sprung into action. They unloaded the crate but, in doing so, accidentally opened the door. To their horror, the next thing they knew, there were ten tiny tortoises crawling along the station platform.

Later, the station manager demanded to know how they had managed to lose the entire consignment of tortoises. The head porter explained: 'There was nothing we could do. They were just too quick for our lads.'

Actual Comments Left In US Forest Service Suggestion Boxes By Backpackers:

Escalators would help on steep uphill sections.

A small deer came into my camp and stole my bag of pickles. Is there a way I can get reimbursed?

Instead of a permit system or regulations, the Forest Service needs to reduce worldwide population growth to limit the number of visitors.

Found a smouldering cigarette left by a horse.

Too many rocks in the mountains.

The coyotes made too much noise last night and kept me awake. Please eradicate these annoying animals.

A McDonald's would be nice at the trailhead.

An airline pilot with poor eyesight had always managed to pass his vision tests by memorizing the eye charts beforehand. One year, however, the doctor used a new chart that the pilot had never seen before and the game was up. The pilot proved to be as blind as a bat.

The doctor was curious as to how he had managed to fly a plane for so many years without incident. 'For example, how do you taxi the plane out to the runway?'

'Well,' said the pilot, 'it's really not that difficult. All you have to do is follow the instructions of the ground controller over the radio. Besides, all the landmarks have become quite familiar to me over the years.'

'I can understand that,' said the doctor. 'But what about take-off?'

'Again, a simple procedure. I just aim the plane down the runway, go to full throttle, pull back on the stick, and off we go!'

'And once you're aloft?'

'Oh, everything's fully automated these days. The flight computer knows our destination, and all I have to do is hit the autopilot and the plane pretty much flies itself.'

'But I still don't see how you land!'

'Oh, that's the easiest part of all,' said the pilot. 'All I do is use the airport's radio beacon to get us on the proper glide path. Then I just throttle down and when the co-pilot screams in terror, I pull the nose up, and the plane lands just fine!'

A travel agent looked up from his desk to see an elderly lady and an old gentleman peering in the shop window at the posters showing the exotic destinations around the world. The agent had enjoyed a good week and the dejected pair looking in the window filled him with a rare sense of generosity.

So he called them into his shop and said: 'I know that on your pension you could probably never hope to have a foreign holiday, so I am sending you off to a fabulous resort at my expense, and I won't take no for an answer.'

He then asked his secretary to write two return flight tickets and book them into a five star hotel. The pair gladly accepted the offer.

About a month later the lady returned to the shop.

'And how did you enjoy your holiday?' asked the travel agent.

'Oh, it was wonderful,' she said. 'The flight, the hotel, the resort, they were all excellent. That's why I'm here: I've come to thank you. But one thing puzzled me. Who was that old guy I had to share the room with?'

A Swiss man, looking for directions, pulled up at a bus stop where two Americans were waiting.

'Entschuldigung, koennen Sie Deutsch sprechen?' he asked. The two Americans just stared at him blankly.

'Excusez-moi, parlez-vous Français?' he tried. The two continued to stare.

'Parlare Italiano?' No response.

'Hablan ustedes Espanol?' Still nothing.

As the Swiss guy drove off, disgusted, one American turned to the other and said: 'Y'know, maybe we should learn a foreign language.'

'Why?' said the other. 'That guy knew four languages, and it didn't do him any good.'

A passenger on a cruise ship spotted a bearded man on a small island, shouting and desperately waving his hands. The passenger sought out the captain and asked: 'Who is that man?'

'I don't know,' said the captain, 'but every year when we pass, he does that.'

Jack said to his friend Bob: 'I reckon I'm about ready for a holiday. But this year I'm going to do it a little different. The last few years, I've taken your advice about where to go. Three years ago you told me to go to Majorca. I went to Majorca and Susan got pregnant. Then two years ago, you told me to go to the Bahamas, and Susan got pregnant again. Last year you suggested Greece, and, blow me, Susan got pregnant again!'

Bob asked: 'So what are you going to do this year that's different?'

Jack said: 'This year I'm taking Susan with me.'

A scoutmaster was teaching his scouts about survival. 'What are the three most important things you should bring with you in case you get lost alone in the desert?'

Hands went up, suggesting food, matches, and so on, but one boy said: 'A compass, a canteen of water, and a deck of cards.'

'Why those items?' asked the scoutmaster.

The boy replied: 'The compass is to find direction, and the water to prevent dehydration.'

'Yes, I understand that, but why would a deck of cards help you if you were stranded alone in the desert?'

'Well, you know how it is,' said the boy. 'As soon as you start playing solitaire, someone is bound to come up behind you and say, "Put that red four on top of the black five."'

Visiting his cousin in the valley, an old hillbilly was fascinated by the railroad. He had never seen a train before and so when one came whistling and steaming down the track towards him, it needed his cousin to drag him to safety at the last minute.

'You could have been killed there!' said the cousin. 'Lucky I was around!'

The cousin carried the shaken hillbilly back to his cabin to recuperate. The cousin put a kettle on the stove to make some tea and then went outside to chop some wood. He returned to find the hillbilly raining blows on the kettle with the butt of a shotgun.

'Why are you smashing my kettle?' demanded the cousin.

'These darned things are dangerous,' said the hillbilly. 'I'm killin' this one before it gets a chance to grow up!'

The navigator of the QE2 was steering the ship through dense fog. Suddenly he turned to the captain and said: 'Sir, I think something is wrong with our compass.'

'Why do you say that?' asked the captain.

'Because we've just been overtaken by a number 36 bus!'

A farmer and his wife went to an air fair. The farmer had always been fascinated by planes and asked the pilot of a light aircraft how much it would be for a ride.

'A hundred and fifty dollars,' said the pilot.

'I can't afford that,' said the farmer. 'That's a real shame cos I've always wanted to go up in one of them things.'

The pilot was moved by his enthusiasm. 'I tell you what I'll do – I'll make a deal with you. You and your wife can ride for free provided you don't make a sound at any time during the flight. But if you make a sound, it'll cost you the full hundred and fifty.'

The couple agreed and climbed into the plane. The pilot really showed off, performing loops, dives and twists. Half an hour later, when he came in to land, he asked the farmer if he'd enjoyed it.

'It was great!' said the farmer. 'Fantastic!'

'Well, I want to congratulate you on your bravery,' said the pilot. 'You didn't make a sound for the entire trip.'

'It was a close call though,' said the farmer. 'I nearly said something when my wife fell out!'

Making her first airplane trip, a young woman found herself a window seat in a no-smoking area and settled down. A few minutes later, a man came over and insisted that she was in his seat, but she flatly refused to move. In the end he said: 'Okay, lady, if that's the way you want it, you fly this plane!'

Among a group of tourists travelling Ireland, one woman was constantly complaining. The bus seats were uncomfortable; the food was terrible; the weather was too hot; the weather was too cold; the hotels were awful – to her mind, everything was wrong.

When the group arrived at the site of the famous Blarney Stone, the tour guide said: 'Good luck will be following you all your days if you kiss the Blarney Stone. But unfortunately it's being cleaned today and so no one will be able to kiss it. Perhaps we can come back tomorrow.'

'We can't be here tomorrow,' moaned the unpleasant woman. 'We have some other boring tour to go on. So I guess we can't kiss the stupid stone.'

'Well now,' said the guide, 'it is said that if you kiss someone who has kissed the stone, you'll have the same good fortune.'

'And I suppose you've kissed the stone?' sneered the woman.

'No, ma'am,' replied the guide, beginning to lose his patience with her, 'but I have sat on it!'

Shortly after a routine takeoff, the flight attendant noticed a male passenger sweating profusely and biting his nails.

'Sir,' she asked sympathetically, 'could I get you something from the bar to calm your nerves?'

He nodded his head feverishly, so she brought him a whiskey, which he knocked back straight away.

Twenty minutes later, she was again making her rounds of the passengers when she spotted the same man grinding his teeth and gripping his hands anxiously. He looked on the verge of a breakdown.

'Would another drink help?' she asked. 'I'll make a special exception for you.'

The man nodded frantically, so she fetched him another whiskey.

Half an hour later, she heard the man sobbing.

'My, you are in a state!' she said. 'I've never seen anyone so afraid of flying.'

'I'm not afraid of flying,' he stammered.

'Then, what's the matter?'

'I'm trying to give up drinking.'

What happened to the survivors of a collision between a red ship and a blue ship? – They were marooned.

A plane was delayed for nearly an hour on take-off. When it eventually took to the air, the passengers asked the flight attendant the reason for the late departure.

'Well,' she explained, 'the pilot was worried about a noise he heard coming from one of the engines and it took us a while to get a new pilot.'

An airline stewardess was just finishing her standard safety briefing to passengers. 'In the event of a water landing, your seat cushion may be used as a flotation device.'

At this, a male passenger called out: 'Hey! If the plane can't fly, why should I believe the seat can float?'

A British woman phoned the lost property office of a coach company to report that she had lost a vulture on a journey from London to Manchester.

'Right, madam,' said the clerk. 'And what colour is the vulture?'

During the 1960s space race, NASA decided that it needed a special ballpoint pen capable of writing in the zero gravity confines of its space capsules. After years of research and development, the Astronaut Pen was produced at a cost of a million dollars. The Soviet Union, faced with the same problem, used a pencil.

A husband and wife were travelling on holiday in Scotland. As they approached Kirkcudbright, they started arguing about the pronunciation of the town. The argument raged until they stopped for lunch. As they stood in the restaurant, the husband asked the girl behind the counter: 'Before we order, could you please settle an argument for us? Would you please pronounce where we are, very slowly?'

The girl leaned over the counter and said: 'Burrrr . . . gerrrrrr . . . Kiiiing.'

It was mealtime on a small budget airline. 'Would you like dinner?' asked the flight attendant.

The passenger said: 'What are my choices?'

The flight attendant replied: 'Yes or no.'

A husband and wife were relaxing on the beach on holiday when the wife suddenly exclaimed: 'Oh my God! I've just remembered I left the oven on!'

'Don't worry about it,' said her husband reassuringly. 'The house won't burn down. I've just remembered I left the bath running!'

With an hour to wait before his flight to Los Angeles, a man was propping up the bar, downing a succession of whiskeys. He was sweating profusely and his hands were shaking. Seeing his obvious distress, a priest came over to try and calm him down.

'Are you nervous about flying?' asked the priest.

'N-n-nervous? I'm t-t-terrified. I j-just kn-know the p-plane is g-going to c-crash and we're all g-going to d-d-die!'

'Is this your first time flying?'

'No, I fly c-cross-c-country all the time. It's my j-j-job.'

'Why don't you ask your boss if you can drive cross-country instead?'

'He'd n-never let me d-do that.'

'Why not?'

'Because I'm the p-p-pilot.'

A husband and wife were on safari in Kenya.

'Look,' said the husband, 'lion tracks! You see where they go and I'll find out where they came from.'

A travel writer was checking out of his Canadian hotel when he spotted an Indian chief sitting in the lobby.

'Who's that?' the writer asked the hotel manager.

'Oh, that's Big Chief Forget Me Not. He's ninety-five and has a fantastic memory – he can remember every single detail of his life.'

Intrigued, the writer went over to the chief and tried to engage him in conversation.

'Hi there,' said the writer.

Preoccupied with carving a wooden tool, the chief mumbled a scarcely audible reply.

'Can you tell me what you had for breakfast on your twenty-first birthday?' persisted the writer.

'Eggs,' said the chief, and he carried on with his carving.

The travel writer recounted this story to a number of people and was advised that the correct way to address an Indian chief was not 'Hi there' but 'How?' Six months later he was staying at the same

Canadian hotel and, to his amazement, Big Chief Forget Me Not was
still sitting in the lobby.

The writer went over to him and said: 'How?'

'Scrambled,' said the chief.

Genuine Comments From Flight Crews:

Anything left behind will be distributed evenly among the flight attendants. Please do not leave children or spouses.

Folks, we have reached our cruising altitude now, so I am going to
switch the seat belt sign off. Feel free to move about as you wish, but
please stay inside the plane till we land. It's a bit cold outside.

We ask you to remain seated as Captain Kangaroo bounces us to the
terminal.

We are pleased to have some of the best flight attendants in the
industry — unfortunately none of them are on this flight.

There may be fifty ways to leave your lover, but there are only four
ways out of this airplane.

As we prepare for takeoff, please make sure your tray tables and seat
backs are fully upright in their most uncomfortable position.

Smoking in the lavatories is prohibited. Any person caught smoking in
the lavatories will be asked to leave the plane immediately.

Ladies and gentlemen, welcome to Amarillo. Please remain in your
seats with your seatbelts fastened while the captain taxis what's left of
our airplane to the gate.

Your seat cushions can be used for flotation, and in the event of an
emergency water landing, please take them with our compliments.

In a great desert in a far off land lived a band of nomads. Their leader,
Benny, had risen to his rank due almost entirely to his magnificently
bushy beard. For his people believed that a man's strength and courage
came from his beard, and thus the man with the biggest and finest
beard was named as their chief. But after leading the band for many
years, Benny began to feel uncomfortable wearing the beard in the hot,
dusty climate. He wanted to shave it off, so he called a meeting of his
council to seek their opinion.

Hearing that he wanted to shave, the councillors were shocked. One
said: 'Do you not remember the ancient legend, sire? The leader who
removes his beard is cursed and made into a piece of earthenware.'

Benny had heard the legend but, being a forward thinker, he had
always scoffed at the tale. So he disregarded the warning and went
ahead and scraped away his once magnificent beard. However as the

final whisker was cut off, a huge dust storm rose up. It lasted only a few seconds but when it cleared, a man-sized clay vessel stood on the exact spot where their leader had been just moments earlier.

Consequently, the council knew the legend must be true and concluded: 'A Benny shaved is a Benny urned.'

Waiters

A wine waiter asked his two customers: 'Red or white, gentlemen?'
  The first said: 'I'll have red.'
  The second said: 'Me, too – and make sure the glass is clean.'
  A few minutes later the waiter returned with the drinks: 'Two red wines. Which one asked for the clean glass?'

Two men were in a restaurant and ordered fish. The waiter brought a dish with two fish, one noticeably larger than the other.
  The first man said: 'Please help yourself.'
  The second said: 'Okay,' and took the larger fish.
  After a tense silence, the first complained: 'You see, if you had offered me the first choice, I would have taken the smaller fish.'
  His companion said: 'What are you moaning for? You've got it, haven't you?'

A man went to a restaurant in Spain. He ordered the house special and was brought a plate with potatoes, corn and two large meaty objects.
  'What are these?' he asked the waiter.
  'Cojones, señor,' said the waiter.
  'What exactly are cojones?'
  'They are the testicles of the bull who lost at the arena this afternoon.'
  Overcoming his initial reservations, the man decided to try this local delicacy and found it very tasty. Indeed he liked it so much that he returned the following night and ordered the house special again. The waiter appeared with a plate of potatoes and corn, but this time the two meaty objects were considerably smaller. Nevertheless the man ate them and thoroughly enjoyed them.
  'What were they?' he asked the waiter afterwards.

'Cojones, señor.'

'No, I had the cojones yesterday and they were much bigger.'

'Ah yes, señor, but the bull does not lose every time.'

A man went into a delicatessen, took a seat at the lunch counter and ordered a corned beef sandwich.

The waiter said: 'Corned beef sandwich is not on the menu, but I can get you a sandwich with corned beef in it. We call it our Thursday Special.'

'What's a Thursday Special?'

'A triple decker with corned beef, tongue, bologna, tomato, lettuce, onion, pickle and mayonnaise, on toasted raisin bread.'

The customer was becoming exasperated. 'I don't want all that. Can't I just have a piece of corned beef between two slices of white bread?'

'Sure. No problem,' said the waiter. Calling across to the sandwich man, he sang out: 'One Thursday special. Make it one deck, hold the tongue, bologna, tomato, lettuce, onion, pickle and mayonnaise, and make the raisin bread white, untoasted!'

A man and a woman were sitting in a restaurant when the waitress noticed the man sliding down his chair and under the table. The woman appeared unconcerned but the waitress felt she ought to say something.

'Excuse me,' said the waitress, 'I think your husband just slid under the table.'

'No,' replied the woman coldly. 'My husband just walked in the door.'

Two businessmen went into a diner and ordered two drinks. Then they produced sandwiches from their briefcases and started to eat. Seeing this, the waiter became agitated and marched over to inform them: 'Sorry, but you can't eat your own sandwiches in here!' The two men looked at each other, shrugged their shoulders and exchanged sandwiches.

A guy had told all of his friends about the great steak he had eaten in a city centre restaurant the previous day, so they decided to join him and find out whether the place really served steaks as large and delicious as he had described.

The group found a table near the back of the restaurant. After scanning the menu, they ordered, and waited hungrily for their gigantic steaks. But to their disappointment, the waiter brought out some of the smallest steaks they had ever seen.

The guy who had recommended the place in such glowing terms was hugely embarrassed and confronted the waiter: 'Yesterday when I came here,' he said, 'you served me a big, juicy steak. Today, however, when I've invited my friends along, you serve miniature steaks! What's going on?'

'Yes, sir,' replied the waiter, 'but yesterday you were sitting by the window.'

'What flavours of ice cream do you have?' asked the customer.

'Vanilla, strawberry, and chocolate,' replied the trainee waitress in a hoarse whisper.

Trying to be sympathetic, the customer said: 'Do you have laryngitis?'

'No,' said the waitress, 'just vanilla, strawberry, and chocolate.'

A pretty waitress came over to take a man's order.

'I want a quickie,' he said.

Appalled, she slapped him around the face. When she had regained her composure, she asked him again: 'Now what would you like?'

'I want a quickie,' he said.

Once again she slapped him hard around the face.

She decided to give him one last chance. 'For the final time, what would you like?'

'I want a quickie,' he replied.

She slapped him around the face again and went to fetch the manager. Meanwhile a customer at the next table leaned over and whispered to the man: 'I think you'll find it's pronounced quiche.'

Waiter, there's a fly in my soup!

No, sir, that's a cockroach; the fly is on your steak.

Waiter, there's a fly in my soup!

It's OK, sir, there's no extra charge.

Waiter, there's a fly in my soup!

Force of habit, sir. Our chef used to be a tailor.

Waiter, there's a fly in my soup!

Couldn't be, sir. The cook used them all in the raisin bread.

Waiter, there's a fly in my soup!
  Sorry, sir. I must have missed it when I removed the other four.

Waiter, there's a dead fly in my soup!
  Yes, sir, it's the hot water that kills them.

Waiter, there's a flea in my soup!
  Tell him to hop it.

Waiter, I'd like a cup of coffee with no cream.
  Sorry, sir, we're out of cream. How about with no milk?

Waiter, I can't seem to find any chicken in this chicken soup.
  Would you expect to find angels in angel cake?

Waiter, your tie is in my soup!
  That's all right, sir, it's not shrinkable.

Waiter, this soup tastes funny.
  So why aren't you laughing?

Waiter, send the chef here. I wish to complain about this disgusting meal.
  I'm afraid you'll have to wait, sir. He's just popped out for his dinner.

Waiter, this water is very cloudy.
  No, sir, you just have a very dirty glass.

Waiter, you're not fit to serve a pig!
  I'm doing my best, sir.

A plane was flying through the jungle when the engine stalled. The pilot ejected and drifted gently down but unfortunately he landed in a large cooking pot. The chief of the tribe summoned his servant and asked: 'Waiter, what's this flier doing in my soup?'

A man in a restaurant ordered a bowl of vegetable soup, but after a couple of spoonfuls he noticed a circle of wetness on the tablecloth directly beneath the bowl.

  Calling over the waiter, he said: 'It's wet down here. The bowl must be cracked.'

The waiter said: 'You ordered vegetable soup, didn't you?'

'Yes.'

'Well, maybe it has a leek in it.'

After finishing his meal, a restaurant customer checked his pockets and left a tip of three pennies. As he put his coat on, the waitress said: 'You can tell a lot about a man by the tip he leaves.'

'Really?' asked the man, intrigued. 'What does my tip say?'

'Well,' said the waitress, 'this first penny tells me you're a thrifty man.'

'That is certainly correct,' said the man proudly.

'This second penny tells me that you're a bachelor.'

Surprised at her perception, he said: 'Yes, that is also true.'

'And this third penny tells me that your father was one too.'

A customer was continually bothering a restaurant waiter. First he asked for the air conditioning to be turned up because he was too hot, then he asked for it to be turned down because he was too cold. This went on for about half an hour, but the waiter never refused the request and, even though he was forever going to and fro, he always kept his temper.

Eventually another customer asked the waiter why he didn't simply throw the pest out.

'Oh, I don't mind,' said the waiter. 'Anyway, we don't even have an air conditioner.'

After taking her young son to lunch in a smart restaurant, a woman noticed that there was still a lot of food left over. So she asked the waiter: 'Please could you put the meat in a bag for the dog?'

'Wow!' said the boy jumping to his feet. 'Are we getting a dog?'

A man went into a café and sat down. He noticed that the special of the day was cold chilli, so when the waitress came to take his order, he asked for a bowl of the cold chilli.

'I'm sorry,' said the waitress, 'the gentleman next to you got the last bowl.'

'I'll just have coffee then,' said the man.

After a while he noticed that the customer next to him was finishing a big steak but the bowl of cold chilli was still there. 'Are you going to eat that bowl of chilli?' he asked.

'No.'

'Would you sell it to me?'

'No, but you can have it for free.'

So he took the chilli and began to eat it, but when he got about halfway through, he noticed a dead mouse in the bowl and promptly vomited the chilli back into the bowl.

The other man said: 'That's about as far as I got too.'

The Following Have Been Seen On Menus Around The World:

Dreaded veal cutlet with potatoes in cream (China)

Sweat from the trolley (Europe)

Battered saucepans and fried hormones (Japan)

Chessburger (Poland)

Toes with butter and jam (Bali)

Muscles of Marines/Lobster Thermos (Cairo)

Special cocktails for the ladies with nuts (Tokyo)

Rather burnt land slug (Thailand)

Salad a firm's own make; limpid red beet soup with cheesy dumplings in the form of a finger; roasted duck let loose; beef rashers beaten up in the country people's fashion (Poland)

Fried fishermen (Japan)

Grilled lamp ribs (Barcelona)

Strawberry crap (Japan)

Children soup (India)

French fried ships (Cairo)

Pork with fresh garbage (Vietnam)

Teppan Yaki – Before Your Cooked Right Eyes (Japan)

Special today – no ice cream (Switzerland)

Foul English breakfast (Greece)

Weather

An Indian tribe asked their chief in autumn whether the forthcoming winter was going to be cold. He didn't really know the answer, but said that it probably would be cold and advised the members of the village to stock up on supplies of firewood anyway. Being a very thorough chief with the welfare of his people at heart, he then phoned the National Weather Service and asked: 'Is the winter going to be cold?'

'Yes, quite cold,' answered the weatherman.

Hearing this, the chief returned to his people and urged them to speed up the wood collection.

A week later, he called the National Weather Service again. 'Is it going to be a very cold winter?' he inquired.

'Yes,' said the weatherman. 'It looks like it's going to be a very cold winter indeed.'

Armed with this information, the chief returned to his village and ordered his people to find every scrap of wood they could.

Two weeks later, he phoned the National Weather Service once more. 'Are you absolutely sure the winter is going to be very cold?'

'Absolutely,' replied the weatherman. 'The Indians are collecting firewood like crazy!'

A tourist spent two miserable weeks in a Scottish hotel. Every day the weather was cold and damp. On his final day, he asked a small boy: 'Does the weather around here ever change?'

'Don't ask me,' said the boy. 'I'm only seven!'

An Irishman was battling through a terrible thunderstorm with a friend when the sheer effort caused him to suffer a heart attack.

'Quick,' said the Irishman, 'I'm dying. Fetch me a rabbi.'

'What do you mean, a rabbi?' said his friend. 'You've been a Catholic all your life.'

'I know,' said the Irishman, 'but I wouldn't want to drag the Father out on a night like this.'

A motorist was carefully picking his way through the floodwater following a day of torrential rain when he spotted a man's head sticking out of a large puddle.

The motorist slowed down and called out: 'Do you need a lift?'

'No thanks,' said the man. 'I'm on my bike.'

A British meteorologist posted to Italy became notorious for his inability to predict the weather accurately. If he forecast sun, it rained; if he forecast snow, it was gloriously hot. His infamy reached the stage where the local newspaper monitored his blunders on a daily basis and duly informed its readers that he had been hopelessly wrong about the weather on no fewer than three hundred and one occasions in the course of the previous year. His employers realized that his position had become untenable and so they fired him.

Hoping that news of his demise had not reached Scotland, he attempted to rebuild his career by applying for a job as a weather forecaster in Edinburgh. At the interview they asked him the question he had been dreading, namely: 'Why did you leave your previous job?'

He answered simply: 'The climate didn't agree with me.'

It was a terrible night. The wind was howling and the rain was lashing down. The streets of the city were deserted and a local baker was just about to shut up shop for the night when a little man entered the shop, carrying an umbrella that had blown inside out. Even though he was wearing two sweaters and a thick coat, he still looked wet and bed-raggled.

As he loosened his scarf, he said to the baker: 'May I have two bagels to go, please?'

'Just two bagels?' queried the baker, astonished. 'Nothing more?'

'That's right. One for me and one for Bernice.'

'Bernice is your wife?' asked the baker.

'What do you think?' snapped the little man. 'My mother would send me out on a night like this?'

A Hollywood director was shooting a big budget movie on location in the desert. One day an old Indian came up to him and said: 'Tomorrow rain.' And sure enough, the next day it rained.

A few days later, the old Indian appeared on set again, sidled up to the director and said: 'Tomorrow storm.' And sure enough, the following day there was a terrible storm, which brought a temporary halt to filming.

The director was hugely impressed by the old Indian's weather predictions and told his secretary to put the tribesman on the payroll. However, after a number of other successful forecasts, the Indian didn't show up for three weeks. Eventually the director sent for him, saying: 'I have to shoot a big scene tomorrow and I'm relying on you. What is the weather going to be like?'

The old Indian shrugged his shoulders. 'Don't know. Radio broken.'

Women

A man was walking through the woods when he stumbled across a lamp. In time-honoured tradition, he picked it up, rubbed it, and out popped a genie who granted him three wishes.

'I'd like a million dollars,' said the man. And POOF! A million dollars appeared.

'And what is your second wish?' asked the genie.

'I'd like a new Ferrari,' said the man. And POOF! A gleaming new Ferrari suddenly appeared.

'And for your third wish?'

'I'd like to be irresistible to women.'

And POOF! He was turned into a box of chocolates.

What do you call a woman with a screwdriver in one hand, a knife in the other, a pair of scissors between the toes on her left foot, and a corkscrew between the toes on her right foot? – A Swiss Army wife.

God said: 'What's the matter, Adam? You look so miserable all the time.'

Adam said: 'I'm bored having nobody to talk to.'

'Right,' said God, 'I'm going to give you a companion. She will be called a woman. This person will gather food for you, cook for you, and when you discover clothing, she'll wash it for you. She will always agree with whatever you say. She will bear your children and never ask you to get up in the middle of the night to take care of them. She will not nag you and will always be the first to admit she was wrong when you've had a disagreement. She will never have a headache and will freely give you love and passion whenever you need it.'

'She sounds great,' said Adam. 'But what will a woman like this cost?'

'An arm and a leg,' said God.

Adam thought for a moment. 'What can I get for a rib?'

The rest is history . . .

Female version:

First Woman: Oh, you got a haircut! That's so cute!

Second Woman: Do you think so? I wasn't sure when she gave me the mirror. I mean, you don't think it's too fluffy-looking?

First Woman: Oh God, no! No, it's perfect. I'd love to get my hair cut like that, but I think my face is too wide. I'm pretty much stuck with it how it is, I think.

Second Woman: Are you serious? I think your face is adorable. And you could easily get one of those layer cuts – that would really suit you. I was going to do that except that I was afraid it would accentuate my long neck.

First Woman: What's wrong with your neck? I would love to have a neck like yours: anything to take attention away from my awful shoulder line.

Second Woman: Are you kidding? I know girls that would love to have your shoulders. Everything hangs so well on you. You're like a walking fashion catalogue. But look at my arms – see how short they are? If I had your shoulders, I could get clothes to fit me so much easier.

Male version:

First Man: Haircut?

Second Man: Yeah.

Two men were propped up against the bar at the end of a heavy drinking session.

'Tell me,' said one. 'Have you ever gone to bed with a really ugly woman?'

'No,' replied the other. 'But I've woken up with plenty!'

A male charity collector knocked on a woman's front door and asked her if she had any old beer bottles.

She was highly indignant. 'Do I look as if I drink beer?' she snapped.

The collector looked at her and said: 'So, have you got any vinegar bottles?'

What's the best way to get a youthful figure? – Ask a woman her age.

A man was sitting alone in his office one night when a genie popped up out of the filing cabinet and asked: 'And what will your third wish be?'

The man looked at the genie and said: 'Huh? How can I be getting a third wish when I haven't had a first or second wish yet?'

'You have had two wishes already,' maintained the genie, 'but your second wish was for me to put everything back the way it was before you made your first wish. Thus you remember nothing because everything is the way it was before you made any wishes. You now have one wish left.'

'Okay,' said the man, 'I don't believe this, but what the heck! I've always wanted to understand women. I'd love to know what's going on inside their heads.'

'Funny,' said the genie as it granted his wish and disappeared forever. 'That was your first wish, too!'

Two men were admiring a famous actress. 'Still,' said one, 'if you take away her fabulous hair, her magnificent breasts, her beautiful eyes, her perfect features, and her stunning figure, what are you left with?'

The other replied: 'My wife.'

First, God created Earth, then he rested.

Then he created Man, then he rested.

Then he created Woman, and no one has rested since!

After examining a female patient, a doctor took the woman's husband to one side.

'I'll have to be honest with you,' said the doctor ominously, 'but I don't like the look of your wife.'

'Me neither,' said the husband. 'But she's a smashing cook and great with the kids!'

Two women in their sixties – fierce rivals in high society – met at a posh party.

'My dear,' said the first patronizingly, 'are those real pearls?'

'They are.'

'Of course,' continued the first, smiling, 'the only way I could tell would be for me to bite them.'

'Yes,' countered the second, 'but for that, you would need real teeth.'

With a plane about to crash into a mountain, a female passenger stood up and shouted: 'If I'm going to die, I want to die feeling like a woman.'

Then she took off her top and cried: 'Is there anyone on this plane who is man enough to make me feel like a woman?'

Hearing this, a man stood up, took off his shirt and said: 'Iron this, love.'

Women's Dictionary:

Argument n. A discussion that occurs when you're right, but he just hasn't realized it yet.

Airhead n. What a woman intentionally becomes when pulled over by a policeman.

Barbecue n. You bought the groceries, washed the lettuce, chopped the tomatoes, diced the onions, marinated the meat and cleaned everything up, but he 'made the dinner'.

Childbirth n. You get to go through thirty-six hours of contractions; he gets to hold your hand and say 'focus . . . breathe . . . push.'

Clothes dryer n. An appliance designed to eat socks.

Diet drink n. Something you buy at a late-night shop to go with a half-pound bag of peanut M&Ms.

Exercise n. To walk up and down a shopping mall, occasionally resting to make a purchase.

Grocery list n. What you spend half an hour writing, then forget to take with you to the store.

Hairdresser n. Someone who is able to create a style you will never be able to duplicate again.

Lipstick n. On your lips, colouring to enhance the beauty of your mouth. On his collar, colouring only a tramp would wear.

Valentine's Day n. A day when you dream of a candlelit dinner, diamonds and romance, but are lucky if you get a card.

Waterproof mascara n. Comes off if you cry, shower or swim, but will not come off if you try to remove it.

Work

The office junior's first task every day was to take the boss a hot cup of coffee, but each morning, much to the boss's annoyance, the cup arrived two-thirds full. The lad explained that in his rush to deliver the coffee hot, he always ended up spilling some of it along the corridor between the coffee machine and the boss's office.

No matter how much the boss complained, he never received a full cup of coffee and eventually he became so frustrated that he threatened to deduct the boy's pay by one-third if he continued to serve short measures. The next morning for the first time, the boss was finally presented with a full cup of coffee. This continued for the remainder of the week, causing the boss to compliment the boy on his new technique.

'It's nothing,' said the lad. 'I simply take a mouthful of your coffee when I'm standing next to the machine and spit it back into your cup when I get outside your office.'

The managing director was scheduled to speak at an important convention, so he asked Jenkins, one of his employees, to write him a punchy, twenty-minute speech. When the MD returned from the big event, he was livid.

'What's the idea of writing me an hour-long speech?' he raged at Jenkins. 'Half the audience walked out before I was finished.'

Jenkins was baffled. 'I wrote you a twenty-minute speech,' he said. 'I also gave you the two extra copies you asked for.'

A man at a job interview was asked what he thought his greatest qualities were.

'My motivational skills, I think. At my last job everyone always said they had to work twice as hard when I was around.'

A carpet fitter decided to take a cigarette break after finishing the first of several rooms he had to do. Finding the packet missing from his pocket, he began searching the house until he spotted a small lump beneath the carpet he had just fitted. The lump was right in the middle and, not wanting to rip up all that work just for a packet of cigarettes, he simply walked over and pounded the lump flat.

At the end of the day, he was loading his tools onto the truck when he noticed the packet of cigarettes on the dashboard. Just then the lady of the house called out: 'Have you seen my parakeet?'

Trying to surprise her husband, an executive's wife stopped by his office. She found him with a secretary sitting on his lap.

Without hesitating, he dictated: '. . . and in conclusion, gentlemen, shortage or no shortage, I cannot continue to operate this office with just one chair.'

The boss of a small firm reluctantly told four of his employees: 'I'm going to have to let one of you go.'

The black employee said: 'I'm a protected minority.'

The female employee said: 'And I'm a woman.'

The oldest employee said: 'Fire me, pal, and I'll hit you with an age discrimination suit so fast it'll make your head spin!'

They all turned to look at the young, white, male employee who thought for a moment before saying: 'I think I might be gay . . .'

Office Memo:

Subject: Casual Fridays

Week 1 – memo 1

Effective this week, the company is adopting Fridays as Casual Day. Employees are free to dress in the casual attire of their choice.

Week 2 – memo 2

Spandex and leather micro-miniskirts are not appropriate attire for Casual Day. Neither are string ties, rodeo belt buckles or moccasins.

Week 3 – memo 3

Casual Day refers to dress only, not attitude. When planning Friday's wardrobe, remember image is the key to our success.

Week 4 – memo 4

A seminar on how to dress for Casual Day will be held at 4pm Friday in the cafeteria. A fashion show will follow. Attendance is mandatory.

Week 6 – memo 5

As an outgrowth of Friday's seminar, a twelve-member Casual Day Task Force has been appointed to prepare guidelines for proper Casual Day dress.

Week 13 – memo 6

The Casual Day Task Force has now completed a thirty-page manual entitled 'Relaxing Dress Without Relaxing Company Standards.' A copy has been distributed to every employee. Please study the chapter 'You Are What You Wear' and consult the 'home casual' versus 'business casual' checklist before leaving for work each Friday. If you have doubts about the appropriateness of an item of clothing, contact your CDTF representative before 7am on Friday.

Week 18 – memo 7

Our Employee Assistant Plan (EAP) has now been expanded to provide support for psychological counselling for employees who may be having difficulty adjusting to Casual Day.

Week 20 – memo 8

Due to budget cuts in the Human Resources department, we are no longer able to effectively support or manage Casual Day. Therefore Casual Day will be discontinued, effective immediately.

It was a baking hot day in the office. The temperature was nudging a hundred outside and a really foul smell was wafting around the room. As the odour grew more intense, the fourteen-strong workforce began to suffer.

Eventually one man said pointedly: 'Clearly someone's deodorant isn't working.'

A guy in the corner called out: 'Well, it can't be me because I'm not wearing any.'

A man went to apply for a job. After filling out the various application forms, he waited anxiously for the outcome. The employer read the forms and said: 'We do have an opening for people like you.'

'Great. What is it?'

'It's called the door!'

Having finally run out of patience, the boss called a young employee into his office. 'It has not escaped my attention that every time there's a home game at the stadium, you have to take your aunt to the doctor.'

The employee looked thoughtful and said: 'You know, you're right, sir. I didn't realize. You don't suppose she's faking it, do you?'

A humble office clerk called Norman boasted to his boss that he knew everyone in the world who was worth knowing. Celebrities, royalty, politicians: he claimed to be personal friends with each and every one.

Needless to say his boss didn't believe him, so Norman offered to introduce him to one of his celebrity friends.

'Would you believe me if I took you to Arnold Schwarzenegger's house?' asked Norman.

'Maybe,' replied the boss.

So they drove off to Schwarzenegger's mansion, and Arnie came to the door to greet them. 'Hey, Norman, my friend, how are you doin'?'

They stayed for lunch and a chat and afterwards Norman turned to his boss and said: 'Now are you convinced?'

'You just got lucky,' sneered the boss. 'Arnie's a friendly guy.'

'How about if I introduced you to Madonna? Then would you believe that I know everybody?'

'Perhaps.'

So they travelled to London where Norman took his boss to Madonna's house.

'Norman, great to see you again!' said Madonna warmly. 'Who's your friend?'

'This is my boss,' said Norman.

'Come in, both of you. Any friend of Norman is a friend of mine!'

Two drinks later they left. 'Now do you believe me?' asked Norman.

'Not really,' said the boss churlishly. 'I bet you tipped her off in advance and paid her to pretend she knew you.'

Norman had one trump card still to play. 'How about if I showed you I was friends with the Pope?'

'Well,' conceded the boss, 'I have to say that would be pretty impressive. I guess if you could appear on the Vatican balcony with the Pope, I'd finally be convinced that you know everyone in the world worth knowing.'

So the pair travelled to Rome. The boss waited in St. Peter's Square while Norman went into the Vatican. A few minutes later, sure enough, Norman appeared on the Vatican balcony alongside the Pope.

After his public appearance, Norman rushed back down to the square to learn his boss's reaction, only to find that he had fainted.

'What happened?' asked Norman.

'I was fine,' said the boss groggily, 'until the man next to me said: "Who's that on the balcony with Norman?"'

On his first day in the office, a young trainee picked up the phone and said: 'Get me a coffee!'

The voice on the other end boomed: 'You idiot, you've dialled the wrong extension! Do you know who you're talking to, you fool?'

'No,' said the trainee.

'This is the managing director!'

'And do you know who you're talking to, you fool?' responded the trainee.

'No.'

'Good.' And the trainee put down the phone.

A boss collared one of his employees and said: 'I know you were skiving yesterday. You were out playing golf!'

The employee retaliated: 'That's a damn lie, and I have the fish to prove it!'

Boss: Do you think you can handle a variety of work?

Applicant: I ought to be able to. I've had eight different jobs in the past three months.

Differences Between You and Your Boss:

When you take a long time, you're slow.
When your boss takes a long time, he's thorough.

When you don't do it, you're lazy.
When your boss doesn't do it, he's too busy.

When you make a mistake, you're an idiot.
When your boss makes a mistake, he's only human.

When doing something without being told, you're overstepping your authority.
When your boss does the same thing, he's using his initiative.

When you take a stand, you're being stubborn.
When your boss takes a stand, he's being firm.

When you're on a day off sick, you're always sick.
When your boss has a day off sick, he must be very ill.

When you apply for leave, you must be going for an interview.

When your boss applies for leave, it's because he's over-worked.

When you're out of the office, you're skiving.

When your boss is out of the office, he's on business.

A man arrived at work with both ears bandaged.

'What happened to your ears?' asked his foreman.

'Well,' he explained, 'yesterday I was ironing a shirt when the phone rang and I accidentally answered the iron.'

'That explains one ear, but what about the other one?'

'For God's sake, I had to call the doctor!'

Boss: If you could have a conversation with someone, living or dead, who would it be?

Applicant: The living one.

Three weeks after a young man had been hired by a top hotel, he was called into the personnel manager's office.

The manager said: 'You told us you had two years' experience at the Dorchester, followed by three years at the Ritz, and that you had organized royal banquets. Now we find that your only previous job was serving in McDonald's!'

'Well,' said the young man. 'In your advert you did say you wanted someone with imagination!'

Bill asked Alf about his new job.

'It's the worst job I've had in my life,' said Alf.

'How long have you been there?'

'Three months.'

'Why don't you quit?'

'No way. This is the first time in twenty years that I've actually looked forward to going home in the evening!'

A female worker told her boss she was going home early because she didn't feel well. Since the boss was just recovering from illness himself, he wished her well and said he hoped it wasn't something that he'd given her.

'So do I,' she said. 'I've got morning sickness!'

A trade union leader was reading his grandson a bedtime story: 'Once upon a time and a half . . .'

A businessman arrived home exhausted one evening and slumped on the sofa.

'You poor darling,' said his wife tenderly. 'You must have had a terrible day.'

'You're not kidding,' he replied. 'The computer system crashed and we all had to think for ourselves.'

Negotiations between union members and their employer were at an impasse, the union denying that their workers were flagrantly abusing the sick leave provisions set out by their contract.

Then one morning at the bargaining table, the company's chief negotiator held up a newspaper. 'This man,' he said, 'called in sick yesterday.' There on the sports page was a photo of a supposedly ill employee who had just won a local golf tournament with an excellent score.

Everyone present waited for a response from the union negotiator. After a moment or two he broke the silence by saying: 'Just think of the score he could have made if he hadn't been sick.'

A newly promoted boss decided to stamp his authority on the office by attaching a sign to his door that read: 'I'm the Boss.'

A few days later a colleague took a phone call for him and relayed the message to him in front of the rest of the staff: 'Your wife rang – she wants her sign back.'

An employee went to his boss and said: 'Is there any chance I could have tomorrow off? My wife wants me to help clear out the attic and the garage, and then to fix the guttering.'

'I'm sorry,' said the boss. 'You know we're short-staffed. I can't let you have the day off.'

'Thanks, boss,' said the employee. 'I knew I could count on you!'

Reviewing a potential employee's application form, the manager of a large retail store noted that the candidate had never previously worked in that field.

'I must say that for a man with no experience, you're certainly asking for a high wage.'

'Well,' replied the applicant, 'the work is so much harder when you don't know what you're doing.'

After sixteen years with the company, a man was so excited about his promotion to vice president that he bragged about to his wife for weeks on end. She became so fed up with his posturing and preening that she eventually felt obliged to take him down a peg or two.

'Your new title means nothing,' she said. 'It's just for show. These days virtually every organization has a string of vice presidents. Why, even the grocery store on the corner has a vice president of peas!'

'I don't believe you,' he said. 'You're just jealous. You're making it up.'

'OK then. Go ahead. Phone the store.'

So he rang the corner store and said in mocking tones: 'Can I speak to the vice president of peas?'

'Certainly,' said the operator. 'Dried, tinned or frozen?'

Out of the Office Replies:

You are receiving this automatic notification because I am out of the office. If I was in, chances are you wouldn't have received anything at all.

I am currently out at a job interview and will reply to you if I fail to get the position. Be prepared for my mood.

Sorry to have missed you but I am in hospital having a frontal lobotomy so that I may be promoted to management.

I am on holiday. Your e-mail has been deleted.

Thank you for your message, which has been placed in a queuing system. You are currently in 286th place and can therefore expect to receive a reply some time in June.

I will be out of the office for the next two weeks for medical reasons. When I return, please refer to me as 'Sandra' instead of 'Steve'.

On his first morning in new premises, a young businessman began sorting out his office. He was in the middle of arranging his desk when there was a knock at the door. Eager to imply that he had gone up in the world and that business was brisk, he quickly picked up the phone and asked the person at the door to come in. A tradesman entered the office, but the young businessman talked into the phone as if he were conducting an important conversation with a client.

'I agree,' he said. 'Yes, sure . . . Absolutely no problem . . . We can do that.'

After a minute, he broke off from his imaginary conversation and said to the tradesman: 'Can I help you?'

'Yes,' he said. 'I'm here to hook up the phone.'

Two men were talking about their jobs. One said: 'The company where I work is installing a computer system and it's going to be putting a lot of people out of work. Have they started that at your place?'

'Oh, we've had computers for three years,' said the other. 'But they can't replace me because nobody has been able to figure out exactly what I do!'

A registered nurse had become disenchanted with her place of work, and so she handed in her notice. Since there was a shortage of nurses in the area, she didn't anticipate any problems in finding another job. She e-mailed cover letters to dozens of potential employers, attaching her CV to each letter. Three weeks later, she was disappointed and bewildered that she had not received even one request for a job interview.

Finally she received a message from a prospective employer that explained why she had not heard from anyone else. It read: 'Your CV was not attached as stated. I do, however, thank you for the vegetable lasagne recipe.'

The boss called one of his employees into the office. 'Michael,' he said, 'you've been with the company for twelve months. You started off in the mailing room. Just one week later you were promoted to a sales position, and one month after that you were promoted to district sales manager. Just four months later, you were promoted to vice president. Now it's time for me to retire, and, despite the fact that you haven't been with us for long, I want you to take over the running of the company. So what do you say to that?

'Thanks,' said the employee.

'Thanks?' replied the boss. 'Is that all you can say?'

'Oh, I'm sorry. Thanks, Dad.'

Unwritten Laws Of The Office:

A pat on the back is only a few centimetres from a kick in the pants.

You can go anywhere you want if you look serious and carry a clipboard.

The more crap you put up with, the more crap you are going to get.

When the bosses talk about improving productivity, they are never talking about themselves.

There will always be beer cans rolling on the floor of your car when the boss asks for a lift home from the office.

Anyone can do any amount of work provided it isn't the work he is supposed to be doing.

The longer the title, the less important the job.

Machines that have broken down will work perfectly when the repairman arrives.

The last person that quit or was fired will be held responsible for all mistakes.

Important letters that contain no errors will develop errors in the mail.

If it weren't for the last minute, nothing would get done.

Once a job is fouled up, anything done to improve it makes it worse.

The authority of a person is inversely proportional to the number of pens that person is carrying.

You will always get the greatest recognition for the job you least like.

No one gets sick on Wednesdays.

A secretary arrived at work late for the third day in a row. The boss summoned her to his office.

'Now look, Samantha. I know we had a fling for a while, but that's over. I expect you to behave like any other employee. Who told you that you could come and go as you please around here?'

The secretary replied coolly: 'My lawyer.'

Boss: Are you able to do anything that other people can't?

Applicant: Yes, I'm the only person that can read my handwriting.

A group of employees were required to attend a fire safety meeting at which an official from the fire department demonstrated the correct way to operate an extinguisher. He told them: 'Pull the pin like a hand grenade, then depress the trigger to release the foam.'

He then asked for a volunteer to have a go at putting out the little fire that he had lit in the parking lot. When nobody rushed forward, he picked on a young woman hiding nervously at the back. Occupying centre stage, she completely forgot everything he had told her, including how to pull the pin. Seeing her unease, the fire official hinted: 'Like a hand grenade, remember?' Hearing this, she pulled the pin and hurled the extinguisher at the blaze!

One by one the directors of a finance company were called into the chairman's office until only the newest, most junior executive was left sitting nervously outside. Finally it was his turn to be summoned. He entered the office to find the chairman and the other eight directors seated solemnly around a table.

Suddenly the chairman turned to the young man and asked: 'Have you ever slept with Miss Parkes, our secretary?'

'No, certainly not.'

'Are you absolutely sure?' persisted the chairman.

'Absolutely. I've never laid a finger on her.'

'You'd swear to that on the Bible?'

'Yes, I swear I've never had a sexual relationship with your secretary.'

'Good. Then you can fire her.'

A new young salesman was asked to report to the manager's office. The manager explained: 'We have a critical shortage of typists, and I'd like you to help out. I'll give you a little test. Here, type this.' And with that, the manager handed him a pamphlet to copy and a sheet of paper, and pointed to a desk across the room. On the desk were a typewriter and an adding machine.

Reluctant to become any sort of typist, even a temporary one, the salesman deliberately typed slowly and inaccurately, making as many mistakes as he could. He then handed the sheet of paper back to the manager who gave it little more than a cursory glance before commenting: 'That's fine. Report for work in the typing pool tomorrow.'

'But aren't you going to check the test?' asked the worried salesman.

The manager said: 'You passed the test the moment you sat down at the typewriter instead of the adding machine!'

Phillips came into the office an hour late for the third time in a week. The boss was waiting for him.

'What's the story this time, Phillips?' he bellowed. 'Let's hear a good excuse for a change.'

Phillips sighed. 'Everything went wrong this morning, sir. The wife decided to drive me to the station. She got ready in ten minutes, but then the garage door got stuck and we couldn't get the car out. So I ran for the bus, but it was struck by a meteorite on the way into town. Everyone else on the bus was killed, but I staggered out of the debris and flagged down a police helicopter. Unfortunately the helicopter smashed into an overhead wire, electrocuting the pilot and sending me plunging into the river. I managed to swim to the shore and hailed a lift to the station from a despatch rider. But yards from the station we swerved trying to avoid a dog and I was thrown into the back of a dustcart. Luckily it was coming this way, but we had to stop off at every house to make the collections, and that's why I'm an hour late, sir.'

'You'll have to do better than that, Phillips,' said the boss, disappointed. 'No woman can get ready in ten minutes.'

A boss collared one of his employees strolling in to work at half past ten in the morning.

'You should have been here at nine,' he growled.

'Why? What happened?'

A salesman called into an office to see a business customer, but found there was nobody about except for a large dog emptying the waste paper baskets. The salesman stared at the animal, wondering if his mind was playing tricks on him.

Eventually the dog looked up and said: 'Don't be surprised. This is part of my job.'

'This is incredible!' exclaimed the salesman. 'Does your boss know what a gem he has with you? A dog that can talk!'

'Please don't tell him I can talk,' said the dog. 'He'll have me answering the phones as well!'

At a job interview, an office manager asked a female applicant whether she had any unusual talents. She said that she had won several prizes in crossword puzzle and slogan-writing competitions.

'That's very good,' said the manager, 'but we want somebody who can be smart during office hours.'

'Oh,' said the applicant. 'That *was* during office hours.'

'Do you believe in life after death?' the boss asked one of his employees.

'Yes, sir.'

'That's good, because after you left work early yesterday to attend your grandmother's funeral, she dropped by to see you!'

A highly successful businessman had a meeting with his new son-in-law. 'As you know, I love my daughter and it is my pleasure to welcome you into the family. To demonstrate our belief that you will make our daughter happy, I am making you a fifty-fifty partner in my business. All you have to do is go to the factory every day and learn the operations.'

The son-in-law interrupted: 'I hate factories. I can't stand the noise.'

'I see,' said the father-in-law, somewhat taken aback. 'Well, then you'll work in the office and take charge of some of the operations.'

'I hate office work,' protested the son-in-law. 'I can't abide being stuck behind a desk all day.'

'Wait a minute,' said the father-in-law, beginning to lose patience. 'I just made you half-owner of a prosperous firm, but you don't like factories and you won't work in an office. What am I supposed to do with you?'

'Easy,' said the young man. 'Buy me out.'

Why is Christmas like a day at the office? – You do all the work and a fat guy in a suit gets all the credit.

The boss told the successful job applicant: 'Congratulations. You start at a hundred and fifty a week, and in six months your salary goes up to two hundred.'

'Great,' said the applicant. 'I'll come back in six months then.'

A man walked into the human resources department of a large company and handed in his job application. As the executive scanned the CV, he noticed that the applicant had been fired from every post he had ever held.

'I have to say,' remarked the executive, 'your work history is terrible. You've been fired from every job.'

'Yes,' agreed the man.

'Well, I'm afraid it's not very impressive. Can you name one positive aspect to such a dismal employment record?'

'Yes. At least it shows I'm not a quitter!'

A company security guard was told by his bosses to find some method of preventing employees using the side door of the factory. So he put up a sign saying 'Please do not use this door' but everyone ignored it. Then he erected a sign that read 'Using this door will activate an alarm' but still everybody ignored it and carried on using that door. Next he put up a sign saying 'Anyone using this door will be subject to a fifty dollar fine' but still the workforce ignored it. In desperation he hired an artist to draw a picture of a vicious-looking Rottweiler and pinned up a 'Beware of the dog' sign above the door but still employees walked in and out of the door as they pleased.

Just when he was about to admit defeat, he had a brainwave and put up a new sign on the door. From the moment the notice appeared, not one worker used that side door again. The sign read simply 'Wet paint'.

A situations vacant ad called for an experienced lumberjack and at the job interview the applicant was asked to describe his experience.

'I've worked in the Sahara Forest,' he said.

The personnel manager looked puzzled. 'You mean the Sahara Desert?'

'Sure, that's what they call it now!'

Rules of Work:

Never give me work in the morning. Always wait until 4.00 and then bring it to me. The challenge of a deadline is refreshing.

If it's a real rush job, run in and interrupt me every ten minutes to inquire how it's going. That helps. Or even better, hover behind me, advising me at every keystroke.

Always leave without telling anyone where you're going. It gives me a chance to be creative when someone asks where you are.

If my arms are full of papers, boxes or books, don't open the door for me. One day I might need to learn how to function as a paraplegic, so opening doors with no arms is good training.

If you give me more than one job to do, don't tell me which is the most urgent. I am psychic.

Do your best to keep me late. I adore this office and really don't have anywhere else to go. I have no life beyond work.

If I do a job that pleases you, keep it a secret. Otherwise, it could mean promotion.

If you don't like my work, tell everyone. I like to be talked about.

If you have special instructions for a job, don't write them down. Instead save them until the job is almost done. No point in confusing me with useful information.

Never introduce me to the people you're with. I have no right to know anything. In the corporate food chain, I am plankton. When you refer to them later, my shrewd deductions will identify them.

A boss was laying down the law to one of his employees for being late yet again.

'Do you know when we start work in this office?' he said.

'No,' replied the employee. 'They're usually hard at it by the time I get here.'

A man went for a job as a signalman on the railways and was told to meet the inspector at the signal box for an interview.

The inspector kicked off the interview with a tough question: 'What would you do if you realized that two trains were heading for each other on the same track?'

'I would switch the points for one of the trains.'

'What if the lever broke?' asked the inspector.

'Then I'd rush down from the signal box and use the trackside manual lever.'

'What if it had been struck by lightning?'

'Then I'd run back into the signal box and phone the next signal box further along the line.'

'What if the phone was engaged?'

'In that case, I'd rush down out of the box and use the emergency phone by the level crossing.'

'What if that was vandalized?'

'Oh well, then I'd run into the village and fetch my brother Brad.'

The inspector was stumped by this answer and asked: 'Why would you do that?'

'Because he's never seen a train crash.'

A shop steward stood up before the gathering of the workforce to announce the results of protracted negotiations with the employers. 'From next week,' he told his members triumphantly, 'your wages will increase by sixty per cent, you will each get a company house and car, and you will only have to work on Wednesdays.'

'What!' came a cry from the back of the hall. 'Every bloody Wednesday?'

'I'm never going to work for that man again!' said the female employee.

'Why, what did he say?' asked her friend.

'You're fired.'

The boss asked a new employee his name. 'Stuart,' replied the young man.

The boss scowled. 'I don't know what kind of namby-pamby place you worked at before, but we don't use first names here. In my view, it breeds familiarity, which ultimately leads to a breakdown in authority. So I always call employees by their last names only – Smith, Brown, Jones etc. They in turn refer to me only as Mr Harris. Understood? Right. Now that we've got that straight, what's your last name?'

'Darling,' replied the young man. 'My name is Stuart Darling.'

'Okay, Stuart, the next thing I went to tell you is . . .'

Every morning a man took the ferry to work, but one day his watch stopped and he thought he was running late. He rushed to the dock and saw the boat ten feet away. Taking a run at it, he jumped and, with a superhuman effort, just managed to land in the boat. The captain looked at him quizzically and said: 'If you had waited another minute, we'd have docked.'

At a job interview, the employer was weighing up the applicant's potential.

'You see,' said the employer, 'in this job we need someone who is responsible.'

'Then I'm your man,' replied the applicant eagerly. 'At my last job, whenever anything went wrong, they said I was responsible.'

Employee Evaluation Reports:

When she opens her mouth, it seems that it's only to change feet.

Since my last report, he has reached rock bottom and has started to dig.

His men would follow him anywhere, but only out of morbid curiosity.

A gross ignoramus – a hundred and forty-four times worse than an ordinary ignoramus.

He doesn't have ulcers, but he's a carrier.

He has a knack of making strangers immediately.

I would not allow this associate to breed.

This employee is not so much of a has-been, but more of a definite won't-be.

Works well when under constant supervision and cornered like a rat in a trap.

He brings joy to others, when he leaves the room.

When his IQ reaches fifty, he should sell.

If you see two people talking and one looks bored, he's the other one.

A photographic memory, but with the lens cover left on.

He would be out of his depth in a puddle.

A prime candidate for natural de-selection.

Has two brains: one is lost, the other is out looking for it.

This young lady has delusions of adequacy.

If he was any more stupid, he'd have to be watered.

It's hard to believe he beat a million other sperm.

If you gave him a penny for his thoughts, you'd get change.

She sets low personal standards and then consistently fails to achieve them.

Some drink from the fountain of knowledge; he only gargled.

It takes him two hours to watch Sixty Minutes.

This man would have to study for a month to pass a urine test.

This employee is depriving a village somewhere of its idiot.

The wheel is turning, but the hamster is dead.

What Employee Evaluation Comments Really Mean:

Accepts new job assignments willingly . . . Never finishes anything.

Delegates responsibility effectively . . . Passes the buck.

Alert to company developments . . . Office gossip.

Uses time effectively . . . Clock watcher.

Strong adherence to principles . . . Stubborn.

Average . . . Not too bright.

Competent . . . Able to get work done with help.

Slightly below average . . . Stupid.

Regularly consults with supervisor . . . Pain in the ass.

Gets along well with superiors . . . Crawler.

Socially active . . . Drinks heavily.

Straightforward . . . Blunt and insensitive.

Uses all available resources . . . Takes office supplies home for personal use.

Identifies management problems . . . Complains a lot.

Inspires the co-operation of others . . . Gets everyone else to do his work.

Is unusually loyal . . . No other firm wants him.

Meticulous in attention to detail . . . Nitpicker.

Keen sense of humour . . . Tells dirty jokes.

Quick thinking . . . Offers plausible excuses.

Listens well . . . Has no ideas of his own.

Demonstrates qualities of leadership . . . Has a loud voice.

Unblemished character . . . One step ahead of the law.

Should go far . . . Please.

Will go far . . . Boss's relative.

A young man, hired by a supermarket, reported for his first day at work. The manager gave him a broom and told him to sweep the store.

'But I'm a university graduate,' he protested.

'Oh, I'm sorry,' said the manager. 'I didn't know that. Here, give me the broom, I'll show you how.'

A worker was given the job of painting white lines down the middle of the highway. On his first day, he painted six miles; on his second day, he did three miles; and on his third day, he painted less than a mile.

The foreman was not pleased. 'How come you're doing less each day?' he demanded.

'Because,' said the worker indignantly, 'each day I keep getting further away from the can of paint!'